ZEPPO

ZEPPO
The Reluctant Marx Brother

ROBERT S. BADER

APPLAUSE
THEATRE & CINEMA BOOKS
Essex, Connecticut

APPLAUSE
THEATRE & CINEMA BOOKS

An imprint of Globe Pequot, the trade division of
The Rowman & Littlefield Publishing Group, Inc.
4501 Forbes Blvd., Ste. 200
Lanham, MD 20706
www.rowman.com

Distributed by NATIONAL BOOK NETWORK

British Library Cataloguing in Publication Information available

Library of Congress Cataloging in-Publication Data

Names: Bader, Robert S., author.
Title: Zeppo : the reluctant Marx brother / Robert S. Bader.
Description: Lanham : Applause, [2024] | Includes bibliographical
   references and index.
Identifiers: LCCN 2024011832 (print) | LCCN 2024011833 (ebook) | ISBN
   9781493087969 (cloth) | ISBN 9781493087976 (epub)
Subjects: LCSH: Marx, Zeppo, 1901-1979. | Actors—United States—Biography.
   | Comedians—United States—Biography. | Talent scouts—United
   States—Biography.
Classification: LCC PN2287.M5423 .B33 2024 (print) | LCC PN2287.M5423
   (ebook) | DDC 792.702/8092 #a B—dc23/eng/20240618
LC record available at https://lccn.loc.gov/2024011832
LC ebook record available at https://lccn.loc.gov/2024011833

Contents

PREFACE

I N THE SUMMER OF 1974, I INVITED GROUCHO MARX TO MY BAR MITZVAH. He did not attend. Whatever made me think a frail eighty-three-year-old man would fly from California to New York to attend a party for a kid he didn't know was likely the result of my adolescent obsession with the Marx Brothers. I figured if he could only know how much of a fan I was, he would surely come. But I wasn't too disappointed. None of the Beatles came either. However, several elderly Jewish men—a few of whom smoked cigars and resembled Groucho—did manage to attend the affair.

For some reason I was not discouraged and still felt compelled to contact the other surviving Marx Brothers. That fall, when I learned that Zeppo Marx lived in Palm Springs, California, I located the Palm Springs phone book at the New York Public Library. He was listed. (I later figured out this was probably in case any young ladies were trying to reach him. He had little interest in hearing from thirteen-year-old Marx Brothers fans.) With great poise I picked up the phone a few days later and dialed his number. The voice on the other end said, "Hello?" and I said, "May I please speak with Zeppo Marx?" I had thought about this opening line for quite some time and decided it was as polite and professional as it could be. The voice on the phone replied, "He's not here." This was followed by a loud click. But the voice sure sounded like the one that left out a Hungerdunger in *Animal Crackers*. I checked the cassette recording I'd illicitly made at the Sutton Theatre when the film had a theatrical reissue that summer and was convinced that I'd just gotten the brush from Zeppo himself.

A few weeks later I heard my father bellow, "Who the hell called California?" when the phone bill arrived. In 1974—years before everyone had a cell phone and could call anywhere in the country very inexpensively—my less-than-a-minute, long-distance call to Zeppo Marx accounted for a significant portion of our normally modest phone bill. My efforts to contact the surviving Marx Brothers were ended by one phone bill just before I could take a shot at Gummo. Just as well, though. At the time I had no reference recording to authenticate his voice.

My curiosity about Zeppo got absorbed into my general Marx obsession, but I always wondered about him. What did he do after leaving the Marx Brothers? If he had spoken to me that day, I would have asked him why he wasn't in *A Night at the Opera*. In retrospect I must admit he made the right move by hanging up on me. But it was a reasonable question from a kid who had only just seen that film for the first time and was hoping to see Zeppo pop out of that steamer trunk with Harpo and Chico. He was so good in *Monkey Business*. How could the Marx Brothers take another ocean voyage without him? I would spend the next several decades researching the Marx Brothers, getting to know their children, and learning all I could about them. The culmination of this quest for Marxian knowledge was the publication of my book, *Four of the Three Musketeers: The Marx Brothers on Stage*, in 2016. There was quite a lot to pack into that rather hefty book and certain sacrifices were made to ensure that readers could lift it. Among the topics only touched on slightly were Zeppo's life before and after his time in the Four Marx Brothers.

His story is very different from his brothers, starting with the notable change of venue for his childhood. While the other boys all came of age in New York City together, Zeppo was moved to Chicago as a boy and roamed the streets alone while Groucho, Harpo, Chico, and Gummo were traveling America's vaudeville circuits. Over the years I had heard about a college professor working on a Zeppo biography and hoped it would get published. This fellow contacted me in the mid-1990s—a couple of years after the publication of *Groucho Marx and Other Short Stories and Tall Tales*, an anthology of Groucho's lost writings that I had edited. I met with him at the New York Public Library for the Performing Arts at Lincoln Center and provided him with some of my research. I never heard from him again. I tried to reach him a couple of times to see where he was with the book. His email bounced back, and his phone had been disconnected. This seemed completely in line with Zeppo's reaction to my adolescent phone call.

Around twenty-five years later Zeppo's son Tim, by this time a good friend, called me to discuss a new prospective Zeppo biographer. While well-intentioned, this man just didn't have a lot of familiarity with the subject and would have needed to really start from scratch. Tim, having learned a lot about his father from reading *Four of the Three Musketeers*, said, "You should write the Zeppo biography." It didn't take much persuading from Tim to get me started. I already had a wealth of information about Zeppo's early life that didn't make it into *Four of the Three Musketeers*. I also had some very interesting material about his life after the Marx Brothers that was outside the scope of that earlier book.

With a good head start I began doing research and found more surprises about Zeppo than I thought possible. It has often been suggested that Zeppo was the funniest brother off stage. I'm in no position to judge that but I'm pretty sure he had the most unusual and interesting life of any of the Marx Brothers. Zeppo's life played out like an adventure story featuring a very restless hero—or antihero, depending on your sensibilities. Being pushed into show business probably saved Zeppo's life. His best friends from his teen years in Chicago spent much of their adult lives in prison, and one of them was killed in a police raid. He was on that path when vaudeville interrupted his burgeoning life of crime on the streets of Chicago.

Zeppo was a frequent object of ridicule during his show business career, and the passage of time has done little to help his legacy. Once a punchline for his brothers and critics, Zeppo is now a convenient pop culture reference synonymous with being useless, unfunny, or expendable. A 1999 episode of the popular television series *Buffy the Vampire Slayer*, titled "The Zeppo," concerns a character—referred to as "the Zeppo of the group"—being deemed unimportant. A 1992 episode of the hit situation comedy series *Cheers* reveals that the dour, humorless Lilith character's favorite Marx Brother is Zeppo. She says, "Isn't Zeppo hysterical? The way he just stands there without expression or reaction. Boy, that cracks me up."

Even when Zeppo is praised, there seems to be some obligation to knock him a bit. Film critic James Agee, reviewing Kyle Crichton's 1950 Marx Brothers biography in *Films in Review* wrote, "I have never seen anyone give Zeppo adequate appreciation in print, and had hoped to find that here, but no; except in the excellent illustrations his peerlessly cheesy improvement on the traditional straight man is never recorded." In *The Marx Brothers: Their World of Comedy*, Allen Eyles wrote, "Zeppo, the fourth Marx Brother is not so interesting, but he is worth having for all his awkwardness just because he is one of the family." In *The Comic Mind: Comedy and the Movies*, Gerald Mast discusses Zeppo's contribution to the first five Marx Brothers films: "Zeppo added a fourth dimension in the Paramounts as the cliché of the straight man and juvenile, the bland, wooden espouser of sentiments that seem to exist only in the world of the sound stage." Mast goes on to say, "Zeppo was a parody of the romantic juvenile—too schleppy, too nasal and too wooden to be taken seriously." Okay, Zeppo's good but only because he's cheesy, not so interesting, awkward, bland, schleppy, nasal and wooden. Got it.

So why then are the first five Marx Brothers films—the ones they made for Paramount before Zeppo left the act—widely considered their best? Could it be the presence of Zeppo? Whatever his individual contribution amounts to, there is no mistaking his value in making the Marx Brothers a quartet—The FOUR Marx Brothers—as they were in vaudeville and on Broadway in perhaps their peak period. They work best as a foursome, often breaking down into two separate teams—Groucho and Zeppo, Harpo and Chico. Zeppo is easily overlooked but at least one bona fide movie star saw something in him that was universally missed by others. Cary Grant saw the Marx Brothers in vaudeville when he was still known as Archie Leach and was working as an acrobat. According to biographer Marc Eliot, Grant believed Zeppo's foil timing was a big part of the act's success. Grant also took to dressing like Zeppo and wearing his hair in the same style. But Cary Grant stood alone. There weren't many non-fictional characters who'd say Zeppo was their favorite Marx Brother.

With a small handful of exceptions, most people who knew Zeppo Marx are gone. Telling his story in anything more than a cursory manner is difficult. And he would be perfectly happy with that because to him none of it was anyone's business. Once he got out of the Four Marx Brothers, he felt no obligation to participate in any form of publicity and gave very few interviews. He told a friend late in his life that he wouldn't put any of his stories down on paper or on tape because he was sure he'd be sued. But his story—and all its deviations from the traditional story of the Marx Brothers—is well worth investigating. If the story of the Marx Brothers is a triumphant show business tale, Zeppo's is a dimly lit film noir based on a gritty crime novel.

Robert S. Bader
Los Angeles, California
April 2024

INTRODUCTION

B EING AROUND ZEPPO MARX WAS OFTEN DIFFICULT FOR PEOPLE CLOSE to him—even going back to his childhood. Once he was able to live on his own terms and by his own rules, life was never difficult for Zeppo— although being close to him never got any easier for other people. Being in charge meant everything to him. Being successful was the icing on the cake, but success had been just out of his reach until he took matters into his own hands and refused to rely on anyone but himself. He'd certainly been a part of something very successful, but it wasn't his success.

Being the fourth of the Four Marx Brothers was never especially interesting to Zeppo. The sixth Marx brother by birth and the fifth to survive infancy, he had big dreams; but pressure to go along with plans that did not coincide with his own controlled him for many years. When he finally broke free it was as if he had to make up for lost time. Zeppo's restless and peripatetic nature took him from juvenile delinquency to a variety of careers that would seem impossible for one man. Automobile mechanic, vaudevillian, Broadway and movie star, real estate salesman, screenwriter, talent agent, horse breeder, manufacturer, inventor, builder, professional gambler, citrus rancher, and commercial fisherman. And he succeeded at almost all of them, making and losing a couple of fortunes. Nat Perrin, a Marx Brothers' writer and friend told author Charlotte Chandler, "Zeppo was a gambler and a very smart guy in business. Highly underrated, a success in most of everything he did except the Marx Brothers. . . . He's a man of many varied abilities, but people just don't seem to realize it. . . . [H]e probably was the unhappiest with the Marx Brothers because he was the low man on the totem pole."

It's a commonly accepted theory that the arrival of talking pictures not only destroyed many silent film careers but also countless vaudeville stage careers. Vaudeville had been struggling for several years courtesy of the rise of the movie industry. Films began emerging as popular entertainment on vaudeville bills during the silent era, with the initial effect being the replacement of a couple of acts on a bill by a film. Eventually vaudeville theaters stopped booking live acts in favor of the more affordable option of booking only films. The combined effect of talkies and the growing popularity of legitimate stage musicals sealed vaudeville's fate by the late 1920s. Although it survived in other forms for several more years, vaudeville essentially ground to a halt with the premiere of *The Jazz Singer* in October 1927.

Vaudevillians able to make the transition to Broadway and talking films were few and far between. Numerous headliners were forced to find other ways to make a living. Acrobats, comedians, singers, magicians, and dancers suddenly found work in factories or as salesmen. Some could not cope with their sudden loss of stardom, and there was a high suicide rate among former vaudevillians. Had the Four Marx Brothers ended with the death of vaudeville, Zeppo would have been fine. The same would not have been true for his brothers, who by that point were ill-equipped for anything other than show business.

The small group of vaudevillians who had found some success on Broadway soon found themselves in talking pictures. Among this select group were the Four Marx Brothers, who had survived a sometimes-tumultuous vaudeville career to become the stars of three Broadway hits. But within the Four Marx Brothers was an even more select group of vaudeville and Broadway survivors. It wasn't even a group. It was one man. The sole survivor of vaudeville and Broadway who went on to success in talking pictures but didn't want any part of it was Zeppo Marx. Drafted into the act at age seventeen to replace his brother Gummo—another reluctant vaudevillian—Zeppo was with the act for its greatest period of success, as the team made the leap from vaudeville to Broadway, eventually relocating to Hollywood for movie stardom.

Zeppo was the accidental Marx brother when he joined the family. He became the accidental Marx Brother in a completely different sense seventeen years later when he joined the act. In both cases this was through circumstances he was unable to control. The poor timing of his birth would later be useful—not for him, but for his mother. She didn't need a fifth son in 1901, but she desperately needed a fourth Marx Brother in 1918.

In the early days of the Depression, Zeppo Marx had it made. He was famous and the money was rolling in—even though his share of it was considerably less than those of his brothers Groucho, Harpo, and Chico, who employed him. Any number of vaudevillians forced into a mundane existence in America's dwindling Depression-era workforce would have given anything to be in Zeppo's comparatively underpaid shoes. He may have been easily mocked as the least important Marx Brother, but he did a fine job with what little he was given to do in the act. And Zeppo was paid a handsome salary by the standards of the day. Who would throw that away? Perhaps a man who had gone through his life without ever having the opportunity to decide anything for himself. Or maybe a man who resented working for his brothers at a salary he considered unfair in comparison to their earnings as owners of the act. Zeppo could have made a good argument for either case.

Zeppo's repudiation of a life in which his mother and brothers controlled him was long overdue by the time he quit the Marx Brothers. But Zeppo wouldn't be happy with just his independence. He would need complete autonomy in control of his future destiny. Perhaps it was overcompensation for the years he spent without any control. He was thirty-three years old when he quit the act. He had been the fourth Marx Brother for roughly half of his life—and his brothers never made him an equal partner in the business, keeping him on salary for sixteen years as they were one of the highest paid acts in vaudeville, on Broadway, and in movies. Leaving the act, Zeppo had a lot to prove—to his brothers and to himself. While some out-of-work vaudevillians were forced into factory work, Zeppo Marx would eventually own a factory. After his departure made the Four Marx Brothers a trio, Zeppo never spent a single day in the employ of anyone but himself. He needed to have absolute control, but he also needed to make more money. A lot more money than he made as a Marx Brother. And a lot more money than the other Marx Brothers made. He'd spent enough of his life being controlled. Zeppo Marx ultimately became uncontrollable.

CHAPTER ONE

The Accidental Brother

MINNIE MARX, THE FORMER MIENE SCHOENBERG, CELEBRATED HER thirty-sixth birthday a few months before Herbert Manfred Marx's birth. She was already the mother of four boys, ages eight, ten, twelve, and thirteen. Another son had died in infancy, so Herbert represented Minnie's sixth pregnancy. Herbert's middle name was given to honor the dead child.

Herbert was born on February 25, 1901, around a month before Minnie's eldest child Leonard's fourteenth birthday. Leo, as he was commonly known, had by this time already discovered the joys of women and gambling. He would acquire the name Chico from "chasing chicks." Leonard started life with an advantage his brothers didn't enjoy. He arrived following a series of tragedies that took a toll on his mother in the summer of 1886. The death of six-month-old Manfred on July 17 was preceded by Minnie's sister Pauline LeFevre being committed on March 16 to what was then indelicately called the Lunatic Asylum at Blackwell's Island.[1] She would die there on August 25. Pauline's husband Julius had died on July 26.[2] But during that awful summer of death, Minnie also learned she was pregnant. All this child would need to do to be her favorite was stay alive, which Leonard, born in March 1887, managed to do—sometimes against all odds, as later in life his gambling and womanizing would result in plenty of people thinking about killing him. The tragedy continued for Minnie when her sister Jenny Zimmerman became ill with an abscess and died of septicemia on November 26, 1888—three days after the birth of Minnie's next son, Adolph, who grew up to become Harpo and ran a close second to Leonard for his mother's affection.

Minnie did not lose any loved ones around the times her next two sons were born.[3] Julius, born in October 1890, and Milton, born in October 1892, never overcame the feeling of not being their mother's favorite. Neither of them got the piano lessons or the favorable treatment Minnie reserved for Leonard. Adolph was sweet and never jealous and was doted on by Minnie. The formerly youngest member of the family, Milton—later known as Gummo—celebrated his eighth birthday four months before Herbert's arrival and spent a good deal of his childhood suffering from various illnesses. When Minnie became obsessed with the idea of putting her sons on the vaudeville stage—mostly possible through the talents of her son Julius, later Groucho—Herbert was around three years old. His lack of show business potential at that point resulted in his mother not paying very much attention to him. Adolph also failed to display any noticeable talent and Minnie's interest in him was limited to whatever she could muster for a kid the entire neighborhood considered an idiot. But Herbert grew up with a large and loving family, crowded into an East 93rd Street apartment in Manhattan's Yorkville neighborhood. The apartment could barely hold the assemblage of Marxes, Schoenbergs, and other relatives Minnie and her husband, Sam "Frenchy" Marx, stuffed into it. Grandparents, aunts, uncles, and cousins all doted on little Herbie as, one by one, his older brothers left the apartment.

Minnie came from a large family with ten children—eight girls and two boys. Five of her sisters died young, which was not uncommon at the end of the nineteenth century, but the five siblings who survived would produce twenty-two children between 1877 and 1902. Their mother's side of the family provided the Marx Brothers with sixteen Schoenberg cousins during that period—although, like Manfred, three died in infancy. Minnie's sister Sara Heyman was seven years older and had seven children. The two youngest Heyman children, Louis and Adolph were close in age to Minnie's older children. Adolph Heyman, a few years younger than his cousin Adolph Marx, began calling himself Arthur years before his cousin also took the name. (The point became moot when Minnie's Adolph dropped Arthur in favor of Harpo.) Another sister, Hannah LeFevre, two years older than Minnie—and married to a cousin of sister Pauline's husband—had two children, Lou, and Polly. They were a few years older than Leonard and Adolph, and particularly close to the Marx family due to occasionally living with their mother at the Marx apartment. (Hannah's two early marriages were tempestuous and brief. She eventually remarried and Julius Schickler, her third husband, would become very close with his Marx nephews in the coming years.[4]

The youngest of Minnie's siblings—Heinemann—became Henry, then Harry, in America. He married Marie Levy on March 15, 1896, and their son Joseph was born on November 22, suggesting either a premature birth or a hastily planned wedding for propriety's sake. This was not an unusual situation in the Marx and Schoenberg families, or in society in general, at the time. What was unusual, and perhaps looked upon curiously, was the decision in 1899 to turn Henry Schoenberg into Harry Shean and send him out into the world of vaudeville after another of the Schoenberg children, Abraham Elieser Adolph, had found fame and success on stage as Al Shean.[5] Minnie pushed Harry into show business hoping he would duplicate the success of his brother. He didn't. A September 25, 1899, *Detroit Free Press* review of Harry's performance as a Hebrew dialect comedian in *On the Stroke of Twelve* was not something Minnie could quote in trying to get Harry some bookings: "Harry Shean presented a colorless and amateurish caricature of the conventional money lender of stage literature." By all accounts, Harry was an ordinary man who mostly worked at menial jobs. His ill-fated foray into vaudeville served as a test run for Minnie's plan to turn her sons into vaudeville successes. All she'd need to do would be get them better reviews.

Harry and Marie had become parents again with the birth of their daughter Florence in 1898, and they welcomed their daughter Jennie into the family on October 3, 1900, the day after Julius's tenth birthday. Their son Lawrence would follow in 1902. Marie and Harry's two younger children would be the cousins with whom Herbert would play as a boy.[6] The notion of Harry supporting his growing family with his limited show business skills seemed unlikely. Cooler heads prevailed and he listed his occupation as a "useful man" in the dry goods business in the 1900 census. Harry and Marie settled with their growing family in Queens where Harry operated a lunch wagon. The family of Harry and Marie Shean as young Herbert knew it during his childhood was very much like his own: four children, a housewife mother, and a hard-working father—Harry running his lunch wagon, Frenchy plying his trade as a tailor. These were two very typical immigrant families in turn of the century New York—one in Manhattan, one in Queens. Weekend family gatherings could be in either place, or with the even larger Heyman family, also in Manhattan. Herbert became accustomed to large family gatherings and his playmates were his cousins and neighbors close to his own age, not his brothers. Herbert's aunts—Hannah, Sara, and Marie—played large roles in his early childhood. Minnie relied on these women a lot, and they were almost like mothers to Herbert when Minnie focused her energy and attention on show business.

Minnie's parents, Fanny and Lafe Schoenberg, lived with the family. But only six weeks after Herbert's birth, Fanny died at the age of seventy-two. Within a few years Leonard would head out on his own, and then came

Minnie's plan. Many vaudevillians came into the profession by necessity. What other options did they have? As the children of immigrants—in an environment barely concerned with child labor laws—most received little or no formal education once they were old enough to work. Talent was not a requirement for a career in turn-of-the-century vaudeville. Many came into it because it was the family business. Others because it just wasn't all that difficult to get started in small-time vaudeville. And it was a much better option than manual labor. For the Marx Brothers it was a combination of all those factors. As each of the five boys came of age, he would dutifully have a bar mitzvah—largely in deference to their maternal grandfather, who appears to have been the last member of the family to pay much attention to Judaism. Asked in 1978 by BBC interviewer Barry Norman if being Jewish was important to the family, Zeppo replied, "No. . . . We didn't go to church or things like that. But we were Jews and we stuck up for the Jews. . . . They were oppressed, and they had struggled for many years, and we took their side. That's the only reason. We were not religious."

Fanny and Lafe Schoenberg had been entertainers in Prussia before emigrating to the United States. He was a magician, ventriloquist, and circus strongman. She was a singing harpist. Four of their ten children attempted show business careers at various times. For their seventh child—daughter Minnie— success as a performer was not to be. But for Minnie Marx vaudeville became a religion. And her spiritual advisor was her younger brother Adolph, who had struck gold in show business as Al Shean. Al, his wife Johanna, and their son Larry lived in the northern suburb of Mount Vernon—only fourteen miles from the Marx family's Yorkville apartment, but culturally it was much farther away. There would have been two more cousins close in age to Herbert had Al and Johanna's twin girls Marie and Selma, born in 1900, survived infancy.[7] Uncle Al was rich, successful, and lived in a mansion. His family frequently traveled with him on tour, so while Larry was only four years older than Herbert, they didn't spend much time together in New York.

As the mother of four boys in various stages of juvenile delinquency and a new baby, Minnie was unable to pursue her own show business dream, but Al's early success convinced her that her boys could be stars. This belief was based on very little evidence of talent. Her middle child, Julius, could sing and was earning some money on Sundays in a Protestant church choir by 1904. (Minnie didn't let Judaism stand in the way of her son singing in a church.) Leonard was already out on his own when Minnie put her plan in motion, but he was a good piano player, and would play a part in the plan soon enough. Adolph was considered a lost cause by Minnie and a fool by almost everyone else.

As Al Shean's star continued to rise Minnie saw his success as a gateway into show business for the rest of the family. Harry may not have made it as a Hebrew dialect comedian, but Minnie remained optimistic. Her next move was to pair Milton in an act—at around age seven—with his Uncle Harry. The story of Milton's very brief vaudeville partnership with his uncle was the subject of an oft-told family legend. Harry attempted to follow in his father's footsteps as a ventriloquist, but unable to learn the craft, he stuffed the undersized Milton into a hollow dummy. Disaster ensued when Harry poked a hatpin into the dummy's leg to prove it was really a dummy and hit the wrong leg—the one with both of Milton's legs in it. The scant evidence of this act suggests it may have only lasted a week or two. As good a story as it is, there is also the possibility that the concept of the act was that Harry was playing a fake ventriloquist and the deception was known to the audience by design. But that would just be a lousy act. The family legend is much better when the enraged audience is added to the mix.

Minnie had big plans for her sons and remained optimistic about her brother Harry. The fact that Harry had no discernible talent, paired with the fact that he was allegedly almost completely deaf did not stop Minnie. In the surprisingly open field of vaudeville, Harry Shean found work. To Minnie this was a sign. All her boys could hear perfectly well and at least one of them showed some signs of talent. Julius had some success singing in vaudeville as a teenager, and Minnie again drafted Milton into service. Milton showed no indication that he had any ability as a performer, but if Harry Shean could get bookings because his brother was Al Shean, Milton could ride on Julius's coattails. This was common in vaudeville. Al Jolson's brother Harry worked the circuits for years with an act that was generally considered terrible. (Harry Jolson started in show business before his younger brother Al but was quickly eclipsed by him and traded on his success for years.) Magician Harry Houdini's younger brother took the name Hardeen and was often billed as Houdini's brother, going so far as to perform much of Houdini's act. Having a brother in the business was a major steppingstone in vaudeville.

The correlation of a bar mitzvah and a vaudeville debut is not farfetched in the Marx family. Both Julius and Milton were working on stage at the age of fourteen—fresh from their bar mitzvahs. They were now considered men under Jewish law, so in Minnie's mind they could ride railroad trains across the country and earn livings as singers. (Of course, Minnie was not averse to claiming her boys were young enough to ride the rails for the children's fare as they advanced into their teen years.) Exactly what Leonard was up to at the age of fourteen is conjecture, but by all accounts, he was far from a boy in his behavior. Adolph simply roamed the streets of upper Manhattan and worked odd jobs throughout his teen years. Once Minnie had established Julius and Milton in an act that she controlled, she was inspired to get work in vaudeville for someone with even less interest than talent. Adolph was in her sights.

Minnie used the early success Julius had in small-time vaudeville to get him a better job with Gus Edwards, an important impresario and songwriter. As Julius was on the cusp of his own success, Minnie made a deal. She enrolled Milton in Ned Wayburn's Training School for the Stage with courses in vaudeville and created an act with Wayburn starring her successful son Julius and the novice Milton. With another Wayburn pupil, Mabel O'Donnell, they formed Ned Wayburn's Nightingales in May 1907. By the end of the year Minnie was able to force Wayburn out and take control of the act, which she renamed the Three Nightingales. Minnie was now in charge, and in June of 1908 she plucked the aimless nineteen-year-old Adolph from his latest odd job and put him in the act—whether he wanted to be in it or not. She also replaced Mabel O'Donnell with Lou Levy. The Four Nightingales were born and so was a family business. Her sons learned that it was nearly impossible to stand in the way of Minnie's dream. Adolph didn't put up much of a fight. He recognized immediately that there was no point. He had been drafted.

The Four Nightingales debuted a few months after Herbert's seventh birthday, leaving him as the last brother in the no-longer-crowded apartment when the act hit the road. Suddenly Herbert didn't have to share a bed with any number of his brothers. When Minnie occasionally went on the road with the act, Herbert was left with Frenchy, his grandfather and the occasional aunts, uncles, and cousins who would often stay at the apartment. Structure and discipline were in short supply for the youngest member of the family during this period. There were enough relatives hitting the road in vaudeville that it seemed completely natural to Herbert. At home, Herbert enjoyed learning magic tricks from his show business veteran grandfather. Hannah's son Lou Shean—another namesake of Al Shean—had already started his own vaudeville career. Hannah's daughter Polly managed to resist the show business bug as did Sara's entire family, but now Herbert could see two uncles, a cousin and three brothers out on the road performing. In the next few years, he would see his mother, Aunt Hannah and his seldom seen brother Leonard take to the vaudeville stage. It couldn't have been that much of a surprise when his time finally came.

While much of Herbert's childhood was like that of his older brothers, enough of it wasn't to give him a decidedly different start in life. For one thing, he never developed a close relationship with a sibling like the one enjoyed by

Adolph and Leonard that remained for the rest of their lives as Harpo and Chico. Similarly, Julius and Milton were extremely close and remained so as Groucho and Gummo into their eighties. Herbert was a lone wolf in many respects, and this remained a core trait of the adult Zeppo. But Herbert did see one of his older brothers as a role model.

All the boys considered Frenchy to be practically another brother, as opposed to a father figure or role model. He was sweet and easygoing and struggled with the notion of disciplining his sons. Minnie was clearly the boss, although Frenchy could at least claim autonomy in the kitchen. When Leonard would make an appearance at the 93rd Street apartment, Herbert was awestruck. Leonard began leaving home for extended periods shortly after Herbert was born, so they never really spent a lot of time together. But Leonard's stories of his adventurous life of gambling and womanizing on the road struck a chord in young Herbert. If he understood that Leonard's travels at this point were usually the result of outrunning his bookies and finding piano-playing jobs in whorehouses, Herbert didn't care. Leonard was practically a god to him.

The Four Nightingales did well without reaching the level of success enjoyed by Al Shean, but Minnie remained optimistic. She was convinced that her act being stuck in the grind of small-time vaudeville circuits couldn't have had anything to do with the quality of a singing quartet in which only two of the members—Julius and hired hand Lou Levy—could sing. It must have been something else. Minnie concluded that having the act based in New York was the problem. The act and the family would move to Chicago to be at the center of vaudeville. This would open the western half of the country for the Four Nightingales.

Minnie, Frenchy, Adolph, Julius, Milton, and Herbert arrived in Chicago in late 1909 along with Hannah and her husband, Julius Schickler. They rented an apartment at 4649 Calumet Avenue. Harry and Marie and their children, and Sara and her husband Gustave Heyman and their children, all remained in New York.[8] These aunts, uncles and cousins had been an important part of eight-year-old Herbert's life—in some cases more important than his own mother and brothers. But that was not considered when Minnie decided that the family had to leave New York to help the Four Nightingales. This was the likely point at which Herbert's lone wolf tendencies blossomed. He embarked on a path that would make him a far more dangerous juvenile delinquent than any of his brothers had ever been.

CHAPTER TWO

The Fifth Son Also Rises

HERBERT WAS EIGHT YEARS OLD WHEN THE MARX FAMILY ARRIVED IN Chicago. They had traveled slowly while the Four Nightingales played a string of dates in the fall of 1909 that would get them from New York to Chicago by the end of the year. Rather than spending several months on the road with the Four Nightingales, eighty-six-year-old Lafe Schoenberg moved into Al Shean's home in Mount Vernon. He took a comparatively luxurious train ride to Chicago with Al's wife Johanna in December. Al was booked with his partner Charles Warren at the Marlowe Theatre at 63rd Street and Stewart Avenue—just a few miles from the new Marx home. Lafe soon rejoined the Marxes in their new Chicago address.

Shortly after the family arrived in Chicago, Adolph changed his name to Arthur and Minnie made another decision.[1] Why should the act only be paid as a quartet when the family had two additional singers? Minnie and her sister Hannah joined the act, which was rechristened the Six Mascots. A local boy named Fred Klute rounded out the sextet that also included Julius, Adolph, and Milton.[2] Klute had no stage experience, but Minnie had never let that stop her before. Klute's father operated a tavern in their new Chicago neighborhood, so it's possible that Minnie saw some advantage in having a saloonkeeper as a friend. If Herbert was keeping score, his mother, two uncles, a cousin, and an aunt had now been on vaudeville stages as had three of his brothers. Sara Heyman was Minnie's only surviving sibling to never set foot on a stage. Minnie probably wondered about the talents never displayed by her five dead sisters.

In their first few months in Chicago, the Six Mascots were able to play locally for weeks at a time, taking advantage of the unusually large number of vaudeville houses in and around the city. The reduction in travel expenses immediately made the Chicago move seem like a great idea. *Continuous Performance*, a biography of theater owner A. J. Balaban, quoted him about Minnie as manager of her sons' act in the family's early days in Chicago. "Whenever there was an open split-week in their bookings, she'd slip them to me at a 'cut,' sharing with me the benefit of a home-town booking that eliminated traveling expense." Chicago was a land of opportunity for the act, but eventually the Six Mascots had to hit the road. Aunt Hannah's husband, Julius Schickler, traveled with them as an advance man—and occasionally a seventh member of the act—so Herbert was left at home under the lax supervision of Minnie's now eighty-seven-year-old father, and Frenchy. It didn't take long for Herbert to figure out that roaming the streets of Chicago was a lot more fun than showing up at school. Being the youngest of five boys certainly toughened up Herbert and he became pretty good with his fists. Boys his own age were no match for him. At home he was little Herbie, easy to pick on. On the street he was known as Buster Marx. He was the first Marx brother to pick up a nickname and was respected by his peers because, if provoked, he could knock a kid on his backside quickly.

Bert Cahn, a childhood friend, spoke about Zeppo's boyhood days in Chicago in an August 8, 1979, *Palm Beach Post* interview:

[W]e called him Buster because of his Buster Brown haircut. . . . We became sort of pals. He was in my room in school. He was full of mischief and did many silly things, but we were like two peas in a pod as I was no angel either. He'd get in more scraps than a junkman. He was anything but a sissy. He'd fight at the drop of a hat.

One hot August day, the two of us decided to go swimming in Lake Michigan about two miles east of where we lived. There was no beach at the location. We'd just jump off the breakwater. We swam until we got tired and started walking home. Try to imagine a very hot day, with both of us thirsty as hell and not a cent between us. Suddenly, on approaching an ice cream parlor owned by a Greek, Zeppo said, "How would you like an ice cream sundae?"

"Whaddaya mean?" Cahn said. "We got nuttin'." "Don't worry about it," Zeppo said reassuringly. "The guy who owns the store is a friend of my mother's and he'll collect from her." So, Bert and Zeppo went into the ice cream parlor and ordered two sundaes. "I was in heaven and enjoying it with all the gusto a ten-year-old kid could summon," Cahn said. Cahn noticed that his friend Zeppo was eating quite rapidly but thought nothing of it. Suddenly Zeppo turned toward the door, cried, "Hello, Joe" and dashed out of the store. It took only seconds for Cahn to realize that he had been left holding the bag. He decided it would be prudent to absent himself.

"Out I dashed after him, with the Greek running along the counter trying to cut me off," Cahn said. "Luckily, there was a cigar counter at the end, so I was out of reach. I got out the door and ran as far as I could until I thought I was safe." Cahn went to Zeppo's house with murderous thoughts on his young mind. Zeppo, being a clever lad, sensibly refused to come out. "Just think, I was his friend, and he left me holding the bag like that," Cahn said.

With Buster Marx's adventures in Chicago far from her mind, Minnie concerned herself with the flailing Six Mascots. They gradually developed a better act than the one in which two women in their mid forties played schoolgirls—the roles Minnie and her sister Hannah took in the act. The act was evolving from a singing act into the schoolroom comedy act that would soon put the Marx Brothers on their path to stardom. By the beginning of 1911 the act was known as the Three Marx Brothers and Company, and they starred in "Fun in Hi Skule," a classroom comedy sketch. Minnie had retired from performing to focus strictly on management—and maybe getting Herbert to school occasionally. Aunt Hannah remained in the act until she finally abandoned her stage career just as the fall vaudeville season began in 1912. In the summer of 1911, Leonard arrived in Chicago with singer Aaron Gordon, the partner he'd teamed with when they met as song pluggers in Pittsburgh. Minnie struggled to get the new act vaudeville bookings and by the beginning of the fall season she had paired Leonard with Aunt Hannah's son, Lou Shean. Minnie now had two acts based in Chicago. As it had with Aaron Gordon, Leonard's reckless lifestyle proved too challenging for even his cousin Lou Shean, a vaudeville veteran by this point, who could do without the aggravation and the danger. Compulsive gambling and womanizing on the road could cause serious problems for Leonard's partners.

With his third partner, Moe Lee, Leonard's vaudeville career took the turn Minnie was hoping for. They did good business as Marx and Lee in the summer of 1912. That fall, Marx and Lee joined the family act to form the Four Marx Brothers and Company. Their new show—an immediate success—was a tabloid musical called *Mr. Green's Reception*. A tabloid was essentially a truncated version of a full-length show cut down for presentation as a vaudeville show. Some of these tabloids were versions of current Broadway hits and others—like *Mr. Green's Reception*—were original creations in the tab format.

With Leonard now based in Chicago, and more relatives passing through town, the Marx family moved out of their rental apartment on Calumet Avenue and bought a three-story brownstone at 4512 Grand Boulevard.[3] The house was only a short walk from the Calumet apartment, so Herbert's adventures on the neighborhood streets were unaffected. The new house had a basement large enough for a pool table, so Herbert would have the advantage of not having to hang around the local poolrooms as his brothers had to in New York. The family was now successful enough to have their own poolroom. And with Leonard and Arthur in the house, they even had their own pool hustlers.

The success of the Four Marx Brothers inspired Minnie, now a successful producer, to branch out with additional acts. The most obvious source of talent was her own family. Having already proven with Milton and Arthur that desire and skill were not essential for vaudeville success, Minnie decided to give her brother Harry another chance to emulate the great Al Shean. After a few unsuccessful show business ventures on his own Harry shut down his lunch wagon in Queens and moved his family to Chicago. Minnie created an act for Harry called the Orange Blossoms and, in the spring of 1913, this terrible act hit the road and made a bit of money. Minnie did even better with her nephew, Lou Shean—partly feeling as though she owed him another chance because of his brief and dangerous partnership with Leonard. He toured the country in a show called *The Duke of Bull Durham*, which did good business for a while.

The only problem with Minnie's new successes was that she was offering theater managers package deals. If a manager booked the Orange Blossoms or *The Duke of Bull Durham*, they could also have the Four Marx Brothers. Booking fees were adjusted accordingly, so if a theater projected losses on the act with Harry Shean or Lou Shean, they would make up for it by paying a little less for the guaranteed box office success of the Four Marx Brothers. Naturally, this did not sit well with the Four Marx Brothers. Leonard, the only brother who could get any consideration out of Minnie, gradually took control of the act away from her. The failure of the Orange Blossoms and *The Duke of Bull Durham* followed almost immediately.

Minnie had rechristened herself Minnie Palmer around this time and remained active as a vaudeville producer and manager while the Marx Brothers mostly managed themselves—always being careful enough to promote the notion that Minnie was in charge.[4] Regardless of the Palmer name, Minnie made sure everyone in vaudeville knew who her sons were. With the success of the Four Marx Brothers, Minnie saw strength in numbers with acts like the Six American Beauties and the Seven Parisian Violets. She even renamed Harry's act the Eight Orange Blossoms. And where was she getting these American Beauties, Parisian Violets, and Orange Blossoms? One of the advantages of the new house was that it had plenty of space. Minnie advertised for aspiring chorus girls to come to Chicago and learn the trade at her home during the summer break in the vaudeville season. With a flock of pretty, young girls in a house with its own poolroom, there was little chance of her sons ever leaving the premises. For Herbert it was his first real chance to spend a significant amount of time with Leonard. And Herbert liked what he saw. He was quickly turning into a pint-sized version of his oldest brother.

The family also bought a car around this time. Herbert developed an affinity for all things mechanical and learned how the engine worked. He learned so well that he even figured out how to start a car without the key—in the era of the newly invented car key, which locked the ignition even though cranking the engine was still required. Stealing cars was a two-man job and Herbert and his schoolmate Joey Bass were a team. Joey had been getting into trouble long before he teamed up with Herbert. He made the local papers when he was twelve and nearly died because of his mischief. Joey had climbed a telephone pole on a dare and touched a live electrical wire. The shock threw him to the ground, but he survived. (Joey was briefly paralyzed, which resulted in his younger brother Ernie beating him in the hospital in retaliation for prior bullying.) The streets of Chicago were an automotive showroom for Herbert. He and Joey took their neighborhood friends on joyrides, abandoning the cars they borrowed wherever they tired of them. The question for Minnie was whether Herbert was better off being around Leonard or cruising the streets of Chicago in stolen cars. In a BBC interview near the end of his life, Zeppo recalled his Chicago boyhood. "I was a real bad boy. I carried a gun and stole automobiles." He came under the influence of Joey's brother, Louis Bass, who was two years older. "This boy was an older boy. . . . I loved to be with him because he was so tough, and I sort of felt that if I got in any trouble, he'd protect me."

Herbert was far from unique in his early life of crime. The Chicago streets were filled with youth gangs and underage crime when the Marx family arrived in town in 1909. Four years later a *Chicago Tribune* story titled "Chicago's Boy Gangsters, Its Greatest Menace" dated November 2, 1913, set the scene: "There are hundreds of gangs in Chicago. The membership of these gangs runs into the thousands. Most of the gangsters are youngsters from the age of 10 to 18." Herbert met the Bass brothers shortly after the family arrived in Chicago. The neighborhood had two dominant gangs—the 39th Street gang and the 43rd Street gang. The Marx home on Grand Boulevard was between 45th and 46th

Streets, putting Herbert squarely in 43rd Street gang territory, along with the Bass brothers, who lived nearby at Wabash Avenue and 42nd Street. The *Tribune* story quoted John H. Witter, superintendent of the Chicago Boy's Club: "The gangster is usually a young fellow who to all appearances is harmless. He is a boy of 16 or 18, and when met on the street shows nothing of the criminal. But he is a criminal. He is a thief, a petty thief to begin with. As he reaches the age of 17 or 18, he becomes a more dangerous criminal." To put it mildly, Herbert was at risk.

When the Four Marx Brothers hit the road for the new vaudeville season in August 1913, Herbert was a full-blown juvenile delinquent. Groucho's son Arthur wrote in *Son of Groucho*, "Zeppo had a good left hook and was nimble afoot from the training of trying to outrun the local truant officer." Minnie only knew one way to get her son under control, but he was still a bit too young for vaudeville. On occasion, when Al Shean was on tour, Johanna and Larry would make extended visits to Chicago and stay with the Marx family. Larry Shean was a cousin that Herbert looked up to and he usually stayed out of trouble when Larry was around. When the Four Marx Brothers were on the road there just weren't many people at the house able to keep Herbert off the streets.

On January 5, 1914, the Four Marx Brothers opened a weeklong engagement at the Willard Theatre in Chicago—only a few blocks from the Grand Boulevard house. The *New York Clipper* on January 10 noted the proximity of the theater to the Marx home and reported, "On Monday they sang special songs for their friends, which brought down the house." The Sunday evening performance at the Willard on January 11 was Herbert's vaudeville debut. He did a solo spot singing "Where Did You Get That Girl," a current popular song written by Harry Puck and Bert Kalmar. (Kalmar would later collaborate with Harry Ruby on numerous songs for Marx Brothers shows and films.) For Minnie, Herbert's debut amounted to an intervention. She had gotten him off the street for at least one night. The *New York Clipper* wrote, on January 24, "Herbert Marx, youngest of the Marx Brothers, will change the title of the act from the Four Marx Bros. to the Five Marx Bros. as soon as he completes school. He appeared at the Willard one night recently and scored . . . big."

Herbert was still six weeks away from his thirteenth birthday when he appeared at the Willard. Completing school did not seem likely. If he was still too young to join the Marx Brothers, he was perfectly happy running around Chicago with the Bass brothers. If he was on tour in vaudeville at least Minnie would know where he was. On February 24 Herbert made another appearance with his brothers in Gary, Indiana. The day before the four-day engagement at the Orpheum Theatre began, an advertisement in the *Gary Evening Post* announced a "Special Attraction." Herbert Marx, the fifth Marx Brother, "Chicago's Boy Soprano" would appear for one night only. The trip to Gary was likely a birthday celebration for Herbert, who turned thirteen the day after his performance.

The Four Marx Brothers played in the Chicago area frequently in the spring of 1914, and Herbert saw his brothers regularly. But when they were away from Chicago Herbert continued getting into trouble. On May 1 and 2, Minnie got Herbert out of Chicago for a couple of days. She took him to Joliet, forty-five miles away, to appear with the act at the Orpheum Theatre. She again promoted the addition of her youngest son to the act. Her press release appeared in *The Joliet News*: "[T]he youngest brother of this talented family, who is in his six-teenth year, and who has just finished his studies in Chicago, joins the company at matinee tomorrow and as a lyric tenor will add still another specialty."

There could be a few reasons why Minnie would lie about Herbert's age. There had been a lot of controversy about putting children on the stage and the Gerry Society, an organization dedicated to preventing and exposing the exploitation of children, was making a lot of noise about vaudeville. At the same time, Chicago's truancy and juvenile delinquency problems had become worse. The juvenile court was overcrowded with gang and petty theft cases, and on March 18, 1914, a new boys' court was opened for cases involving boys aged seventeen to twenty-one. This took a lot of pressure off the juvenile court, which promptly started rounding up younger truants. If they could catch up to Herbert, he would be a prime candidate for incarceration in what was known as the Parental School. It was opened in 1902 in the remote northwest corner of Chicago, adjacent to the municipal tuberculosis sanatorium. Hundreds of hooky-playing Chicago boys spent between eight months and two years in this facility, which was essentially a combination of a school and a prison. Any boy there would be discharged upon reaching the age of fourteen, but there was a political movement working toward increasing the age to sixteen. With debate going on about the age at which a child could legally be out of school, and truant officers fanning out across their neighborhood, Minnie took no chances. She got Herbert to Joliet and advertised him as "the Fifth Marx Brother—Chicago's 16-Year-Old Tenor." To Minnie's way of thinking, any truant officers reading the vaudeville press would know to leave Herbert alone.

Herbert was now part of Minnie's show business plan, but he wasn't ready for the road yet. When he returned to Chicago, he would be thirteen again and would be required by his mother to attend school regularly to get into the act, which, contrary to his later recollections, he very much wanted to do. Al Shean's son Larry, a few years older than Herbert, was again staying in the Marx home. He was a good student and positive influence on Herbert, who wrote a letter to his brother Julius on the road on November 23, 1914. Julius likely received it at the Lyric Theatre in Birmingham, Alabama later that week:

> Julie. Dear brother, how are you feeling? I hope you are well. How is everything? I hope you hurry and come home. I am having a fine time with Larry. When are you coming home? Mama told me that you were going to play the Majestic. . . . I have not much to write but enough to assure you I am getting a lot of chicken nowadays. Dear brother Julius, give my regards to all. I am getting along fine in school and at home. I am a good boy now and glad of it. Goodbye. Your loving brother Herbert.

Herbert had not made a complete transformation from juvenile delinquent to honor student. While he did spend less time with the local criminal element, he remained pals with Joey and Louis Bass. The big change was going to school every day, which was all it took to keep the truant officers away. He'd still have time to steal the occasional car with his buddies. Buster Marx was still a tough kid on the streets and if anyone made any cracks about him going to school, they could count on getting punched in the face. Herbert got into a lot of fights—as did a lot of boys his age at the time. The prevailing attitude was "boys will be boys." But even so, Herbert was a more frequent fighter than most.

When he did go to school, Herbert was a good student. He developed an early appreciation of books and would later proudly own a fine collection of first editions. Like most boys his age, Herbert was inspired by the work of Mark Twain, whose death in 1910 resulted in numerous new editions of *The Adventures of Tom Sawyer* and *The Adventures of Huckleberry Finn*. Herbert found he had much in common with Huck Finn, whose favorite pastimes included not going to school, "borrowing" boats, and fishing. Herbert would later become an avid fisherman—possibly the result of his admiration of Twain's celebrated juvenile delinquent character. There were several instances of runaway boys Herbert's age attracting the attention of Chicago's newspapers. It was frequently reported that these boys were emulating Huckleberry Finn. Herbert didn't need to run away from home to live this fantasy life. The lack of supervision at home allowed him to indulge in his Huck Finn lifestyle while enjoying a roof over his head and three square meals a day.

The end of the school year coincided with the end of the vaudeville season. On May 29, 1915, *The Grand Rapids Press* reported that Herbert was heading straight from school to Michigan to join the Four Marx Brothers: "During their Grand Rapids engagement, their youngest brother who is just out of school, will make his professional debut. He has had several tryouts and is said to be one of the cleverest in the lot." The act opened at the Empress Theatre in Grand Rapids on May 31 as a quartet, but Herbert was on stage the following day and the rest of the week. *The Grand Rapids Press* covered his arrival on June 2, albeit with his age incorrectly listed:

> The youngest of the Marx Brothers, ten-year-old Herbert, arrived Tuesday from school in Chicago and appeared in the musical revue, *Home Again* at the Empress. He is a clever little lad and his appearance in everyday school attire and his frank, unaffected boyishness ingratiated him at once in the favor of the audiences. This is the second time that he has appeared publicly on stage. He expects to return to school in the fall.

Herbert had turned fourteen a few months before his appearance in Grand Rapids. Perhaps the locale was no accident or coincidence. Julius made his professional debut in Grand Rapids ten years earlier at the age of fourteen—and the occasion marked the end of his formal education. But at least publicly, the stated intention was for Herbert to continue in school. At the end of June, Leonard, Arthur, Julius, and Milton came home to Chicago for their summer vacation. But it would be a shorter break than usual. Minnie had an idea about giving Herbert a real chance to experience vaudeville without missing school. There was some hope that Herbert would be the first member of the family to graduate from high school, so any vaudeville work would need to be in the summer. But if higher education wasn't in Herbert's future, Minnie would be perfectly happy to expand the act into the Five Marx Brothers.

After a seven-week vacation, the Four Marx Brothers along with their youngest brother would hit the road for a one-month tour of Michigan. A few weeks before the tour started Herbert and Milton visited their cousin Lou Shean, who was vacationing at Park Beidler, a resort at Lake Goguac in Battle Creek. On July 25, 1915, Herbert sang a few songs at a local cabaret. This seemingly insignificant event managed to get reported in the *Battle Creek Moon-Journal*: "One of the regular entertainers at the cabaret was singing and had started upon the chorus of a well-known popular song, when a new voice was heard, coming from a different section, and continued until the end of the piece, ending in high tremolo tenor. A thunder of applause greeted this and all present looked to see where the voice came from. One of the other members of the cabaret troupe saw Marx through one of the side windows and succeeded in inducing him to come in and sing several selections for the audience."

This little episode seems like a carefully orchestrated piece of publicity. The newspaper item noted that Herbert's appearance had taken the cabaret by storm. Presumably a fourteen-year-old kid interrupting a performance would not be pleasing to the audience or the performers on stage. But Herbert was one of Minnie Marx's sons and this was no spontaneous outburst by Herbert. Milton and Herbert returned to Chicago before debuting with the Five Marx Brothers. Playing split weeks, they appeared in eight cities—Lansing, Saginaw, Kalamazoo, Jackson, Bay City, Flint, Battle Creek, and Ann Arbor. It would be the only instance of the act being billed as the Five Marx Brothers. Herbert's integration into the act was simple. The Four Marx Brothers had been successfully touring in *Home Again*, a show written for them by their uncle, Al Shean. The second act featured a party with several musical performances. Herbert sang a few songs in this context and appeared in a couple of other small bits added to the show.

The first local review, from the Bijou Theatre in Lansing, Michigan, on August 15, 1915, got Herbert's age wrong, and noted, "Master Herbert, who is about twelve, sings four or five ballads well and shows promise of development." At their next stop in Saginaw, the local paper commented on the new quintet: "The Four Marx Brothers are presenting an entire change of bill this season. There are now five of them, Leonard, Arthur, Julius, Milton, and a kiddie brother who perhaps is not yet christened as his name does not appear on the artistic menu cards handed out to Franklin Theatre patrons Thursday night when they went to see the brotherhood in *Home Again*." Apart from not knowing Herbert's name the writer gave him a positive review: "Number Five makes his debut in a vocal specialty and his performance is such as to place him in line for full membership in the brotherhood."

A reporter in Kalamazoo appears to have taken the time to speak with Herbert and wrote, "The new Marx—the youngest brother—who appeared on the theatrical horizon for the first time at the Sunday performance, sang nicely and gave evidence that he will soon be ready to take his regular turn along with the other four. He is only fourteen years old and will return to his home in Chicago when school season starts. In the meantime, he is having the time of his young life, just traveling and watching his brothers entertain the crowds."

For his baptism of fire Herbert experienced a grueling schedule. The tour ran from August 15 through September 11. There were no days off and most of the days featured three performances—a matinee and two evening shows. Herbert may have been having a good time on the road, but he also had to have noticed how hard his brothers worked. After the final show of the tour in Ann Arbor, the entire family returned to Chicago. For the Four Marx Brothers it was just a short rest. They opened in San Francisco on September 19. Herbert most likely wanted to go with them, preferring the hard work of vaudeville over the more mundane option of going to school. But it was certainly not Herbert's decision to make, and he returned to school—at least for a while.

CHAPTER THREE

The Juvenile Six

AN IMPORTANT DEVELOPMENT DURING HERBERT'S CHILDHOOD WAS
the opening of the Ford Motor Company's Chicago Assembly Plant
in 1914. The sprawling facility was located at 39th Street and Wabash
Avenue—a short walk from the Marx home on Grand Boulevard. Herbert's
fascination with cars kept him around the Ford plant, and he learned everything
he could about engines in the hope that he could work at the plant someday.
When Herbert cut school during the fall semester in 1915, he was more likely
to be found near the Ford plant than roaming the streets with Joey and Louis
Bass. Fixing cars had suddenly become more interesting than stealing them. Still
too young to work at Ford, Herbert learned that lying about his age was more
difficult on a Ford job application than it was in vaudeville. But Herbert now had
a dream of his own that had nothing to do with vaudeville. He had already experienced the road conditions and the grind of vaudeville. He preferred the idea of
joining the Ford team of 350 workers at the plant, which had added a salesroom
and a service department since the opening. Ford employees had a profit-sharing
plan and could earn as much as five dollars a day. The plant even had its own
movie theater. (It was mostly used to show visitors how cars were assembled at
the plant, but employees were occasionally treated to a film screening.)

Herbert was still being groomed by his mother for a career on the vaudeville
stage, but the possibilities he saw at the Ford plant were enough to make him
less interested in show business. When Groucho and Gummo jointly purchased
a used Chalmers automobile, they had a pint-sized mechanic at home to keep
it running. In *Groucho and Me*, Groucho wrote, "I suppose there are any number
of mechanically minded geniuses around the country who are born with an
instinctive flair for machinery. Zeppo was one of these freaks. He could take an
engine apart, grind the valves, adjust the timing and clean out the carbon with

no more fuss or effort than I would use in sharpening a pencil." Groucho also mentioned that the Chalmers would often mysteriously become inoperable, forcing him and Gummo to find alternate means of transportation. Each time Herbert would proceed to drive the repaired Chalmers around Chicago the moment they left the house.

Occasional periods of good behavior could never keep Buster Marx out of trouble for very long. In the Marx Brothers' authorized 1950 biography, Kyle Crichton wrote, "Minnie had only lately rescued him from a State Street pool-room, where he was assistant manager and associate of a circle of friends who were later to cost Cook County a fortune in cell space. Zeppo was the handsomest of the brothers and the possessor of a scintillating wit and a splendid right cross. . . . At a mass meeting called by the school principal at the request of fearsome parents, only one question had been asked: 'Has any boy in this room been struck by Herbert Marx?' Every hand went up."

When he turned fifteen in February 1916, Herbert was much less of a concern for the truant officers, and he quit school in the middle of the ninth grade.[1] But there was still the Chicago Police Department to worry about. In July, while his brothers were home on their summer break, Herbert managed to get into a fight that resulted in all five Marx Brothers being arrested. To Minnie's dismay this incident was covered by the *Chicago Examiner* and picked up by *Variety* in their July 21 issue, where the show business paper noted fifteen-year-old Herbert's age as sixteen, probably the result of Minnie's previous billing of him as Chicago's Sixteen-Year-Old Tenor. Details of the fracas appeared in the *Examiner* on July 18:

> The Four Marx Brothers were at liberty in jail yesterday. Only members of the theatrical profession can be at liberty and in jail at the same time—because "in jail" means "in jail" and "at liberty" means "temporarily disengaged from professional activities." The Marx Brothers are a vaudeville team.
>
> They went swimming yesterday at the Fifty-First Street beach, and they all declare that J. J. Kelly, a lifeguard, beat the youngest brother, Herbert, for playing ball in the water.
>
> The four brothers combined in an attack on Kelly, who was rescued by the police. Then the brothers, clad in bathing suits, were taken to the Hyde Park police station, where they remained until they were given bond.

It can't be known more than a century after the fact if Minnie's next move came because of Herbert's latest brush with the law, but it is certainly not inconceivable. When the Four Marx Brothers opened the fall season at the Le Grand Theatre in Chicago on August 21, 1916, there was a new act on the bill with them. This act accompanied them to Indiana for three-day engagements in Elkhart and Richmond, and a one-night stand in Hammond, but was never heard from again. The act was "Buster Palmer," a juvenile singer. Any resemblance to Herbert Marx was unavoidable. Minnie had combined her vaudeville surname with Herbert's neighborhood nickname, and he was instantly on a vaudeville bill. But why not as Herbert, the fifth Marx Brother? It was all part of Minnie's latest plan, which may have been necessitated by the Four Marx Brothers preferring not to take Herbert on the road with them for the fall season in 1916. Apart from Herbert's occasionally criminal behavior, they likely had other reasons. While crisscrossing the country and visiting almost every theater along the way, the Four Marx Brothers also made a habit of visiting every poolroom and whorehouse along the way. Their fifteen-year-old brother joining them in these activities could land them in jail. Minnie's solution was to send Herbert out on tour, but as part of another act. This would keep him out of his brothers' hair, and he would earn a salary that did not come out of the Four Marx Brothers' revenue.

Minnie Palmer and Minnie Marx were one and the same, but they also lived separate lives. By the time Herbert was singing on stage as Buster Palmer, Minnie Marx barely existed, having been completely overwhelmed by Minnie Palmer. One of the main reasons Herbert had hardly any parental supervision at home was that Minnie Palmer had set up her office in the Crilly Building at 35 South Dearborn Street. The building was the hub of vaudeville in Chicago. Practically every agent, manager and circuit had an office there. Thurman Dwight Pepple— known professionally as T. Dwight Pepple—was a vaudeville agent, producer, and one-time actor based in Ohio. When he came to Chicago in October 1913, he rented space in Minnie Palmer's office. But Minnie would not rent office space to just anyone. There had to be something in it for Minnie besides rent money.

By the time T. Dwight Pepple arrived in Chicago, Minnie was enjoying great success with tabloid musicals. With the Four Marx Brothers leading the way, she sent several of these shows out on the road after the initial success of the Marx tab *Mr. Green's Reception* in 1912. Maurice L. Greenwald, who had been the road manager of Minnie's tabloid *Running for Congress*, went into the tabloid production business with T. Dwight Pepple. Minnie was not threatened by her friends and associates producing their own tab shows. They learned the business from her. She ran ads in the trade papers touting herself as "Minnie Palmer—Queen of Tabloids" and she really was for a while.

Tabloids were a great business for managers and agents who could stock the casts of these shows with three or four of their acts. But that could present a problem for independent small-time acts who had trouble finding work, as openings on bills became scarce during the tab craze. It was not uncommon for a tabloid to replace as many as five acts of an eight-act bill. Some—like *Mr. Green's Reception*—could fill an entire bill. One of the many small-timers who lost job opportunities because of tabloids was Minnie's nephew, Lou Shean. Lou's brief partnership with his cousin Leonard as Shean and Marx in the 1911–1912 season had ended with Lou fearing for his safety as the occasional gunshot fired at Leonard by an angry husband or father got a little too close. Lou worked as a burlesque comic until Minnie put him in her tab show *The Duke of Bull Durham*. T. Dwight Pepple's first order of business working out of Minnie's office was to find a new job for Lou Shean. To this point, Pepple was known for putting together all-girl acts like the Colonial Minstrel Maids, which tended not to have openings for German dialect comedians like Lou Shean. More challenging was Lou's health. He had to stop working for several months because of an eye ailment that left him unable to leave his room for six weeks. But before Pepple could put Lou Shean to work, he and Minnie created their first act together. The Five Rose Maids—a group of attractive young female singers and musicians— was more typical of the acts Pepple had been working with. Minnie's efforts to "class up" the act included the placement of roses all over the stage.[2]

T. Dwight Pepple was cut from the same cloth as Minnie. Determination won out over every obstacle, and he was almost as optimistic in the face of failure as Minnie. They also shared a penchant for extreme nerve in advertising. Minnie would occasionally put phrases like "world famous songwriters" into an ad for the Four Marx Brothers when they were barely famous in the American Midwest and had not written any songs. Pepple would bill his mediocre *All Girl Revue of 1916* as "the *Ziegfeld Follies* of Vaudeville." This was a man Minnie could do business with. An early advertisement for the Five Rose Maids billed them as the "classiest act in vaudeville."

A month after moving into Minnie's office, Pepple and Lou Shean were the producers of the new tabloid musical, *The Parisian Revue*. The following spring, Pepple and Shean revamped Pepple's old show *A Night at Maxim's*, and when Lou's health permitted, he joined the cast of both shows. Pepple also created several shows that didn't require him to find jobs for Minnie's relatives. In the fall of 1916, when Minnie needed to put Herbert into an act, she turned to

T. Dwight Pepple, who by this time had become successful enough to get his own office a few doors down the hall from Minnie's. Pepple first needed to see what the boy could do, so Minnie set up the showcase for "Buster Palmer" on the bill with the Four Marx Brothers.

Pepple and Greenwald had been casting all-girl shows like *Southern Porch Party* and the *Song and Dance Revue* when they met the three Kashner sisters from Cleveland, Ohio. Two of them, Fay, twenty-five, and Marvel, twenty-one, had been working in vaudeville as a singing act for several years. The youngest, Ida, eighteen, worked as a child actress and had recently joined her sisters in their singing act. The dancing Harris Brothers—George, twenty-five, and Victor, twenty-two, were well known to Minnie. They had spent two seasons with the Four Marx Brothers between 1912 and 1914. When Minnie put Buster Palmer on a couple of bills with the Four Marx Brothers for Pepple to see, she also had the Harris Brothers on those bills. Pepple and Greenwald—with some help from Minnie—created a new act for the fall season in 1916. Pepple and Greenwald supplied the Kashner Sisters, and Minnie supplied the Harris Brothers and Herbert Marx. They called the act the Juvenile Six, although Herbert was the only actual juvenile in the group. Having a pair of twenty-five-year-old "juveniles" in the act harkened back to Minnie's early days as a producer. When the Three Marx Brothers were touring in their classroom sketch "Fun in Hi Skule" in 1911, twenty-two-year-old Arthur and Minnie's forty-nine-year-old sister Hannah played school children.

The Juvenile Six, like the Marx Brothers before them, were not above stretching the truth. Lying was as important as talent in vaudeville. The Kashner sisters not only lied about their ages—claiming to be nineteen, eighteen, and sixteen—they also called themselves the Karlmer Sisters. The act ran fifteen minutes and afforded the three separate acts within it brief chances in the spotlight. After a song by the full sextet, the Harris Brothers danced. The Karlmer Sisters followed with a couple of songs before Herbert took a solo spot that would typically include a pair of popular current songs. "What Do You Want to Make Those Eyes at Me For (When They Don't Mean What They Say)" had recently been introduced in the Broadway show *Follow Me*. "You're a Dog-Gone Dangerous Girl" had been featured in Al Jolson's show at the Winter Garden Theatre. Both were considered novelty songs and were presumably made more novel when sung by a fifteen-year-old.

The finale was again a sextet number, this time featuring the group doing a Scottish song in appropriate Scottish attire. The act's reviews often remarked about the staging. They were sometimes billed as "a novelty in black and white," which referred to the two-tone backdrop and the costumes designed to blend with it. The act also traveled with some advanced electrical lighting effects built into their scenery. This aspect of the Juvenile Six comes directly from the Minnie Palmer playbook. The Four Marx Brothers' scenery for *Home Again* got a lot of attention from critics, mostly because the boat featured in the dock setting was on wheels surrounded by cardboard waves and would leave the dock at the end of the first act.

After opening in Chicago at the Lincoln Hippodrome on September 21, 1916, the Juvenile Six hit the road for a season in small-time vaudeville. They covered most of the country over the next nine months, starting in the Midwest and working their way east through Ohio and upstate New York before turning around and heading north for a grueling trip around the far-flung Ackerman and Harris circuit through North and South Dakota, Montana, and Idaho before heading down the West Coast. This infamous slice of vaudeville was known to performers as the "death trail" due to the long distances between cities on the circuit. The Juvenile Six also had the extra misfortune of working the "death trail" in December and January.

As large parts of the country experienced the coldest winter in thirty-seven years, there was also a coal shortage to make it worse. Adding to their general misfortune, snow delayed their train and the Juvenile Six failed to arrive in Lewistown, Montana, in time for a scheduled one-night stand on December 26, 1916. Herbert and his costars rang in 1917 with a New Year's Eve show in frigid and windy Butte, Montana. Even in their leanest years, the Marx Brothers never played the dreaded Ackerman & Harris circuit. Herbert was paying his dues. The Juvenile Six made it out of the cold and got to enjoy several weeks of mild weather on the West Coast with dates in San Francisco, San Diego, and Los Angeles before working their way back to Chicago through Colorado, Missouri, Arkansas, and Iowa.

Reviews for the Juvenile Six were generally positive. But occasionally a critic aired his grievances with the act. A review in *The Sacramento Bee* from February 1, 1917, said, "The Juvenile Six are effectively staged as far as costumes and setting are concerned and the young performers are fairly clever, but their immaturity is responsible for a conspicuous lack of stability, smoothness and finish in the act." That same day *The Sacramento Star* reviewed the same performance: "A novel black and white impressionistic setting is used by the Juvenile Six. They open with a clever sextet number, followed by some of the best soft shoe dancing seen in many a month. Clever song numbers are given, and the act closes with a rousing Scotch chorus and solo in costume. It's a neat act." One man's hit is another man's flop.

Reviews generally appeared in local papers the day after an act opened. The summary of the show that appeared in advance of the opening was supplied by the theater—which received it from the circuit that booked the act. This basically meant that the acts supplied their own advance press notices. Minnie Palmer was a notorious self-promoter and specialized in outrageous lies and effusive praise when it came to selling her acts. Before the Juvenile Six even got off the train in East Liverpool, Ohio, this item ran in the *Evening Review* on November 4, 1916:

> This is a very clever act composed of three boys and three girls who are real artists presenting their incomparable style of songs and dances. The act is enhanced with beautiful scenery and electrical effects and the ability of these child performers is said to be wonderful, in fact it is considered the best juvenile act on the American stage. No one can well afford to miss this great big treat.

Minnie's incessant hyping of her sons and her other acts added to her legend. The stories of her throwing her allegedly untalented sons into show business may have had a tinge of truth in the cases of Harpo and Gummo, but in a rare moment of candor on the subject, Groucho was quoted in Arthur Marx's book *Son of Groucho*: "That's a lot of horseshit. Sure, Mom gave us a little push. But *we* did all the work. *We* were the ones with the talent." Harpo was more of a company man when he was quoted in the *Columbus Sunday Dispatch* on October 1, 1916: "We are Minnie Palmer's sons. Our mother expected us to make good—so we had to do it." Herbert was now officially part of his mother's expectations. He'd given Minnie's dream a try and did quite well at it, garnering favorable reviews and sending home his salary as his brothers had in their early vaudeville travels.

On January 12, 1917, while Herbert was in Walla Walla, Washington with the Juvenile Six on the so-called death trail, there was an eruption of gang violence and real death in his Chicago neighborhood. Likely, Herbert would have been in the middle of it had Minnie not sent him on the road. Two rival gangs got into a brawl in front of Schaeffer's Ice Cream Shop at the corner of St. Lawrence Avenue and 43rd Street. Louis Bass got knocked down and beaten up in the brawl. He ran home, came back with his gun, and shot and wounded twenty-two-year-old Joseph M. Mahoney, who died a week later. Louis fled, but Joey Bass was held as a witness. Louis was eventually found hiding at his aunt's house and taken into custody. Louis claimed he shot Mahoney in self-defense—failing to explain why he ran home to get his gun before defending himself. Somehow, the charge was reduced to manslaughter, and Judge Joseph H. Fitch of the Cook

County Superior Court acquitted Louis on May 3, 1917. Louis Bass ran out of luck with the court system after that. He was in and out of trouble and prison for the rest of his life.

Zeppo told BBC interviewer Barry Norman a slightly mixed-up version of the Louis Bass story in 1978, conflating the January 1917 shooting with an important incident in his life that would not take place until June 1918. He told a story about a double date he and Bass were to go on that Minnie made him break so he could join the Four Marx Brothers in Rockford, Illinois:

> We were dating a couple of girls at that time, and we were dating about two or three times a week, in the evening, and we'd go take them out to the park, and go in the bushes. Well, what boys and girls do in the bushes. . . . We had no money to go to a motel or hotel. So, this particular night we had a date. . . . I couldn't keep the date with my friend and so I called him and told him and he said "[A]lright, I'll keep the date with the two girls," which he did and the two girls had two boys there that were brothers and they found out about us, and they were over at the park waiting for us. . . . They got a hold of him and beat the hell out of him and they knocked him down, and they kicked him, kicked him in the face and everything, and he pulled out a gun and killed [one of them]. Now I would have been there too, and with my buddy, I'd have done the same thing and I'd have gotten into the same trouble.

The facts about the shooting of Joseph M. Mahoney as reported in the Chicago papers in January 1917 are reliable, and Herbert Marx was nowhere near Chicago at the time. Could Louis Bass have killed two neighborhood kids in separate incidents more than a year apart? Doubtful. The Mahoney shooting probably had nothing to do with Herbert and his friend getting intimate with a couple of girls in the bushes of a neighborhood park. But the Mahoney shooting was over two girls who were alleged to have snitched on some gang members. *The Chicago Examiner* reported on January 14, 1917, that the girls were seventeen-year-old Grace Shaw and nineteen-year-old Olive Van Valkenburg. These girls may be the two girls Louis Bass and Herbert had been to the bushes with. And Mahoney may have beaten up Louis Bass previously because of that. More will probably never be known, but Louis Bass killed someone in front of dozens of witnesses and was miraculously acquitted. Herbert Marx didn't require an acquittal to be available when Minnie needed him in the spring of 1918. He knew he'd been lucky to be far from Chicago when the shooting occurred.

CHAPTER FOUR

What's in a Name?

WHEN THE JUVENILE SIX RETURNED TO CHICAGO IN THE SUMMER of 1917, the first thing the now sixteen-year-old Herbert Marx did was get himself a job at the Ford Motor Company in the service department. The one season existence of the Juvenile Six would be quickly forgotten. Much had changed at home while Herbert was on the road. The United States was getting closer to entering World War I, and in the spring of 1917, the Selective Service Act put the Four Marx Brothers in a precarious situation. On June 5, while Herbert was in Detroit with the Juvenile Six, the Four Marx Brothers registered for the draft in Chicago. Herbert, now old enough to work at Ford, was still too young to be drafted.

The Juvenile Six had never been intended to be an ongoing venture. The fact that only one member of the sextet was really a juvenile finally became a problem with the June 1917 draft. George and Victor Harris registered for the draft in Detroit two days before the act opened there at the Miles Theatre. According to their draft cards, they had already secured new jobs for the upcoming fall season with producer Lew Canter. But by the summer of 1918, the Harris brothers had traded life on America's vaudeville stages for life on the battlefields of France. Victor Harris was wounded in the Argonne Offensive, the deadliest battle in the history of the United States Army.[1] After the war, Victor returned to show business but George did not. Minnie hoped deferments would keep her draft-aged sons from following the same path as the Harris Brothers.

The first Marx family draft deferment came in the form of a wife with a baby on the way. The Marx Brothers had gotten women pregnant before, but Minnie was eager to prevent her sons from getting married, so abortions were her favored solution. Wives could only minimize Minnie's control of her sons and—more importantly—the act, which was slowly slipping away from her anyway. Betty Karp went on a date with Leonard in Brooklyn in March. When she contacted him to let him know he was going to be a father, Minnie had her take the train to Chicago, where they were married on August 3.[2] As this was going on, Minnie heard about agricultural and farming deferments, so she bought a chicken farm in La Grange, just outside of Chicago in June. Leonard and Betty moved into the Grand Boulevard house and the rest of the family moved to the farm. Julius avoided the draft because of his poor eyesight, and Milton and Arthur registered as farmers. For the moment, none of the Marx Brothers were heading off to war.

The farm was around fifteen miles from the Grand Boulevard house, so Herbert split his time between the farm and house while working at Ford. Time at the farm was also useful in keeping Herbert away from his street gang buddies in the old neighborhood. Julius, Milton, and Arthur spent that summer at both locations as well. Around this time the family purchased a used Scripps-Booth automobile, which frequently required service. If Herbert needed the car, he would repeat the trick he used on Groucho and Gummo's old Chalmers by disabling the engine and miraculously repairing it after his brothers found alternate transportation. This was impractical. Kyle Crichton wrote of Herbert's solution to his transportation problem:

> Zeppo gave up on the Scripps-Booth and began borrowing cars. These belonged to strangers and were taken without permission, but Zeppo made a point of returning them after a few hours with only such minor dents as might be acquired from a passing encounter with a truck. He was driving a Cadillac one day with the car loaded to the eaves with admiring young friends when a policeman hailed him at Randolph and State. The fat was in the fire.
>
> They were hauled off to the jug and things looked bad. Minnie hurried down to find herself surrounded by an indignant mob of mothers and fathers. Each asserted vehemently that their sons had never in their lives considered an illegal action until brought under the influence of Herbert Marx.

It was during this period that Herbert acquired the name Zeppo. The Four Marx Brothers had been rechristened as Groucho, Harpo, Chico, and Gummo during a Galesburg, Illinois, poker game in May 1914 by an obscure vaudeville comedian named Art Fisher. The various explanations for Zeppo's name over the years have ranged from plausible to improbable. But the version favored by at least a few of the Marx Brothers' children involved Herbert's resemblance to sideshow performer and circus freak William Henry Johnson, also known as Zip the Pinhead. Zip evolved into Zippo, and eventually Zeppo. Naturally this was not flattering to young Herbert, who would come up with some of the more implausible explanations for his name years later. Monkeys, acrobats, chimps, clowns, zeppelins—anything was better than a circus sideshow freak!

Having an older brother can be challenging. Having four of them left Herbert with a nickname derived from a man who could at best be considered as being outside of any form of polite society at the time for a variety of reasons—race, appearance, and mental capacity topping the list. William Henry Johnson, the son of African American slaves, was also sometimes billed as the Original 'What-Is-It?' and worked in circus sideshows for many years. He may have suffered from microcephaly, a condition in which the head and brain are underdeveloped, causing limited mental capacity and a misshaped head. But he also may have just had an odd-shaped head and acted the part.

Before the coverup began, the derivation of Zeppo's nickname was openly discussed. At the point where the Four Marx Brothers began using their nicknames professionally, reporters naturally wanted to know how they were acquired. Beginning with the fall 1925 opening of their second Broadway show, *The Cocoanuts*, the Four Marx Brothers were shown in the cast listings of programs as Groucho, Harpo, Chico, and Zeppo. They'd only used the names causally, and mostly among themselves, prior to that.

On May 23, 1926, an item in the *Brooklyn Daily Eagle* asked, "Why are the Marx Brothers, the comedians in *The Cocoanuts* at the Lyric Theatre, using nicknames instead of their real names?" The paper went to the source for information. "'The answer is simple,' says Groucho, who always acts as spokesman for the group. 'We want to be different and attract unusual attention.'" Asked specifically about Zeppo, Groucho provides a compelling piece of evidence that would soon disappear from the record. "Zeppo was named for a freak in a circus which visited a farm where we used to live as boys." The Marx Brothers had an unusually long summer break in 1917 and didn't work from late April until mid-August, spending most of that time at the farm in LaGrange. William Henry Johnson was with the Barnum & Bailey circus at this time and spent a large part of that summer performing in Illinois, with stops in Chicago, Danville, Rockford, and Aurora. This would be the point at which the Marx Brothers saw Zip the Pinhead and decided he looked like Herbert. If the circus or any of its performers visited the Marx farm, there's no documentation of it, but Groucho told a reporter in 1926 that it happened.[3]

Herbert feebly denied this story in the coming years, and his brothers eventually played along and phased out the sideshow freak angle, but early on the truth kept coming out. In a March 1931 interview for Hubbard Keavy's syndicated "Screen Life in Hollywood" column, Harpo added a disturbing detail. Herbert "got a new name when his playful brothers once shaved his head and decided that he resembled Zep, a sideshow freak." (Clearly there's more to Herbert's later stated reluctance to join the act than just wanting to work as an auto mechanic.)

The *coup de grâce* in the Zip the Pinhead narrative came from Zeppo himself. An interview from the Boston tryout run of *The Cocoanuts* at the Tremont Theater finds a *Boston Globe* reporter in a dressing room shared by Harpo and Zeppo. The narrative is almost identical to the one Groucho shared in the *Brooklyn Daily Eagle*. The *Globe* article states, "Zeppo was named for a freak in a circus who visited a farm where the four used to live as boys." The article also quotes Harpo. "'The freak's name in the circus was Zippy,' he explained, 'but we changed it to Zeppo for Herbert here, and I swear the freak was insulted and didn't like the idea one bit.'" Then, for perhaps the only time, Zeppo confirmed the tale. "Zeppo, at the moment in a discussion with Sam Harris, came out long enough to admit the truth of this." After this one weak moment, the story—no matter who was telling it—evolved into one of the implausible variations. Anything but a circus freak. Older brothers could be cruel. In Herbert's case, multiply that by four and add in a forcible shaving of the youngest brother's head.

One of the more unusual versions of the nickname story came in a 1933 feature from the British magazine, *Film Weekly*. "It was left for Herbert, the last to join the little band, taking the place of another of his brothers, to choose a name for himself, and in doing so he set a pace in craziness which set the standard for the act. He once spotted a circus sideshow billed as 'Zeppo—Half Monkey, Half Man.' And he took his name from this." It would be highly unlikely that this version of events was supplied by Zeppo.

By the time the Marx Brothers hired Kyle Crichton to write their 1950 authorized biography, they couldn't agree on a single explanation for Zeppo's name. Chico and Gummo ascribed it to their use of hick farmer names, saying it evolved from first calling him "Zeb." Groucho went with the alleged popularity of the German Zeppelins being used in World War I. (Was this really a big deal in Chicago? And what possible connection could there be to Herbert?) Harpo took the sideshow freak theory to another level in the Crichton book, saying Zeppo was named after a sideshow freak named Zippo the Dog-Faced Boy.

In August the Four Marx Brothers began the 1917–1918 vaudeville season with Chico's new wife Betty added to the cast. Herbert stayed in Chicago and continued to work at Ford. It seemed like he had become the first member of the family to overcome Minnie's plan. After a full season on the road, Herbert had won his freedom from vaudeville and was hoping to work his way up to a better position at Ford. He had even outgrown the gang life of the Chicago streets, although he was still friendly with the Bass brothers and didn't stay completely out of trouble. But the war raged on, and draft deferments were harder to come by with each successive draft. It became clear that at some point the Marx Brothers would run out of luck. Betty left the show before the start of a December Orpheum circuit tour and returned to Chicago to await the start of the next generation of the Marx family.

Minnie somehow had the idea that Betty would be a good person to keep Herbert in line when she wasn't around. How she came to this conclusion—considering that Betty was only a few years older than Herbert—can only be attributed to Minnie's endless supply of optimism. In *Growing Up with Chico*, a biography of her father, Maxine Marx wrote that Zeppo quickly become fed up with being bossed around by Betty and

> decided to scare her a bit. One morning when they were driving back from a shopping expedition, Zeppo speeded along on an ice-slicked road. Betty pleaded with him to stop, sure that they would crash. Miraculously, nothing happened, but when Betty got back to the farm, she wrote Chico that Zeppo had almost caused her to lose the baby. Chico was the only one who could control the youngest of the Marx Brothers. Zeppo, shaken up by a letter he received from the irate Chico, nevertheless had the chutzpah to ask him for any of his old suits. This patched things up between them; Chico admired a hell-raiser anyway— and a brother, after all, was a brother.

Herbert stopped scaring Betty and Chico's military deferment was secured on January 13, 1918, when Betty gave birth to Maxine. Groucho's eyesight was still not to Uncle Sam's liking, but farmers Gummo and Harpo were not raising sufficient chickens to impress the draft board. Something needed to be done.

As far back as his days as Milton in the Three Nightingales, Gummo was not very interested in being on stage. He'd developed a stammer and had trouble delivering his lines. He worked hard to overcome it but still never became comfortable on stage. But he was as loyal to Minnie's plan as any of his more interested and talented brothers. Minnie's dream of the act becoming the Five Marx Brothers had already taken a step backward when Zeppo went on the road with the Juvenile Six instead of the Four Marx Brothers. A quintet was looking unlikely, and the quartet's survival was now in jeopardy thanks to World War I. When it became clear that one of the brothers needed to go into military service, Gummo either eagerly volunteered or accepted that his mother shipped him off to the army because he was the least important member of the act. Accounts differ. Minnie turned to Zeppo, who described being drafted into the act in an interview with Richard J. Anobile for *The Marx Bros. Scrapbook*:

> I was then working as a mechanic for the Ford Motor Company. I never did care about show business. But my mother called me up to tell me that Gummo was leaving for the army and that she wanted to keep the name "the Four Marx Brothers" intact. She insisted I join the act and that's what I did. I did have a bit of experience in that I had done a little singing and dancing as part of a cheap boy and girl act.

That fleeting reference to a cheap boy and girl act seems to be the only historical acknowledgment that Zeppo ever made of the Juvenile Six. In his BBC interview Zeppo elaborated on getting that fateful phone call from Minnie.

> She says[,] . . . "this is important to me and to our whole family" so I acquiesced, and I joined the boys in Rockford, Illinois. I got right on, right on the stage, didn't know what the hell to do, but Gummo danced and did some straight lines, so I ad-libbed some of the lines and they gave me some of the lines. . . . [T]he dancing I didn't do because I didn't know the routines.

The Rockford engagement began on June 6, 1918. It was half of a split-week and Gummo and Zeppo both appeared with the act for those three days and the three-day engagement in Madison, Wisconsin that followed. After breaking Zeppo in, Gummo spent the duration of the war as a supply sergeant in Chicago and was discharged in the fall when the Armistice was signed. He had wanted to get out of the act for years. The combination of World War I and Zeppo no longer being considered a child facilitated Gummo's escape from vaudeville. The season ended and Zeppo returned to work at Ford for the summer, but his fate was sealed. He was now one of the Four Marx Brothers, and he would be heading out on the road as part of the act in September.

The fall vaudeville season in 1918 was like no other. The Spanish Influenza epidemic shut down most of vaudeville, but the Four Marx Brothers initially tried to carry on with a new show. It seemed to them that *Home Again* had been played in just about every vaudeville theater in the country for the last four years. With the creation of a new show, Zeppo had some hope that he could do more than simply take the place of Gummo, who filled a role created for a brother with skills that, by his own admission, were limited.

Several members of the Marx family have claimed that in private life Zeppo was the funniest brother. He would seem perfectly suited to joining a comedy team, but Zeppo was always the first to acknowledge that there was no room for a fourth comedian in the act. Chico's daughter Maxine described Zeppo's sense of humor as occasionally cruel. By way of example, she cited a story passed down by Chico. When it became clear that the new show, *The Cinderella Girl*, wasn't very good and would be scuttled in favor of reviving *Home Again*, Zeppo's frustrated comment to his brothers was this: "Do you want me to stammer Gummo's lines?" Brothers could be cruel to one another, and they had no problem giving him a nickname based on his alleged resemblance to a sideshow freak, but Zeppo seems unnecessarily mean at the expense of the generally kindhearted Gummo.

With *The Cinderella Girl* (sometimes known as *The Street Cinderella*), the Four Marx Brothers attempted to make the leap from vaudeville to the legitimate stage with a self-produced musical show. They debuted it in Benton Harbor, Michigan, on September 26, 1918, and never went any further with the show. The combination of World War I, the flu epidemic, and a weak script doomed *The Cinderella Girl*. But the plot, as described in local Benton Harbor papers, indicated that a substantial role had been created for Zeppo.

A pretty street singer named Amoleta and her brother Harpo pass the hat to make ends meet. Harold Hammer (Zeppo) loves Amoleta and dreams of success in the stock market. Chico Saroni is also in love with Amoleta and dreams of owning a three-chair barber shop. Harold's father (Groucho) disapproves of his son's dreams and supports Saroni in his quest for Amoleta. But this only spurs Harold on. He achieves success and marries Amoleta.

Zeppo's character was central to the plot in a way that Gummo's never was. Gummo also played Groucho's son in *Home Again*, but his primary function in the show was to give Groucho someone to bounce lines off. Apart from singing and dancing, Gummo's main contribution to *Home Again* came in the form of lines like "But Father . . ." and "Yes, Father but what about . . ." Gummo was the prototypical vaudeville straight man. *The Cinderella Girl* was to be a new opportunity for the Four Marx Brothers—now featuring a fourth brother with a chance to display some real musical comedy skills. But it was not to be.

Several weeks of Midwestern bookings for the show in October and November were canceled and attempts to retool *The Cinderella Girl* were abandoned. Vaudeville was slowly recovering from the effects of the war and the flu epidemic as the Four Marx Brothers accepted their fate and gave up on their plans for the legitimate stage. Instead, they revised *Home Again* to take advantage of Zeppo's presence and slightly expanded the role of the fourth brother. They renamed the show *'N' Everything*, but it was still essentially *Home Again*. Zeppo was disappointed about going back to filling Gummo's minimal slot after a brief chance in a substantial role. Travel was problematic as the waning days of the war and the flu epidemic severely compromised the railroads, so they played the show exclusively in the Midwest—staying in Illinois, Indiana, Ohio, and Michigan—until February 1919, when they embarked on a lengthy tour that would take them across the United States and Canada.

CHAPTER FIVE

The Reluctant Vaudevillian

O N FEBRUARY 3, 1919, THE FOUR MARX BROTHERS OPENED AT THE
Palace Theatre in Chicago with their not exactly new act. *Variety*
summed up the situation in their February 7 review of the show: "The
act is billed as 'The Four Marx Brothers in Their New Revue.' It is really not a
new revue—it's the old revue with new scenery, new gowns, new gags, new songs
and a new Marx Brother, Herbert Marx, who replaced Milton Marx."

The act worked through the summer of 1919, skipping the normal vacation
vaudevillians customarily took for most of July and August, thereby cutting their
losses from the *Cinderella Girl* debacle. In November Gene Maddox, a dancer
who had been with the Marx Brothers since 1917, left to form a "boy and girl"
act with dancer Al Gibbs. Maddox had been Gummo's dancing partner in the
show, and she continued being featured in a dance number with Zeppo after
Gummo's departure. She had also been Zeppo's love interest in the ill-fated *Cinderella Girl*. There were several new faces with the act in 1919, but it wouldn't be
any of them who would replace Gene Maddox as Zeppo's dance partner.

Ruth Johnson had no experience on the stage, but this was never an imped-
iment for the Marx Brothers. Minnie had put inexperienced relatives and neighbors on stage in the past. Ruth had been living with her parents on Calumet
Avenue around a mile from the Marx home on Grand Boulevard. Her parents
divorced, and her mother remarried in 1919. Twenty-two-year-old Ruth briefly
lived in a Chicago boarding house but was in New York when she met Zeppo
around the time the Marx Brothers learned that Gene Maddox was leaving the
act. He told BBC interviewer Barry Norman, "[T]here was quite a nice pool
room, the ladies used to go there, and I saw this blonde, she was very pretty, and
I really got stuck on her just by seeing her, and I said, 'Jesus, I bet I could make
a dancer out of her.' So, I talked to her. I said, 'Would you like to go in show

business,' and she said yes. I said, 'Can you dance?' She said no. I said, 'Well, I'll teach you.' So, I got her the job." Zeppo learned very quickly that when it came to chasing women, being one of the Four Marx Brothers had certain advantages.

Living on the road most of the time, the Marx Brothers had very few rules about women. One that was frequently broken involved avoiding stray bullets in small towns by staying away from the local girls. There were certainly plenty of pretty girls in the act and on the bill with them in every city. Girlfriends had always been fair game and that generally meant that sooner or later Chico would have a dalliance with a brother's latest girlfriend. Chico's daughter Maxine explained that the first serious and unbreakable rule they imposed was that wives were off limits. Apparently, this was necessary because shortly after Chico married Betty, one of his brothers made a move on her. But without a marriage license a Marx Brother could lose a girl to a brother if he took his eyes off her for a minute. So, it came as no surprise when, shortly after becoming Zeppo's new dance partner, Ruth found herself another Marx Brother for offstage romance.[1]

Betty told Groucho's biographer Hector Arce, "I think Ruth discovered that perhaps Zeppo didn't count for much in the act. She was using her head. She may have liked Zeppo better at first, but she discovered Zeppo wasn't making as much money as Groucho. When Groucho went for her, I didn't see that Zeppo was broken-hearted." It was an early example of Zeppo's growing resentment about his status as a salaried employee of his brothers. When he replaced Gummo he was not given an equal share of the act. To be fair, he joined one of the most successful acts in vaudeville and did not build that success from nothing as his brothers had. But now his financial standing in the act was costing him girls. Zeppo may not have seemed broken-hearted to Betty, but his pride would not have allowed him to show his feelings on the rejection.

Zeppo's previous dance partner was petite. The February 7, 1919, *Variety* review called her, "Little Gene Maddox." Zeppo told Barry Norman in the BBC interview that "she weighed about 102 or 103 pounds and the dance that I did was acrobatics and I'd throw her around and I'd catch her and all of that." Ruth was the right size to be Zeppo's dance partner in the beginning, but from his comments in that interview sixty years after Ruth dumped him for Groucho, it seems Zeppo may have never gotten over the slight. What he remembered most about Ruth was her weight.

It seems like she didn't eat too much before she met me and kept putting on weight and of course finally she got pregnant. Now she's up to 135 and I'm pretty strong . . . but to lift her up in the air . . . and then throw her around and put her legs around my waist, and spin very fast, it was getting more difficult all the time. But I couldn't say anything. Groucho had married her and now she was up to around 145. It was ridiculous. It finally got so she couldn't get her legs around my waist to hold on with her feet when I'd spin her. I was constantly after Groucho to let me get another girl. But she wanted to do the dance. I got very angry. I was the younger brother. I didn't have that much to say, although it was my number. So, I spun her one day and—I think she got up to 150 pounds—and I spun her so hard that she couldn't hold on and she flew out . . . across the stage and into the orchestra pit. That finished her. . . . and I got another partner.

To add to Zeppo's frustration, Gene Maddox rejoined the act in January 1920, but Ruth kept her spot in the dance number with Zeppo. According to Hector Arce, Harpo one day suggested that the modestly talented Ruth be replaced. "'The girl stays,' Groucho snapped. 'I'm going to marry her.'" Ruth and Groucho were married on February 4, 1920. The Marx family had moved back to New York in November 1919 and Groucho and Ruth returned to Chicago to be married at the home of Ruth's mother and stepfather. It was hastily arranged to fit into a break before they started a western tour. Minnie and Frenchy were vacationing in Florida, and the few surviving photos of the day don't show any of the groom's brothers in attendance.[2] Writer Jo Swerling was the best man. *Variety* reported, on February 6, "Julius Marx (Four Marx Bros.) is to be married this week in Chicago to Ruth Terrel, non-professional." The fact is that she had been dancing in the act for a few months. And *Variety* used her stage name—which randomly alternated between Terrel and Tyrell—in the report. If calling Ruth "non-professional" was an inside joke, Zeppo probably laughed loudest.

When she became pregnant, Ruth was probably no longer being whirled around the stage by Zeppo, who may have been exaggerating about her with the benefit of sixty years of hindsight and being one of the last survivors from the act at the time of the BBC interview. He may also be conflating the incident with a very similar one, that featured neither him nor Ruth, that was documented in the *New York Sun* on May 20, 1919—several months before Ruth joined the act.

Yesterday at the Palace, two of the cutups in the act of the Four Marx Brothers, '*N' Everything*, did a swan dive off the stage, making a beautiful landing on the head of one of the musicians. As it seemed to be the kind of head designed to break falls, they arose unhurt without even their reputations damaged. The accident befell Arthur Marx, the red headed clown of the company, and Gene Maddox, who's a girl. The pair were whirling about in a dance, shaking the shimmy so violently that in a moment they had slipped into the trough of the stage, several footlights had popped out—raising the expense of the production enormously—and they had popped off the stage in the most offhand manner.

It is entirely possible that two different dancers in the Marx company were thrown into the orchestra pit during the 1919–1920 season by two different Marx Brothers, but it is more likely that Zeppo borrowed the story about Harpo and Gene Maddox to fit with his "Ruth was fat" narrative. But that wasn't even the most unflattering thing he said about her in the BBC interview. Asked about Ruth's relationship with Groucho, Zeppo said,

> She was very stupid, and it was difficult for Groucho to tolerate stupidity. He liked bright people and at the beginning, of course, it must have been sexual attraction . . . because it couldn't have been mental. She was not bright, and I guess they had regular quarrels that married people have. . . . I don't think Groucho was the easiest man to live with. . . . He put people down, especially a woman like that who was stupid.

Zeppo acknowledged that losing Ruth to Groucho caused some strain in his relationship with Groucho, but only for a short time. The dancing became tougher for Ruth in the aftermath of moving on to Groucho. Zeppo was rough with her and hoped she would voluntarily give up the dance spot. This, probably more than anything else, got Zeppo his next dance partner. In *Son of Groucho*, Arthur Marx—also Ruth's son—wrote,

> Like his brothers, Zeppo could never be very serious on stage and when he discovered that Mother didn't have much of a sense of humor, he used to take great delight in finding ways to torment her. For example, when Zeppo realized that my mother couldn't extricate herself from a back-bend position very gracefully under her own power, he'd let her struggle with the problem herself for what seemed like an interminable length of time before he'd condescendingly pull her to her feet. This was embarrassing to Mother, and at the conclusion of their act there would be an unpleasant scene in the wings.

The backstage battles continued, and Groucho frequently had to make tentative peace between his new wife and youngest brother. Zeppo had reasons other than Ruth's dancing and her romantic rejection of him to be unhappy. He'd been the fourth Marx Brother for more than two years and was still trying to make something more out of Gummo's part than was ever intended. But his situation would soon improve.

With their return to New York in the fall of 1919, bookings were primarily kept close enough to home that the Marxes were able to live in their own apartments for a few months. The temporary elimination of lengthy train rides reduced some of the backstage tension. After a short tour of New England and upstate New York, the Four Marx Brothers rang in 1920 with a month of performances in Manhattan, Brooklyn, and Newark before embarking on an Orpheum circuit tour that would start in the Midwest and take them to the West Coast. Newlyweds Ruth and Groucho honeymooned on the tour. Zeppo recovered from losing Ruth quickly as he joined Harpo and the married but wandering Chico in pursuit of young female vaudeville fans across the country.

Zeppo explained three-sheeting, a common vaudeville technique for meeting women, to Barry Norman in the BBC interview. A three-sheet was a large poster used in the front of theaters that listed the acts on the bill.

> When you're outside of theatres you see these posters with the names of the people . . . and we go out after the show . . . we get dressed quickly and go out and stand by these three-sheets and when the girls pass by, of course some of them nodded. That was all that was necessary.

In his vaudeville memoir, *Much Ado About Me*, Fred Allen discussed three-sheeting: "Many good-looking vaudeville actors, after each matinee, dressed hurriedly and rushed out to stand in front as the audience left the theater. As the girls came out, the male peacock preened himself, hoping to catch the attention of one of the corn-fed belles."

When three-sheeting didn't yield results, Zeppo shared an alternative source for female companionship on the road. "We'd always wind up in a whorehouse. Chico played the piano, and Harpo would do something, and Groucho would sing, and they loved us. These hookers, they just loved us—and usually for free. We entertained them, and they'd come see the show all the time. That was part of our routine." At least in the early days of his marriage, Groucho took his vows more seriously than Chico, so while touring with his new wife in the company, Groucho reduced the Marx Brothers' whorehouse act to a trio.

If the act on stage sometimes also seemed like a trio, it was because Zeppo had little beyond straight lines, his dance number, and a few songs in the show. But by 1921 he could be considered a vaudeville veteran, having the season with the Juvenile Six under his belt as well as nearly three years with the Four Marx Brothers. He had learned a lot and had talent that was not being utilized. He explained his acceptance of the situation to Barry Norman:

> I wanted to be a comedian and there wasn't an opportunity at all for me to be a comic. They had a very difficult time getting funny stuff for three boys. . . . If I thought of a good joke or thought of a good piece of business, I would contribute that, but I felt frustrated because I couldn't do the things that I was thinking up for them to do, and rightly so. I didn't resent it at all. But every time I walked out on the stage, I felt I was cheating because I wasn't doing a good job. . . . I also had the feeling that they were carrying me along because I was their brother.

Groucho summed up Zeppo's role in brutally frank terms in *The Marx Bros. Scrapbook*: "He was a funny guy off stage, but he wasn't a funny guy on stage. He was the juvenile, and the juvenile doesn't have any funny lines. In the plot, he's supposed to fuck the leading lady, the young girl. Zeppo was the romantic lead. That's all."

Jack Benny, who toured with the Marx Brothers in 1920 when he was still calling himself Ben K. Benny, roomed with Zeppo on the road and spoke of him in an interview with Richard J. Anobile for *The Marx Bros. Scrapbook*:

> Zeppo was the kind of fellow who was always funny at parties. But when he was with the team, he ended up with all the straight material. He never had an opportunity to find out if he could be funny on stage. Maybe he could have been, but he never had a chance to prove it. But to me, Zeppo off stage was like Groucho on stage.

Benny and Zeppo spent a lot of their offstage time together during that 1920 Orpheum tour, and one incident has taken on a life of its own, having been told and retold so frequently that each new version became less accurate than the one before. It was customary for prominent Jewish families to invite Jewish vaudevillians passing through their towns to their homes for a traditional Friday night sabbath dinner. When the tour came to Vancouver for the week of March 8, 1920, local businessman David Marcowitz invited the Marx Brothers to his home. Only Zeppo took him up on the offer, and he brought Jack Benny with him. The youngest of the three Marcowitz children, fourteen-year-old Sadya (later anglicized to Sadie Marks) would marry Jack seven years later. She would eventually change her name to Mary Livingstone and become his onstage partner.

Writing in the March 1945 issue of *Radio Mirror*, Mary told her version of the story. "Zeppo Marx, leaving the vaudeville theater where Jack and the Marx Brothers were sharing top billing to call on my older sister, Babe, thought he would have some fun when Jack—a stranger in town and lonesome—asked him if his date had a sister. 'Sure thing,' replied Zeppo invitingly, 'and a looker!' Jack came along expecting a date with a gorgeous girl and his 'date' turned out to be me!" In the posthumously published memoir *Sunday Nights at Seven*, completed by his daughter Joan, Jack Benny recalled the fateful evening.

> Zeppo, the youngest brother, talked me into going to this party. He said he knew some fascinating Vancouver girls and it would be wild, with Canadian ale, Canadian rye, Canadian women and Canadian whoopee. I told him I didn't like wild parties and I didn't like wild women. He talked me into going with him.
>
> We drove to a large frame house on the outskirts of the city. When we entered, much to my relief, we were in a nice family home. Zeppo's wild party was just in his imagination. It was his idea of a put-on—I would expect a wild evening and be disappointed. Instead, it was Zeppo who was disappointed in my reaction."[3]

Under various titles, the Four Marx Brothers had been starring in *Home Again* since the fall of 1914. The act in 1920 may have been called *'N' Everything*, but the reality was that it was *Home Again* with new songs. Harpo may have invented new sight gags from time to time, and Groucho and Chico occasionally worked their best ad libs into the show; but other than the songs and the fourth Marx Brother, not much had changed since 1914. Zeppo seamlessly replaced Gummo and *Home Again*, the reliable vehicle created for them by Al Shean, rolled on. By 1921 they all thought it was time for a new show. (They'd thought that in 1918, but the failure of *The Cinderella Girl* led them right back to *Home Again*.) In the past, Minnie had even placed advertisements looking for a suitable new script for the Marx Brothers. It would ultimately come from another vaudeville veteran who had appeared on several bills with them in the past.

Herman Timberg's vaudeville career started in 1906 when he was a child performer in the original Gus Edwards school act. (The early Marx act "Fun in

Hi Skule" was one of the many imitations of this act.) By 1919 Timberg was moving away from performing and started a production business with a well-known partner financing him: lightweight boxing champion Benny Leonard. Timberg had worked on a bill with the Marx Brothers as recently as December 1920 and was very familiar with their act. He also had a keen eye for talent, and it was obvious to him that Zeppo was underutilized. With financing from Benny Leonard, and the Marx Brothers in the market for a new show, Timberg wrote *On the Mezzanine Floor.*

The opening scene was a revelation. In a theatrical manager's office, Zeppo outlines a show he wants to produce as Groucho, Harpo, and Chico each arrive at the office to audition, disrupting Zeppo's pitch. For the first time the Marx Brothers truly function as a quartet of equals. Zeppo has an opportunity to be funny, delivering snappy dialogue and getting a few good laughs. He isn't overshadowing any of his brothers, but he has clearly graduated to a role that was simply way beyond Gummo's capabilities. Fast patter—in this case entirely in rhyme—would not have been written for an actor with a stammer, and that scene had a lot of it. Had material like this been offered to them before Zeppo was in the act, another member of the cast would have been pitching the idea to the manager and Gummo may have opened the door to the office before disappearing into the background until the next song or dance.[4]

The final performance of *'N' Everything* on January 22, 1921, at Keith's 81st Street Theatre in New York was followed by three weeks of rehearsal and the premiere of *On the Mezzanine Floor* at Poli's Capitol Theatre in Hartford, Connecticut, on February 14. In early April, the Four Marx Brothers filmed their ill-fated movie debut. They starred in a never-released two-reel short called "Humor Risk," which seems not to have survived. They had a lot more confidence in the new show and their partnership with Herman Timberg. The Marxes' new producer Benny Leonard appeared in the show on opening night and would make additional guest appearances on the road when his fight schedule permitted. Timberg developed a bit of business in which the champ sparred with the Four Marx Brothers. This routine had to be modified after the first performance. According to Kyle Crichton, Zeppo "clipped Benny so smartly with a right cross that Mr. Leonard was enraged." The bit quickly became Benny Leonard sparring with three Marx Brothers while Zeppo played the referee. Buster Marx was still good with his fists.

CHAPTER SIX

A Guy Could Get Used to This

*O*N THE *MEZZANINE FLOOR* REFRESHED THE ACT—IN LARGE PART DUE TO Zeppo's expanded role. The show Zeppo pitches to Mr. Lee, the theatrical manager in the opening scene, comprises the rest of the show. A plot was never especially important in a Marx Brothers show. It was just a device upon which to hang the specialty numbers and routines. The admittedly slight story of the show within the show centers around Groucho's character, Mr. Hammer, trying to marry off his oddly named son Quinine, played by Zeppo, to the daughter of a wealthy widow. Hammer claims to have arranged the marriage years before with the girl's father. The girl inherited the hotel where the story unfolds. The premise that the girl must marry a musician is introduced and Quinine—who asks the girl to call him Bobby—can't play an instrument. Hammer summons a pair of musicians from the local union and introduces them as his other sons. He calls Chico "Geshveer"—the Yiddish word for ulcer. Quinine proclaims his love for the girl, Dorothy, and wants to marry her. But Dorothy's mother insists her daughter marry a musician, so Harpo is chosen as the groom after they see his harp solo. The hotel detective turns out to be Dorothy's guardian and he is played by Ed Metcalfe, the actor who played the theatrical agent in the opening scene. At the finale, the detective breaks character and becomes Mr. Lee again. He proclaims that the plot of the show is terrible. The cast sings the finale, and the curtain comes down.

> Girls: Mr. Hammer, Mr. Hammer, we have some news for you. Mr. Lee has packed his trunk and said that he was through. He leaves for home today.

Hammer: Are you sure he went away? Well, believe me when I say he was the worst one in the play.

Girls: Mr. Hammer, Mr. Hammer, he doesn't like the plot.

Hammer: No one's going to worry about the little plot we got.

Detective: (enters)

Hammer: (to Detective) Goodbye, goodbye, I hate to see you go.

Detective: Goodbye, goodbye, and what a terrible show.

(Enter Bobby and Dorothy)

Bobby and Dorothy: What's the matter, what's the matter?

Hammer: He doesn't like your act.

Detective: I like the patter.

Bobby and Dorothy: Well, what's the matter?

Detective: I didn't like the way your story ended.

Bobby and Dorothy: What did he say?

(Chico enters)

Detective: And I don't like your dialect.

Chico: For twenty a week, what do you expect?

Detective: It sounded good when you first read it to me. Now here's the only remedy that I can see. You'll have to go into a great big dance, and they'll forget about the rest.

Company: Give us a chance and we'll do our best.

Hammer: (to orchestra leader) Say, leader, play feather your chest.

Detective: I've even played a part for you.

Hammer: That's what made the show so good.

Company: We thank you, Mr. Lee.

Hammer: What do you think of me?

Detective: I don't use that kind of language.

(Harpo enters)

Detective: Who is the guy that plays the harp? He should have more to say.

Hammer: Once we let him say two words and they pinched us right away.

Detective: You'll have to go into a great big dance, and I'll come up and help you out.

Company: Thank you, Mr. Lee. Play a dancing melody and we'll go over with a shout.

Zeppo's romantic interest in the show was played by Herman Timberg's sister, Hattie Darling. She was an accomplished violinist, so Timberg wrote a specialty for her. Chico hypnotizes her, and she is suddenly able to play the violin. The show was filled with bits of business like that. It was essentially a series of vaudeville turns linked by dialogue sequences concerning the arranged romance. The main deviation from *Home Again* was the inclusion of key scenes involving Zeppo's character. He even gets a few jokes of his own. When asked to play Mendelsohn's "Spring Song," he asks who wrote it. Since *On the Mezzanine Floor* was also conceived as a starring vehicle for Herman Timberg's sister, the show has scenes featuring only Zeppo and Hattie Darling.

Bobby: Oh, Dorothy. I'm so glad we're alone. I want to tell you something.

Dorothy: That you are not a musician.

Bobby: How did you know?

Dorothy: Mendelsohn's "Spring Song." Mother wants me to marry that red-headed boy.

Bobby: You just do as she tells you.

Dorothy: I don't understand you. What do you mean, Bobby?

Bobby: Just this. I want them to try to marry you to him. He can't even speak two words. He can't even say "I do," and I know your mother

49

would not allow you to marry a man who can't talk. Oh, Dorothy, you do love me, don't you?

Hammer: (sticks head out of center room and interrupts) Quinine, did you shine my shoes with my nightgown?

One of the features of *On the Mezzanine Floor* was a two-tiered set with several windows from which Groucho would occasionally pop out with a wise crack or non sequitur. This afforded him many opportunities to throw in new lines when he wasn't featured prominently. Reviewing the new act in *Variety*'s March 18, 1921, issue when it played at the Palace in New York, critic Bell noticed the new approach without necessarily attributing it specifically to Zeppo's increased role. "Arthur Marx, the silent comic of the family, hasn't as much to do in a comedy way as in the former Marx turn, the meat being more evenly distributed. Julius, the eldest, shines as usual with a constant flow of wise cracks, apparently for the most part, impromptu, but all distinctly funny."

If there was any doubt that Zeppo's role in *On the Mezzanine Floor* remained the least consequential among the brothers despite it being the best role the fourth brother ever had, it was removed when Harpo became ill and was unable to perform for three weeks in June and July of 1921. Cast member R. C. McClure effortlessly filled Zeppo's role and the versatile and capable Zeppo was called upon to fill in for Harpo, which he did without incident in Baltimore, Philadelphia, and Boston. The harp solos were removed, but Zeppo still had to display enough rudimentary harp skill to play the bits that advanced the plot. Reviews were good and no one noticed Harpo's absence.

Zeppo had been with the act long enough to have learned how to fill in for each of his brothers, which over the years would occasionally become necessary. When this happened just about anyone from the chorus could become the temporary Zeppo. The least valuable Marx Brother occasionally saved them from disaster. By the time Zeppo played Harpo's part in the summer of 1921, his biggest problem in the show had resolved itself when the very pregnant Ruth left the company in the spring to await the July birth of Groucho's first child.

After an extended stay on the East Coast, *On the Mezzanine Floor*—sometimes billed as *On the Balcony*—headed out on the Orpheum circuit, covering the western half of the United States and Canada for the fall 1921 season, concluding with a return to New York and another engagement at the Palace Theatre. Had they just gone home to rest after the Palace, their lives would have been much easier. But they accepted a month-long engagement in London in

June and July of 1922 and that was complicated. The Four Marx Brothers had become one of the highest paid acts in vaudeville. Their 1920 Orpheum circuit salary of $1,500 per week had ballooned to $2,750 by early 1922. The Orpheum and its eastern partner, the Keith-Albee circuit, crafted carefully worded contracts that required performers to get their permission to work for anyone else. The expectation was that if they wanted to work in the summer, it should be for the circuit that was paying their handsome salary all year. They played London without permission and came home to find themselves blacklisted by the two major circuits.

Zeppo, still on salary and not a decision maker in the act's business, could only watch in frustration as the act could not find sufficient bookings in the fall of 1922. They ultimately settled for the new renegade vaudeville circuit formed by the Shubert brothers, who dominated the legitimate theater business, but were ill-equipped to operate a vaudeville circuit. The Four Marx Brothers salary would be $2,000 per week from an organization that teetered on the brink of bankruptcy on a regular basis. How the act's finances affected Zeppo's salary is not documented, but his lack of involvement in the decisions that made the act's price plummet had to make Zeppo wonder what sort of position he would have had at Ford had he never joined the act. Since joining the Four Marx Brothers, Zeppo had experienced some major disasters: *The Cinderella Girl*, "Humor Risk," the London trip that got the act blacklisted, and the Shubert vaudeville debacle that was now crashing down on them. If the reason for keeping Zeppo from being a partner was that Gummo had endured the hard times and Zeppo joined a successful act that didn't struggle, the reasoning was certainly flawed.

The Marx Brothers had purchased the Herman Timberg and Benny Leonard interests in *On the Mezzanine Floor* for $10,000 to become the sole owner of the act. Again, Zeppo was not involved in this transaction. He remained an employee of the show, which was retitled *The Twentieth Century Revue* for its one season on the Shubert vaudeville circuit. The show was perpetually in financial trouble—as was the case with most of the Shubert vaudeville shows. *The Twentieth Century Revue* limped along for months before being put out of its misery by the sheriff in Indianapolis, who attached the box office receipts and confiscated the scenery and costumes to cover some of the show's debts. When it was all over, the Four Marx Brothers were still blacklisted by Keith-Albee and Orpheum. Unemployment loomed, and the brothers briefly considered careers outside of show business. Only one of them possessed any marketable job skills, but things had not quite reached the point where Zeppo needed to ask Ford for his old job.

With no other options, the Four Marx Brothers took a job in a summer revue in Philadelphia. To the great surprise of all involved, this show facilitated the rebirth of the Four Marx Brothers. *I'll Say She Is* left Philadelphia after a summer of sold-out performances and continued to pack theaters around the country for nine months. The only place to go from there was Broadway, where *I'll Say She Is* opened at the Casino Theatre on May 19, 1924. Suddenly the formerly blacklisted, unemployable vaudeville act known as the Marx Brothers was the toast of the town. And Zeppo seemed much less like the expendable Marx Brother. Starting with *The Cinderella Girl* and *On the Mezzanine Floor*, he was a much more important part of the act. He may not have been as funny on stage as his brothers, but he was on stage—with and without them—quite a lot in *I'll Say She Is*.

The show opened with the now familiar "Theatrical Manager's Office" sketch, which had opened *On the Mezzanine Floor* and *The Twentieth Century Revue*. A new comedy scene written for the quartet, and featuring Groucho as Napoleon, was the highlight of the show. Zeppo had vastly improved the plight of the fourth Marx Brother since Gummo's days of struggling to spit out his lines. Getting banished from vaudeville turned out to be the best thing that ever happened to the Four Marx Brothers. Long train rides were replaced by luxurious Manhattan apartments and invitations to dinners and parties with people like George Gershwin, columnist Franklin P. Adams, and future New York Mayor Jimmy Walker. Almost overnight, the Four Marx Brothers were among New York's most in-demand celebrities, and they rubbed elbows with New York's elite. Prohibition was in full swing and being roundly ignored in speakeasies all over town. The nightlife after the shows let out began at midnight, and the fun usually lasted until sunrise. Groucho, now a husband and father, did not partake. Chico, also a husband and father, was not going to pass up this much fun. Along with Harpo and Zeppo, he enjoyed his celebrity status—including the fringe benefits of chorus girls and flappers who were anxious to meet the Marx Brothers.

As one of Broadway's newest stars, Zeppo was invited to visit the Paramount studio in Astoria and ended up with a bit part in an Adolphe Menjou film. His brief appearance in *A Kiss in the Dark* was in a garden party scene featuring several other Broadway personalities.[1] After closing on Broadway, *I'll Say She Is* went back on the road for another five months. The tour began in Boston, where Zeppo made some news. On February 25, 1925—his twenty-fourth birthday—*The Boston Globe* reported that Zeppo was engaged to a twenty-year-old local woman. "Announcement was made yesterday of the engagement of

Miss Kay Austin of 42 Warren Street, Roxbury, to Herbert Marx, one of the Four Marx Brothers featured in *I'll Say She Is* at the Majestic Theatre."The newspaper item claimed they met because the young woman had read an interview in which Herbert proclaimed himself a "woman hater" and wrote to him insisting he was wrong. Miss Austin clearly did not have any insight into how Herbert entertained himself in his spare time while *I'll Say She Is* was on Broadway for almost nine months. Whatever relationship they had did not outlast the seven weeks the show spent in Boston. But Miss Austin recovered quickly enough. In April 1926 she married an actor and seven months later gave birth to a daughter.

The tour ended in June and the brothers enjoyed a much-needed summer vacation as a new show produced by Sam H. Harris went into preparation for the fall season. The success of *I'll Say She Is* earned the Four Marx Brothers a chance to work with the best playwright in the business—George S. Kaufman. But according to Kaufman biographer Scott Meredith, he wasn't the first choice.

> When Harris phoned the comedians to say that he would produce their show, he told them at the same time he was sending a blackout writer right up to do some new sketches for them. A blackout writer was the last thing in the world the Marxes wanted. They had plenty of comedy sketches and bits of their own, and furthermore, the employment of a blackout writer sounded as though Harris was contemplating a revue, whereas they wanted a genuine, plotted play and a real playwright to write it. They decided to deal with the blackout writer in their own way.
>
> When the man arrived, they insisted he remove his coat, and Zeppo, who was a bodybuilding enthusiast at that time and had bulging, rippling muscles, stepped up close to him. "I'll wrestle you to a fall," said Zeppo threateningly. "You write two shows for us or none." The writer, a small man, retrieved his coat and disappeared into the night, and it was after Harris heard of this that he called Kaufman.

Kyle Crichton identifies Zeppo's wrestling opponent as Richard Atteridge, who had worked on several successful Shubert-produced shows during the period. Kaufman's oft-quoted line suggesting he'd rather write a show for the Barbary apes may have been inspired by Zeppo's wrestling challenge. But Kaufman came on board and brought in Morrie Ryskind, who in this instance would be an uncredited collaborator. Both writers recognized that *I'll Say She Is* was really a vaudeville show—a series of sketches with a story so unimportant to the proceedings that audiences would be hard pressed to describe it after seeing the show. In his autobiography Ryskind noted,

> Zeppo was a continuing problem. There just wasn't any way to squeeze another comedic personality into an act that already had Groucho, Harpo, and Chico. Zeppo couldn't sing or dance or play a musical instrument, and although he was the best looking of the brothers, he still fell short of matinee-idol status. So, with all the avenues closed to him, there wasn't anything left for him except to play the straight man. George and I tried our best to invent some business that would more fully incorporate him into the act, but we were being pressed for a late fall opening which stopped us cold. The best we could do for Zeppo was give him the thankless role of a hotel clerk. It was the smallest role he ever played with the team, but he accepted the role without complaint.

Zeppo's brief period of near equality on stage had begun with *The Cinderella Girl* and would end with *I'll Say She Is*. It would all be downhill from there. Ryskind's assessment of Zeppo's abilities may have been extreme since he acquitted himself well in the shows where he had a chance to do more than a handful of straight lines. But in the world of Broadway and the musical theater of the 1920s, being adequate was not enough. Kaufman and Ryskind marginalized Zeppo because when they looked at the Four Marx Brothers, they saw a very talented trio with a lot of possibilities. According to Ryskind, the odd man out was a good sport about the whole thing. While Zeppo "might have been one comedian too many on stage, off stage he was by far the wittiest of the brothers. This would have given him a valid reason for brooding about his fate, but until he made his break from the act, he deferred to the best interests of the group. But that would have never been true of Harpo and Chico, who demanded that every one of each other's musical solos be matched by one of his own."

Everyone around the Marx Brothers accepted that Groucho would get the most to do and would be the favorite of the writers. But Chico's wife Betty warned her husband about the risk of being marginalized by Groucho. In a 1981 interview Betty said,

> Groucho was very selfish about his work. I said to Chico one day, "Look, you're busy running around playing the horses and playing cards, and Groucho's around with the writers. And Groucho's fighting for his part to be bigger and bigger. And pretty soon you'll be a Zeppo

and have nothing to do because he'll write you out." So, I said, "Be smart and go and protect yourself. You go in and sit in with the writers."

In *Growing Up with Chico*, Maxine Marx shared the disastrous result of Chico following Betty's advice.

The next day he came home in a rage. "Betty, don't ever interfere with me and my brothers again! Just remember one thing: There's only room for two prima donnas in the act. Not three. Groucho and Harpo need the limelight. I just need the act to be good." "I didn't mean any harm," Betty said. "I just thought you deserved better." "Well, next time keep your ideas to yourself. You almost broke up the Marx Brothers."

About her Uncle Zeppo Maxine added, "He was funny. Everyone knew that, yet his humor was too much like Groucho's to fit into the act. Groucho never liked that particular comparison—he hated to share the spotlight with anyone. So, Zep was left out and had to play the banal romantic leads that we all knew he was much too good for." In *The Cocoanuts* he didn't even get that much. The role of a hotel clerk relegated the importance of the fourth Marx Brother back to the Gummo era. But Zeppo was a good soldier, and he accepted the lifestyle of a Broadway star without really being one. In *The Cocoanuts* he truly was carried along by his brothers, but no one seemed to have any problem with it.

CHAPTER SEVEN

Love and the Fourth Marx Brother

THE *COCOANUTS* OPENED ON BROADWAY ON DECEMBER 8, 1925, AFTER six weeks of fine tuning in Boston and Philadelphia. To no one's surprise it was a smash hit in New York and would head out on the road in the fall of 1926. Three days before the final Broadway performance at the Lyric Theatre, the *New York Times* on August 4 reported that Zeppo was engaged.

> Herbert Marx, the youngest of the four brothers of that name and the one known as Zeppo in *The Cocoanuts*, has become engaged to Marion Bimberg, actress who goes by the stage name of Marion Benda. The engagement, it is said, will be formally announced on Sunday at the home of Mr. Marx's brother Julius in Great Neck.
>
> Miss Benda succeeded Fania Marinoff in *Tarnish* and has been in pictures for Famous Players-Lasky. Mr. Marx has long appeared with his brothers in vaudeville and musical shows. Miss Benda said last night that the marriage would probably not take place until after *The Cocoanuts* has closed its road tour, which starts in September. She will continue on the stage, having been engaged for a Chicago company of *Love 'Em and Leave 'Em*.

An item in the *Brooklyn Daily Star* said they met at Paramount where Marion was costarring in a film with Thomas Meighan. Since Zeppo likely only worked at Paramount for a day or two filming his brief appearance in *A Kiss in the Dark*, there's an incredibly small window when this could have taken place in early 1925. But it becomes even more unlikely when considering that there is no evidence of Marion ever appearing in any Famous Players-Lasky films at Paramount, let alone starring with Thomas Meighan, who was a big star at the time. If she worked at Paramount at all it would have been as an uncredited extra.[1]

Marion Ruth Bimberg was born on December 6, 1903, in New York City. Her Russian immigrant parents, Rebecca and Louis Bimberg, were living the American dream. Louis was prospering with the American Oilcloth Company, a business he cofounded in 1900 and owned with his brother Alexander. He and Rebecca had two more children—Jessie Sarah, born in 1906, and Alan Joseph, born in 1908. The family settled in an affluent section of Brooklyn before moving to White Plains, an upscale Westchester suburb. But Louis was involved in a scandal when Marion was ten years old that put everything the Bimbergs had in jeopardy.

On March 28, 1914, Louis and Alexander Bimberg were arrested on a train while traveling through Trenton, New Jersey. They had been implicated in an arson plot. The manager of their Salem, New Jersey, plant claimed that the Bimberg brothers agreed to pay him $10,000 to burn down the plant so they could collect on an insurance policy. The claim was made solely by the plant manager, Joseph Campbell, who told authorities he had a signed contract with the Bimbergs for the arson job. Despite this seemingly ridiculous piece of evidence—who signs a document agreeing to pay someone to torch their business?—the brothers were put in jail and could not raise the $30,000 bail. Eventually the bail was reduced, and they were released after spending several weeks in prison awaiting their trial. The plant—which was never actually burned down—had been closed when the Bimberg brothers were arrested. They sold the American Oilcloth Company in August 1914. The company was reported to be worth $300,000 but was sold for $100,000.

After a couple of postponements, the trial finally concluded in a hung jury in March 1915. Evidence against the brothers included a phony audio recording of them allegedly planning the crime with Campbell. It became clear that the Bimberg brothers had been framed by their own stockholders, who were attempting to take over the company. They were fortunate to get a jury that recognized the dubious quality of the evidence. The charges were finally dropped in January 1916, but Louis Bimberg's reputation and finances were in tatters. He did manage to hang on to some Manhattan real estate and briefly lived in an upper west side apartment. He may have been asked to leave the family home by an unsympathetic Rebecca who was ashamed of her husband even though he was exonerated. He persevered and started his own linoleum business. Soon the family was living on West 96th Street in an apartment large enough for the five of them and two live-in servants. The 1925 New York State census lists the

Bimberg family living on West 86th Street and shows all three of the children as college students. But Marion had left college to pursue a stage career by 1922.

From September 1922 to April 1923 Marion was enrolled at the American Academy of Dramatic Arts, the first acting school in the United States. It was founded in 1884 by Franklin Haven Sargent, a Harvard University speech and elocution professor, and therefore was commonly known as the Sargent School. During Marion's time at the school, Spencer Tracy was also enrolled. Among the numerous illustrious graduates of the Sargent School are Edward G. Robinson, Cecil B. DeMille, William Powell, Kirk Douglas, Lauren Bacall, and Pat O'Brien. An audition was required to get in and it was not inexpensive. Presumably Louis Bimberg still had some money after his earlier financial downfall.

Marion likely appeared in the Sargent School's productions at the Lyceum Theatre but made her proper professional debut shortly after the end of her second semester. She got a job with the Harder and Hall Stock Company and appeared at the Trent Theatre in Trenton, New Jersey, from May to July 1923 in a variety of productions as part of the Trent Players. She then got a small part in the comedy *Home Fires*, which had a brief Connecticut tryout run in Stamford and New Haven before opening a forty-nine-performance run on Broadway at the 39th Street Theater on August 20, 1923. The show moved briefly to the Ambassador Theatre shortly before closing. Marion had gone from completing two semesters in acting school to a part in a Broadway show in four months. *Home Fires* closed on September 29 and Marion quickly got another part. She was hired by well-known producer Jules Hurtig for his new comedy, *Fraid Cat*. For a brief time, stardom must have seemed within Marion's reach. But after November tryouts in Scranton, Wilkes-Barre, Allentown, Patchogue, and Wilmington, *Fraid Cat* closed without making it to Broadway.[2]

Marion next joined the cast of the hit drama *Tarnish*, which starred Fredric March, at the Belmont Theatre on March 24, 1924, but only appeared for the last six weeks of the seven-month run. She did not travel with the cast of *Tarnish* for an extended Chicago run that summer, but her brief association with the show was significant enough to be mentioned in the *New York Times* announcement of her engagement. She remained in New York, where at some point, she met Zeppo, who had just returned from the post-Broadway tour of *I'll Say She Is* in June 1925. They discovered a shared love of horses and went riding early in their courtship. (Marion was an experienced rider, having been given lessons as a young girl. Her equestrian interests were not dampened by an early accident in which she broke her back when thrown from a horse.) Their romance was interrupted in October when Zeppo went back on the road for the out-of-town tryouts of *The Cocoanuts* in Boston and Philadelphia. While Zeppo was in rehearsals for *The Cocoanuts* that summer, Marion got a part in a show called *Mission Mary* that was to open in October, but she was cut from the cast before the out-of-town tryouts. Just as well because the show never made it to Broadway. Marion rejoined the cast of *Tarnish* in December for brief runs in Toronto and Baltimore. By the time she got back to New York in January 1926, *The Cocoanuts* was a month into its 276-performance Broadway run.

Exactly how Zeppo and Marion met is a mystery with many conflicting clues. Several newspaper items have vastly different explanations—all presumably provided by Zeppo and Marion, likely through the publicist for *The Cocoanuts*. There's much confusion surrounding Marion's stage career because there were two women working in New York theater using the stage name Marion Benda during this period. It was this other Marion Benda who appeared in *The Ziegfeld Follies* and dated Rudolph Valentino.[3] Zeppo's fiancée would occasionally be erroneously placed by the press in *The Ziegfeld Follies*. If Marion protested, it wasn't too vigorously. Padding her résumé could only help further her ambitions. The circumstances of Zeppo meeting Marion become even murkier with the questionable suggestion from Maxine Marx that Marion was Betty Marx's cousin. Marion and Betty were both children of Russian immigrants, but if they were indeed related, they were probably distant cousins at best.

When Zeppo and Marion eventually married, the Universal Service press syndicate sent out an item with the headline "Marx Brother Weds Musical Comedy Star" datelined April 12, 1927. The article provides another version of the couple's first meeting. "The young comedian first saw Miss Benda when she played opposite Thomas Meighan in a motion picture. He met her a year later and persuaded her to desert the films for the stage." The reality is that the actress formerly known as Marion Bimberg had a very minor, if not promising, stage career before meeting Zeppo. There's no evidence of her doing any film work. She had not appeared in any musicals nor was she a star. The Universal Service article surprisingly acknowledges the falsehood of its own headline in its final paragraph: "Marion Benda of *Rio Rita*—no relation to Zeppo's bride—was showered with phone calls, notes, telegrams and flowers today congratulating her." It is one of the very rare instances of the press pointing out that there were two women named Marion Benda active at the time, and that the one who was a musical comedy star was not the future bride of Zeppo Marx.

When Zeppo and Marion announced their engagement in August, news of Marion being cast in the Chicago company of the Broadway hit *Love 'Em and Leave 'Em* was noted. The show had opened on Broadway on February 1, 1926, at the Sam Harris Theatre and it seems that Marion may have briefly had a small part—perhaps through the influence of her new boyfriend, who was appearing in a hit show produced by Harris. But there is no documentation of her being in the Broadway cast. She may not have even been in the Chicago production, which opened on August 29. If she took the job, she only had it briefly because she joined the road company of *The Cocoanuts* and opened with the show in Washington on September 20.

The Marx Brothers had instituted a "no wives in the act" rule because of some friction caused by Ruth and Betty, but Marion, not yet a wife at this point, was given special consideration—partly because she was an experienced actress who had been getting work on her own, and partly because his brothers were aware of Zeppo's growing desire to get out of show business. They wanted to keep him as happy as possible, since he was still a salaried employee, and they were being paid phenomenal sums of money as Broadway stars. It was import-ant for them to keep the name of the Four Marx Brothers intact, and it would remain this way while Minnie Marx was still around. Having Zeppo's fiancée in the chorus was much easier than giving him a piece of the action or having him leave the act. For Marion, being on the road with Zeppo would have an added benefit. She'd be able to keep an eye on him. Since joining his brothers on the road, Zeppo had become a very prolific protégé to his brother Chico in the womanizing department. But if Zeppo was anything like Chico, a fiancée couldn't slow him down. Chico prided himself on his ability to outfox Betty. Zeppo studied under a master.

After single weeks in Washington, Baltimore, and Cincinnati, *The Cocoa-nuts* settled in for a ten-week run in Chicago. The cast celebrated Christmas in Milwaukee and rang in the new year in St. Louis. The next three months took the show all over the Midwest. When *The Cocoanuts* finally got close to New York for a week in Newark, New Jersey, Zeppo and Marion decided not to wait for the end of the tour. The show opened at the Shubert Theatre in Newark on April 11, 1927. The following afternoon, Zeppo and Marion were married at the Chalfonte Hotel on West 70th Street in Manhattan. Two days later, under a photo of the newlyweds, a caption in the *Brooklyn Citizen* provided yet another completely fabricated version of the circumstances of Zeppo and Marion meet-ing, saying they "resumed a childhood romance when they met again in *The Cocoanuts*." After the ceremony the wedding party hurried back to Newark for the evening performance. In lieu of a honeymoon, the happy couple spent the next seven weeks with *The Cocoanuts* in Brooklyn, Atlantic City, Philadelphia, and finally New York, where the tour ended on June 4 at the Century Theatre. A month later press reports indicated that Zeppo would be producing vaudeville acts for the Keith-Albee circuit with prominent agent M. S. Bentham, who numbered among his clients W. C. Fields, Clark and McCullough, Bert Lahr, and future Marx Brothers film costars Oscar Shaw and Mary Eaton. But there's no indication that Zeppo was ever involved in a Bentham production.

After nearly four months off, *The Cocoanuts* was set to go back on the road for a second season of touring. This time the show would make it to the West Coast where the Four Marx Brothers planned to explore movie opportunities. Marion did well enough during her first season on the road to earn a promotion. She was relieved of chorus work and took a featured role in the show—a role that required her to do more on stage than her husband.[4] Zeppo may have wanted to get out of show business, but he now had an ambitious wife angling for stardom. Marion was being promoted—certainly with help from the show's publicist—as a rising star. A November 24, 1927, newspaper clipping promoting the show's upcoming week at the Broadway Theatre in Denver was carefully preserved in Marion's collection of memorabilia from her stage career. The headline of the article states, "Miss Benda Entered Musical Comedy by Romance Route." It provides yet another variation on the story of how Zeppo and Marion met.

Miss Benda gave up the dramatic stage for musical comedy when Cupid entered the scene. And the story of the romance of Marion Benda and Zeppo Marx is as good as any fiction. The first time that Zeppo saw Miss Benda was when she was playing the second feminine lead in *Tarnish*, and he decided then and there that this was a girl he wanted to meet. But *Tarnish* closed before Zeppo had the opportunity to know her.

Some time passed and one day the Marx brother noticed a girl playing in a film with Thomas Meighan and decided that she was none other than the girl whose acquaintance he had desired to make. This time he decided that there would be no waiting. He went to the Lambs club and asked Meighan about Miss Benda. The next day the cinema star introduced her to Zeppo. At that time, she was working for Paramount in its Astoria studio. That was the beginning of a friendship that led to selection of rings.

Whatever may be true in this account of Zeppo meeting Marion can easily be separated from what is demonstrably untrue. It would have been nearly impossible for Zeppo to have seen Marion in *Tarnish*. She only appeared in the last 48 of the 255 performances of the show at the Belmont Theatre during its final six weeks on Broadway. For those six weeks Zeppo was on tour with *I'll Say She Is*. For Marion's first week in *Tarnish*, Zeppo was in Atlantic City and the next week in Washington. The following two weeks find him in Baltimore, and for the closing two weeks of *Tarnish* he's in Brooklyn and Philadelphia. The only possible performance Zeppo could have attended would have been the Thursday matinee on April 24, 1924, while *I'll Say She Is* was at the Shubert Crescent in Brooklyn, where matinees were on Wednesdays and Saturdays. *Tarnish* had the unusual schedule of Thursdays and Saturdays for matinees. And this possibility would require the assumption that someone doing eight shows a week would spend an afternoon seeing another show before heading over to Brooklyn for his own performance that evening.

As for the Thomas Meighan angle, there could be something to it because his name comes up frequently in the various tales of Zeppo meeting Marion. But it strains credibility that Meighan would have the ability to immediately contact an extra from a film he'd made as much as a year earlier, although some versions of this tale have Marion still working at the Paramount studio and Meighan introducing them there. In much the same way as the story of Zeppo's nickname has become a *Rashomon*-like tale, the meeting of Zeppo Marx and Marion Bimberg will likely remain a collection of contradictory tales describing the same incident. As the press item from Denver pointed out, "the romance of Marion Benda and Zeppo Marx is as good as any fiction." And if it wasn't, every effort was made to make it so.

CHAPTER EIGHT

Not the Brightest Light on Broadway

FOR ALL THE EFFORT PUT INTO MARION'S CAREER—BOTH BY HER AND the Marx Brothers' publicists—it pretty much ended once the second road tour of *The Cocoanuts* concluded on February 4, 1928, in San Francisco. Five days later, the Four Marx Brothers began a short West Coast vaudeville tour with an abbreviated show consisting mostly of a few highlights from *The Cocoanuts* and the "Theatrical Manager's Office" sketch. Marion continued traveling with the company but did not perform in the show they called *Spanish Knights*. They also brought the show to Chicago where the season ended earlier than usual on April 21, 1928. It had been a whirlwind honeymoon. Mr. and Mrs. Zeppo Marx spent most of the first year of their marriage on the road.

The trip to the West Coast fueled rumors that the Marx Brothers would soon be making movies. First National, Universal, MGM, and United Artists were all mentioned in press reports. There was talk of a screen test and a filmed version of *The Cocoanuts*. But this was all premature speculation. Zeppo was still interested in finding a better paying job than being the salaried Marx Brother. Rumors about movies and Zeppo's departure were nothing new. A report in *Billboard* from November 13, 1926, said, "Zeppo Marx may leave the Four Marx Brothers when the Chicago run of *The Cocoanuts* is finished. He plans to go into straight comedy." In theory it would not have been a bad idea for him to work alone or with Marion instead of his brothers—at least financially. But the family pressure to keep the quartet intact won out. After a long summer break there would be a new Marx Brothers show heading for Broadway in the fall of 1928.

Rehearsals for *Animal Crackers* began in mid-August. Zeppo once again did not complain about the paucity of material created for him by writers George S. Kaufman and Morrie Ryskind. Ryskind addressed the situation in an interview for *The Marx Bros. Scrapbook*: "Kaufman and I would try to throw a line to Zeppo if we had a situation. But there weren't many of those. We were interested in what the audience was interested in, and they wanted funny scenes. Zeppo was involved with the love story, and nobody cared a lot about love stories." For the record, Zeppo wasn't involved in the love story of *Animal Crackers*. He had not been the "romantic lead" frequently referenced in descriptions of the team since *On the Mezzanine*, which by the time of *Animal Crackers* was ancient history. His job was to be there for Groucho to bounce lines off. At least Bert Kalmar and Harry Ruby came through with a song that would become a signature number for the Four Marx Brothers. "Four of the Three Musketeers" at a minimum guaranteed Zeppo a moment in the spotlight at every performance of *Animal Crackers*.

Just before *Animal Crackers* opened there were reports that a deal had been arranged between the Four Marx Brothers and Paramount on a filmed version of *The Cocoanuts*. Initially Paramount made a deal with Sam Harris, the producer who held the rights to the show. The studio had to make a separate deal for the services of the Four Marx Brothers, who were represented by the William Morris Agency. William Morris Jr., son of the agency's founder, was handling negotiations with Paramount. In *The Agency: William Morris and the Hidden History of Show Business*, author Frank Rose described him: "Morris was a dapper young man, clear-eyed and handsome and stylish enough to invite comparison to Mayor Jimmy Walker and the Prince of Wales. But he wasn't much of a salesman." He concluded, "Morris showed less aptitude for agenting than some of his clients."

Various accounts credit Chico with brokering the deal with studio head Adolph Zukor while William Morris Jr. observed quietly, but Paramount executive Walter Wanger provided a vivid account of the negotiation between Zukor and Zeppo when he was interviewed for the 1970 book *The Real Tinsel*. According to Wanger, Zeppo displayed the skills of an experienced agent. In getting Zukor to raise the Marxes' fee from $75,000 to $100,000 Zeppo first flattered the narcissistic mogul, who hadn't even agreed to the $75,000.

> Zeppo walked over to Mr. Zukor. "Mr. Zukor," he said, "this is one of the greatest moments of my life. I've always wanted to meet you. You are the one showman in the world. When I think of what you did for Mary Pickford, of what you've done for pictures, I can't tell you how thrilled I am to meet you." He went on like that for ten minutes, and the old man started to melt. When he got all through, Zukor wanted to know, "So what's the trouble between Walter and you?" "Mr. Zukor," Zeppo answered, "all our lives we've worked to perfect this one show. This is our first show on Broadway. It's a big hit. All our jokes are in

it, everything we've ever done. We're willing to make a picture for you, give you all our material, all our services, and all those marvelous gags—the whole thing for one hundred thousand dollars." One hundred thousand dollars was never mentioned. I sat there and gasped. Zukor turned to me. "Walter, what's wrong with that?" And that's how the deal was made.

As for William Morris Jr., Frank Rose wrote, "The incident at Paramount, where he sat mute while Zeppo Marx sold Adolph Zukor on *The Cocoanuts*, was hardly out of character. Morris hated agenting. He was shy. He was lousy at making chitchat. Nothing about him suggested a showman." Zeppo was the opposite of Morris in almost every way and the Zukor incident demonstrated his business acumen and all the skills needed to be a good agent. With little to do on stage in the new show, Zeppo had proven to be more valuable to his brothers off stage with his deft handling of Adolph Zukor.

Animal Crackers opened to the expected rave reviews and the usual press celebrations of the Marx family. *New York Herald Tribune* theater critic Percy Hammond offered an odd tribute to Zeppo on November 11, 1928:

One of the handicaps to thorough enjoyment of the Marx Brothers in their merry escapades is the plight of poor Zeppo Marx. While Groucho, Harpo, and Chico are hogging the show, as the phrase has it, their brother hides in an insignificant role, peeping out now and then to listen to plaudits in which he has no share. Among the *Animal Crackers* of the title Zeppo is but a goat. A handsome fellow of the "juvenile" type, he is able in song, dance, and elocution, yet he cuts a small figure in the family revels. When, if ever, he is noticed by the press it is with disdain. Reviewers have said of him that he makes the Marx quartet a trio, and that he is an appendage to a fraternity already overladen. I seldom read criticism of the drama for the reason that dull reviewers bore me, and bright ones make me envious. Therefore, I may be wrong in suspecting that this is the first good notice Zeppo ever got in a newspaper.

Sometimes as I watch him tiptoeing around the outskirts, unobtrusive, though not diffident, I admire him for the proud humility with which he performs his inglorious office. In *Animal Crackers*, for instance, he sings his little song and dances his little dance as if he were a useful if not important atom in the proceedings. Subdued, and I fear a trifle forlorn, he shows no evidence of forgetting his lot in self-pity. The silence that greets his own conscientious efforts seems to be as sweet to him as the uproar that welcomes the accomplishments of Groucho, Harpo, and Chico. He asks his brilliant brothers foolish questions in order that they may answer with clever retorts and then he retires backstage until they need him again. Although he is a Marx as much as any of them, he never allows that distinction to interfere with the privileges of his more aggressive kinsmen.

As *Animal Crackers* rolled along on Broadway, the New York newspaper columnists could always count on the Marx Brothers to fill a column with real and imagined tales of their comings and goings. The show had a publicist feeding material to the newspapermen just to make sure the public knew the Marxes were still holding court nightly at the 44th Street Theatre months after their opening. This had also been true of *I'll Say She Is* and *The Cocoanuts*. What was different with *Animal Crackers* was the sudden media interest in Zeppo. *New York Journal-American* columnist O. O. McIntyre wrote of Zeppo in his widely syndicated "New York Day by Day" column on December 16, 1928:

Young Mr. Marx is in the billing and that is almost all. In his fleeting appearances on the stage, he seems not at all disturbed by his insignificance while his brothers merrily hog the show. It seems to me he is far more distinguished for his diffident humility than his brothers are for their highly advertised humor. And given a decent chance he would, I venture, give his brothers a run for popularity.

Critics and columnists writing about *Animal Crackers* seemed less inclined to beat up on Zeppo—even if his status in the act hadn't really changed. A March 28, 1926, *Jewish Daily Forward* review of *The Cocoanuts* featured glowing descriptions of the comedic gifts of Groucho, Harpo, and Chico. Rounding out the quartet, the critic could only add "And Zeppo is the fourth one—I'm sorry that that's all I can say for him." Perhaps the easy jokes about the fourth Marx Brother had run their course. With *Animal Crackers*, the sympathetic Zeppo press continued into the new year in Mark Hellinger's *New York Daily News* column "Behind the News" on January 3, 1929:

Theatregoers know all about Groucho, but few of them know Zeppo, who is content to remain in the background and watch his three brothers garner the glory. Zeppo, however, is an extremely shrewd real estate operator. He doesn't care as much for the stage as he does for the business world. Accordingly, his chief interest in life lies in the various real estate deals he has helped swing in recent years."

There seems to have been a concerted effort to call attention to Zeppo—even if it meant calling attention to his virtual nonexistence in *Animal Crackers*. It could have been Marion's influence, or perhaps Zeppo was laying the ground-work for his future away from the act. His press notices routinely included mention of his burgeoning real estate business—although no press agents or columnists wrote of Zeppo's desire to earn more money than his wealthier brothers were paying him. Filming of *The Cocoanuts* began in early February, shooting during the day, with *Animal Crackers* still doing excellent business on Broadway at night. One can only hope that Zeppo was paid a fair bonus for getting Adolph Zukor to increase the Marx Brothers price for making the picture.

The constant specter of Minnie hung over Zeppo's dream of leaving the act. The brothers all felt they owed a lot to their mother, and she couldn't get enough of them. *Variety* columnist Nellie Revell reported a Minnie Marx sighting in her March 27, 1929, column: "Mrs. Marx, mother of the Four Marx Brothers, in a fourth-row seat, watching the performance of *Animal Crackers* at the 44th Street. 'Tis said that she has missed only three performances during the engagement." Zeppo wasn't going anywhere while his mother was coming to see him on Broadway every night.

The task of turning a Broadway musical into a sound film was fraught with challenges in 1929. Sound recording and camera mobility were still being perfected. But the main issue was that Broadway musicals ran for well over two hours on stage. Significant portions of the show would need to be eliminated to make a ninety-minute film. The first casualty of the trimming was Irving Berlin's music. There would simply be far fewer songs in the film. The next victim of the cutting was the already small role of Zeppo. Quick results in truncating *The Cocoanuts* came with the elimination of the first two musical numbers in the show. The first, "The Guests," featured Zeppo's hotel clerk character Jamison singing about—oh, the irony—real estate.

So, this is Florida
Where land is booming
And ev'rybody has a little to sell
The climate is delightful
The natives tell us so

But living here is frightful
We'd like to have you know
That lovely Florida,
The land of sunshine,
Is not so lovely
Stopping at a bum hotel.

Although "The Guests" wasn't in the show on opening night, it was added soon after and hundreds of Broadway and touring performances of *The Cocoanuts* opened with Zeppo singing this song and the following one, "The Bellhops," in an elaborate number featuring him and sixteen dancers set in the hotel lobby seen in the film. Zeppo's other featured number, "Florida by the Sea" made it into the film but without Zeppo singing it. His dialogue scenes were also trimmed. If Zeppo had been marginalized on stage, he'd be barely visible on screen.

After the final Broadway performance of *Animal Crackers* in April and a brief vaudeville run with selected scenes from the show, Zeppo looked forward to concentrating on his real estate business during the four-month break until *Animal Crackers* hit the road in September 1929. In April, as the Four Marx Brothers were appearing in their vaudeville turn at the Palace Theatre, for what was reported as the highest salary ever paid to a vaudeville act at the Palace, Marion briefly resuscitated her acting career only a few blocks down Broadway at the Majestic Theatre. She had not been on stage since the final performance of *The Cocoanuts* more than a year before. The *New York Daily News* reported on April 21 that "Marion Marx, wife of Zeppo, one of the Four Marx Brothers will join the cast of *Pleasure Bound* tomorrow night. But it's for two weeks only. Mrs. Marx is a novelist, and she wants to absorb stage atmosphere for a book." By this point the other Marion Benda had become marginally famous for having been with Rudolph Valentino the night he died, and there could be no inference of nepotism for her being cast in a non-Marx show, so Marion used the name Marion Marx professionally.

Pleasure Bound was a Shubert Brothers musical comedy revue that starred Jack Pearl, Phil Baker, Aileen Stanley, and the vaudeville team of Shaw and Lee. Whatever Marion contributed during her two-week engagement is a mystery. Zeppo was again unable to see Marion's performance. The Four Marx Brothers performed at the Palace or the Riverside on each day of Marion's two weeks at the Majestic. The whole thing seems odd, especially since Marion should have absorbed plenty of stage atmosphere during her years working on Broadway and then on the road with the Marx Brothers. If she ever started writing a novel there is no trace of it anywhere. Marion's last performance in *Pleasure Bound* was on May 4, 1929—the same day the Four Marx Brothers gave their final performance of the season at the Riverside Theatre.

The filmed version of *The Cocoanuts* premiered during their run at the Riverside, so they all went to see it the day after they closed. Initially skeptical about the film, the brothers put aside their misgivings as it became a tremendous hit over their long summer break. They were now assured a new career in the movies. But that didn't change Zeppo's plan to get out of the act. It would just be a little more complicated. Although Minnie was long retired as the manager of the Four Marx Brothers, it was understood that she considered the word "Four" as essential to the act as the word "Marx."

Zeppo and Marion had taken an apartment at 169 East 78th Street and they spent a good deal of time and money that summer turning it into a luxurious salon where they could entertain guests.[1] The *Animal Crackers* tour was scheduled to begin on September 20 in New Haven, Connecticut, and rehearsals began in August. Sam Harris rented the run-down Casino Theatre—where *I'll Say She Is* had its Broadway run five years earlier—as a rehearsal space. Early on Friday, September 13, Minnie and Frenchy were driven by their chauffeur from their home in Queens to the old theater at 39th Street and Broadway so they could attend the afternoon rehearsal before heading uptown for dinner with Zeppo and Marion. Groucho rushed home to his family in Great Neck as soon as the rehearsal was over. Chico and Betty headed to a weekend party at Adolph Zukor's estate in Rockland County, and Harpo had plans elsewhere in Manhattan, as did Gummo. But they would all frantically scramble to Zeppo's apartment before the night was through.

The brothers had all started to notice that Minnie was growing weaker each time they saw her. But she still retained the enthusiasm for the act that they remembered from their childhoods. At the rehearsal that day she joked with a few reporters about going on the road occasionally to make sure her boys were giving good performances. But she also made comments about her own mortality. After enjoying a hearty meal and a few vigorous games of ping-pong with Zeppo and Marion, Minnie and Frenchy called for their chauffeur and headed back to Queens. As they drove across the Queensborough Bridge, Minnie became ill. She had the presence of mind to tell Frenchy that she was having a stroke. Frenchy ordered the chauffeur to turn the car around in the middle of the bridge and head back to Zeppo's apartment. Zeppo called a doctor and all his brothers, who each arrived at the apartment in short order. But nothing could be done. Minnie had suffered a cerebral hemorrhage. The brothers laid her to rest two days later.

Five days after their mother's funeral, the Four Marx Brothers were on stage at the Shubert Theatre in New Haven as scheduled. Minnie would never have tolerated a cancellation. The act was her life and the best way for her boys to celebrate it was to keep the act together. In the short term this would be fine, but Zeppo was conflicted. An August 31, 1926, item about the Four Marx Brothers in Wood Soanes's *Oakland Tribune* column, "Curtain Calls," referred to Zeppo's crushed ambitions:

> Zeppo, the youngest, wanted to be a businessman with a lot of people working for him and a special room to hold conferences. And he might have achieved these dizzy heights, but his brother Gummo went to war and on return refused to act any more, going into the dress business. Naturally there had to be Four Marx Brothers and Mother Marx, who rules the roost, drafted Zeppo. And that's the story.

Efforts to present Zeppo as an equal persisted in the press during the Broadway years. A January 22, 1926, article in *The American Hebrew* stated, "Zeppo's inclusion in the team was first actuated merely by a desire to keep the family together. Now he is indispensable." Zeppo knew better but his thoughts of leaving the act could only be thoughts while Minnie was around. Her death suddenly made it at least seem possible.

CHAPTER NINE

Wall Street Lays an Egg

THE JANUARY 1929 ISSUE OF *THEATRE MAGAZINE* CONTAINED A PIECE called "Confessions of the Marx Brothers." Press items of this sort were usually devoid of anything serious. But the fourth Marx Brother's question-and-answer session is surprisingly revealing. It reads like a transcript of Zeppo talking to a therapist.

What is your function in the family? "The fifth wheel of the Marx Brothers. The spare. Pushed into show business when the fourth, Gummo, broke into the war."

Information volunteered: "My career on the stage is practically ruined, because I am afraid of my brothers. I'm the youngest, and from the moment I first went on I would look at them, who had already been established as comedians, and if I caught them smiling, even good-naturedly, over what I was saying or doing, I would become self-conscious to the point of unhappiness. For quite a while I've been in the real estate business, on the side, and that's to what I'm going to devote myself when this show closes. I won't even go on tour. I'm not suited to the musical comedy stage; should have been in straight comedy, and not with my brothers. They make me feel so self-conscious that I suffer. It's developed an inferiority complex in me."

"I like to sing, but I haven't a good enough voice to carry the juvenile lead, and the other lines were not written for me, so you can't blame Mr. Harris for not wanting to take a chance. I can go out and sell a house as calmly as that, because I'm not self-conscious there, but the moment I step out on the stage I defeat myself."

How did you get your name, Zeppo? "We had a farm in Illinois, and they nicknamed me Zeke—and then when I came to the stage, Zeppo. No reason for it. Just the same as me being in *Animal Crackers*."

If Zeppo really believed he would be leaving the Four Marx Brothers when *Animal Crackers* closed on Broadway, he was mistaken. He was still controlled by a fair amount of family pressure and there was no reason to put the value of the act at any risk. Announcing his plans to a magazine reporter may have been his way of testing the idea out on his brothers, who were having none of it. At least no one cared if he didn't want to tell the Zip the Pinhead story.

In the immediate aftermath of Minnie's death there was a full season of *Animal Crackers* on the road to deal with, so any thoughts of making the Four Marx Brothers a trio would have to wait. But an additional obstacle presented itself only weeks after Minnie's death. The stock market crash of 1929 affected the Marx Brothers in different ways. Groucho and Harpo suffered significant losses—with Groucho seeing his portfolio worth an estimated $250,000 vanish nearly overnight. (He had been buying on margin, so his investment was significantly less.) Chico, who spent his weekly salary on gambling and women before the sun set on payday simply laughed off the stock market as a sucker's bet. But Zeppo viewed things in much the same way as many working Americans. He was lucky to even have a job. His brothers were each pulling in $2,000 a week touring in *Animal Crackers*, but he was on salary at $500 a week. This was a very healthy wage in 1929, but his plans of doing much better on his own now seemed less likely. His little real estate business was doing well enough before the crash, but with the entire economy in turmoil, his *Animal Crackers* salary kept Zeppo solvent.

A November 10 *Pittsburgh Press* item offered a typical post-crash summary of Zeppo's situation:

Zeppo Marx, youngest of the Marx boys, at the Alvin in *Animal Crackers*, has a sideline. He sells real estate during the off months, when not employed at the theater as one of the quartet that has put the cracker in *Animal Crackers*. Zeppo Marx two seasons ago fell in love and married. As the head of a family, he developed the age-old urge to own a home. At the present time he holds title to six different apartment houses in the Bronx. That he has what is called the salesman instinct can be attested from the fact that he sold his manager, Sam H. Harris, a piece of property."

Being in the theater kept Zeppo around people who had money after the crash. Apart from *The Cocoanuts* and *Animal Crackers*, producer Sam Harris had several other successful shows touring and on Broadway. He had also owned the Sam H. Harris Theatre, which housed a few other Broadway hits during the period, so he was able to buy some property from Zeppo—even if it was just a polite gesture.[1] Throughout the *Animal Crackers* tour local newspapers regularly ran feature stories about Zeppo, usually pointing out his importance to the act. It was almost as if his brothers were responding to Zeppo's unburdening in *Theatre Magazine*. On November 24, the *Detroit Free Press* headlined their Zeppo piece "Although He Does Least, Zeppo Has Hardest Job of All." The challenges of Zeppo's job are detailed:

> A "straight man," for the benefit of those who should know but may not, is the actor who makes straight the way for a comedian's wise-cracks. It is he who bats out fungoes for the funny man to catch, snaps back the ball for the funny man to carry and is then buried under the heap of laughter which follows. Ordinarily he goes through a routine as standardized and nowhere near as energetic as a chorus girl's. But when you are playing straight for the Marx Brothers, those avid devotees of ad libbing, no two nights' performances are the same. Trying to figure out what Will Rogers is going to say next would be reasonably simple compared with trying to anticipate Groucho's and Chico's remarks on all topics and Harpo's eloquent and ever-changing pantomime.

If the brothers were trying to make Zeppo feel better about his position in the act it probably had less effect on his decision to stay than the economic conditions as the Great Depression began. The tour continued until the first week of April 1930, so Zeppo was paid roughly $14,000 over the twenty-eight weeks that *Animal Crackers* was on tour. As the holiday season approached in 1929 and the show headed into the Midwest, the *New Republic* described "a winter of unemployment and suffering." In New York men broke police station windows just to get a warm bed and a meal with their night in jail. On March 7, 1930, President Herbert Hoover assured the nation that, "all the evidences indicate that the worst effects of the crash upon unemployment will have passed within the next sixty days." He was wrong. That same day Communists rallied in major cities across the country with speakers denouncing the capitalists who had taken away the jobs of working people. In New York's Union Square, a crowd of thirty-five thousand protesters met police brandishing nightsticks as they marched to City Hall to confront Mayor Jimmy Walker, a living symbol of the Roaring Twenties excess that ushered in the crash. On this day of turmoil, the Four Marx Brothers went on stage at the Shubert-Rialto Theatre in St. Louis, probably unaware of the riot in New York City. March 7 was a Friday, so Zeppo visited the box office and collected his $500. He would remain quiet on the topic of leaving the act for the foreseeable future.

Had Zeppo entered the job market in early 1930, he would have found that show business was still his best bet. A single man with a vaudeville act could make several thousand dollars a week, but that would be for the rarest of stars. The bottom end of the scale was $50 a week. A retail salesclerk was pulling in between $17 and $25 a week. A cashier could earn between $25 and $40. In Hollywood the General Casting Bureau, which had been established in 1926 and sent actors to work at all the studios, had twelve thousand actors registered. They were all looking for one of the roughly seven hundred jobs per day that were available. If a lucky actor got one of the jobs, the pay ranged from $40 to $150 a week. An experienced leading man, who would not need to go through the General Casting Bureau, commanded a salary between $75 and $350. At $500 a week Zeppo Marx may have felt underutilized, but he was in no way underpaid. If he had indeed tried his hand at working without his brothers in light comedy, he would not have automatically been at the top of the pay scale. He may have thought his brothers should have cut him in for a full share in the Four Marx Brothers, or maybe given him a chance to be worth a full share, but from their perspective they were being quite generous with their youngest brother. This situation plagued Zeppo for years.

The tour ended in Cleveland on April 5 and the brothers were back at the Paramount studio in Astoria to start filming *Animal Crackers* a few weeks later. Zeppo remained on salary as Paramount paid $150,000 for the Four Marx Brothers to appear in their second film, which would premiere at the Rialto Theatre in New York on August 28. After filming was completed in early July, Zeppo returned to his other life as a Manhattan real estate broker. His combined income from real estate and the Marx Brothers put Zeppo in a financial position that would be enviable to most people, but he lived in the shadow of his much richer brothers. When the compulsive gambler Chico needed money, he was not above preying on Zeppo when Groucho and Harpo reached their limit with him. Zeppo was becoming as much of a gambler as Chico—although with generally better results. Harpo's son Bill compared the gambling acumen of his uncles in his book *Son of Harpo Speaks!*:

I remember my Uncle Chico being competitive through his astounding grasp of mathematics. His satisfaction from gambling came from his ego-driven desire to show off his God-given abilities in front of any kibitzers on hand. He could remember every hand of cards he was ever dealt, and he would tell you the serial number from a dollar bill you gave him to memorize twenty years ago. On the other hand, my Uncle Zeppo wasn't into the action to "win" the contest. He just wanted to beat the crap out of you.

Rehearsals for the Marx Brothers' return to vaudeville put an end to their extended summer vacation as they prepared for an October opening. Their new show, *The Schweinerei*, consisted of highlights from *I'll Say She Is*, *The Cocoanuts*, and *Animal Crackers*. It was probably not an accident that the show was structured to feature Zeppo in a more substantial way than the Broadway shows had. They used the concept of Groucho hosting a wedding reception—an idea borrowed from *The Cocoanuts*—with Zeppo as the groom, as he had been in *On the Mezzanine Floor*. The inclusion of the "Theatrical Manager's Office" sketch also assured Zeppo some duty beyond being the straight man. The tour was scheduled for ten weeks, with the Marxes reaching their highest weekly salary yet at $9,000 a week. In an unexpected turn of events, this tour would provide Zeppo with a chance to be the star of the act—albeit briefly and in disguise.

After trying out the show in Queens and Brooklyn, they opened a two-week run at the Palace on Broadway before heading out on the road. The night before their November 8 opening in Chicago, Groucho was hospitalized with severe abdominal pain. He was suffering from acute appendicitis. The following morning an operation was performed, but the opening day matinee went on as scheduled with Groucho in the hospital. *Variety* reported on November 12: "Zeppo Marx who usually works straight assumed his brother's trick mustache and cutaway and gave a creditable performance Saturday matinee with the public unaware of the missing member. Seemingly it was Zeppo who was absent. Sudden switch had all three of the performing brothers doing each other's stuff to fill the gap." A report in *Billboard* on November 15 was either an obvious mistake or a late and futile attempt at a coverup. "Zeppo Marx of the Four Marx Brothers was stricken with acute appendicitis. . . . The Marx Brothers opened at the Palace Saturday with the audience ignorant of the fact that Zeppo was missing."

Zeppo shared his perspective on the experience with Charlotte Chandler for her book, *Hello, I Must Be Going: Groucho and His Friends*.

I didn't understudy him or anything, because who expected it? . . . I had to do Groucho five times a day at the Chicago Theatre, which I did. Actually, some of his friends didn't even realize it was me. They thought it was Groucho. They came backstage, and they wanted to see Groucho. But, anyway, it got pretty bad after a few days, because I never smoked cigars, and I'd smoke those goddamn cigars every day. I used to vomit every day after the last show—four or five shows a day, you know, and it was very difficult. But, anyway, I knew I could do it. And this frustrated me more, because I knew I could get laughs, but I wasn't allowed to with the Marx Brothers.

Zeppo's ability to cover for Groucho appeared to solve a difficult problem, but the power brokers of the RKO vaudeville circuit were not as grateful as they could have been. They canceled the following week's booking in Cincinnati while they tried to get the Four Marx Brothers to accept a reduction in salary for providing only three brothers. This controversy caused the advertising for the remainder of the Chicago run to be changed from "the Four Marx Brothers" to "the Marx Brothers"—a change that Zeppo had been arguing for behind the scenes regarding his departure with little success. With the canceled week in Cincinnati left open for Groucho to recover, the tour resumed in Cleveland on November 22. The Marxes assured RKO that Groucho was fully recovered and that he would be on stage for all performances. But they got caught having Zeppo fill in at two of the four daily performances. RKO reduced their pay and canceled the scheduled second week in Cleveland.

They finished the tour in Boston and Detroit with Groucho fully recovered and Zeppo relinquishing his brief turn in the spotlight. For all the trouble caused by the substitution, the one thing everyone—including Groucho—agreed on was that Zeppo did such a fine job that most people were unable to notice Groucho's absence. For Broadway shows, Actors' Equity required the production to employ an understudy for each featured actor. On the rare occasions when Groucho missed Broadway or Equity tour performances—notably the week of the Stock Market Crash—Sam Goldman, an obscure vaudevillian hired by Sam Harris for his physical similarities to Groucho, filled in. Understudies not being required for vaudeville shows resulted in Zeppo filling in for each of his brothers at one time or another. But they'd been mostly working on Broadway or in Equity shows for the past six years, so there had not been many opportunities for Zeppo to demonstrate his peculiar skill in imitating his brothers. During the Broadway run of *The Cocoanuts*, there had been a strange item placed in

Billboard—probably by the show's publicist—stating that Gummo had "been made a general understudy for the quartet." Apart from Gummo having been out of show business for eight years by that point, the suggestion that the admittedly least-talented member of the family possessed the skills to step in for even Zeppo—who had replaced him and made something more of the job—was ridiculous. That Zeppo could really step in for any of his brothers was remarkable. After reading about his new assignment in *Billboard*, Gummo probably stayed far away from the Lyric Theatre.

Six days after the final show of the RKO tour in Detroit, the Four Marx Brothers sailed for England where they would perform an abbreviated version of *The Schweinerei* at the Palace Theatre in London as part of *Charles B. Cochran's 1931 Varieties*. It was on board the SS *Paris* on Christmas Eve 1930—as they were about to sail from New York for their London engagement—that three Marx Brothers made a critical career decision that would alter the lives of the Four Marx Brothers. A three-picture contract with Paramount was signed that would require them to make movies not based on their stage shows. While the contract allowed for those movies to be made in New York or Hollywood, it was generally acknowledged that they would be relocating to Hollywood upon their return from England. Preparations for the move began before they sailed.

Zeppo's signature is on the contract alongside those of his brothers. But this was merely to assure his continued participation in the Four Marx Brothers. There is nothing in the contract specifying exactly how the "artists"—as they're called in the agreement—will split the money, which in this case amounted to $200,000 per picture and 50 percent of the net profits. The payments by the studio, as outlined in the contract were "payable to the order of Julius H. Marx, for the account of the Marx Brothers." Zeppo was a signatory to a contract that was expected to generate in excess of a million dollars, but by a separate agreement with his brothers, would remain their salaried employee. And forget about that New York real estate business, kid. You're moving to Hollywood.

CHAPTER TEN

Hooray for Hollywood

THE MARX ENTOURAGE ARRIVED IN LONDON ON DECEMBER 30 AND SET up headquarters at the Savoy Hotel. After one warm-up show in a theater outside of London, they had some time to relax before the January 5 opening at the Palace. Zeppo may have still harbored mixed feelings about being in the act, but the free trip to London was certainly agreeable to him and Marion. As they strolled the London streets, they became interested in an unusual breed of dog they'd never seen before. After learning that the dogs were Afghan Hounds, Zeppo and Marion were soon talking to Phyllis Robson, who would write about the encounter in the December 1940 issue of *Kennel Review*:

One day a very nice young man and a pretty wife called on me in London. I did not catch their name, they wanted to talk about Afghans and that was enough for me. They told me they'd been 'round the pet shops but could not see anything they liked. In one shop they saw a copy of the *Dog World* giving my address as editor so popped into a taxi and came along to ask my help. They told me they wanted a dog and a bitch that they could breed from and with good coats and light colored.

We must have talked for half an hour, and I drew up a list of kennels I suggested I would visit with them and then somehow California was mentioned, and the young man said, "You know I only work six months in the year." "Aren't you lucky," I replied, "and just what do you work at?" He said, "Films," so I said, "Do you mind telling me your name?" He said, "Marx." Then knowledge came to me as the Marx Brothers were fulfilling a contract in London and I said, "Don't tell me you are one of the Marx Brothers." To which he replied, "Yes I am, I am Zeppo." So, I replied, "Well, don't you mention your name when you go 'round the kennels, we'll ask prices and if they are too high, I will tip you the wink."

A photo of Zeppo and Marion walking one of Phyllis Robson's Afghan Hounds in Hyde Park appeared in the London newspapers, and through her efforts, they became the owners of a pair of show-quality Afghans—Westmill Omar and Asra of Ghazni. The dogs soon appeared on stage at the Palace. During the London, run American newspapers broke the news that the Four Marx Brothers would be relocating to Hollywood upon their return and would start shooting their new film around April 1. They gave their last London performance on February 1, and Harpo sailed for New York that night from Southampton. The rest of the family—now including Asra and Omar—enjoyed an extra week in Europe and sailed on February 8 from Cherbourg, France. They arrived in New York on February 14 and made their final preparations for the move to Hollywood.

Harpo, the first to arrive in California, rented a villa at the Garden of Allah at 8152 Sunset Boulevard. The famous Hollywood landing spot for new arrivals advertised itself as "the ultimate in luxurious modern living accommodations" and offered hotel rooms, apartments, and four- and five-room villas—all completely furnished. Zeppo and Marion liked what they saw and took a large apartment there after briefly renting a three-bedroom house on Rodeo Drive.

It was around this time that Zeppo and Marion parted company with Omar and Asra. They still owned the dogs when Omar placed second in the hound variety class at the Del Monte Kennel Club Show in June. Zeppo also brought the dogs to the set at Paramount that summer. But by the time of the Santa Barbara Kennel Club Show in July, the dogs were owned by George S. Thomas, a well-known dog judge and trader from Boston. (Omar won a best in breed ribbon at the show.) For Zeppo and Marion, it was likely a case of there not being enough space for the dogs at their new apartment, or that caring for a pair of prized show dogs—particularly Afghans with their coats needing a lot of grooming—was too much work. Both were probably factors in their decision. The dogs would also be a problem if the Marx Brothers were to go back on the road.[1]

Other Garden of Allah residents at the time Zeppo and Marion moved in included director Edwin H. Knopf, playwright John Howard Lawson, composer and pianist Sergei Rachmaninoff, screenwriter S. J. Perelman, and actress Lila Lee. Marion and Lee became close friends in those early days at the Garden of Allah. When gossip columnist Sheilah Graham wrote the book *The Garden of Allah* in 1970, she interviewed Marion. Lila Lee became more notable for the series of scandals that overshadowed her long film career, and Marion had quite a story to add to Lee's legacy. In the book, Graham was careful about using names and in true gossip column tradition was deliberately vague.[2]

A wife of one of the Marx Brothers was called from the Garden at four in the morning by an actress who had been a statuesque silent-film star and was then working infrequently in the talkies. "I'm dying," she moaned. "You've got to come over, I'm dying."

Mrs. Marx hastened over. She was far from dead, but her bed, her gown, and her body were covered with blood. The sadist, who is now dead—the father of a famous current young film actress—had made little cuts all over her with razor blades. Cutting soft flesh was his particular hang-up. There was lechery at the Garden, but nothing as cruel as this. The same man was always pretending to commit suicide. They would take bets at the Garden on whether he would surprise himself one day and succeed. He died of natural causes two decades later.

Lila Lee moved into the Garden of Allah shortly before Zeppo and Marion. She had just returned to Hollywood after spending some time in an Arizona sanatorium—officially for treatment of tuberculosis, but more likely for treatment of substance abuse. Lila's sadistic boyfriend was screenwriter John Farrow, the father of Mia Farrow. John Farrow would become more prominent in Hollywood as a director and the husband of Maureen O'Sullivan a few years later. Farrow was engaged to Lee, but she broke it off due to his rampant infidelity.

The frequent threats of suicide could have been made by Farrow, who had enough scandals of his own to make anything plausible. But Graham also could have attributed some characteristics of Lee's former husband James Kirkwood Sr. to her nameless sadist in the book. Kirkwood not only threatened to take his own life on several occasions, but he also threatened to kill Lila Lee and John Farrow. Sheilah Graham also attempted to interview Groucho about the Garden of Allah, but all she got out of him was one usable quote: "I didn't mix with that lot. I didn't fraternize. I was a family man."

Zeppo and Marion did have one neighbor at the Garden of Allah that socialized with Groucho. In fact, S. J. Perelman had recently arrived in Hollywood to work on the new Marx Brothers movie, *Monkey Business*, at Groucho's behest. While the brothers settled into their new homes—Groucho in Beverly Hills and Chico in Malibu—a script for the film was being developed by what would become a revolving team of writers. Groucho's first suggested writers, Perelman and Will B. Johnstone, worked on the story for six weeks as various gag men and additional writers—including Groucho's friend Arthur Sheekman—threw ideas around. The result was loosely based on the early Marx vaudeville show *Home Again*.

Perelman wrote about working on *Monkey Business* in a November 1961 article in *Show* magazine: "Zeppo, the youngest was never a concern, since he was always cast as the juvenile love interest. His speeches were usually throwaways like 'Yes, Father' or song cues on the order of 'I think you have the loveliest blue eyes I've ever seen.'" While it was commonly said that Zeppo was the "juvenile love interest," this simply wasn't true regarding *The Cocoanuts* and *Animal Crackers* on stage or screen. When *Monkey Business* was released, it came as a surprise to many that Zeppo was far from marginalized this time. In his *New York Evening Post* column, "The Moving Picture Album," playwright Robert E. Sherwood told of attending a Glendale, California preview of the film:

> The really big news concerning *Monkey Business* is that it imposes the burden of the love interest on the hitherto understressed shoulders of Zeppo Marx. It is a prodigious responsibility, for Zeppo has to be dashing, romantic and, at the same time, the brother of Groucho, Harpo and Chico—an impossible task, which he undertakes with his usual uncomplaining fortitude.
>
> Someday someone should write a character analysis of this heroic soul, Zeppo, who is content to go down to posterity as "that other Marx." There is a famous story of how, during the rehearsal of *Animal Crackers*, Sam H. Harris approached him and asked, "Can't you get a little more variety into your performance?" which provoked Zeppo to inquire, "Just how many ways are there of saying 'yes'?"

While Zeppo was filming *Monkey Business*, Marion found herself before the cameras too. Shortly after the Marxes arrived in Hollywood, Louella Parsons noted in her column on March 25, "Eddie Cantor, who is a very good friend of the irresistible Marx Brothers, is seen about with them swapping jokes." Cantor was preparing *Palmy Days*, his second sound film—the followup to the hugely successful *Whoopee!* Robert Benchley and Morrie Ryskind, both old friends of the Marxes, were brought out to Hollywood to work on the script and took rooms at the Garden of Allah, which Ryskind described in his memoirs as "the stopping-off place for all of the New York literary expatriates during studio assignments and divorce settlements," adding that "the noise, laughter, music and mating calls were loud and continuous each and every night."

Production of *Palmy Days* began in late May. Cantor and producer Samuel Goldwyn publicized their search for pretty girls to appear in the picture. Among those who got early career breaks in the film were Paulette Goddard, Betty Grable, Virginia Grey, and Toby Wing. It wouldn't take long for Eddie Cantor to notice Zeppo's pretty wife—but if he didn't, Marion knew people working on the film, including some of her neighbors at the Garden of Allah.

On May 17 the *Los Angeles Times* reported that Cantor attended an afternoon of golf, swimming, and tennis at a barbeque luncheon at the Beverly Hills estate of Jack Warner. Zeppo and Marion were among the numerous movie people there. Within days Marion was on the set of *Palmy Days* shooting a scene with Eddie Cantor. It was an uncredited bit part, but Marion—unlike most of the other girls selected for the picture—had a speaking role. It didn't lead to any other movie work, although Louella Parsons reported in July that Marion would be having a screen test. In her brief scene in *Palmy Days*, Marion handles herself well and shows enough promise to at least get another chance. Perhaps Zeppo's desire to get out of the movies did not mix well with any desire Marion had to get into them.

Monkey Business was released in October and Zeppo's larger role in the film was noticed in many of the positive reviews. *The New Yorker* suggested, "the generally somewhat slighted Zeppo" was given more to do in *Monkey Business* "as a favor perhaps, for having been good and quiet for so long." Zeppo and Marion traveled to New York in September and the Four Marx Brothers attended a preview screening of their new film at the Rialto Theatre on September 23. During this trip they also all attended the premiere of *Palmy Days* at the same theater.

Preparation had begun for another lucrative vaudeville tour. With three hit movies under their belts, the Four Marx Brothers now commanded their highest-ever salary—$10,500 per week. In the waning days of vaudeville, it took a generous salary to get movie stars to perform on stage. Naturally Zeppo did not share in that figure and was once again working for his brothers as a salaried employee. On November 3 *Variety* made light of that situation: "Zeppo now never knows his weekly salary until three days after payday, when there's another conference over that without Zeppo allowed in on it."

Zeppo was making a good living in the employ of his brothers, but he was still bothered by his position within the act. Jokes at his expense in the press presented a danger when combined with Zeppo's volatile temper. There seems to have been a campaign to make Zeppo a more valuable and useful Marx Brother during the team's early Hollywood period. (He didn't object to relocating, so there may have been some agreement to increase his role.) For the vaudeville tour that followed immediately after the release of *Monkey Business*, the first film to really give Zeppo a chance to shine, they resurrected and updated a piece of material from *I'll Say She Is* that was a true showcase for the quartet. The sketch from the play called "Napoleon's First Waterloo" was expanded and updated into a full vaudeville show called *Napoleon's Return*. The tour began in mid-October and concluded on January 14, 1932, at the RKO Albee Theatre in Brooklyn, where Zeppo gave his last scheduled stage performance as a member of the Four Marx Brothers. He was contractually obligated to appear in two more films for Paramount but had no such commitment to any further touring. Had his brothers accepted another lucrative stage offer after the Paramount commitment was honored, there was no guarantee Zeppo would have cooperated.

Still looking at other career opportunities, Zeppo was suddenly being singled out for his versatility in publicity pieces—usually arranged by Paramount publicist Teet Carle. A July 1932 *Photoplay* story—"The Nuttiest Quartette in the World" by Sara Hamilton—included this testimonial to Zeppo:

> Forced by necessity of plot, to be just a handsome juvenile, few know that Zeppo has, next to Groucho, the keenest, quickest wit of any ten thousand men. Young, handsome, married, Zeppo it is who goes in for swankiness, Rolls-Royces and town houses. While the others live in extreme modesty. He plays the piano, the saxophone and a swell game of bridge. Many a radio contract as a "crooner" has young Zeppo Marx turned down. His voice is astonishing. And it's noticeable, too, that at a gathering it's Zeppo at whom they laugh most. His quick wit surprising those who expect this Zeppo to be as unfunny off the screen as on.

While true that Zeppo was funny, lived well, and appreciated the finer things in life, it doesn't seem that he really turned down many offers to be a radio crooner. But he may have briefly considered this option. On April 17, 1932, he was heard singing with the Raymond Paige Orchestra on the CBS radio program *California Melodies* from the Los Angeles studio of station KHJ. It appears to be his first and last such appearance. The show regularly featured singing movie stars like Irene Dunne, Mae Clarke, and even Mickey Mouse, who appeared a few weeks before Zeppo. Mae Clarke's *Frankenstein* costar Boris Karloff also made an appearance, so the show was not all about the singing.

Zeppo suddenly putting himself into the highly competitive arena of the radio crooners while Bing Crosby and Russ Columbo dominated the airwaves would not be a solution to his career problem. He'd become friendly with Crosby when they met at Paramount and discovered their mutual love of horse racing, boxing, and gambling. Zeppo was also friendly with Columbo and when he died tragically in 1934, Zeppo and Crosby were among the pallbearers at his funeral.

His singing was certainly good enough for Marx Brothers movies, but Zeppo knew he was no Crosby or Columbo. He wasn't looking for a way out of the Four Marx Brothers to become mediocre at something else. Zeppo was in large part motivated by a desire to show his brothers that his abilities stretched far beyond those required for the role of fourth Marx Brother. Mostly, he wanted to make more money than they did.

When the brothers got back to Hollywood after the *Napoleon's Return* tour, rumors began circulating that Zeppo would be leaving the team—not surprising considering how frequently Zeppo told reporters exactly that. But Paramount had a big hit with *Monkey Business* and a contract with the Four Marx Brothers. Paramount executive B. P. Schulberg issued a statement to columnist Louella Parsons that she ran on January 12: "The boys get here with wives, aunts, uncles, dogs, cats, etcetera, later in the month to start work on *Horse Feathers*, their latest picture." The statement left out Frenchy, who had been living at the Garden of Allah, splitting his time between Harpo's villa and Zeppo's apartment. Hector Arce, in his authorized biography, *Groucho*, told a tale about Frenchy from this period that is both amusing and melancholy:

> During the course of filming, Zeppo would retire early, since he had to be up at six every morning. There would be no one up to trade small talk with whenever Frenchy returned home. One night, he rang the doorbell. A sleepy Zeppo stumbled to the door. "Pop, for Christ's sake, where's your key?"
>
> "I must have lost it," Frenchy replied.
>
> "All right," his son said. "I'm getting you another key. So stop ringing the bell and waking us up."
>
> A couple of nights later, the doorbell rang again. Zeppo stumbled to the door of the darkened house and opened it. There stood his father. "Didn't I give you a key?" he asked.
>
> "Sure," Frenchy said, holding it out, "here it is."
>
> "Then why did you ring the bell?"
>
> "I wanted to see if somebody was home," this funny-sad little man said.

Marion and Zeppo found a place more to their liking and moved out of the Garden of Allah. They briefly stayed at Chico's house in Malibu before taking occupancy at their new place. In March 1932 Zeppo and Marion rented the apartment just vacated by Clark Gable at the recently built Colonial House at 1416 North Havenhurst Drive in West Hollywood. Silent screen star Margaret Livingston, notable for having appeared in F.W. Murnau's *Sunrise*, was one of the owners of the building, which would become a Hollywood landmark. She'd married orchestra leader Paul Whiteman in 1931, and Zeppo occasionally referred to Whiteman as his landlord. Early tenants included William Powell, Ernst Lubitsch, Carole Lombard, Norma Talmadge, and Cary Grant. It was a residence befitting an up-and-coming movie star.

The *Los Angeles Times* described the building while it was under construction:

The style of the architecture is to be French Colonial, and the main foyer will be finished in the same design. The building is divided into apartments ranging from three to eight rooms each and will be oper-ated as an unfurnished apartment building. The apartments are being decorated in different styles ranging from French Colonial to the mod-ernistic; special attention is being given to the tile work, all bathrooms being designed with specially made tile.

The Colonial House more accurately reflected Marion and Zeppo's taste and style than had the free-for-all, transitory atmosphere of the Garden of Allah. The building was a symbol of Hollywood success. In Budd Schulberg's 1941 novel *What Makes Sammy Run?*, the obsessively driven character Sammy Glick—allegedly based on any one of several ruthless Hollywood moguls (perhaps even the author's own father B. P. Schulberg)—bolsters his image by renting an apart-ment at "the fashionable Colonial House just off the Sunset Strip" described as "one of the smallest in the building and even that must have been way beyond his means." Zeppo had more in common with Sammy Glick than an address.

Before production began on *Horse Feathers*, Zeppo attempted to start another career while riding out his obligation to Paramount and his brothers—and for this latest idea being at Paramount was very convenient. On May 10, 1932, *Variety* reported that Zeppo had a script treatment at the studio. Being surrounded by screenwriters at the Garden of Allah could have inspired him. He wrote "Tom, Dick and Harry" in collaboration with novelist and screenwriter Gouverneur Morris, who was his new neighbor. Next door to the Colonial House, Morris had an apartment at 1414 North Havenhurst Drive. He was the great grandson of the identically named founding father who was one of the authors and signers of the Constitution of the United States.

Twenty-five years older than Zeppo, Morris was a wealthy, successful writer of novels and short stories who had been recently working on film scenarios. The West Hollywood apartment was but one of his residences. Morris lived primarily at a large palatial estate in Monterey. In addition, his wife's family had a coconut plantation in Tahiti. Gouverneur Morris was also the president of the Monterey Bank. Zeppo's taste for the finer things found a kindred spirit in Gouverneur Morris, and they began spending a lot of time together. Zeppo and Marion also rented a beach house in Malibu for the summer and Morris and his wife Ruth were frequent weekend guests there.

Marion had demonstrated excellent taste and skill in furnishing their Manhattan apartment and relished the opportunity to decorate their new home. Decorator to the stars Harold W. Grieve had been a set designer and art director on several films. Among his screen credits are *Ben-Hur: A Tale of the Christ*, *The Thief of Bagdad*, and *Lady Windermere's Fan*. But he gave up working in movies and forged a very successful career decorating the homes of stars and directors for decades. Along the way he married silent film star Jetta Goudal, who was also a decorator. Working with Grieve and Goudal, Marion and Zeppo turned their Colonial House apartment into such an exquisite home that it was featured in *Architectural Digest* shortly after they moved in. Marion was really the driving force in this area. She had come from the wealthy environment created during her father's successful times. For Zeppo the most important piece of furniture during his adolescence was the pool table Minnie put in the basement of their house in Chicago. But the influence of new friends Gouverneur Morris and Harold Grieve helped Zeppo develop an appreciation of things like antique furniture and first editions.

Harold Grieve was the same age as Zeppo, born only a few weeks earlier. He had a successful movie career in various studio art departments but was driven to leave it all behind for a career as his own boss doing something he enjoyed more than movie studio work. This could not have gone unnoticed by Zeppo. Morris also worked for himself and was a great success. With his experience at Paramount and his friendship with Morris, Zeppo believed his future was in writing movies rather than appearing in them. After failing to interest Paramount or any other studio in "Tom, Dick and Harry"—a story about three orphaned brothers adopted by different families—Zeppo and Morris went to work on another treatment. "A Pair of Shoes" was a story of marital infidelity and murder that also found no takers at the Hollywood studios. There would be no further collaborations between Zeppo and Gouverneur Morris, although they remained friends and neighbors.

Production of *Horse Feathers* had begun in March, and once again Zeppo's role was more substantial than it had been in the past. Paramount was eager to replicate the successful formula that made *Monkey Business* a box-office hit. S. J. Perelman returned as part of the writing team and when production was halted on April 10 after Chico was injured in an automobile accident, Zeppo found his new collaborator. Perelman and Zeppo, who had become friendly while neighbors at the Garden of Allah, began work on a treatment called "Roller-Coaster." Not discouraged by his inability to sell the two dramas he wrote with Gouverneur Morris, Zeppo tried another. For all the talk about Zeppo being a funny guy off screen, and Perelman's reputation as one of the country's top humorists, it seems odd that they didn't try to create a comedy. "Roller-Coaster" revolves around a love triangle involving two rival amusement park operators and one's attempt to kill the other by sabotaging a roller coaster. Once again, there were no takers at any studio.

While Zeppo was actively seeking a solo career of almost any kind, his brothers were trying to make his role in the Four Marx Brothers more significant. Not more significant than their own, but something interesting enough to keep him happy and part of the team. Literary agent George Bye had been successful in placing several of Groucho's writings in various magazines and was instrumental in getting his first book, *Beds*, published in 1930. Bye represented writers like Franklin P. Adams, Alexander Woollcott, James M. Cain, and Theodore Dreiser. But he also represented stage and screen stars like Eddie Cantor and Moran & Mack. His client list even included boxer Gene Tunney. Groucho asked George Bye to investigate radio opportunities for the Four Marx Brothers and on April 11, 1932—the day after Chico's accident—Bye presented NBC with an offer and a script.

The twelve-page script—simply titled "Four Marx Brothers Radio Sketch"—was written by Morrie Ryskind and Will B. Johnstone. Conceptually it is not unlike the "Theatrical Manager's Office" sketch in that it allows each of the brothers to effectively introduce himself. Even more unusual than a role for Zeppo nearly equal to those of his brothers is the remarkable inclusion of lines of dialogue for Harpo. When the straight man confronts Harpo with the line, "Harpo Marx! But I thought you never talked." Harpo replies, "Well, I never could talk, but now a German fellow is teaching me English, so I'm a brother too." When Zeppo is told he's the only brother that talks English, he responds, "That's not my fault. I picked it up from the boys in the gutter."

George Bye offered the show—which would air three times a week for thirteen weeks—to NBC for the sum of $15,000 per week, a total of $195,000 for the series. Presumably Zeppo's arrangement with his brothers would have had him remain a salaried employee rather than a participant in this windfall. Bye arranged for the Four Marx Brothers to perform the script for NBC executives in his office, and they were impressed—even with Chico performing from a wheelchair. An NBC interoffice memo dated April 27 states, "Mr. Peterson went down to Mr. Bye's office, and heard the Marx Brothers do this script. He fell off his chair, it was so funny. Of course, he was able to see them too, which means a lot, but even so as we read the copy, we thought it was grand." But the price was ultimately too high, and NBC was unable to interest any sponsor in the services of the Four Marx Brothers at their asking price. The radio voice of Harpo Marx would never grace the airwaves, although he would later whistle, honk, and strum his way through several broadcasts.

Production on *Horse Feathers* resumed in June, and the film was released in August. No one really equated the success of the film with Zeppo's improved standing within the team. He was still chasing his screenwriting dream as his ticket out of the Four Marx Brothers. After failing to interest any studio in three collaborative dramas, Zeppo made his last attempt as a movie scenario writer by himself—and it was a comedy.

Even a casual comparison of the treatment for Zeppo's "Muscle-Bound" to his previous efforts reveals that Gouverneur Morris and S. J. Perelman were probably responsible for getting Zeppo's first three film scenarios on paper. But what "Muscle-Bound" lacks in professionalism as a written work is balanced by its apparent marketability. *Variety* reported on October 11, 1932, that Universal was interested in it as a vehicle for Slim Summerville and Zasu Pitts. But the silly story of a country doctor who accidentally concocts a liniment that provides enough strength and endurance to win a six-day bicycle race ultimately joined Zeppo's other treatments on Hollywood's prodigious pile of unsold film ideas. "Muscle-Bound" made the rounds and was seen by enough studio people to have possibly had its main story idea stolen. First National's 1934 Joe E. Brown film *6 Day Bike Rider* has enough elements of Zeppo's story to make the case, but it could also be a coincidence given the popularity of six-day bike races at the time.

Four unsold film treatments in one year were enough for Zeppo. It became clear in 1932 that he was neither a radio crooner nor a screenwriter. For the moment he still had one more film to make after completing *Horse Feathers* at Paramount before he could escape the Four Marx Brothers.

CHAPTER ELEVEN

The Great Race

O NE OF ZEPPO'S EARLIEST PASSIONS WAS THE AUTOMOBILE. HAD MIN-
nie not dragged him away from his job as a mechanic at Ford in
Chicago when he was a teenager, there's a good chance he would have
continued to pursue a career in the automotive field. But he also could have
continued his career as a small-time hoodlum. Getting him away from Chicago
was the critical thing that would save Zeppo.

Zeppo's early days in show business coincided with the continued criminal
activities of his boyhood friend Joey Bass, who would also end up in California.
While Zeppo was making plans in Hollywood, Bass was on his way to the California State Prison at San Quentin, where he was incarcerated from March 1933
until he was paroled in January 1935. For Bass, stealing cars with Herbert Marx
as a teenager led to a string of arrests for embezzlement, securities fraud, grand
theft, and passing bad checks. Maybe vaudeville wasn't the worst thing that
could have happened to a troubled kid with a penchant for juvenile delinquency.
Life could have been very different for Joey Bass had his mother harbored an
unfulfilled burning desire to be on the stage.

Zeppo never lost his love for tinkering with engines, and once he was making a solid living, he was a frequent purchaser of luxury cars. Zeppo saw in Errett
Lobban Cord the future he might have had if not for show business interrupting
his life. E. L. Cord, as he was more commonly known, had been a mechanic,
race car driver, and car salesman. In 1924 he became the manager of the failing
Auburn Automobile Company in Indiana. He turned the company around and
would soon own it, along with several other transportation-related businesses.
Cord put his name on a line of luxury cars manufactured by Auburn, and his top-
of-the-line model for 1930—the Cord L-29 Phaeton Sedan—found an enthusiastic customer in Zeppo Marx. The Four Marx Brothers were photographed in

Zeppo's new car for the April-May 1930 issue of the automotive magazine *The Accelerator*. With a price tag of $1,695, the L-29 was a relative bargain. The first car ever to have front wheel drive also featured a 125-horsepower, 298-cubic-inch, inline eight-cylinder engine, and three-speed manual transmission. This was a reasonably priced car for the motor enthusiast who might not have had the resources to afford something like the 1930 Cadillac V16 Roadster—with its newly introduced sixteen-cylinder engine and price tag of $5,350. The Cord L-29 was plenty of car for Zeppo—at least in 1930.

In Hollywood, Zeppo and Chico together acquired a 1928 Mercedes-Benz S 26/180 Boattail Speedster, which was regarded as the finest sporting car of the era. Chico, Betty, Zeppo, and Marion—arriving at the home of Al Jolson and Ruby Keeler to play bridge—spotted a 1931 Duesenberg Model J parked on Sunset Boulevard. No longer the teenaged Chicago car thief of bygone days, Zeppo could only admire the car, which he assumed belonged to Jolson. Zeppo soon learned that the Duesenberg belonged to Hollywood agent and fellow car enthusiast Phil Berg, who with his actress-wife Leila Hyams, was also a guest for bridge night at Al Jolson's house.

Interviewed in *Automobile Quarterly* in 1980, Berg recalled the evening:

> [S]oon enough the conversation turned to these powerful-looking machines and which one of them was faster. Chico, who never would miss a chance to make a bet for a few thousand dollars, challenged me, and I challenged him back. . . . So, we decided to climb into our respective cars then and there and to head for Santa Monica. The first one to get to the beach would win.

Leila Hyams and the other wives adamantly insisted there be no street racing and a safer method of settling the matter would be worked out.

Zeppo and Marion began socializing with Phil Berg and Leila Hyams and their evenings together usually turned into boring affairs for Marion and Leila as the two men endlessly talked about their cars. Zeppo boasted about his skill as a mechanic and said that he could make the Mercedes run faster and better than Berg's Duesenberg. Berg was incredulous and these discussions would usually become heated. They arranged a race and a $1,000 wager to settle the matter. As word of the race between Berg's American-made Duesenberg and the German-made Mercedes belonging to Zeppo and Chico got around, all of Hollywood became interested. As the race approached, it was reported in the gossip columns that $25,000 in bets had been placed. Chico was more interested in the gambling. Zeppo took over the automotive aspects of the contest.

Phil Berg was yet another self-made success in Zeppo's sights as he envied the independence of friends like Gouverneur Morris and Harold Grieve, and admired E. L. Cord from afar. Berg, a year younger than Zeppo, had made himself a millionaire by the age of twenty-six. In Hollywood Berg would become famous as an agent for inventing what would come to be known as the "package deal." He would acquire a script or story rights; get actors, a writer, and a director interested in the project; sign them up; and then sell the whole thing to a producer. Among the more well-known Berg package deals would be *Mrs. Miniver* and *Rebecca*—both Oscar winners for Best Picture—and the *Andy Hardy* and *Dr. Kildare* franchises.

Initially with partner Bert Allenberg, and then on his own, Berg also represented many top stars, including Gary Cooper, Deanna Durbin, Wallace Beery, Olivia de Havilland, and Clark Gable. Zeppo soon learned that Berg bought his car from E. L. Cord, who had acquired the Duesenberg Motors Company in 1926. Cord had been liquidating his Duesenberg inventory as the Depression began hurting the luxury car business. Cord, recently on the cover of *Time* magazine, was renting a home very near Phil Berg and Leila Hyams's home while Cordhaven, his thirty-two-thousand-square-foot mansion with sixteen bedrooms and twenty-two bathrooms on eighteen acres on North Hillcrest Road in Beverly Hills, was being built. Berg not only bought a Duesenberg for himself, but he also managed to sell several to his clients, endearing himself to E. L. Cord.

The Duesenberg-Mercedes race was set for 5 a.m. on September 25, 1932, at Muroc Dry Lake in the Antelope Valley around a hundred miles north of Los Angeles. The unusually hard surface of the dry lake—an endorheic desert salt pan in the Mojave Desert—was the principal reason for the eventual construction of Edwards Air Force Base around it. The hard natural surface was able to support landings of the heaviest aircraft. It was also an ideal surface for auto racing and sported a five-mile circular track. The race would be three laps around the course. *Los Angeles Examiner* columnist Harriet Parsons wrote, on September 23: "Zep and Phil, besides putting up a grand apiece, have spent plenty stripping their cars for action. Film folks are taking sides violently and backing up their opinions with sizable wagers. . . . And you'd be amazed at how many celebrities are planning to stay up till dawn for the event."

E. L. Cord took great interest in the race, as it would be bad for business if his car were to lose. If Zeppo thought he was on a level playing field, he was mistaken; although, like Cord, he was also on the cover of *Time* magazine shortly before the race. But unlike Cord, Zeppo was pictured in a large garbage can with his brothers. Cord put his Auburn-Cord-Duesenberg racing team to work on Berg's car and hired Eddie Miller, who had raced for Cord's team in the Indianapolis 500, to drive the Duesenberg. Miller knew the course well. He had driven a twelve-cylinder Auburn in a five-hundred-mile race at Muroc in August.

Zeppo hired German-born mechanic Joe Reindl to drive his Mercedes. Reindl operated the Hollywood Spring and Axle Company, a foreign motor repair shop on Sunset Boulevard, and serviced the cars of many movie stars. Reindl was the best Mercedes-Benz man in Los Angeles, but he was up against the service department of the company responsible for building the Duesenberg. Both cars were streamlined by having their bumpers, fenders, running boards, and windshields removed. Zeppo and many other car experts believed the smaller, lower, and much lighter Mercedes would leave the comparatively enormous Duesenberg in the dust.

Gummo's son Bob recalled an automotive invention that would have served Zeppo's Mercedes well had it not been a complete disaster. Gummo, himself an occasional inventor, and Zeppo developed a nonskid tire together.

> Dad and Zeppo set up a demonstration for the executives of the tire companies who were in Akron, Ohio. Zeppo drove the car with the new skid-less tires down a steep hill. When the car reached the spot where Dad and the executives from the tire companies stood, Zeppo applied the brakes. The tires gripped the macadam roadway with a vengeance. The non-skid treads were a phenomenal success! The car, however, ran right out of the tires and went hurtling down the hill sans tires.

Zeppo left the preparation of his car for the race to Joe Reindl.

Zeppo's friend Mae Sunday—the former daughter-in-law of celebrated baseball player turned evangelist Billy Sunday, and a frequent social companion to many Hollywood figures—chartered a Greyhound bus to bring many movie people to the race. She threw an all-night party on Saturday that led right into the early Sunday morning event. Among the screen star revelers were Bebe Daniels and her husband Ben Lyon. Ben served as the official starter of the race, driving his Lincoln twelve-cylinder Phaeton as the pace car. In the predawn darkness, the gathering crowd included Al Jolson, Ruby Keeler, Clark Gable, Carole Lombard, Mae West, Wallace Beery, at least another Marx Brother or two, and around a thousand other interested onlookers.

Ben Lyon's Lincoln kicked off the thirty-five-mile-per-hour rolling start, and Joe Reindl had Zeppo's Mercedes briefly ahead in the first lap. But the more experienced Eddie Miller quickly guided the Duesenberg into the lead. The *Los Angeles Times* reported the result on October 2: "Getting away together at thirty-five miles an hour, the two cars careened neck and neck around the five-mile circle. Only inches separated them at the five-mile mark. Then the Duesenberg forged ahead and finished far in the lead." The Duesenberg's average speed in the race was reported at 102.5 miles per hour, with a top speed of 108. The *Los Angeles Record* reported Miller's gracious explanation of his victory: "[I]t was the Gilmore Red Lion gasoline that gave him the necessary edge to win, so evenly matched were the cars in power and speed." Presumably this was not a free endorsement. Oil tycoon Earl Gilmore, who helped set up the race, was on hand and a Gilmore Red Lion checkered flag signaled the end of the race.

Almost immediately plans were underway for a rematch. The *Los Angeles Times* reported on October 7 that the second Zeppo Marx–Phil Berg race would take place at the Legion Ascot Speedway at Valley Boulevard and Soto Street in Los Angeles. Opened in 1924, the track became known for its numerous deadly crashes. By 1933 six drivers had been killed there. By the time it was shuttered in 1936 the number of fatalities had reached twenty-four. The track earned the nickname "Killer Track," with one of the curves becoming known as "King of the Grim Reapers." The second race set for October 12 was barely even noticed by the press. It was an added attraction to a card of professional races. On the day of the race, the *Illustrated Daily News* made clear that this was purely an exhibition. "Both cars will circle the track as fast as possible, but it has been found impossible to race the two cars because of their size and weight." Columnist Dan Thomas reported Leila Hyams thoughts about her husband's amateur auto racing, saying, "[S]he's going to have the car fixed so it won't go that fast. She's afraid Phil will get into another race with someone and be killed."

After the Muroc race Zeppo was gracious in defeat. He and Marion continued to socialize with Phil Berg and Leila Hyams, and even vacationed with them in Palm Springs. There were no hard feelings, but it was clear that E. L. Cord corrupted an amateur race by elevating Berg's car to professional racing caliber. Having Eddie Miller drive the Berg car was the automotive equivalent of adding Lou Gehrig to the lineup of the underdog baseball team in a little league game. Years later Zeppo may have laughed at the irony of Eddie Miller ending up in the movie business as a journeyman electrician at MGM. Zeppo's car also got into the movies. The Mercedes was seen in the 1935 MGM film *Sylvia Scarlett* with Katharine Hepburn and Cary Grant.

Phil Berg happily took Zeppo's $1,000—or more if the gossip columns had any real information—but Zeppo was not especially worried about gambling losses. In Palm Springs, as stars headed to the desert to avoid the cold weather in Hollywood that fall, there were a lot of high stakes bridge and backgammon games being played and Zeppo held his own. Also vacationing in the desert in the fall of 1932 were Phil Berg and Leila Hyams, who introduced Zeppo and Marion to another agent, Milton Bren. Bren and his wife Marion were part of the Hollywood bridge crowd. Bren, with his partner Frank Orsatti, was also a successful agent and half of the Bren-Orsatti agency. Zeppo noticed the lavish lifestyles enjoyed by Milton Bren and Phil Berg. These men didn't necessarily have much more knowledge of the movie business than he did. Berg had recently taken on a partner, Bert Allenberg, after having been on his own since starting his agency in 1927. The agency business looked good to Zeppo. It was another option to consider. Bert Allenberg became a partner in a successful agency. Why not Zeppo Marx?

With the Marx Brothers on hiatus as Paramount made plans for their final film due under the 1930 contract, Zeppo was enjoying his leisure time—and winning a lot of money—while exploring future opportunities. With no sponsors willing to meet the radio price for the Four Marx Brothers, Groucho and Chico took to the airwaves as a duo on NBC's *Five Star Theatre*. They debuted on November 28. The following day *New York Daily News* columnist Sidney Skolsky reported, "Zeppo Marx hit the gambling tables last week for more than Groucho and Chico received for their broadcast last night." Zeppo's reputation as a gambler didn't portray him as the genial, happy-go-lucky reckless loser that Chico seemed to be. Maxine Marx wrote in *Growing Up with Chico* of overhearing Douglas Fairbanks, Jr. remark, at around this time, that Chico was bad enough, "but the one I can't stand is Zeppo. He plays for blood, and I think he's crooked besides."

Zeppo and Marion widened their social circle as they waited for word about the next picture, which Zeppo was sure would be his last. Frequent visitors to their Colonial House apartment in the fall of 1932 included neighbor Alice Glazer (the former wife of writer-producer Barney Glazer), Mae Sunday and her constant companion Dave Harris, and Gary Cooper—recently back in Hollywood after ten months abroad with his married girlfriend Countess Dorothy Di Frasso, formerly American heiress Dorothy Caldwell-Taylor. MGM producer Irving Thalberg and his wife, actress Norma Shearer joined the group occasionally for bridge or backgammon, as did Milton and Marion Bren. Zeppo played high stakes bridge with Irving Thalberg, Milton Bren, and Phil Berg, but when the women played, there was considerably less money involved. Louella Parsons ran an amusing item in her column:

> Here is a rough idea the way checks travel in Hollywood bridge circles. Skeets Gallagher paid Mae Sunday a $15 bridge debt. Mae in turn, handed the check to Marion Bren to pay a $15 loss. Milton Bren borrowed it from Marion to hand over to Zeppo Marx as payment of a debt. Mrs. Zeppo collected it from her husband to give to Bebe Daniels.

Bridge had become a phenomenon and it had taken hold in Hollywood in a big way. Much was made of the story of a Kansas City housewife who shot her husband dead during a bridge match with a neighbor couple in 1929. He misplayed a hand, she complained about his lousy bridge playing. He slapped her and she got a pistol and killed him. She was later acquitted, providing bridge enthusiasts with plenty of laughs over misplayed hands. Harpo encouraged his close friend Alexander Woollcott to write an essay about the so-called "Bridge-Table Murder," and Woollcott included it in his 1934 book, *While Rome Burns*. Zeppo took his bridge game very seriously, and there were plenty of people in the community who preferred not to play with him.

The man most responsible for the popularization of bridge, Ely Culbertson, came to Hollywood in early 1933 to make a series of short films at RKO. He quickly met some of the town's best players. Lionel Barrymore threw a bridge party honoring Culbertson. Seen playing with him in a widely circulated newspaper photo of the event were Bebe Daniels, Joe Schenck, and Zeppo. At another table Chico played in a foursome with Mrs. Culbertson. Culbertson had made bridge big news by accepting challenges and generally beating everyone. When Zeppo and Chico challenged him, Culbertson accepted, and a pair of matches was set. Invitations were sent for a match at Paramount on February 22 and another at RKO the following day.

Then Culbertson had second thoughts—probably after playing with Zeppo and Chico at the Barrymore party. He claimed to have thought the Marx challenge was a joke, and he was astonished to learn they were serious about it. Chico was quoted in wire service stories saying, "We are disappointed that he withdrew. I have a new system that will beat Culbertson. I challenge him to a match with a $5,000 side wager." Culbertson was not known to have turned down any other challengers, but he ducked the Marxes, who were among Hollywood's best players.

Zeppo and Marion became closest for a time with another pair of social bridge players, Richard Arlen and his wife Jobyna Ralston. The two couples spent Christmas together at Lake Arrowhead, skiing, skating, and gambling with Walter Huston, Reginald Denny, Warren William, and their wives. Zeppo was known within this circle as a serious gambler and a great practical joker. On Christmas Eve columnist Dan Thomas wrote, "After receiving telephone invitations from an 'executive' of a well-known airline to make free trips east, a number of stars were all set to take vacations in the near future. And then it was discovered that the big-hearted guy was Zeppo Marx. The vacation plans were canceled."

As 1932 drew to a close, the fun and games ended for Zeppo. On December 26 Frenchy suffered a heart attack at around the same time Paramount announced that the Four Marx Brothers were going back to work on a new film to be called *Cracked Ice*. But all was not going according to plan with Paramount and the Marx Brothers. The studio was having financial problems and had tried unsuccessfully to renegotiate the advance on *Horse Feathers*. Rumors began appearing in the press that the Four Marx Brothers would be making films elsewhere as soon as their new film at Paramount was completed. Zeppo was not part of any of these discussions.

In February 1933 *Variety* reported that the new Marx picture was to be called *Grass Hoppers* and would begin shooting in March. But the Marx Brothers had other ideas. Paramount violated their contract by transferring the agreement to a newly formed subsidiary company as part of a financial reorganization as the studio teetered on the brink of bankruptcy. The Marx Brothers refused to work for another company under the contract and formed their own. They announced that they would make their next film independently. Zeppo saw an opportunity to leave without violating any contracts. But everyone else thought the team needed to remain a quartet—in large part to honor Minnie's wishes, even though she had been dead for more than three years.

The stress affected Frenchy as much as any of the brothers, and he suffered another heart attack on March 7. His death on May 11 came amid the trouble with Paramount, and Zeppo trying to convince his brothers that any new deal for the team be as a trio. Zeppo accompanied Frenchy's body on the train to New York. His brothers were already there, looking for their next project in case things with Paramount didn't work out. Frenchy was laid to rest next to Minnie, and on the day of his funeral Paramount and the Marx Brothers agreed to settle their differences by signing a new contract for the one remaining picture—now called *Duck Soup*. They would settle the financial differences from the original contract later.[1] The delays extended the hiatus well past the point where Zeppo expected to be done with making Marx Brothers movies, but he still hadn't settled on what he would do with his independence once he had secured it.

Zeppo and Marion had become very close to Carole Lombard during this period. Apart from Lombard's mother, Marion was her closest confidant as she and William Powell decided to get a divorce after only a couple of years of marriage. When Lombard abruptly left town in July 1933 to establish residency in Nevada, where a divorce could be expedited, she wrote to Marion:

> Marion Darling,
> I didn't call you before I left as I just couldn't talk to anyone. Remember when I saw you at the Colony. I know you wondered why I acted so strangely. Well, I was right in the middle of all of it. I knew if I talked to you, I would instantly go into hysterics. So dear, I didn't go anywhere near you. Believe me it's ghastly to go through, and I hope to God I never have to do it again. I want to try to tell you now. Only one thing I want you and Zeppo to know is it was all very beautifully done, and Junior and I will always be the best of friends. It was inevitable so I thought it best to end it while we both had love in our hearts for each other. Sweet, I brought a few things with me and the white fur rug you gave me was one of them. It makes it easier having a few things around you that your friends gave you. Have taken a cottage at Lake Tahoe at last. It is beautiful up here. And God, Reno is too, too dreadful. If you have time write me at Brockway, California. Forgive me and understand. I love you both so much. Call Junior and ask him out. I know he will be lonely. Will write soon.
> Devotedly,
> Carole

Seeing Lombard and Powell split up troubled Marion. Lombard wrote in another letter, "[W]hen two people are basically as difficult as Bill and me in every way it's quite impossible to find common ground . . . As much as I love Bill, we are so wrong for each other." Marion could say with great conviction that she and Zeppo were very compatible and got along like best friends six years into their marriage. Divorce had not been a subject she wanted to confront even though she knew Zeppo had never given up his extracurricular activities with other women. He was discreet, but it was painful for her. Powell was faithful in his marriage to Lombard, but they split up because they lacked everything else Marion had with Zeppo. Marriage was becoming something of a balancing act for Marion.

CHAPTER TWELVE

How to Succeed in Business
without Really Trying

A NEW BUSINESS VENTURE UNEXPECTEDLY MATERIALIZED FOR ZEPPO AS a result of attending the boxing matches at the American Legion Stadium. Always looking for inside information before placing bets, Zeppo befriended fight manager and matchmaker Charlie MacDonald. MacDonald had a 50 percent interest in a failing Hollywood café that had opened in May 1933. Recognizing the excellence of the location—6327 Hollywood Boulevard near Vine Street—Zeppo bought MacDonald's half of the business for $10,000 in July. But Zeppo didn't just like the location. He had a vision for the place that could turn it into a goldmine.

The other 50 percent of Perry's Brass Rail was owned by Bob Perry, an actor and retired boxer whose career in movies dated back to the early 1920s. By 1933 Perry, who had previously been in the restaurant business in New York as the owner of Perry's Grill, was working mostly as an extra in uncredited bit roles. Perry's Brass Rail was floundering when Zeppo became Bob Perry's partner. The opening of Perry's Brass Rail—and Zeppo's interest in it—was the result of the impending repeal of Prohibition, which had been a key item in the Democratic party's platform in the 1932 presidential election. The Cullen-Harrison Act—commonly called the "Beer Act"—had been passed by Congress and signed into law by President Franklin D. Roosevelt on March 22, 1933.

The sale of alcohol had been illegal in the United States since January 17, 1920. Before the Twenty-First Amendment fully repealed Prohibition in December, states were authorized by the "Beer Act" to allow the sale of low-alcohol beer—with no more than 3.2 percent alcohol content—in restaurants. Roosevelt famously remarked when signing the bill, "I think this would be a good time for a beer." The public agreed and there were suddenly lines outside establishments selling 3.2 beer. Bob Perry began selling the low-alcohol beer with sandwiches—the sandwiches in this case being a barely edible formality to make the beer sales legal. (The "Beer Act" required food to be served with alcohol.)

Like everyone else in Hollywood, Zeppo knew plenty of places to enjoy illegal liquor without being bothered by anyone silly enough to enforce Prohibition in Los Angeles. But operating a legal beer parlor in the heart of Hollywood and inviting a bunch of celebrities seemed like a real moneymaker. Shortly after Zeppo completely revamped the operation with a "Gay Nineties" theme, *Variety* reported that Perry's Brass Rail had "developed into Hollywood's hottest night-spot." That *Variety* item from August 1, 1933, also detailed Zeppo's makeover:

> Marx installed a flock of singing waiters, rouged their snozzles and pasted handlebar mustaches over their lips. He got behind the bar himself, both for advertising and protection, and the spot was off to a fast second start. Now it's a hangout for the picture mob who find the place a laugh resort.
>
> How long it will last is anyone's guess, but the boys are spreading the word that Marx got his investment back in three weeks, and the closing notice isn't up yet. Zeppo Marx is the juve of the Marx Brothers. He is not a comedian, just a bridge player with crap shooting on the side.

The gambling reference had become common in the press, and Zeppo seems to have encouraged it—or at least not protested. He knew how to publicize Perry's Brass Rail and the gossip columnists—usually an annoyance to him—became his free publicity machine. Louella Parsons cooperated, reporting this "Snapshot of Hollywood" in her column: "The singing waiters at Bob Perry's Brass Rail greeting Gary Cooper with a special song. This unique Hollywood 'jernt' is crowded to the doors every night. The waiters, ex-vaudevillians, double in brass, singing, tap-dancing, jigging between serving beer and sandwiches."

The "Gay Nineties" theme wasn't just a random idea. In September 1932 Florence Eldridge threw a "Gay Nineties" costume party for her husband Fredric March's birthday. Nearly every major star in Hollywood turned up at the party in costume. Zeppo and Marion were there, as was Groucho—who came as a "Gay Nineties" police officer. The Hollywood community was still talking about the Fredric March party when Zeppo bought into the restaurant several months later. Zeppo was certainly an idea man. He put Fredric March's birthday party and his friend's investment in a failing café together in his mind and saw the potential.

Columnist Devon Francis wrote in the *Venice Evening Vanguard* on September 27: "Getting into the Brass Rail is like trying to crash the bargain basement on dollar day, but it's worth the trouble. There's Nancy Carroll, Joe E. Brown and Jack Oakie. Over here is Harlow and Texas Guinan. And at the back, of all persons, John Barrymore!" Ethel M. Taylor, in *The Van Nuys News*, called the Brass Rail "[j]ust another one of those 'different' places that have resulted from the beer act." But she also pointed out the main attraction that Zeppo knew would separate it from every other beer joint. "Here one finds a bit 'ritzier' crowd, with a good smattering of full dress worn by folks 'enroute home' about 12 bells."

Zeppo's vision of the place as a stomping ground for movie people who didn't want to risk being in a raided speakeasy after a party or a premiere was precisely what Perry's Brass Rail became almost immediately after he took over.[1] Of course, Zeppo, Marion, and their friends became regulars; and none of them missed the irony of Mae Sunday enjoying a beer. Her former father-in-law, Billy Sunday, championed Prohibition and even called for its reintroduction after it had been repealed.

Zeppo made the transformation of Perry's Brass Rail look easy. It was a high-profile success, but once he'd done it, there was no challenge left in the venture—other than the normal annoyances of being in the restaurant business. He sold his interest at a significant profit in November 1933 to Wilson Atkins, whom he'd likely met through the actor Tom Kennedy, who had appeared in *Monkey Business*—and more than three hundred other films. Kennedy became Atkins's partner in Perry's Brass Rail, which they renamed the Hollywood Brass Rail when they bought out Bob Perry in March 1934. The new owners moved the establishment down the block to 6321 Hollywood Boulevard. Zeppo's influence remained, and the celebrity clientele continued to be part of the attraction. An advertisement for the new location mentioned the "$3,000 ventilating and heating system" as well as "charcoal broiled steaks" and "entertaining waiters." But most prominent in the ad was the acknowledgment of "the tremendous support given us by the general public which includes the 'WHO'S WHO' of the stage and screen and sports world."

An ironic twist to Zeppo's involvement in the Brass Rail came shortly after he sold his share of it. Sam Bischoff, producer and studio supervisor at Warner Bros.—and a regular at the Brass Rail—bought a story idea from Paul Finder Moss and Jerry Wald, new arrivals in Hollywood. The story, originally titled "Hot Air" was turned into the First National film *Twenty Million Sweethearts*, in which a singing waiter is discovered working at Perry's Brass Rail and becomes a radio star. The film—which stars Pat O'Brien, Dick Powell, and Ginger

Rogers—includes an exterior shot of the original Perry's Brass Rail and a brief appearance by Bob Perry as its manager. There's a tiny hint of Zeppo having some involvement in the film: Marion appears as an uncredited extra in a scene shot at a studio recreation of the interior of Perry's Brass Rail. It was Jerry Wald's first feature film story credit and marked the beginning of his long career in Hollywood as a writer and producer. Zeppo, unable to sell any of his four screenplay ideas, probably should have tried a story about his restaurant.

The success of Perry's Brass Rail seemed like the solution to Zeppo's career problem. He easily could have left the Four Marx Brothers to become a very successful restaurateur. The timing was perfect—one more movie and straight into the restaurant business full time. But Zeppo got out of Perry's Brass Rail as quickly as he got in. He knew he could do much more but had not yet settled on where his talents could best lead him. After spending the holidays skiing, skating, and gambling in Lake Arrowhead, Zeppo and Marion returned to the reality of Hollywood and his position as the fourth—and lowest paid—Marx Brother.

There was still the matter of *Duck Soup*, which as originally conceived before the delay in production, had a sizable and interesting role for Zeppo. His character was going to be Groucho's son—as it was in *Horse Feathers*—and he would be involved in a romantic story line, even singing a duet with costar Raquel Torres.[2] (In *Horse Feathers*, Zeppo sang to Thelma Todd, but not with her.) But that all changed when the Marx Brothers refused to make the picture when their contract was breached. By the time they returned to the studio with a new contract, there was a new script that reduced Zeppo's role to the insignificance he'd grown accustomed to before the Hollywood move and his emerging relevance in *Monkey Business* and *Horse Feathers*.

During the first story conferences for what became *Duck Soup*, *Los Angeles Evening Herald Express* columnist Harrison Carroll wrote, on February 24, 1933,

> Dozens of stories are told of the Marx Brothers conferences. Latest is about the writer who was submitting dialogue for their approval. He read a six-line speech. They asked him who it was for. "Zeppo," he replied. "Cut it down to 'Well, er,'" snapped Groucho.

A typical Groucho wisecrack in February became a reality by July, when filming of *Duck Soup* finally began. By that point it was clear that the Marx Brothers would soon be a trio. Even Zeppo made light of being returned to his former status on screen. The movie fan magazine *Shadoplay* quoted him in a report from the set: "Zeppo, handsome young straight man of the four brothers, wanders about in resplendent uniform. 'I've got a line to say in this picture somewhere. I saw it in the script. Is it time to say my line?' he keeps asking no one in particular." Zeppo was not bothered by his reduced role in *Duck Soup*, as it afforded him more time for other ventures like Perry's Brass Rail. By the time the Four Marx Brothers finally made the film, Zeppo was already thinking of them as a trio.

Zeppo's self-confidence and sharp sense of humor allowed him to make jokes about his unimportance to the Marx Brothers, but his comments to Richard J. Anobile in 1973 are not humorous and reveal a sense of guilt for being handed a career he hadn't earned.

> I was getting very neurotic at going on stage, doing something I didn't want to do. Taking money for something for which I didn't think I was deserving. I kept thinking that I had the job because my parents wanted to keep the Four Marx Brothers together. I either had to get out and do something or else wind up with a nervous breakdown.

Leaving the Four Marx Brothers wasn't just about proving himself capable of more than his meager roles on screen. Zeppo was in his early thirties and had been under the control of his family for his entire life. It would be surprising if this hadn't affected his mental health.

Paramount's publicity people were probably among the last to know *Duck Soup* would be Zeppo's last Marx Brothers movie. In the pressbook for the film they created a version of Zeppo that none of the Marx Brothers would have recognized: "Zeppo, despite his 'straight' character, is a most important part of the team. He's an expert gag man and is so splendid at imitating any one of the brothers, that should illness stop one from making an appearance, Zeppo can immediately take his place." Zeppo's ability to fill in for a brother now and then may have prevented a few cancellations in vaudeville, but Groucho wasn't exactly thrilled when audiences were unable to detect Zeppo as his substitute on stage in Chicago three years earlier. The trouble caused by that probably assured that Zeppo's days of filling in for Groucho were over.

While his brothers and the studio made a last-ditch effort to make Zeppo feel better about his role in the Four Marx Brothers, no one seems to have considered offering him a full partnership in the team or a chance to contribute more than a handful of straight lines to *Duck Soup*. The three films made in Hollywood restored their billing to the Four Marx Brothers—after the film versions of *The Cocoanuts* and *Animal Crackers* billed them simply as the Marx Brothers. This may have had something to do with Zeppo's earlier threats to leave the act, and perhaps some promises made with the new Paramount contract. But the fact remains that over the course of the five Paramount films Zeppo's screen time pales in comparison to any other Marx Brother and totals well under an hour.

As production was completed on *Duck Soup* the Hollywood rumor mill began running with the news that the Marx Brothers would either become a trio or would all be going their separate ways. *Daily Variety* ran a front-page story on October 28, 1933, claiming that the Four Marx Brothers had split up. This was not the sort of publicity Paramount was looking for as *Duck Soup* was about to be released. To keep the studio and his brothers happy as the film rolled out, Zeppo held back any news about his future. But with his freedom now clearly on the horizon, Zeppo's thoughts again turned to Phil Berg. They had a lot in common—each man loved to gamble, had a glamorous wife, and a fast car. But Berg had achieved a level of financial independence that Zeppo envied.

Likely influenced by Berg's success in turning book and stage properties into films, Zeppo made his first foray into the business end of the movies. On December 30, 1933, Louella Parsons reported that Zeppo had purchased the screen rights to Margaret Deland's best-selling 1906 novel *The Awakening of Helena Richie*, which had been the basis of a Broadway play in 1909 and a film starring Ethel Barrymore in 1916. Parsons wrote, "He is about to take a flyer and make an independent production. Any number of famous actresses have been seen on the stage in this play and Zeppo expects to induce one of our Hollywood favorites to play the emotional lead. Provided of course, he gets a suitable lead."

Either Zeppo or Louella Parsons was misinformed. There hadn't been a production of *The Awakening of Helena Richie* in years. The 1909 Broadway production starring the forgotten Canadian actress Margaret Anglin seemed to have been quite enough. In October Hollywood columnist Sidney Skolsky had reported, "Zeppo Marx went to a bookstore and asked for $200 worth of first editions." He had developed an interest in rare books through his friendships with Gouverneur Morris and Harold Grieve and had recently learned that Phil Berg was also a collector. Like Berg, Zeppo hoped to find some film possibilities in forgotten books. But shopping for first editions as if buying meat by the pound suggests something less than the erudition normally associated with collecting rare books. If Zeppo read *The Awakening of Helena Richie* and believed the dated melodrama had the makings of a good movie, he was not alone in his assessment. The story concerning a woman who leaves her husband after he kills their child was sold to MGM by Zeppo in May 1934 as a vehicle for Helen Hayes. But the film was never made. Hollywood apparently considered the 1916 silent version of *The Awakening of Helena Richie* to be in no need of a remake.

While still trying to find interest in his newly acquired literary property, Zeppo branched out with another venture that might prove useful if he were to follow the path of Phil Berg and Milton Bren into the agent business. On February 4, 1934, Zeppo and theatrical producer-director Dickson Morgan announced that they had founded the Westwood Theatre Guild. Their plan was to produce new plays featuring motion picture talent. Zeppo filled an impressive advisory board with friends like Sam H. Harris, Bebe Daniels, Ben Lyon, Gouverneur Morris, Carole Lombard, Robert Montgomery, William Powell, Richard Barthelmess, and Gloria Swanson. The board also included Edmund Lowe, Lilyan Tashman, George Fitzmaurice, Lewis Milestone, King Vidor, Lowell Sherman, Gregory La Cava, Richard Dix, Frank Borzage, and Adolphe Menjou. Ground was broken on a new theater on San Vicente Boulevard and the Westwood Theatre Guild set up offices in the El Paseo Building in Westwood. A month after their announcement, Dickson Morgan and Zeppo had received seventy-six new play manuscripts and promised to select the best ten for production.

Dickson Morgan began producing some of the plays at different small theaters around Los Angeles almost immediately. But Zeppo's name and any mention of the Westwood Theatre Guild disappeared from the press notices. Zeppo had a press notice of his own, and it was the bombshell he had long promised. A *Daily Variety* cover story on March 27, 1934, formally announced his departure from the Four Marx Brothers:

> From now on, as far as the stage is concerned, it is the Three Marx Brothers. Zeppo is responsible for creating the trio as he has bought an interest in the Bren & Orsatti agency and will devote his time to selling talent. Firm will be known as Bren, Orsatti & Marx.

A few weeks before the news became public Zeppo explained his position in a frequently quoted letter to Groucho, who was in New York with Chico doing their radio show. "I'm sick and tired of being a stooge. You know that anybody else would have done as well as I in the act. When the chance came for me to get into the business world, I jumped at it. I have only stayed in the act until now because I knew that you, Chico and Harpo wanted me to." Groucho's less frequently quoted response appeared in show business newspaper columns across the country, and did not reveal any concerns he may have had about the act:

Dear Zeppo,

Now that you have decided to turn crooked and become an agent, let's hope that you become a good one even if you have to turn honest. It's going to complicate things terribly for us, particularly on sleeper jumps. In the old days there were four of us and we could split up peacefully, two to a berth. Now we're three and there's bound to be bad feelings and discord with two sharing one berth and one sleeping alone. On the other hand, it will give you a chance to sit out front and see if we're really as bad as you always said we were. Hoping this finds you booking more acts than there are in show business, one of the surviving three musketeers,

Groucho"

As definitive as Zeppo was about making the Marx Brothers a trio there was an item in the July 1934 issue of *Hollywood* that suggested at least one imaginative reporter wasn't ready to accept the news. Zeppo, it was reported, "is not entirely deserting his mad brethren. When stage and picture roles call, he'll hang an 'Out to lunch' sign on the office door and take his place as the fourth spoke in the family wheel." If she hadn't been dead for five years, Minnie would have been suspected of planting something that ridiculous.

The news came as no surprise to anyone close to the Marx Brothers, or anyone paying attention to the gossip columns, where Zeppo's imminent departure from the team had been a topic since the Broadway days. In the months leading up to the official announcement, columnists got in their last shots, resurrecting some of the more amusing tales of Zeppo's apparent uselessness as a Marx Brother. On August 10, 1933, syndicated columnist Harrison Carroll reached back to the Broadway period for a tale that would later be borrowed by Groucho:

Zeppo once thought of quitting the stage for a business venture with Gummo. The Four Marx Brothers were in the midst of negotiations with Sam Harris, and that showman objected strenuously. It was a trade name, "The Four Marx Brothers," he argued, and he wanted the whole quartet.

After much talk he not only gave in but agreed to pay the same salary for the three.

Chico shook his head, exclaimed: "No, no, it will cost you $1,000 more a week to get rid of Zeppo."

Zeppo's announcement brought an end to the Four Marx Brothers—a unit that had been in business since 1912. Zeppo had replaced Gummo as the fourth brother along the way, but in either aggregation the role never amounted to much. Gummo's lack of desire and ability served to define the role in the nascent days of the team. Zeppo, capable of much more, was locked into the limited role that was tailored to Gummo's inadequacies as a performer. By the time Zeppo joined the act, they were too successful to make any substantial changes. On stage he really wasn't much more than the warm body Minnie Marx needed to keep her sons' salary at vaudeville's quartet level. That scenario followed Zeppo to the Broadway stage and Hollywood—with the occasional moment of slightly larger importance thrown in now and then to keep him from complaining too much. Could he have become a star in his own right? Speculation about what Zeppo could have been had he been given a proper chance will remain speculation. He will also remain the butt of the jokes and the recipient of the scorn of film critics and analysts of the Marx Brothers.

In the 1968 book *The Marx Brothers at the Movies*, one of the first studies of the Marx Brothers on film, Paul D. Zimmerman and Burt Goldblatt wrote in even-handed terms of Zeppo's fate: "While handsome and blessed with a pleasant tenor, he had the ungrateful task of playing the romantic lead in films that didn't have one. He would appear in the first scene as a hanger-on and rush in at the end to remind the public that there were four Marx Brothers. But he lacked any real flare for performing and had the wisdom to recognize it." Near the end of his life Zeppo told Charlotte Chandler, "the only fun I got out of it was the chorus girls. And laying all of them, or as many as I could. That was the fun I got out of it."

Zeppo didn't lose his appreciation of chorus girls when he left the act. His roving eye—on at least one occasion—caused Marion to exact a bit of revenge, albeit surreptitiously. To do so with less discretion would have lit the fuse on Zeppo's jealous temper and might have deprived Hollywood of one of its greatest leading men well before he'd hit his stride. Clark Gable was a good friend of Zeppo and Marion in their early years in Hollywood. They frequently saw him socially, and he turned up at events like Zeppo's auto race at Muroc. Gable was a close enough friend to surprise Marion's mother and brother at Union Station when they arrived in Los Angeles for a visit. But Gable was rarely with his wife, Ria Langham. Theirs was the best example of a sham marriage Hollywood had to offer. Ria was seventeen years older than Gable. They had lived together when he was struggling, and she was a wealthy widow. They claimed to be married but weren't. Gable wanted to leave her, but she threatened MGM with going to the press. Fearing bad publicity as Gable's star began to rise, the studio reminded him of the morals clause in his contract and pressured him into marrying Ria in 1931.

Although Gable had starred in *No Man of Her Own* with Carole Lombard in 1932, she was still married to William Powell, and Gable and Lombard were not romantically involved until four years later. In fact, they disliked each other in 1932 and did not keep in touch once the film was completed. Lombard told Garson Kanin, "[W]e worked together and did all kinds of hot love scenes and everything. And I never got any kind of tremble out of him at all." Gable had affairs with numerous women including Joan Crawford and Loretta Young—and, for at least a brief fling, Marion Marx. Years later Marion enjoyed telling friends about her romp with Gable and relished the chance to tell them that he wasn't particularly well equipped, or quite the lover millions of movie fans dreamed he was.

Chapter Thirteen

Opportunity Knocks

O N JUNE 10, 1931, SHORTLY AFTER THE FOUR MARX BROTHERS arrived in Hollywood to film *Monkey Business*, Zeppo's past and future collided in a story in the *Los Angeles Evening Express.*

A new booking agency looms upon the film horizon. Frank Orsatti, former real estate broker, Harry Weber and Milton Bren have formed a tri-partnership and announced themselves as representatives of motion picture players, directors, and writers. Both Weber and Bren have maintained separate offices before, but Orsatti is new to the game as an agent.

Harry Weber was well known to the Marx Brothers as an agent and man-ager dating back to their vaudeville days. They'd signed up with him as their booking agent in 1914, and it was not a harmonious relationship. Weber was still booking the Marx Brothers when Zeppo joined the act in 1918. Decades later, when asked about Harry Weber, Groucho described him as "a dirty cocksucker" who "always got ten percent of our salary." Milton Bren was almost as new to the agent business as Orsatti. His start in Hollywood was as an office boy at MGM working for Irving Thalberg. He moved up to a position in the scenario department and eventually was allowed to produce a few short subjects. Bren started his agency only a few months before partnering with Weber and Orsatti. Frank Orsatti, the completely inexperienced partner, would soon play a key role in Zeppo's departure from the Four Marx Brothers. Orsatti had a sketchy pedi-gree that might have caused some people to avoid doing business with him, but Zeppo did not scare easily. He might have even seen a bit of himself in Orsatti.

Frank Orsatti was born in Philadelphia on February 22, 1892, to immigrant parents from Naples, Italy. His father, Morris Orsatti, arrived in the United States in 1878 as a nine-year-old-boy, but not an ordinary one. His family had money. As a young man Morris married and relocated his growing family to Los Angeles where he made a very well financed and rapid rise in the business community. He quickly became the manager of the International Steamship and Railway Company and the vice president of the International Savings and Exchange Bank. He also offered loans to Italian immigrants interested in buying homes. Morris and his wife Mary had seven children. Four of his sons would at various times be talent agents in Hollywood. Frank grew up running with thugs on the streets of Los Angeles. He began a boxing career as a teenager and fancied himself a pool hustler as well. He was first arrested in 1910 for burglarizing a San Diego pool hall.

To this point Frank's life only differed from Zeppo's in that he had a wealthy father. Barely out of his teens, Frank married a prostitute who, he alleged in his request for an annulment, had chased him with a butcher knife. The court told him to wait a year and file a suit for desertion. He didn't need to wait that long. The girl was murdered eight months after the wedding under mysterious circumstances.

Frank's brothers Ernie and Vic were star athletes. Ernie played professional baseball for the St. Louis Cardinals from 1927 to 1935, appearing in the World Series four times and winning it twice. Vic was the star quarterback on the University of Southern California football team. He also played baseball and ran track there. Milton Bren was also on the USC track team, so his first connection to the Orsatti brothers came well before the agency business. Vic quit school to break into the movies in November 1926. He was dating the frequently married Constance Talmadge while she was waiting for her second divorce to be finalized. Her sister Natalie was married to Buster Keaton, who took an interest in Vic. Keaton was operating a semi-pro baseball team and was a pretty good player himself. He was filming *College* and Vic was used as an extra and stuntman in the sports scenes with several members of the USC baseball team.

Keaton and his producer Joe Schenck continued to employ Vic in various jobs on their pictures and Vic played baseball with Buster's team. In 1928 Keaton's operation moved to MGM and Vic met studio chief Louis B. Mayer. When the Cardinals' season ended with a World Series loss to the New York Yankees, Vic brought Ernie to the studio and got him a job as a property man.

Things had been going beautifully for the Orsatti brothers' father Morris until 1920 when his wife caught him with a girlfriend and began legal proceedings with an eye on what she knew was a considerable amount of community property. That would turn out to be the least of his problems. Morris had become a very active bootlegger during the early years of Prohibition. He had a large fleet of ships and was regularly moving liquor between Mexico, Los Angeles, and San Francisco.

In July 1922 Morris was indicted on nineteen counts of attempting to bribe federal Prohibition agents. He was also charged with embezzlement. Morris was eventually convicted and given the heaviest penalty ever imposed in a prohibition case: twenty years in federal prison and $31,000 in fines. He began serving his sentence in March 1925 at the federal penitentiary at McNeil's Island, Washington, as Frank took over his bootlegging business. But the federal government still had an eye on Morris's assets and indicted Frank on income tax charges in May 1928. Frank tried to claim his business was a legitimate real estate company that he operated with his mother, who had successfully separated Morris from a significant portion of his assets over his adulterous behavior. But it wasn't a very convincing story, and Frank had to pay a tremendous amount of money to the government in order to avoid joining his father in prison. Morris ended up serving a little under three years, and the leniency may have come as part of the deal in which Frank essentially went broke paying the family tax debt.

Inevitably, Frank Orsatti ended up on the MGM lot with his brothers and quickly had a new customer for illegal liquor. He became Louis B. Mayer's supplier and was soon a close friend and confidant. Orsatti sought Mayer's advice after telling him about his father and their tax problems and having to give every penny he had to the government.[1]

During the United States Senate's 1951 Kefauver Committee hearings investigating organized crime, Frank Orsatti's name was mentioned several times. In April 1951, *New York Post* columnist Leonard Lyons, covering the hearings, revealed the details of how Orsatti became an agent. Mayer was about to travel to New York and suggested they talk over Orsatti's problems while he drove him to the train station in Pasadena. "We'll think of something on the way," Mayer told him. During the drive Mayer suggested, "Why don't you become an agent?" Orsatti replied that he didn't even have a car or an office. Mayer handed him five thousand dollars and said, "There's your office." When they arrived at the Pasadena station, Mayer handed him the registration certificate for the car and said, "There. Now you're an agent." Orsatti's brothers Vic, Ernie and Al would soon join him in the business.

Mayer wasn't just being generous with his bootlegger. The studios had a lot of problems with agents, and Mayer liked the idea of having one in his pocket.

There had been talk of banning agents from coming onto studio lots. In June 1931 Adolph Zukor restricted agents visiting Paramount to the front offices and attempted to prohibit them from dealing directly with stars, directors, and writers on the lot. Agents began considering organizing a protective association and exploring legal options. A June 2, 1934, *Variety* report on the controversy stated that, "there are currently 81 agents visiting the lots, and, with an average of three working clients each, the lots are knee deep with ten percenters and that considerable studio time is lost as a result of the estimated 250 studio calls a day by these agents." Mayer was generally detested by his studio competitors, but they acknowledged his foresight in simply buying into the troublesome agency business—however surreptitiously—as this controversy swirled around the studios.

As his relationship with Louis B. Mayer evolved, Frank Orsatti began supplying him with more than illegal liquor. Orsatti was arranging liaisons with women for him and helping with other problems. It was a mutually beneficial relationship. Mayer used his influence with judges he'd helped get elected to keep Orsatti's bootlegging associates out of jail. Loyd Wright, a prominent Hollywood attorney—who, incidentally, would later handle Groucho's first divorce—was at one time the president of the California Bar Association. His comments about Mayer collected in FBI files indicate that he considered the MGM boss immoral and unprincipled in part due to his association with the Orsatti brothers, known bootleggers who were also active in the narcotics trade.

In the book *All the Stars in Heaven: Louis B. Mayer's MGM*, author Gary Carey tells of an exchange between Mayer and his business manager, Myron Fox. Fox asked why Frank Orsatti was always hanging around. "'Look,' Mayer answered. 'I've got certain things that have to be done and there are things I can't ask people like you to do.'" When well-known mob figure Pat DiCicco became an agent in the summer of 1933, he worked out of the Bren-Orsatti office. DiCicco was then married to Marx Brothers' costar Thelma Todd, who had appeared in *Monkey Business* and *Horse Feathers*. DiCicco worked for Charlie "Lucky" Luciano, the underworld's foremost purveyor of narcotics. And if Frank Orsatti's underworld credentials weren't convincing enough, testimony before the Kefauver Committee would later reveal that he was also associated with notorious organized crime figures Frank Costello and Benjamin "Bugsy" Siegel.

Harry Weber was out of his partnership with Bren and Orsatti after only four months and long gone by the time Zeppo agreed to buy what was essentially Weber's third of the agency. On March 27, 1934, The *Hollywood Reporter* revealed the financial details: "Zeppo Marx became an artists' manager yesterday at a cost of $75,000 to himself, paying that sum for a third interest in the Bren-Orsatti firm. The office has 77 clients." But did Zeppo have $75,000 and if not, where could he get it? Although he was still the salaried member of the Four Marx Brothers, Zeppo was living quite well in early 1930s Hollywood—while bringing home a fraction of the money his brothers were. Groucho or Harpo could have easily afforded a Malibu beach house for weekends, but Zeppo was the Marx Brother who had one.

When Zeppo left the Marx Brothers and entered the agency business, he basically traded Groucho, Harpo, and Chico for Orsatti, Bren, and DiCicco. Zeppo was friendly with Orsatti and Bren, but he and DiCicco did not get along and had little to do with each other. They participated in an unscheduled added attraction at the Friday night fights at Hollywood Legion Stadium on November 30, 1934. After the main event between Gege Gravante and Harry Serody, Zeppo and DiCicco started throwing punches outside the ring. Public brawls would become a regular part of Zeppo's routine. On April 17, 1936, the *Los Angeles Examiner* reported on an incident at the Trocadero. Zeppo commented on a man who had been bothering Marion:

"Whether he was drunk I don't know," Zeppo said yesterday, "but his actions made me blaze with anger. Probably I'd have hit him even if he hadn't given me further excuse, but he really left me no choice because he aimed a kick at me as I remonstrated with him. As I sidestepped the kick, I punched him. His companion hit me behind the ear."

In *Son of Harpo Speaks!* Bill Marx commented on his pugilistic uncle:

He was easily the most aggressive personality of the brothers. He had a very short fuse, and because of it, would often wind up duking it out with someone twice his size, and still make the fight quite interesting. Zeppo had been a remarkable physical specimen. Pound for pound, he was put together as well as anyone. The chest expansion of the great heavyweight champion of the world, Joe Louis, was two and a half inches. Zeppo's was an astounding six inches. You can't begin to imagine the sight of him puffing himself out like a peacock.

For most people, punching Pat DiCicco would be very dangerous, but Zeppo feared no reprisals from DiCicco's underworld friends—probably because they were also his underworld friends. That no trouble came Zeppo's way for belting Pat DiCicco at a public event was solid evidence of the quality of Zeppo's connections.

He certainly had a reputation as one of the best bridge players in Hollywood and played for high stakes, but Zeppo also had his share of gambling setbacks—particularly in 1934, the year he bought into the agency. He bet heavily on Primo Carnera in the June 14 heavyweight championship fight against the victorious Max Baer. Ten days later the *Los Angeles Times* gossip column "That Certain Party" (credited to the pseudonym "Tip Poff") noted, "Zeppo Marx still paying off his Carnera bets." Probably best that the hot-tempered Zeppo had no idea who "Tip Poff" really was. But the anonymous columnist had also reported on July 17, 1932, under the column title "Don't Quote Me" on Zeppo's winnings: "Zeppo Marx still seems to hold top record as a bridge player in the colony. There was that little matter of some $90,000 that he was reputed to have won last summer, you know. Rumor has it he makes as much money playing cards as some of the other brothers do on their pictures."

Zeppo's apartment at the Colonial House was an impressive home but he left it vacant on weekends. On August 20, 1932, while Zeppo and Marion enjoyed a weekend in Malibu, burglars entered the fifth-floor apartment and helped themselves to jewelry valued at $37,600. Zeppo's neighbor, actress Carmel Myers, had been victimized at the same address on January 17. These were among the first in a series of almost identical crimes. On September 28, Mae West was robbed of her jewelry at gunpoint while sitting in a car in front of her apartment. On October 30, Helene Costello was the victim.

One attempt was foiled when the burglars waited on New Year's Eve at the home of Ruth Chatterton and George Brent. They mistook the maid and her husband for the Hollywood couple as they opened the front door. The criminals were stunned when the maid's husband pulled out a gun of his own and they quickly fled. A few nights later the jewel thieves displayed their sense of humor by robbing the home of Los Angeles district attorney Buron Fitts during a dinner party. Fitts had been making some public remarks about knowing who the perpetrators of the earlier robberies were and promising that he'd soon capture them.

The robberies continued into 1933, with Dorothy Burgess, Betty Compson, William Von Brincken, George Raft, and Aileen Pringle all being relieved of cash and jewelry by a group of very polite well-dressed, masked burglars. But the pattern took an unusual turn when, on June 1, 1933, Zeppo and Marion were victims for the second time—with the take being reported as $30,000. And this time they were in their apartment with Alan Miller—Marion's brother, who had stopped using the name Bimberg during their father's arson scandal.[2]

Miller had just arrived from New York. The doorbell rang and Marion was confronted by two neatly attired men, one of whom covered his face with a handkerchief. They asked to see Zeppo and pushed their way into the apartment as Marion hurried into the kitchen. The *Los Angeles Evening Herald Express* reported that the gunman told Marion, "Listen, you, if you act right, there will be no slugging or rough stuff—it's all up to you."

One man pointed a gun at Zeppo and Alan, and the other followed Marion into the kitchen and held her and housekeeper Lillian Scott at gunpoint. Zeppo, Alan, and Lillian were told to face the wall, and one of the intruders forced Marion to show him where the jewelry was kept. Among the items taken was Zeppo's twelve-carat diamond ring and Marion's platinum bracelet with rubies and diamonds—each valued at around $12,000. The men then asked for Alan and Zeppo's wallets, but they only had a few dollars in cash, and were allowed to keep the wallets. The phone lines were cut, and the criminals proceeded to bind and gag Alan and Lillian with his belt and her apron. Zeppo and Marion were forced into a closet. The thieves moved a heavy piece of furniture to block the closet door and left.

This was the fourth time the gang had hit the Colonial House building. In addition to the previous visit to Zeppo's apartment, and the Carmel Myers robbery, the thieves had been to the apartment of Grace La Rue and Hale Hamilton on the same day as their second visit to Zeppo. The *Los Angeles Times* reported details of this failed attempt. "Hamilton said two men answering the description of the bandits, knocked at the door shortly before 7 p.m., and asked for Miss La Rue. On being informed she was not in, one of the men said, 'tell her the men from the gas company were here. She'll know what we wanted.'"

Curiously, the robbers politely left and moved on to Zeppo's apartment. They chose not to rob Grace La Rue and Hale Hamilton if La Rue was not at home. Perhaps there was concern that Hamilton or the housekeeper would be less cooperative than La Rue. They'd already run into that once before at the Chatterton-Brent home. This suggests that Grace La Rue knew what was going on and simply failed to show up for her planned robbery.

The robberies were the subject of jokes around the studios. Occasionally a joke would become public. Arthur Forde's *Hollywood Filmograph* column contained this item on June 10, 1933: "All the stars gathered on the Paramount lot to hear the thrilling adventures of one of the famous Marx Brothers, who was giving the other three and Maurice Chevalier the account of his second or was it tenth robbery in Hollywood."

Although it was never established as part of the investigation, the victims could have easily been profiting from this scheme with virtually no risk. If they had knowledge that the jewelry would be returned, and the insurance company would pay the criminals to return it, there was plenty of opportunity to turn cooperation into cash. Note that by the spring of 1934 Zeppo Marx—who was the only two-time victim in the jewel robbery scheme—had the money to pay Frank Orsatti and Milton Bren for one-third of their agency. Presumably some of the money would have come from his profit on the sale of Perry's Brass Rail, but that alone would not have been enough. Of course, he could have had a very good run of luck in high stakes bridge games—particularly with Milton Bren, with whom he was known to gamble for large amounts of money, but cooperating in the jewel robberies seems more likely.

Another clue that the stars may have been in on the scheme is that one of the victims was Chico Marx, who was relieved of $15,000 worth of jewelry somewhere in between the gang's visits to Betty Compson and Charles Butterworth. It's easy to imagine Chico asking Zeppo to get him in on the action. Incidentally, Butterworth was also a friend of the Marx Brothers.

Police were able to conclude very quickly that the jewel robberies were the work of one very organized group with specific knowledge of their movie industry victims. There was a finger man involved—a person who ingratiated himself into the community and socialized with the victims. The problem in solving the case initially was that the thieves didn't really want the jewels. They were willing to take 20 percent of the value in payment for the return of the stolen items. This was a good deal for the insurance companies, so there was little pressure to solve the crimes. Zeppo reported his losses to his insurance company after both robberies and was among the cooperating victims who ultimately got their jewels back, leaving their insurers to take the 20 percent loss.

The exception was Mae West, the rare victim who stared down the barrel of a gun and got smacked around by the robbers. As she was removing a bracelet from her arm the clasp jammed and the impatient thief struck her demanding she hurry and hand over the bracelet. Mae reportedly told him, "Relax. You'll get it." Other victims were bound and gagged, locked in a closet, or simply told to face the wall and be quiet. But Mae West got hit. Despite anonymous phone calls warning her not to testify, she appeared in court at the trial of the three men who were ultimately charged. Betty Compson also received telephone threats and refused to cooperate with police.

One of the suspects, Edward H. Friedman, confessed to the Mae West robbery and implicated his accomplices, Morris Cohen and Harry O. Voiler.

Friedman identified Voiler as the mastermind of the plot. Voiler was the "finger man" and the person seated in a car with Mae West when she was robbed by Friedman and Cohen. Voiler, an ex-convict and former theatrical agent had been an associate of notorious Chicago mobster Dion O'Banion and was very skilled at avoiding prison time. In 1930, while managing Texas Guinan's nightclub in Chicago, Voiler was arrested in the shooting death of the club's previous owner but was not prosecuted. By comparison, beating a jewel robbery rap was child's play for Voiler.[3]

But what does all of this have to do with Zeppo buying into Frank Orsatti's agency? Perhaps nothing, but there is an unusual connection that can be established through Voiler's numerous other criminal activities. In September 1933—during the time of the jewel robberies—Voiler was arrested on an unrelated vagrancy charge with two other men: Joseph "Red" O'Riordan and James "Socks" McDonough. McDonough was one of eight men indicted in the 1930 kidnapping of wealthy Agua Caliente betting commissioner Zeke Caress—who was known to frequent some of the same illegal gambling establishments as Zeppo. The others indicted included former Al Capone associate Ralph Sheldon, and Frank Orsatti's older brother Jesse, the proprietor of the Club Royale, an upscale nightclub located at 5355 Wilshire Boulevard. The club was used as a headquarters for the kidnappers, and Jesse Orsatti—who knew the clientele and could point out which customers would make for the most profitable kidnappings—was perfectly positioned as the gang's finger man. The link from the jewel robberies to Frank Orsatti is circuitous, but mobsters tend to work that way.

For a more unusual coincidence, another of the indicted kidnappers was a local gambler and strongarm man named Les Bruneman. He would be gunned down in October 1937 and the newspapers had some fun with the story of him having a check from Chico Marx in his pocket when he was killed. One of the other kidnappers was James Doolin—also known as "Jimmie the Squealer." No imagination is needed to figure out how Doolin acquired his unflattering nickname. Jesse Orsatti, whose nickname was "Cheesy," should not have been surprised when "Jimmie the Squealer" identified him as the finger man.

When Zeppo went into business with Frank Orsatti, Jesse was a guest of the State of California in the penitentiary at San Quentin, where he remained incarcerated until February 1940 on the kidnapping charge. When Jesse Orsatti arrived at San Quentin in August 1933, he met an inmate who had arrived there in March. They had a mutual acquaintance in Hollywood. The other inmate was Joey Bass, Zeppo's boyhood pal from Chicago.

Another remarkable coincidence is the arrival at San Quentin of Steve Palinkas in November 1934. He had been Chico's butler and chauffeur before he was arrested for stealing $73,000 worth of bonds, cash, and jewels from his next employer. Once the police had Palinkas in custody they expressed the opinion that he was part of the Hollywood jewel robbery gang, but he confessed to the later crime and punched his ticket for San Quentin without being charged in the jewel robberies.

It might not be more than circumstantial evidence, but it would be difficult to dismiss a few pieces of this puzzle that appear more than coincidental. Frank Orsatti's brother is the finger man in a kidnapping gang that counts among its members an associate of Harry Voiler, the finger man in the jewel robbery gang that victimized Zeppo Marx twice, shortly before he bought a partnership in Frank Orsatti's agency. Of course, Zeppo got his jewelry back and the gang profited from the insurance company payoff. Is it farfetched to suggest that perhaps Zeppo and the other victims got some cash from the gang for their cooperation? Maybe Zeppo did so well the first time, he asked for the jewel thieves to pay him a second visit.

The Club Royale was also frequented by a lot of movie industry people and a good finger man with an eye for expensive jewelry could have done well there. An aggressive prosecutor might theorize that Zeppo Marx raised the money to buy into Frank Orsatti's business through some harmless larceny with Orsatti's brother. A more extreme suggestion would be that Jesse Orsatti made payments to his brother look perfectly legal by disguising them as Zeppo Marx's business investment.

Variety didn't miss the obvious signs and reported a very plausible theory on the robberies on January 24, 1933:

> Recent stickups and robberies of half-a-dozen picture players have the local police figuring that someone is tipping off the hoodlums just how and when to pull their jobs. In the cases of Zeppo Marx, Mae West, Helene Costello, George Raft, Betty Compson, and William Von Brincken, the victims were ripe for banditry when taken. Each was loaded with cash or jewelry at the time of the stickup.
>
> Affairs have all been too methodical. Miss Compson had just returned home from a party; Miss West had a display of jewelry which she seldom wore; Raft's home was without any occupants on the night it was burglarized and Von Brincken's wife had taken her jewelry out of a vault the day before she was held up.

Coppers believe that someone connected with the picture business or some former picture personality who has had a tough break is working with the mobsters, getting a split on what is taken from the victims.

If the thieves had an inside man helping arrange their victims, it wouldn't have necessarily been someone who'd had a tough break. It could have just been someone raising money to buy into a business.

CHAPTER FOURTEEN

What Makes Herbie Run?

"We operate like any business partnership. Only three of us vote so far.
Zeppo hasn't graduated yet. We pay him a salary."
—CHICO MARX, *COLLIER'S*, JULY 10, 1926

EIGHT YEARS AFTER *COLLIER'S* QUOTED CHICO, THE YOUNGEST OF THE Four Marx Brothers was still an undergraduate. But by all outward appearances Zeppo Marx seemed to be a very wealthy man in 1934. He enjoyed a luxurious lifestyle and lived as well as any movie star with a much higher salary. But delivering straight lines in Marx Brothers movies didn't pay well enough for Zeppo to live the way he did. He was a prolific gambler, and most accounts point to him usually coming out ahead. But how did he suddenly come up with $75,000 in cash and notes to buy a piece of a thriving talent agency?

In 1973 Zeppo told Richard J. Anobile, "I was busted and didn't have a quarter, but I decided I had to do something." He probably wasn't exaggerating. In August 1932 Zeppo earned a few unflattering local headlines when the Sunset Laurel Market sued him over an unpaid $52 grocery bill. Ultimately it didn't matter to Frank Orsatti where Zeppo's money came from. He had his own criminal past and a brother doing time in San Quentin. Milton Bren, on the other hand, was less comfortable about his hard-core gambler bridge buddy joining the firm.

Corporate documents show Bren as president, Orsatti as vice president, and Zeppo as secretary, so Bren presumably had a lot of influence on major decisions. Bren, Orsatti & Marx was short-lived. The partners formally dissolved the agency on June 25 after having officially formed it on April 20. On June 12, 1934, *Daily Variety* reported,

When the Bren-Orsatti-Marx Agency split takes place this week it is understood that Zeppo Marx, who joined the firm recently, will be returned $25,000 cash and his notes for $50,000 (which he was to redeem out of profits) for his interest in the agency. Both Milton Bren and Frank Orsatti are to agree on a division of the clients within the next day or two and each will continue in the business on his own. Marx, it is understood, may join the ranks of one of the larger agencies as an associate, not wanting at this time to go in on his own.

On June 18, the *Hollywood Reporter* disclosed more details of the split: "Milton Bren has taken over more than 50 of the Bren, Orsatti & Marx office clients, and Frank Orsatti will handle 27. Marx has taken five personal clients that he brought into the concern and has been paid back his investment." Groucho, Harpo, and Chico made no secret of the fact that they were helping Zeppo find clients. Marx Brothers' friends and associates Alexander Woollcott, George S. Kaufman, Morrie Ryskind and Moss Hart were among Zeppo's first signings.

Another was writer Norman Krasna, a close friend of Harpo's and an occasional writing partner of Groucho's. Krasna had been one of the playwrights who submitted a manuscript to Zeppo during his brief time as the president of the Westwood Theatre Guild. Zeppo incessantly courted Krasna, who initially begged off, telling Zeppo he already was represented by Charlie Feldman and Ralph Blum. In an often-told Marx family tale, Zeppo was dining in a Hollywood restaurant with Krasna when a drunk began harassing the very unimposing Krasna. Zeppo flattened the guy with one punch and asked Krasna, "Does the Feldman-Blum Agency do that for you?" adding "All for the same ten percent, my friend." Woollcott, Kaufman, Ryskind, Hart, and Krasna were the five clients Zeppo took with him when the Bren, Orsatti & Marx partnership was dissolved.

It's quite possible that Harry Weber had left the partnership so quickly due to the company Frank Orsatti kept. Weber may not have been the most popular agent in town, but he didn't have mobsters, bootleggers, and narcotics dealers hanging around his office. The clean-living and law-abiding Milton Bren also had second thoughts—possibly even exacerbated by the sudden arrival in his office of the totally inexperienced Zeppo Marx, who seemed perfectly comfortable with Orsatti's underworld friends. Bren's resume looked nothing like Orsatti's.

After coming up through the ranks at MGM, and his time as an agent, Bren would go on to become a respected and successful producer for the Hal Roach Studios, MGM, and Columbia. During World War II he would serve as a lieutenant commander in the Coast Guard and then as a destroyer captain in the Pacific Theatre. Orsatti's background and friends probably kept Milton Bren perpetually nervous.

Whatever the reason, Bren, Orsatti & Marx was not to be. Zeppo briefly considered joining the Small & Landau agency but ultimately decided to go it alone. His primary motivation for leaving the Four Marx Brothers was a burning desire to be his own boss, and now he would be. In July of 1934, Zeppo Marx, Inc. was formed with the help of Loyd Wright—the same attorney who would later tell the FBI that Louis B. Mayer was immoral and unprincipled for associating with the Orsattis.[1]

On October 1, 1934, an item in *Variety* seemed to have been planted to shift the onus of the partnership's failure away from Zeppo, noting that "Zeppo's affiliation had nothing to do with the split. After the three-way division, there were three new agencies, where only one existed before, all three partners going into business for themselves." Maybe someone thought placing this in *Variety* was important as a face-saving gesture because Orsatti and Bren, while officially separating into two agencies, remained in the same Beverly Hills office that had been occupied by Bren, Orsatti & Marx. It certainly seemed by appearances that Zeppo was pushed out. Columnist Leonard Lyons got a different version of the breakup from Zeppo in 1952: "'The first thing to remember is that an agent has to be friendly with everybody,' his new partners told him at their first business session. Zeppo then arranged to get his $100,000 back immediately—for he discovered that Orsatti and Bren weren't on speaking terms." If Zeppo paid $100,000—as he frequently claimed years later—the source of the additional $25,000 could have had numerous explanations, but none of them would have been a business loan from a bank. None of the Hollywood trade papers had anything to say about Zeppo's financing. Maybe Zeppo's links to Jesse Orsatti's criminal activities in the period leading up to the deal are all just coincidental. But maybe they're not. It's possible that the whole thing was a setup in which Frank Orsatti agreed to get Zeppo started in the agency business, never really intending to be his partner.

Some people had trouble taking Zeppo's new venture seriously. In his *New York Daily News* column Sidney Skolsky wrote, "The talk about the movie city is that Zeppo Marx became an agent to learn how it feels for an actor to go to work." In the August 26, 1934, *Screen and Radio Weekly*, Grace Wilcox shared a tale from Zeppo's early days as an agent that suggests even Zeppo wasn't taking his new job seriously:

Recently he called up Jack Warner and asked him if he could bring out a "find" for a test. Jack Warner set an hour and a day and told him he would be glad to look the would-be actor over. At the appointed time, Zeppo and his "find" appeared. The "find" went through the necessary routine for a test and when it was finished, Zeppo leaned back, sighed deeply and said: "Isn't he wonderful? Isn't he colossal? Isn't he marvelous?" "Not bad at all—Not bad at all," agreed Jack Warner, in the level voice of a producer who is wondering what he will have to pay. "Who is he, Zeppo?"

"I don't know. I'm just practicing with him!" replied Zeppo, innocently.

That curious announcement about the Bren, Orsatti & Marx breakup not being Zeppo's fault came just as the Marx Brothers signed an MGM contract as a trio. But they did not actually sign with MGM. They signed with Irving Thalberg, who was powerful enough at the studio to have his own production unit and the discretion to offer contracts to people that Louis B. Mayer did not want at MGM. It's impossible to discern what level of power Mayer wielded over Frank Orsatti and his business, but he certainly had some influence considering what they knew about each other, and the fact that Mayer bankrolled Orsatti in the first place.

Mayer's disdain for the Marx Brothers was often referenced by Groucho through the years. Having had no prior business with them, the possibility that Mayer didn't want the Marxes at MGM could have had something to do with Zeppo's intimate knowledge of Frank Orsatti's business—and having knowledge of Mayer's involvement in some of Orsatti's less than legal activities. Film producer and journalist Peter Bart wrote in *Variety* on September 26, 2009, "In the studios' halcyon days, the firings were more colorful than the movies. Frank Orsatti was fired by Louis B. Mayer for running the official studio brothel. The termination was not on moral grounds—Orsatti was siphoning off too much money."

One of Zeppo's first moves with his own agency was to place one of his five writer clients in a movie as an actor. On June 28, 1934, the *Hollywood Reporter* announced the deal: "Universal yesterday wired Alexander Woollcott a bona fide offer to try his hand at acting in pictures. The noted raconteur and critic made a sally at acting in *Brief Moment* on the stage. The studio has offered him a role in *Gift of Gab*. The offer went through Zeppo Marx." Woollcott didn't need to do much acting. In a comedy about a radio personality, he played radio personality Alexander Woollcott. Zeppo would revisit the idea of putting nonactors on the screen. In February 1937 he signed *New Yorker* magazine cartoonist Peter Arno and tried to sell him as an actor. Arno went before the cameras once before resuming his successful cartooning career. He appeared as himself in the Jack Benny film *Artists and Models.* Zeppo may have reminded Benny that he'd introduced him to his wife to get Arno the job.

In August 1934 Zeppo strengthened his agency with the hiring of the experienced agent Walter Kane away from Harry Weber. He also took in one of Milton Bren's closest friends, the respected and experienced Louis Artigue. In September, Zeppo brokered a deal with 20th Century Fox for Norman Krasna to write the screenplay for *The Man Who Broke the Bank at Monte Carlo.* Things started moving quickly as a totally inexperienced agent with a few respected agents in his office was suddenly attracting clients and making deals. A month after the Krasna deal Zeppo negotiated screenwriter Julius Epstein's contract with Warner Bros., where eight years later Epstein would win an Academy Award for his work on *Casablanca.* Zeppo didn't have much trouble picking up his uncle Al Shean as a client. The great vaudevillian who inspired his nephews was now in Hollywood as an aging character actor. In September 1934 Zeppo negotiated a deal for Uncle Al at Warner Bros.

Zeppo seemed to find a niche representing writers in the early days of his agency. He hired Leonard Spigelgass, a scenario editor and producer at Universal, to head the agency's writers' division. Among the first screenwriters signed to the agency was the team of John Bright and Robert Tasker, who were quickly placed with 20th Century Fox and Paramount for a pair of projects. Zeppo was also able to continue cashing in on some of his family connections. New York newspaper columnist Heywood Broun, a longtime friend of the Marx Brothers, arrived in Hollywood looking for film work and was quickly signed by the Zeppo Marx Agency. In July 1935 Zeppo sent Walter Kane, who he would soon promote to vice president, to New York to set up an East Coast office to be headed by Gummo, who was struggling to keep his various business ventures afloat.

Zeppo told Charlotte Chandler,

Gummo was in New York, and he was in the dress business or something and he wanted to go into the agency business. So, my brothers came to me and said, "Jeez, what about Gummo?" So, I said, "All right. We'll open a New York office and let Gummo take over the New York office." So, he opened an office, and he did very well. He got New York actors signed up to our agency, sending them out here and I'd sell them if I could.

Film Daily, on February 13, 1937, took note of the efficiency of the New York office.

> Matching the speed of its coast office, the Zeppo Marx Agency in New York is delivering players, writers and other gilt-edged talent to producers. Gummo Marx, who gets around, is the head man for the office in Manhattanisle. The Gummo Marx service is taking on that certain distinguished quality that is inherent in the name of Marx.

A year after deciding to go it alone in the agency business, Zeppo was successful enough to break ground on a new office building on Sunset Boulevard. More significantly, he would now employ one of his brothers, which had to bring him a certain level of satisfaction. Gummo told Richard J. Anobile, "I had been away from show business for quite a number of years but nevertheless I did very well and managed to send out quite a few people."

High-profile acting clients did not come easily at first. But Zeppo demonstrated creative thinking that caught people's attention. He signed Patricia Ellis, a steadily working but undistinguished Warner Bros. contract player. He was aware of her background in musical theater and her desire to sing. She was in a rut at Warner Bros. and Zeppo booked her for a weeklong singing engagement in Detroit, near her hometown, in November 1936. If nothing else, this was a quick way to earn revenue on representing Patricia Ellis that would eclipse whatever she could earn under her film contract. In the early days of his agency, Zeppo became known as a champion of lost causes, taking on clients with the odds clearly stacked against them. While he did occasionally turn a lowly contract player into a star, the lost causes mostly remained lost.

Zeppo's most challenging client was the celebrated novelist Upton Sinclair, well known as the author of *The Jungle*. In November 1934, after Sinclair's unsuccessful campaign to be the governor of California, the future Pulitzer Prize winner received a wire from Zeppo, saying, "Would like to handle you for a job at a studio. What's your salary?" The studio chiefs would normally have been throwing each other into traffic to get a writer as good as Sinclair, but he was considered poisonous to the industry because of what the fiercely conservative moguls considered his radical politics. While living in Monrovia—not very far from Hollywood—Sinclair had been the Socialist Party candidate for a seat in the House of Representatives in 1920 and the United States Senate in 1922. He also ran in the California gubernatorial races in 1926 and 1930 as a Socialist. He lost each time and was not considered much of a threat. But when he ran for governor in 1934 as a Democrat, he had a far more respectable showing even though he lost to the incumbent Republican, Frank Merriam.

In Hollywood the studios all vehemently opposed Sinclair, and pressured employees to vote for Merriam. At MGM Irving Thalberg produced anti-Sinclair propaganda films depicting hoboes heading to California to cash in on Sinclair's proposed anti-poverty programs and branding him as a Communist. A legitimate case could be made that Irving Thalberg invented "fake news" and destroyed the Sinclair campaign. The purported documentary newsreel-style short films featured actors reading scripts with scenes staged on the MGM lot. Sinclair was going to be a tough sell, but Zeppo signed him up. In her December 17 column Louella Parsons wrote:

> Upton Sinclair, who for months was the boogey-man of the movies when he was running for governor, wants to become one of us. Sinclair has movie ambitions and he's engaged Zeppo Marx, of the Marx Brothers, to represent him in all negotiations. Sinclair will write, if he gets the chance, and I'm told that he had dinner with Samuel Goldwyn and has an appointment with Louis B. Mayer. So, all is going to be too beautiful. Why not? After all, Sinclair is an established writer, and he should be a much better scenarist than politician.

Zeppo's plan wasn't just to get Sinclair a writing job. His idea was to have him star in a film about his gubernatorial race based on his new book, *I, Candidate for Governor: And How I Got Licked*. *Variety* reported that Sinclair "has good stage presence and voice is okay for sound." Hollywood's reaction was predictable. When Sinclair won the Democratic primary, the studios had threatened to relocate the entire industry to Florida if he became governor, rather than suffer under the proposed tax hikes that Sinclair planned to end poverty.

Politically, Zeppo was as liberal as Thalberg was conservative and had no problem representing Sinclair. But the studios had made their position very clear by taking payroll deductions from employees and donating the money to the Merriam campaign. Among the few in Hollywood who spoke up about the dirty political tricks were James Cagney, Fredric March, screenwriter Dorothy Parker, and talent agent Zeppo Marx, the only man in town willing to help Sinclair find work.

Not surprisingly, there were no jobs available at any studio for Upton Sinclair. But rather than harm Zeppo's ability to attract clients, the Sinclair episode gained him the respect of the quietly growing liberal movement in the industry. If nothing else, potential clients learned that Zeppo was fearless.

Sinclair was but one example of Zeppo reaching out in many directions in search of clients. In New York, Broadway columnist Ed Sullivan noted, "Zeppo Marx, wiring local actors to let him handle their Coast business, has burned up Broadway agents." One of Zeppo's early success stories as an agent came from another seemingly lost cause. In September 1934 British actress Wendy Barrie came to Hollywood hoping to land a contract with a studio. She had experienced some early success in England and caught Hollywood's attention with her performance in Alexander Korda's 1933 film *The Private Life of Henry VIII* alongside Charles Laughton and Merle Oberon. But Barrie's first months in Hollywood resulted in unsuccessful screen tests at every major studio other than Paramount. When she signed with the Zeppo Marx Agency, the situation looked hopeless, with Paramount looking like her last chance. Walter Kane and Zeppo went to work. Alva Johnston told the story in an August 15, 1942, *Saturday Evening Post* article, "Hollywood's Ten Per Centers":

> Zeppo and Kane decided that it was necessary to throw the studio into a fit of temporary insanity in which it would sign the actress without a screen test. They finally worked out a plan with a touch of genius. They saw or telephoned everybody they knew—producers, top executives, directors and writers—in all the studios except Paramount. Talking to each man confidently and exclusively, they advised seventy or eighty influential film people that Paramount had a sensational screen test of one Wendy Barrie, a young English Bernhardt.
>
> The Paramount offices were flooded with requests from other studios to see the test of Miss Barrie. Paramount reported that it had no such test. This convinced the other studios that Paramount had uncovered another Garbo or Shearer and was deliberately making a secret of it. After being puzzled and annoyed, Paramount became excited. Al Kaufman of Paramount telephoned to Zeppo one morning to arrange for a screen test. He was told Miss Barrie didn't have time to make one. Kaufman pleaded for a chance to look at her. "I can bring her around at two-thirty this afternoon," said Zeppo, "but be prompt, because I take her to see Goldwyn at three."
>
> Shortly after 2:30 that afternoon, Kaufman signed Wendy Barrie for forty weeks at $1,000 a week. The next day he sent for the two agents. "What have you done to me?" he asked. "We sold you a client,"

said Zeppo. "How can I go to my stockholders," asked Kaufman, "and justify spending forty thousand dollars on a girl who had one small part in England and has been turned down by every other studio in Hollywood?"

This was the first time the agents had known anybody in Hollywood to show any concern over stockholders. After thinking awhile Zeppo said, "Here's what we can do. We'll help you promote her so fast that you can make her a star in six months. Then you can say to your stockholders, 'For a mere forty thousand dollars I've made you a new star.'" The actress was promoted skillfully, and Paramount got its $40,000 back by lending her to other studios. She has been fairly successful in Hollywood ever since.

Shortly after Zeppo got her a Paramount contract, Wendy Barrie appeared in three pictures at the studio, and was also loaned out to Fox, Columbia, MGM, and RKO. To find additional British talent, Zeppo briefly contracted with American-born London-based agent David A. Bader in 1936. Bader had been with Universal in Hollywood for ten years and had served as studio chief Carl Laemmle's personal representative. Not much came of Bader's partnership with Zeppo and he would close his London office in 1938.

Shortly after Groucho, Harpo and Chico made their MGM deal, Groucho told Irving Thalberg he didn't think the scripts he offered were good enough. He wanted the top writing talent they'd had for their biggest successes—like George S. Kaufman and Morrie Ryskind, who happened to be clients of the Zeppo Marx Agency. Groucho had rejected scripts by Bert Kalmar and Harry Ruby—who had been contributors to earlier Marx successes, and Robert Pirosh and George Seaton—who would later write *A Day at the Races*. The basic idea for *A Night at the Opera* was Thalberg's and the story outline for the two rejected scripts was by James Kevin McGuiness, the head of the MGM story department. These were all people Groucho ultimately worked with on very successful plays and films. Whether intentional or not, Groucho set up a situation in which Thalberg had to negotiate with Zeppo to get a script for the new Marx Brothers film.

In his autobiography Ryskind credited his new agent for getting him the job, while managing to get in a dig at the now-former actor's skills in front of the camera. "[T]he biggest factor working in our favor was that Zeppo was no longer part of the act. His part was filled by screen newcomer Allan Jones, whose good looks and excellent voice gave his characterization a dimension that allowed us to advance the story in ways that Zeppo would never have been able to fulfill."

It seems an unfair criticism, since there had been better singers filling romantic lead roles in *The Cocoanuts* and *Animal Crackers* as Zeppo performed his generally thankless tasks. *Monkey Business* didn't suffer from Zeppo being the romantic lead and getting the girl for the one and only time. On the other hand, his commission on Kaufman and Ryskind's salary easily eclipsed what he would have been paid by his brothers had he been in *A Night at the Opera*. Kaufman alone was paid $75,000. Zeppo was now successful enough to make his own Zeppo Marx jokes. He remarked that during negotiations with Thalberg, he gained leverage by threatening to rejoin the Marx Brothers.

Frequent Marx Brothers costar Margaret Dumont was added to the cast of *A Night at the Opera*. Zeppo, who'd known Dumont since she appeared in the stage version of *The Cocoanuts* ten years earlier, saw her potential value as a client. But she was represented by an aggressive young agent at the small Joyce & Polimer Agency named Henry Willson. Zeppo first encountered him in 1933 at Perry's Brass Rail, when Willson arrived in Hollywood as a fan magazine writer.

Zeppo wanted Dumont as a client, and in June 1936 he got her by hiring Henry Willson away from Joyce & Polimer. Willson, a relentless self-promoter, had a keen eye for talent. One of his early successes at the Zeppo Marx Agency was dancer Marjorie Belcher—later known as Marge Champion of the famous team of Marge and Gower Champion. Willson also discovered an attractive high school student named Marilyn Louis, who he renamed Rhonda Fleming. Zeppo also hired the completely inexperienced Solly Baiano in October 1936. Baiano, one of Hollywood's best tennis players, had been working as a violinist in the MGM studio orchestra when Zeppo took a chance on him. With his gambler's instincts, Zeppo played hunches. Baiano and Willson both became valuable employees.

Hiring Walter Kane would continue to pay off for Zeppo. He brought in the agency's first big radio deal in December 1936. The National Biscuit Company and the McCann-Erickson advertising agency were to sponsor a musical comedy program on NBC with Helen Broderick, Victor Moore, and the Buddy Rogers Orchestra. Kane negotiated the stars' contracts for the agency. Radio had become a lucrative source of additional revenue for movie stars, and Zeppo tried to make a deal for the Marx Brothers. A *Hollywood Reporter* item from September 24, 1936, detailed an interesting idea that never materialized:

A deal for the Marx Brothers to star on a full-hour air show sponsored by Axton-Fischer, makers of Spud cigarettes, is expected to finally be closed today in a confab between the brothers and executives of the

Young & Rubicam ad agency. The show would be a script program without guest stars, to start around the first of the year, emanating from Hollywood. Zeppo Marx is agenting.

Even without a Marx Brothers show, radio became a good source of revenue, but the Zeppo Marx Agency's strength at this point remained representing writers and stories. Zeppo sold rights in several plays to major studios while still looking for some star power to put his agency on the map in a big way.

While the Marx Brothers were making *A Night at the Opera*, life imitated art. As Groucho would in the film, Zeppo signed an Italian opera singer to a management contract. He saw great potential in expanding his business outside the walls of the movie studios and signed tenor Paolo Marconi, freshly arrived from La Scala in Milan. With Zeppo as his personal manager, Signor Marconi performed with the Pacific Grand Opera Company. He didn't become the sensation Zeppo was hoping for, but he did ultimately find work in Hollywood as a voice teacher. His studio pupils would include Kathryn Grayson and Deanna Durbin.

Zeppo signed a diverse array of clients and on occasion his connections landed him accomplished people who were in demand. In November 1935 he signed the husband-and-wife screenwriting team of Dorothy Parker and Alan Campbell to a deal at Warner Bros. Zeppo also used his new position to help old friends. He placed Lila Lee, his former neighbor from the Garden of Allah, in the film *Champagne for Breakfast*. Lee was not much in demand by 1935 and worked mostly in forgettable B-pictures, but Zeppo took her as a client.

Zeppo's early success as an agent didn't put an end to the jokes at his expense in the press. When Allan Jones was making his second film as what Morrie Ryskind might have called "the better, more talented Zeppo," Sidney Skolsky ran this item in his syndicated "Hollywood" column on March 28, 1937:

> Chico Marx was listening to Allan Jones complain. "I'm not getting the money I should get," said Jones, "and what is more important, Metro is not giving me the big roles. I don't know what to do." Chico tried to advise Allan. "What you need," said Chico, "is a good agent who will go in and fight for you to get the big, important parts." "Maybe you're right," said Jones. "Zeppo Marx is my agent."

The Allan Jones item is a ridiculous canard. In between *A Night at the Opera* and *A Day at the Races*, Jones played the lead opposite Irene Dunne in Universal's screen version of the Broadway musical *Show Boat*. There were few pictures more anticipated in 1936. For good measure, Jones was also seen in a featured role alongside two of MGM's biggest stars, Nelson Eddy and Jeanette MacDonald, in *The Firefly* that same year. Considering that Jones is mostly remembered today for those two musicals and the Marx Brothers movies he was in, Zeppo did a pretty good job as his agent—especially considering that he arranged for MGM to loan Jones to Universal for *Show Boat*.

Zeppo had arranged another loan of a studio contract player that resulted in a tremendous career boost for the actor—and enough aggravation to cause Zeppo to refuse to even mention the actor's name in later years. Fred MacMurray was playing the saxophone in the California Collegians, making $60 a week when he signed a contract with his first agent, Arthur Lyons. Lyons was successful and well regarded as Jack Benny's longtime manager. He also represented stars like Joan Crawford, Hedy Lamarr, Lucille Ball, and Carole Lombard and songwriters Cole Porter and Jerome Kern. MacMurray had done some uncredited extra work in a handful of films at Fox and Warner Bros. but had no real acting experience. In early 1934, Lyons got MacMurray a six-month contract with Paramount that paid him $100 a week. In unpublished comments from a 1970 interview with *Detroit Free Press* columnist Shirley Eder, Zeppo reluctantly told how he jump-started MacMurray's career:

> I saw him, and I liked his looks, so I asked him if he had an agent, and he didn't have an agent. I don't think he did, anyway. I signed him up, made a contract with him. Now he had been at the studio three months. He only had a couple of more months to go, and he had never been in a picture. They didn't know he was on the lot. So, I went into the front office and said to one of the executives, "What's going to happen to this boy?" They said, "Well, we've never had a part for him." I said, "This boy has great potential."

Zeppo asked his friend Cliff Reid, a producer at RKO, to borrow MacMurray from Paramount and put him in a picture. When Reid called Paramount, he was told they'd never heard of Fred MacMurray. Once Paramount figured out that they had him under contract, the arrangements were made, and Reid cast MacMurray in *Portrait of Laura Bayles* with May Robson. (The film would be retitled *Grand Old Girl*.) *Daily Variety* announced on September 20, 1934, "Fred MacMurray, on Paramount's payroll six months without a part is likely for a loan to RKO-Radio. . . . Zeppo Marx is handling the deal with the player." Zeppo's next move worked out very well for Fred MacMurray. He asked Cliff Reid to buy MacMurray's contract from Paramount. Still not sure who MacMurray was, Paramount decided that if he was good enough for RKO, they had better keep him at Paramount. Zeppo negotiated the renewal of the Paramount contract at a significant salary increase.

Arthur Lyons read *Daily Variety*. His client signing with another agent did not go unnoticed. MacMurray's contract renewal was worth $234,000 over five years. Lyons promptly filed a lawsuit—first for $220,000 in a California State Court, and then upping the ante and changing the venue with a $250,000 suit in Federal Court. The agent's commission on MacMurray's wages would be $23,400. Lyons's suit claimed the additional amount was for damages to his reputation as an agent and exemplary punishment.

Zeppo and Lyons each had their own version of the events. Zeppo simply claimed he had no idea MacMurray had an agent. No one believed that someone as sharp as Zeppo thought that Paramount gave a contract to an unknown saxophone player who had never acted outside of extra work without an agent being involved. It was clear that Lyons got the studio to sign MacMurray. But Lyons took great liberties with the facts, asserting that he had gotten MacMurray the renewal and the larger salary and was entitled to the agent's commission on it. The truth was that Lyons was doing nothing for his client and Zeppo played a hunch and discovered a star.

The suit would be settled out of court on January 24, 1936, but not before Arthur Lyons spitefully hired agent Louis Artigue away from the Zeppo Marx Agency. Zeppo retaliated by signing Ray Milland away from Lyons. Lyons also hired Zeppo's old nemesis Pat DiCicco when he left Frank Orsatti's agency in December 1935. Suffice it to say Arthur Lyons and Zeppo Marx were not friends. Shortly after settling the Lyons lawsuit, Zeppo was back in court with a much smaller problem. Writer Al Boasberg sued him for $3,500 in damages, and an order to prevent Zeppo from claiming commission on his MGM salary because Zeppo didn't get him the job.

Zeppo would move on from his problems with Arthur Lyons, but there would be more trouble with Fred MacMurray. Zeppo came to regard him as greedy and ungrateful. Later Zeppo would privately tell people that he made MacMurray a millionaire and was shown no loyalty in return. With Lyons out of the picture as the lawsuit worked its way through the courts, Zeppo was able to do great things for his client. In the fall of 1934, Zeppo's friend Wesley Ruggles was about to direct a Claudette Colbert comedy at Paramount and the film needed two young, handsome leading men. Also friendly with Colbert, Zeppo suggested his two clients, Fred MacMurray and Ray Milland. These were perfect and inspired casting choices, and the film, *The Gilded Lily*, became a big hit in 1935. MacMurray would go on to make six more films with Colbert.

Zeppo and MacMurray staged a walkout by the star in February 1936 as shooting was about to begin on *The Princess Comes Across*, in which MacMurray was featured with Zeppo's friend Carole Lombard. Zeppo demanded another salary increase before his client would work on the picture. Paramount didn't give MacMurray the salary Zeppo asked for, but they did give him a raise. Zeppo eventually used the success of *The Gilded Lily* to get Paramount to tear up their MacMurray and Milland contracts and give each of them a new seven-year deal with a healthy salary increase. There's no question that Zeppo was effective in representing his clients.

For a time, Zeppo and MacMurray were friendly enough to come up with an invention together. In 1940 they patented a collapsible rubber fishing boat that could be carried like a backpack with room for equipment. MacMurray became a top star at Paramount, and all seemed well until the seven-year contract was about to expire. Paramount reported to the Securities and Exchange Commission that MacMurray earned $347,333 in 1942, as he entered the last year of the contract. That made him the highest paid male movie star in Hollywood. Only Claudette Colbert earned more that year from making movies, being paid $360,000.[2]

MacMurray told Zeppo he wanted a straight five-year contract with a guaranteed salary, no options, and no cancellation clause. MacMurray had become a big enough star to make demands, but this was a challenge for Zeppo. Paramount wasn't agreeable with MacMurray's terms and initially there were no takers for one of the biggest stars in the business who suddenly had a list of unreasonable demands. It took some time, but Zeppo was able to make a deal with Darryl F. Zanuck and Joe Schenck at 20th Century Fox. It was a big money deal for both the star and the agent. It came as a great surprise to Zeppo that MacMurray asked to get out of the contract almost immediately. Zeppo managed to do this for him, forfeiting a significant commission on this guaranteed contract. Then MacMurray decided that since his seven-year Paramount contract had expired, Zeppo was no longer his agent. The Zeppo Marx Agency had become one of the most successful agencies in Hollywood and Zeppo was making a small fortune for his efforts, but Fred MacMurray was the first client that made Zeppo think about getting out of the agency business—but he certainly wasn't the last.

CHAPTER FIFTEEN

Enter Miss Stanwyck

As the Zeppo Marx Agency flourished, the Marx Brothers made a seamless transition from quartet to trio. *A Night at the Opera* was a big hit, and no one seemed to object to Allan Jones in the Zeppo role. It worked so well they repeated the formula for *A Day at the Races* in 1937. But Zeppo's absence from the screen did not necessarily exclude him from the press coverage of a new Marx Brothers movie. Veteran newspaperman Harry T. Brundidge, in the *St. Louis Star-Times* on March 3, 1937, gave readers—who probably didn't ask for one—a Zeppo update: "From the worst actor in history to the best actor's agent in Hollywood—all in four years. He's a hustling, bustling businessman who swept aside the handicaps of bad singing and a receding hair line, to become the most ambitious chap in Hollywood."

The accolades heaped upon Zeppo in the promotion of *Duck Soup* not quite four years earlier were apparently only valid if he didn't quit. Suddenly this formerly integral part of the act was a balding guy who couldn't sing. He was no longer the fourth Marx Brother, but he was still worthy of all the abuse that position entitled him to. He was not to forget that—no matter how much money he made.

The success of the agency should have ended the jokes about Zeppo, the unimportant Marx Brother, but Walter Winchell couldn't resist printing this item in his column a few years after Zeppo had made his last screen appearance:

The Marx Brothers' *Horse Feathers* flicker was revived the other day, and a Broadwayite confessed he couldn't enjoy its comedy because he kept remembering that three of its principals were dead . . . Thelma Todd, David Landau and Zeppo Marx, he said . . . "Zeppo isn't dead,"

corrected a listener, "he's a Hollywood booking agent!" . . . "I know" was
the reply, "but I thought it would be kinder to say he is dead."[1]

It was not lost on Zeppo that had it not been for show business he might
very well have been dead. Zeppo's boyhood friend Joey Bass eventually found his
way to Los Angeles after his discharge from San Quentin. Bass was impressed
by how far Buster Marx had come since he last saw him in Chicago almost
twenty years earlier. His old friend was rich, well connected and had never spent
a day in prison. Bass got out of San Quentin in October 1936. After a brief time
in Portland, where he got married and had a daughter, Joey moved to the upscale
Hancock Park section of Los Angeles. In prison he'd learned to make electrical
signs and briefly worked at an honest trade for the first time in his life—as a
condition of his parole, not necessarily out of any desire to go straight. Ex-
convict sign makers did not live in fancy apartment buildings with live-in maids,
but somehow Joey Bass did.

Sharon McKibben, Bass's daughter, recalls her father operating a nightclub
during their time in Los Angeles. (In his later years Bass proudly told her that
he hired Nat "King" Cole to play piano at the club years before anyone had ever
heard of him.) She also remembers her childhood playmate, Margaret O'Brien.
These recollections and Joey Bass's sudden lifestyle improvements point directly
to the Orsatti brothers—and his shared time at San Quentin with Jesse Orsatti.
The Orsatti Agency signed five-and-a-half-year-old Margaret O'Brien to a contract with MGM in 1942. Her agent was Vic Orsatti. The Club Royale changed
ownership when Jesse Orsatti went to prison, but Frank Orsatti had an interest
in several other Los Angeles nightclubs and Joey Bass probably worked at one
of them. It isn't known to what extent Zeppo was involved with Joey Bass at
this time, but he certainly knew he was in town. They probably connected—their
mutual associations with the Orsatti brothers making it unlikely that they didn't.
Zeppo's later recollection of running into Bass in Las Vegas may simply be mis-
placed. But whether in Las Vegas or Los Angeles, at some point Zeppo learned
the fate of Joey's older brother Louis, the boy he so admired for being tough and
carrying a gun when they were kids in Chicago.

Louis Bass had been in California running numerous swindles involving oil
leases and real estate up and down the coast. In December 1939 he was a fugi-
tive wanted in twenty-one California counties on a variety of charges. He was
hiding out in a San Francisco boarding house and contacted his landlord in Los
Angeles to have his holiday cards forwarded. The landlord gave detectives the
San Francisco address. When the police entered his room on January 3, 1940,

with guns drawn, Louis shot himself in the head. Zeppo would mention the Bass brothers in later interviews, saying that his life could have turned out much like theirs had Minnie not called on him to join the Four Marx Brothers.

Running a nightclub apparently left Joey Bass with plenty of time for other activities. On December 1, 1944, he was convicted of criminal conspiracy to commit grand theft for selling phony oil leases. Zeppo's reunion with his childhood friend would be relatively brief. Joey returned to San Quentin before serving most of his sentence at Folsom State Prison, where he would remain until February 1950.[2]

Zeppo seemed to have an affinity for undesirable people. He moved freely between the social circles of the underworld and the movie business—both of which had their fair share of pariahs and frequently intersected. As if to take pride in his willingness to associate with Hollywood's most vilified outcasts, Zeppo not only represented the blacklisted radical Upton Sinclair, but he joked about it on stage at an event with perhaps the most detested entertainer in the business.

Zeppo first crossed paths with Frank Fay in vaudeville when Fay was at the height of his success as a comedian and master of ceremonies. Apart from being outspokenly anti-Semitic, Fay seems to have gone down in the annals of show business without anyone ever having a kind word to say about him. Fay was an ardent Republican who hated president Franklin D. Roosevelt almost as much as he hated Jews. It wasn't surprising to find Fay on stage at a banquet honoring governor Frank Merriam, the anti-Roosevelt Republican who had defeated Upton Sinclair in a close election months before. But Fay did a little routine at the event with Zeppo—who didn't let his admiration and support for FDR stop him from appearing on behalf of Merriam. And there certainly weren't many Jews lining up to make jokes with Frank Fay.

Based on the account in the *Visalia Times-Delta* on July 15, 1935, Zeppo was once again a straight man, this time setting up lines for Fay.

At a recent "mutual admiration" banquet of members of Governor Merriam's official family and friends, the most popular "joke" was staged by Frank Fay and Zeppo Marx of the stage and screen. It went like this:

Marx: What's that button you're wearing, Frank?

Fay: That's a "Merriam-for-governor" badge.

Marx: Yes, but Merriam has already been elected governor.

Fay: Sure, but I'm having the button changed to read "Merriam for president."

Zeppo wasn't about to support Frank Merriam—or any Republican—against FDR in 1936 or 1940, but the appearance at the Merriam event and his attempt to help Upton Sinclair made clear that Zeppo did not cling to any ideology that might interfere with business. The strange upside to Zeppo's association with Sinclair was that a lot of actors secretly agreed with Sinclair's position that wealthy people and big businesses—like movie studios—should pay more taxes to eliminate poverty.

Many actors, writers, and directors quietly seethed as their beliefs had to remain unspoken because they did not match those of Louis B. Mayer, Irving Thalberg, Jack Warner, or Darryl F. Zanuck. Taking on Upton Sinclair as a client—albeit unsuccessfully—was an unintentional signal to the left-leaning people working in Hollywood that Zeppo Marx might potentially be a good agent for them. Zeppo was a registered Democrat and supported FDR, but like many he opposed FDR running for a fourth term in 1944 and declined to state his party affiliation on his voter registration that year. He eventually changed his affiliation and became a registered Republican. But he was a solid Democrat when he represented Upton Sinclair and simultaneously appeared with Frank Fay at a Republican Merriam event.

Frank Fay and Zeppo were not especially friendly, but they had many mutual friends in the Hollywood gambling community. Both were frequent patrons of the Clover Club at 8477 Sunset Boulevard, near the Chateau Marmont just north of the Sunset Strip. The Clover catered to Hollywood's high rollers; and whenever the Los Angeles vice squad randomly decided to crack down on illegal gambling, the Clover was immune to any trouble by virtue of the hefty payoffs the owners made to the police department. *The Hollywood Citizen-News* reported on a series of raids in December 1933 and noted that the Clover Club was "given a clean bill of fare by deputy sheriffs who visited . . . but reported no signs of gambling." It was that sort of press that drew Hollywood's biggest gamblers to the Clover, which was managed by Eddy Nealis, a Mexican American gangster with several less impressive gambling joints around Los Angeles. The silent partner in the Clover was Zeppo's friend Milton "Farmer" Page, one of the most notorious gangster-gamblers in town. Page had been running gambling houses in Los Angeles since he was a boy, and he would eventually rise to a position of great power in "the Combination"—the mysterious entity that controlled the Los Angeles underworld. Zeppo knew a lot of people with very good connections.

The local high stakes action on sports betting kept Zeppo in regular contact with many notorious figures. Boxing matches in Los Angeles tended to bring out gamblers and movie stars in great numbers. It was only months after the Marx Brothers arrived in Los Angeles that Zeppo and Marion attended the light welterweight championship fight between Tony Canzoneri and Cecil Payne on July 13, 1931, at Wrigley Field. Also in attendance were Frank Fay and his wife Barbara Stanwyck. It is the earliest known documentation of Zeppo and the movie star who would become his most high-profile agency client being together. At this point Stanwyck had an agent and Zeppo probably hadn't yet considered becoming one. But Zeppo and Marion became friendly with Fay and Stanwyck—largely due to Stanwyck and Marion hitting it off. Zeppo—like almost everyone else who ever met him—had little use for Frank Fay unless he was beating him in a card game.

The Stanwyck-Fay marriage was already in trouble by the time the couple crossed paths with Zeppo and Marion. Fay's career was fading and Stanwyck's was on the rise. It would later become an open secret in Hollywood that they were at least the partial inspiration for the tragic couple in the 1937 film *A Star Is Born*. Director William Wellman, who won an Academy Award as the coauthor of the original story, was a close friend of Stanwyck's. As the director of three of her early 1930s films, Wellman had an intimate knowledge of the abuse she suffered at the hands of Frank Fay.

Stanwyck remained loyal to her alcoholic husband, who had become violent as his career floundered. She used her growing star power to create opportunities for Fay, but he just got worse. They adopted a son, Dion, in 1932, hoping it would save the marriage. Ultimately life with Frank Fay proved to be too much for Barbara Stanwyck, and she left him in 1935. She and her son moved into Zeppo and Marion's house shortly after Zeppo and Fay appeared together at the Merriam event.

Marion wrote about her friendship with Stanwyck in the April 1942 issue of *Motion Picture*:

Most friendships start with mutual interests. Ours grew out of simple appreciation of each other's honesty. The mutual interests came later— after she and her little boy, Dion, came to our house to live. At that time, Barbara was desperately unhappy, hardly interested in living. Her whole world seemed to have gone to pieces. She had no faith in the future. No confidence in herself.

One thing that put Stanwyck's mind at ease was that Frank Fay was not likely to show up at the house looking for trouble. He knew about Zeppo's quick temper and that he was very good with his fists. Marion offered friendship and support at a terrible time, and Stanwyck slowly bounced back. Zeppo also began advising her about career matters.

Stanwyck's longtime agent had been Zeppo's nemesis, Arthur Lyons. After the Fred MacMurray debacle, the growing friendship of Zeppo Marx and another of Lyons's high-profile clients might have seemed like a conspiracy to Lyons. Stanwyck felt Lyons had not done a good job for her and was unhappy with the deals he was working on.

Zeppo advised her at first without acting as her agent. When he learned that Cliff Reid at RKO was developing a biographical film about legendary sharpshooter Annie Oakley to be directed by George Stevens, Zeppo recommended Stanwyck for the lead role. Originally in development as *Shooting Star*, the film was eventually retitled *Annie Oakley*. It isn't a particularly important film in the Stanwyck canon, but she was well paid and treated nicely. And Arthur Lyons had nothing to do with getting it for her.

In February 1936—shortly after his lawsuit against Zeppo was settled—Lyons sued Stanwyck over an unpaid commission on a contract. In court Lyons presented a handwritten note signed by Frank Fay as evidence of the agreement. The validity of an agreement scribbled by her bitter former husband became a moot point when Stanwyck appeared in court and testified that the deal was never consummated because the studio was unable to acquire the story rights for the canceled project. She was never paid and therefore no commission was due. Stanwyck prevailed in the case, fired Lyons, and announced that Zeppo was her new agent.

With Zeppo handling Barbara's business affairs, Marion became more involved in her personal life. After her divorce from Frank Fay became final in December 1935, Stanwyck mostly stayed home with her now four-year-old son, Dion. She offered a small glimpse into her life in a September 1936 interview in *Picture Play*.

"What do I do for fun?" she mused. "Oh, I'm a regular nighthawk nowadays. Sometimes, when I'm not working, I'll go out to some of the night spots as often as a couple of times a week. I like to go to the previews. Whenever there's a good play in town, I take it in. I play tennis—or I did until I sprained my wrist reaching after a high one that would have been out, anyhow. I ride horseback occasionally. Most of the time during the day, unless I have appointments, Marion Marx—Zeppo's wife—and I just bum around together. She helped me decorate my house." She paused a second and then, "I suppose as long as I'm giving her billing I might as well tell the truth and shame the devil by admitting that she decorated it. She has marvelous taste in house furnishings."

It was Marion with whom Stanwyck played tennis and rode horses. They were together constantly. A story in the December 1939 issue of *Modern Screen* said, "They are oddly alike. They have the same easy manner, the same dramatic trick of lowering the eyes. Both are difficult conversationalists. It's hard work drawing copy from either of them. They are very quiet. In small towns, Marion and Barbara would be labeled 'still waters.'" Marion and Zeppo got Stanwyck out to nightclubs and parties. Otherwise, she would have hardly gone out. They became a frequently seen threesome at Hollywood nightspots. The tension of being a foursome with Frank Fay was gone, but Marion encouraged Barbara to look for a relationship.

For a night out at the Trocadero in February 1936, Walter Kane—who had been working with Zeppo almost since the inception of the agency and was involved in Stanwyck's contract negotiations—was Barbara's escort for dinner with Zeppo and Marion. The twice-divorced Kane was tall and attractive and was frequently seen in nightclubs and restaurants with clients and starlets of varying degrees of fame. No one mistook Kane—who would later marry actress Lynn Bari—for Barbara Stanwyck's new boyfriend. It was strictly a professional evening and Stanwyck was dining with her agents.

That night at the Trocadero may have been orchestrated by Marion and if she knew rising young star Robert Taylor would be there, it was a brilliant stroke. Stanwyck and Taylor hit it off and expressed admiration for each other's work. They began dating—quietly at first, but soon enough their romance became public. Zeppo, Marion, Stanwyck, and Taylor became Hollywood's newest foursome. The version of Stanwyck's introduction to Taylor as told in the September 1946 issue of *Movieland* suggests the meeting was in no way accidental.

Mrs. Zeppo Marx, wife of Barbara's business agent, was lecturing Barbara: "You never take time off to have fun," Mrs. M accused her. "You're just like Robert Taylor—always working too hard, never going dancing. Come to think of it, I believe you two will hit it off." Whereupon the indignant lady introduced Barbara to Bob.

Once Stanwyck's relationship with Taylor became public, Marion's physical resemblance to Stanwyck resulted in an amusing item in Louella Parsons's syndicated column in July 1938: "Zeppo Marx and Bob Taylor getting a big kick when *The Crowd Roars* preview fans chased Marion Marx for blocks, mistaking her for Barbara Stanwyck."

As Stanwyck's new agent Zeppo had an immediate impact on her career. By January 1937 Samuel Goldwyn had reportedly tested forty-seven actresses for the much sought-after title role in *Stella Dallas*. Zeppo's friendship with Goldwyn and a strong screen test won Stanwyck the role that made her one of Hollywood's biggest stars. This was the type of role she never seemed to get with Arthur Lyons as her agent. On May 16, late in the filming of *Stella Dallas*, Stanwyck and Robert Taylor spent Sunday morning horseback riding with Zeppo and Marion. Barbara's horse stepped in a gopher hole and rolled over on her, badly injuring her knee. But she returned to the set on crutches to finish the picture a couple of days later. Zeppo saw great leverage in Stanwyck's success in *Stella Dallas*, for which she had been loaned out to Goldwyn from RKO. She would earn an Academy Award nomination for her work in the film.

When Stanwyck turned down the lead role in RKO's production *Distant Fields* in January 1938, the studio suspended her. Zeppo issued a statement to the press: "Miss Stanwyck felt the role assigned to her was not suited to her talents, particularly after her casting in *Stella Dallas* for Sam Goldwyn. She is not taking an arbitrary attitude and has asked that she be assigned to a role more suited to her in another picture." Stanwyck eventually returned to work but was deprived of several pay checks as punishment for her independence. Her stand was particularly courageous when considering she took it after Bette Davis had lost a similar battle with Warner Bros. Agents were becoming more powerful, and studios were beginning to see a future where they would not have autonomous control of their stars. But Barbara Stanwyck, with the solid support of Zeppo, took her stand six years before Olivia de Havilland successfully sued Warner Bros. over Jack Warner suspending her for turning down roles she didn't like.[3]

Zeppo had recently purchased a lot in Beverly Hills and was planning to build a new house close to where Groucho and Harpo had their homes. Harpo had married his longtime girlfriend, actress Susan Fleming, and they had just moved into a new house. Susan and Marion had become close and were spending a lot of time together. But Zeppo abandoned his plan to build near Harpo and Groucho. Barbara Stanwyck was also contemplating new living arrangements.

Marion had always dreamed of living on a ranch and breeding horses and suggested to Zeppo that they investigate San Fernando Valley real estate with an eye on property suitable for a ranch. As with any of his ventures, Zeppo went all in. He brought in well-known breeder Harry S. Hart, who had managed the

LeMar Stock Farm and the Swing Along Stables in Lexington, Kentucky. The land they were looking at was a portion of the Benjamin F. Porter Ranch, which had been purchased by Porter as part of a 57,000-acre piece of property in partnership with his cousin George and a group of other investors in 1847. Benjamin F. Porter, who died in 1868, had owned twenty thousand acres in the northwestern corner of the property, which was the least desirable section because it was a great distance from the railroad line. It remained mostly undeveloped. But Harry Hart determined that it was a perfect location for horse breeding, and Barbara came into the venture as a partner.

Zeppo and Barbara paid $200,000 for the property and announced their plans for the business they named the Marwyck Ranch. *The Van Nuys News* reported on November 19, 1936:

> San Fernando Valley will soon be the home of some of America's finest Kentucky thoroughbreds as a result of negotiations being completed this week which involve the purchase of 127 acres of the Porter estate by a syndicate composed of Zeppo Marx, Barbara Stanwyck and Harry S. Hart. The property, which is located at the corner of Devonshire and Reseda boulevards is particularly well adapted to the purpose of its new owners.

Hart, not actually an owner as erroneously reported, and his wife Bertie were hired to manage the business, and like the Zeppo Marx Agency, Marwyck got off to a fast start. Phil Lonergan, the Hollywood columnist for the British magazine *Picturegoer* reported in the January 9, 1937, issue, "All the buildings will be exact replicas of famous horse breeding farms in Kentucky." Permits to build two homes on the property were issued in February 1937 and Harry Hart began stocking the stables. A permit for a third home soon followed.

The new owners sent out invitations to the February 28 opening of Marwyck. *The Van Nuys News* reported

> The day Miss Stanwyck and Zeppo Marx opened the ranch to their friends, she rode out to the foothills with Friend Bob Taylor. . . . First, they stopped for a glimpse of the colt born bright and early that morning. It was all legs and quite timid about being viewed. Then they went on over the hill, past the three homes on the three knolls, and then out of sight, leaving a little cloud of dust in their wake.

Stanwyck discussed Marwyck in the March 1937 issue of *Radio Stars*:

I've bought a ranch in the San Fernando Valley. Marion Marx and I have bought 120 acres together. We're raising horses. Thoroughbreds. We're going to breed horses, besides caring for our own, we're going to breed and train and board horses for other people. I'm building a ranch house out there and will live there most of the time. It's peaceful and quiet. I can have gardens, and it will be wonderful for Dion. It will be home.

Barbara's new home was a 6,500-square foot English manor with French Normandy and Tudor revival elements. In December 1937, *Turf and Sport Digest* described Zeppo's house as "a living memory of the Old South, rising in pillared, white majesty, a bright jewel laid against the mauve velvet of the sheltering Mother Mountains, the Sierra Madres." Maxine Marx described Zeppo's Marwyck house for Groucho's biographer, Hector Arce: "It was the prettiest house I've ever seen. . . . Marion designed it from a movie she saw. It wasn't ostentatious, but the house was totally charming."

Two architects with long lists of celebrity clients worked on the homes. Robert Finkelhor had designed Harpo's home on North Canon Drive in Beverly Hills and one for Bob Hope. Paul Revere Williams would design homes for Cary Grant and Groucho, but Zeppo was far more interested in Williams because he had designed E. L. Cord's Beverly Hills mansion, Cordhaven. It was a way of him displaying how much money he'd accumulated since Cord helped Phil Berg beat him in the 1932 auto race.

Construction at Marwyck intensified in April when Robert Taylor bought an adjacent additional twenty-seven acres of the Porter estate property. On the stable side, Harry Hart never slowed down. *Turf and Sport Digest* wrote,

For a stud farm that has been in operation less than a year, Marwyck can boast an unusual equine population: one stallion, twenty broodmares, ten two-year-olds (most of them in active training), fifteen yearlings, and six weanlings. And in addition, several animals which are kept for pleasure and utility purposes. A large percentage of the racing stock is the property of the owners of Marwyck, but a goodly number are "boarders," to whom group additions are being made almost daily.

One morning the owners of Marwyck found a mangy-looking mule munching on a bale of hay on their property. The mule wore a sign stating, "The Pride of the Marwyck Ranch." It was a gag gift from Carole Lombard.

As Marwyck took shape at lightning speed in the San Fernando Valley, things were moving even faster back at the Zeppo Marx Agency. Star clients like Barbara Stanwyck, Ray Milland, and Fred MacMurray got most of the attention, but the Hollywood trade papers barely went a week without news of a less-celebrated Zeppo Marx client signing a deal somewhere—actors Keye Luke at 20th Century Fox, Helen Vinson at MGM, Alice Reinhart with B. P. Schulberg Productions, John King at Universal, Joan Fontaine at RKO, and newcomer Stanley Morner—soon to be better known as Dennis Morgan—at MGM. Zeppo prided himself on discovering and developing new talent. His representation of Joan Fontaine started when she first arrived in Hollywood using the name Joan Burfield. Early in their careers Judy Garland and Lana Turner were represented by Zeppo. He also signed little-known New York stage actor Richard Bond, who would work steadily in Hollywood for several years.

Representing writers remained a specialty for Zeppo and 1937 was a great year in that department. He sold two Broadway plays to Warner Bros.—*Chalked Out* by Lewis E. Laws and *Jezebel* by Owen Davis, Sr. Laws was the warden at Sing Sing Correctional Facility and several of his books about prison life were adapted into plays and films. *Chalked Out* became the Humphrey Bogart film *You Can't Get Away with Murder* and *Jezebel* earned Bette Davis her second Academy Award as Best Actress. Zeppo also made studio deals for well-known writers like Ben Hecht, Charles Lederer, Bela and Sam Spewack, and Leo Rosten, while also representing writers not as celebrated—Aben Kandel, Barry Trivers, Stephen Morehouse Avery, and Helen Meinardi. He even found film work for a pair of *Variety* writers he was friendly with, Cecelia Agar and Joe Bigelow. Closer to home Zeppo sold Mervyn LeRoy a screenplay called *The Grand Passion*, written by Norman Krasna and Groucho Marx. The film would be released by Warner Bros. as *The King and the Chorus Girl.*

Zeppo also signed Romanian-Gypsy writer Konrad Bercovici and promptly found him work at Universal. Bercovici and Upton Sinclair had been among the expatriate American writers flocking to Paris in the 1920s and Sinclair introduced his friend to Zeppo. Both avowed socialists, the two writers knew Zeppo didn't care about their politics and was only interested in making money with them. They added to the agency's diverse array of clients—which ranged from lowly contract players to big stars. Zeppo negotiated a long-term contract for director George Nicholls at Republic and made a deal for Phyllis Loughton, who ran the MGM talent school. No client was too big or too small for the Zeppo Marx Agency.

Zeppo's brothers had to have noticed his name appearing in *Variety* and *Hollywood Reporter* as frequently as many movie stars. It wasn't long before Groucho,

Harpo, and Chico took the obvious next step after having recommended Zeppo to their friends in need of representation. Irving Thalberg's death during the production of *A Day at the Races* allowed the Marx Brothers to exercise a termination clause in their contract, which stipulated that if Thalberg became unavailable for a certain period, they could end the agreement. Convinced that Louis B. Mayer wasn't interested in them—and it was really a contract with Thalberg that had them at the studio—they opted out of the MGM deal.

On September 23, 1937, *Variety* reported,

> Zeppo Marx is holding confabs with Leo Spitz, prez of RKO-Radio, for the appearance of the Marx Freres in three features to be made by Radio within the next two years. If deal is consummated, first picture will be *Room Service*, George Abbott's legit production in first year of its Broadway run. Radio paid $255,000 for rights to the play.

The deal would ultimately only result in *Room Service*. The underwhelming performance of the film at the box office made everyone involved forget about the other two pictures that could have been made at RKO. But Zeppo tried to sell another film starring his brothers. As the Marx Brothers were engaged in their contract dispute with Paramount in 1933, they attempted to become independent producers of their own film, an adaptation of the Pulitzer Prize–winning musical *Of Thee I Sing*. They were never able to finance it, but a fair amount of work was done with the property before they ultimately signed with Thalberg and made *A Night at the Opera*. The *Hollywood Reporter* on August 29, 1938, announced Zeppo's resurrection of the dormant project:

> The Marx Brothers next picture for MGM will be *Of Thee I Sing*, the George S. Kaufman-Moss Hart stage success with music by George Gershwin. The deal, which is being handled by the Zeppo Marx Agency for the sale of the musical play, is expected to be sealed this week. MGM is reported to be paying $100,000 for the screen rights to this piece.

It would be the second time *Of Thee I Sing* would not become a Marx Brothers film.

Regarding his brothers, Zeppo told Richard J. Anobile, in his interview for *The Marx Bros. Scrapbook,* "When I went into the agency business, I didn't have them. They probably didn't think I was good enough. But a lot of good writers and directors and actors and actresses thought I was good enough. I had 250 clients." He found his brothers difficult to please, adding,

> Whatever kind of deal I would get them, they would want to change and make it different. And Chico was always a little put out because he was the one who always wanted to make deals for the boys. . . . So, the only deal I made was *Room Service*, and I found it so difficult that I didn't want any part of it. . . . I wanted to get away from the Marx Brothers anyway. I didn't want the feeling of them telling me what to do anymore. . . . I was my boss and I told people what to do.

Zeppo vented his frustration to Anobile adding, "[U]p until that time, the most money they ever got was for the deal I made for them. . . . I got them a quarter of a million dollars for four or five-weeks work."

Lucille Ball, a client of Arthur Lyons, costarred with the Marx Brothers in *Room Service*. During the making of the film, she was briefly represented by Zeppo. In the spring of 1977, Ball taught a six-week class at Sherwood Oaks Experimental College in Hollywood. During one of her lectures, she told students that Zeppo asked her to let him know when she heard about any parts she wanted. She never got any of the roles she mentioned and concluded that Zeppo used the information to get those jobs for other clients. Zeppo's failure to place Lucille Ball probably spared him any further trouble with Arthur Lyons. But Ball may have unfairly maligned Zeppo. She was having trouble advancing her movie career for years until radio and television made her a star.

Zeppo had taken his own personal income to another level and proved beyond doubt that he could make a lot more money away from his brothers. He knew the lucrative deal he arranged for them would have only been worth a weekly salary around $700 to him had he still been working in the act—and that would have only been paid while they were shooting a film or working on stage. With the average American worker earning $1,780 a year in 1937, it was a good salary by any measure, but Zeppo was driven by ambition and a desire to make more money than his brothers. According to the April 15, 1939, issue of *Boxoffice*, Zeppo's reported personal income in 1937 was $78,383—or roughly $1.5 million adjusted for the current economy. (He was on an upward track having earned $56,766 in 1936.)

For comparison, Frank Orsatti reported $69,000 and Abe Lastfogel, the head of the William Morris Agency, reported $64,500. They all trailed the top-earning agent that year. Myron Selznick reported $110,825. Zeppo's top clients were among the industry's biggest earners—Barbara Stanwyck at $195,749 and Fred MacMurray at $92,000. Being a successful agent paid well, and so did being a movie star, but in Hollywood there was no doubt who the highest paid man in town was. Louis B. Mayer's reported personal income for 1937 was $1,296,503.

Zeppo took advantage of what seemed to him like an opportunity to make easy money in Hollywood. Ten percent of many salaries simply added up to much more than he would ever earn as an actor. An amusing *Hollywood Reporter* item from August 7, 1937, said,

> Zeppo Marx was walking around a studio lot in gloom. Another agent approached him with "What's the matter, Zeppo?" And Zeppo cracked: "It's not right. Just think of it, all these actors, writers and directors getting 90 percent of their salaries."

After only a couple of years of operation, Zeppo had recently closed his New York office and arranged for agent Leland Hayward to handle any New York business. Gummo told Richard J. Anobile,

> Zeppo came to New York and convinced me that if I was doing so well in New York I could probably do better in California. So, with that, my wife and I packed up and moved west. But when we got here things seemed to change. Instead of me being in charge of the business as I was in New York, I found Zeppo taking over all my people. I discovered I was working for him. I lost all the commission I was getting, and he put me on salary.

Within the agency there was some discontent. In December 1937—only six weeks after Gummo arrived in Los Angeles and set up his desk at the agency—Walter Kane, who had been with Zeppo almost since the very start of the business, quit to start his own agency. Kane had taught Gummo the business thinking he would remain in New York, but his arrival in the Los Angeles office immediately reduced Kane's position in the agency. Working out of Zeppo's new offices at 8732 Sunset Boulevard, Gummo also learned that his newest clients were his brothers. In the Anobile interview Zeppo said, "I told Gummo they were all his. I didn't want any part of it. That was that." Citing their demands and lack of cooperation, Zeppo concluded, "I had too big a business to fool around with them." After Gummo's arrival in Los Angeles, Zeppo quit the Marx Brothers for the second time.

CHAPTER SIXTEEN

This Thing of Ours

THE TYPE OF DISPUTE ZEPPO HAD WITH ARTHUR LYONS WAS VERY COM-
mon among agents. In the spring of 1937, thirteen top agencies formed
a protective association—to protect themselves from each other, it
seemed. They called it the Artists' Managers Guild, and only larger agencies were
initially invited to join. Smaller agencies left out of the organization considered a
separate guild but ultimately decided that defining themselves as being too small
for the Artists' Managers Guild would hurt their businesses.

Pressure from numerous other agents quickly resulted in membership
becoming open to all. On July 10, 1937, *Daily Variety* detailed the mission of
the new organization: "Code of ethics will prohibit client chiseling, limit fees
charged player, provide for cancellation of contract where player is not actually
placed, etc." Along with Zeppo, charter members included his friends Phil Berg,
Leland Hayward, and Frank Orsatti, and at least one agent he didn't like very
much, Arthur Lyons. Other important agents—William Morris, Jr., Myron
Selznick, H. E. Edington, Frank Vincent, Sam Jaffee, Charlie Feldman, Ralph
Blum, William Hawks, M. C. Levee, Morris Small, and Arthur Landau—also
signed on before membership became open to all agents.[1]

Further down in the *Daily Variety* article, the real purpose of the Artists'
Managers Guild was revealed. It should have been the headline: "Contact will be
made with Screen Directors Guild, Screen Actors Guild and other organizations
with view of cooperating and working in unity with all studio organizations,
including Motion Picture Producers Association." The agents were connecting
themselves with labor unions at the precise moment that the studios were having
a major problem with the International Alliance of Theatrical Stage Employees,
or IATSE, the union that represented the industry's craft workers—sound engineers, editors, electricians, prop builders, projectionists, and other technicians.

IATSE was the only union powerful enough to fight back against the unilateral salary cuts imposed by the studios in March 1933 as the Great Depression threatened the studios' very existence. That summer IATSE workers walked out at eleven studios. Some IATSE workers broke ranks and went back to work, and the studios made secret deals with the rival International Brotherhood of Electrical Workers union.

Like many labor actions of the era, order was restored through violence and intimidation. Striking workers at studio gates encountered bands of bat-wielding thugs. Within a week the strike was over. This efficient solution was provided to the studios by Johnny Rosselli, an Italian-born Chicago mobster employed at times by notorious organized crime figures Al Capone and Frank Nitti. Working with Rosselli were small-time Chicago mobsters Willie Bioff and George Browne. Bioff and Browne got their business in Hollywood started by accepting a $20,000 bribe from the Balaban & Katz theater chain in Chicago in 1927. The payment saved the theater owners the expense of wage increases for the members of the stagehand's union, which Bioff and Browne represented.

After learning how the 1933 strike was settled, Frank Nitti called Johnny Rosselli to Chicago and they formulated a plan to take over all the Hollywood labor unions. Browne was installed as the president of IATSE in 1934, and Bioff began working under Rosselli in Hollywood. Rosselli's help with the 1933 union trouble was the start of a lucrative mob business in selling protection to the studios.[2] Further trouble with IATSE in 1937—at the same time the Artists' Managers Guild was formed—came as Rosselli had solidified his position and wielded great power over union operations.

Rosselli's FBI file indicates that the leaders of IATSE could not act without instructions from him. He could secretly cause a problem for the studios and then be paid to make it go away. Through the Artists' Managers Guild, top agents who otherwise did not have access, availed themselves of Johnny Rosselli's influence, if not his services. Agents and unions were generally problems for the studios. With even a tenuous connection to the labor unions—and Johnny Rosselli—an agent gained an additional piece of leverage in negotiations.

It didn't take long for the Artists' Managers Guild to have its first internal breach. On August 13, 1937—around a month after *Variety* reported that the top agents would not behave unethically toward one another—Zeppo filed a grievance against his friend Phil Berg, who had signed actor Wayne Morris away from the Zeppo Marx Agency. Zeppo asserted that Berg also indemnified Morris against any legal action that might result from him signing with the Berg-Allenberg Agency. Within a couple of weeks, the matter was resolved amicably and without any need for the services of Johnny Rosselli. The Zeppo Marx Agency and the Berg-Allenberg Agency would jointly represent Wayne Morris. It was an odd solution in that it appeared to reward Berg for poaching Zeppo's client. Zeppo's friendship with Phil Berg seems to have overcome any desire on his part to bring in Johnny Rosselli, with whom he had an even longer association.

Johnny Rosselli's FBI file contains an unusual connection to the Marx Brothers. A confidential informant "advised that about 1927, he first observed activities of various racketeers and recalled that Jack LaRue, motion picture actor, lost large sum of money to Harpo and Chico Marx of Marx Brothers entertainment team. LaRue would not pay and Rosselli interceded as collector of gambling debt."[3] Shortly after the IATSE trouble in 1937, Rosselli was questioned by police about the murder of Les Bruneman. Bruneman was the mobster-gambler who was gunned down in October that year with Chico's almost certainly bad check in his pocket. A 1949 *New York Daily News* exposé on organized crime in Los Angeles connected a lot of the dots on the Bruneman story:

> During the heyday of the Clover Club on the Sunset Strip, his face was well known to movie colony celebrities. In his safety deposit box at a Hollywood bank his widow found a bank draft signed by Chico Marx and filed a claim for $2,200 against the actor.[4]
>
> Chico said he had never met Bruneman and did not recall executing the draft found by the gambler's widow. He did admit, however, that he had lost a chunk of money gambling early in 1937 and had paid off $4,000 in $1,000 installments.
>
> He didn't say to whom he had lost the money and police didn't seem anxious to ask the $64 question. But Chico, like almost every other celebrity in Hollywood, had been a frequenter of the Clover Club, where Bruneman had worked.

Bruneman's murder wasn't truly solved until mobster Aladena James Fratianno—better known as Jimmy "the Weasel" Fratianno—became a government informant. He explained in 1977 that, although someone was convicted and sent to prison for shooting Bruneman, that man was innocent and had been framed.[5] Bruneman was involved in a dispute over gambling revenue with Rosselli and called people in Chicago to see about having Rosselli killed. The Chicago people immediately told Rosselli, who promptly had Bruneman killed. Without question, Johnny Rosselli was Zeppo's most dangerous friend and the most powerful organized crime figure in his orbit. Rosselli's influence with

IATSE, and his studio connections were also very useful to the Zeppo Marx Agency. And if Rosselli should happen to kill the guy who was probably about to have Chico's check bounce, it was an unexpected bonus.

Chico's $4,000 gambling debt paled in comparison to the money thrown around in high stakes Hollywood poker games. Herman Mankiewicz, the producer of *Monkey Business* and *Horse Feathers* was an occasional player. His biographer, Richard Meryman wrote, "Herman sat at poker tables gambling $100 chips against the industry's chieftains and its most feared players: Joe Schenck, Eddie Mannix, Irving Berlin, Zeppo Marx, Sam Goldwyn, Sid Grauman, Ben Bernie—taciturn circles of watchful men, no jokes, no amenities. Thousands of dollars routinely changed hands in the Malibu mansions." One such game took place in September 1938 at 20th Century Fox executive Darryl F. Zanuck's house. The game was run by longtime Fox producer Sol Wurtzel. Among the participants were Zeppo and several other major Hollywood figures including producers Sam Goldwyn, Jay Paley, and Hunt Stromberg, screenwriter Robert Riskin, director Robert Z. Leonard, 20th Century Fox chairman Joe Schenck, theater owner Sid Grauman, longtime MGM executive Eddie Mannix (better known as Louis B. Mayer's "fixer"—the man who covered up the more salacious problems involving the studio's stars), and Zeppo's fellow Artists' Managers Guild member, Myron Selznick.

Correspondence preserved in Sol Wurtzel's papers provides a rare record of the game's financial details: $62,625 changed hands in one evening of poker. The big loser was Myron Selznick who ended the night with debts totaling $53,400. Goldwyn, Leonard, and Grauman lost more modest amounts—a total of $9,225 between them—and covered their losses immediately. The big winner was Zeppo. By the end of the evening Selznick owed him $35,000. Selznick also owed smaller amounts to Wurtzel, Mannix, Paley, Stromberg, and Riskin.

Wurtzel wrote to Zeppo on November 3, 1938: "I got in touch with Myron Selznick about his loss in the poker game at Darryl's house several months ago. Myron told me he had no money now and cannot pay, and he would like me to advise all of the winners in that game to get in touch with him direct and he would settle with them direct when he is in a position to do so."

The other winners received similar letters and Eddie Mannix advised Wurtzel to maintain the customary practice of the person running the game collecting the money from Selznick and distributing it to the winners. Selznick agreed and Wurtzel again wrote to Zeppo on November 14: "Enclosed herewith find my check for $5,156.80 which represents your proportion of the amount won against the losses paid in the poker game at Darryl's house. There is still due you from Myron $29,843.20." In a letter to Selznick dated February 23, 1939, Wurtzel acknowledged that Selznick had made a separate arrangement with Zeppo for the balance due.

Selznick, who was one of the most successful agents in Hollywood, was desperate for cash. He was involved in a legal dispute with his fourteen-year-old client Freddie Bartholomew over $39,600. The child star's legal guardian, his aunt, fired Selznick in November 1937 and with other representation was able to get his $100,000 MGM salary raised to $396,000. Selznick claimed he was entitled to 10 percent of Bartholomew's new salary and assured his gambling buddies that he would prevail in court, but the suit was eventually dismissed. Zeppo's arrangement with Myron Selznick likely resulted in some of Selznick's agency clients finding their contracts suddenly under the auspices of the Zeppo Marx Agency.

There had been some unusual situations concerning Zeppo, Selznick, and their clients in the past. In May 1938 Warner Bros. screenwriter Jerry Wald went to court to clarify his contract status because three different agents were all claiming commissions from him. Zeppo, who probably become acquainted with Wald at the time his story about a singing waiter at Perry's Brass Rail restaurant was made into the film *Twenty Million Sweethearts*, got him his Warner Bros. contract in October 1934. But Leland Hayward and Myron Selznick were also billing Wald for commissions. It appears some agents occasionally traded or moved clients around—perhaps even as payment for gambling debts. For Zeppo the timing of Selznick's run of bad luck was perfect. The construction of Marwyck was getting expensive.

Myron Selznick and Zeppo were also both active in the thoroughbred horse racing business. Selznick's horse Can't Wait finished third in the 1938 Kentucky Derby. On February 9, 1939, the *Los Angeles Times* reported the earnings of the various celebrity owned racing concerns at the halfway point of the season at Santa Anita. Stables owned by Louis B. Mayer, Howard Hawks, and Bing Crosby topped the list. Selznick was ranked sixth with earnings of $2,000 and two first place finishes. Marwyck was at the bottom of the list with earnings of $50 and one fourth-place finish. Between his agency and his stable, Myron Selznick certainly had things to offer Zeppo in lieu of cash.

As Zeppo and Barbara Stanwyck were building Marwyck, Groucho got involved in a construction project of his own. The original Beverly Hills Tennis Club was founded in 1929 by International Tennis Hall of Fame member Fred B. Alexander and two avid tennis players with Hollywood connections, Larry Bachmann and Milton Holmes.

Bachmann was a novelist and screenwriter who would later become a producer at MGM. Holmes, briefly an actor, had appeared in minor roles in a handful of films in the late 1920s. In addition to tennis, Holmes had another passion: gambling at the Clover Club, where he met numerous Hollywood celebrities and befriended Eddy Nealis and Milton "Farmer" Page. It was rumored that between the Clover and his own operations, Nealis handled $10 million in bets a year. Groucho did not frequent the Clover Club, and he didn't know people like Nealis and Page. It was Zeppo who introduced him to Milton Holmes when Holmes proposed an expansion of the Beverly Hills Tennis Club that would make it a full-service country club catering to Hollywood's large Jewish population. With many of the town's high-class country clubs preferring not to welcome Jews, this idea appealed to Groucho—especially since his teenaged son Arthur was showing signs of becoming a tennis champion.

Zeppo's client, actress Helen Vinson, had recently married British tennis champion Fred Perry. Perry had a prior Hollywood connection, having dated Marlene Dietrich. After a brief time in England, Vinson and Perry moved to Hollywood, and Perry joined Groucho as one of the principal backers of the new Beverly Hills Tennis Club. A December 1936 luncheon announcing plans for the new club featured Groucho as toastmaster and Fred Perry acting as head waiter with Barbara Stanwyck serving as a waitress. The club formally opened on July 11, 1937, with a celebrity doubles match pitting Britain's Fred Perry and Charlie Chaplin against America's Ellsworth Vines and Groucho Marx. The star-studded membership of the club included all the Marx Brothers as well as an array of movie stars, writers, and producers. Marion quickly became the best female tennis player at the club.

When Groucho boasted about Arthur's tennis skills to Zeppo and Marion, Zeppo was skeptical. In *Son of Groucho* Arthur wrote,

Zeppo allowed that "Art might be pretty good for a boy," but then quickly added. "But he's certainly not in Marion's class." "She can't beat Arthur," said Father confidently. "How much would you like to bet?" shot back Zeppo, always eager to risk his money. "A hundred dollars?" Not a betting man himself, Father's complexion turned the color of our white tablecloth. "Put up or shut up!" said Marion as Father hesitated.

They made the bet, and a match was arranged at the club. Arthur described the action: "For the first couple of games I could hardly keep the ball in play. As I looked over at the veranda, I could see Zeppo smirking, and Father, paler than usual, and extremely silent, probably thinking about what he could have done with a hundred dollars if he hadn't thrown it away on me." But Arthur found weaknesses in Marion's game and turned things around. He recalled winning the two-set match, 6–2 and 6–1.

Zeppo did not like to lose a bet, no matter how small, and his competitive nature took over. Arthur continued,

> Zeppo suddenly turned away from Marion, whom he'd been consoling, and said in a loud voice, "Listen, Groucho. The kid may be able to beat my wife, but I'll bet you he can't beat me!" Zeppo was just a "B" player on the men's ladder but being a man and naturally more athletic than the average woman, he figured he could make up in brawn for what he lacked in skill and orthodox strokes. "Okay, double or nothing" replied Father, who, in his euphoria over my victory, was turning into a regular Nick the Greek. Zeppo didn't even bother to put on tennis clothes. He just stripped off the jacket of his Eddie Schmidt suit, loosened his tie, and slipped on a pair of tennis sneakers. He was tougher than Marion. I couldn't bring him to the net and lob, because he had a strong overhead and volley from playing doubles with the "A" players. However, I did manage to outsteady him from the back court, and outlast him, too. His chain-smoking was finally catching up with him. By the time I won the first set, 6–4, and was leading 3–0 in the second, Zeppo had to default from sheer exhaustion. I got a big kick out of watching Zeppo pull a huge roll of bills from his pocket, count out two hundred dollars and hand them over to Father.

Arthur's account may be perfectly accurate. If it isn't the same match described by Groucho's biographer Hector Arce, Arthur's story occurred at another time. According to Arce,

> Arthur, in his mid-teens, had developed into a fine tennis player. Zeppo was a touch better at the time. He bet Groucho that he could beat Arthur. The match went to set point several times with Arthur on the brink of victory, but Zeppo rallied and bested his nephew. [MGM executive] Sam Marx, sitting next to Groucho said, "I bet you beat the hell out of him when you get him home." "No." Groucho corrected. "Halfway home."

Winning or losing two hundred dollars to Groucho meant nothing in Zeppo's world of gambling. He threw that much around in tips on a night at the Clover Club. But his desire to beat Groucho won out over all logic. If Zeppo did beat Arthur at one point, there certainly came a time when Arthur was known to be an excellent tennis player and a nationally ranked member of the junior Davis Cup team, alongside players like Jack Kramer and Ted Schroeder, while still in his teens.

Zeppo didn't usually make bad bets, leaving that sort of gambling to Chico. But betting against Arthur in a tennis match against a top-ranked amateur would have been risky by the time Arthur was around seventeen. Marion, not even at the level of an unranked amateur, was overmatched and Zeppo probably knew it. But just getting the frugal Groucho to wager on anything amused him. Zeppo's competitiveness at tennis extended outside the family. Columnist Art Arthur reported in *The Brooklyn Daily Eagle*, "Zeppo Marx and David Selznick . . . settled a bitter tennis feud by playing far into the night on an unlit tennis court. Zeppo lost but offered a perfect alibi: 'It was too dark . . . and I just can't play the Braille system. Why, I had to strike a match every time I served!'"

A more significant loss around this time came in a court, not on one. Zeppo had signed sixteen-year-old French actress and dancer Olympe Bradna and got her a contract with Paramount. Her parents, Josef and Jeanna Bradna, went to superior court to get their daughter out of the contract with Zeppo, claiming it was invalid because she was a minor when it was signed. (They were perfectly fine with the Paramount contract, they just preferred to not pay the agent who got it for them.) Zeppo answered the suit with a counter claim, saying the girl's parents were responsible for payment of 10 percent of the girl's earnings.

The case went to trial in October 1937 and Zeppo's lawyer claimed that even if the girl had the right to terminate the contract, her parents remained responsible for agent's fees incurred before the termination. The decision came down in favor of the Bradnas on both points and there wasn't much the Artists' Managers Guild could do about it. Signing underage performers was risky. A law had been passed to protect the studios from this sort of thing. California Civil Code Section 36 provided that "a minor may not disaffirm a contract to render dramatic services where the contract has been submitted and approved by the Supreme Court in the county where the minor resides or is employed." But this law made no provision for agents. And there was the added problem that California Civil Code Section 33 provided "that a minor cannot give a delegation of power." This was considered an unsettled issue because if interpreted strictly, no minor could have an agent.

Daily Variety summed up the problem on October 24, 1938. "Many youthful actors and actresses employ agents and business representatives. Large sums of money are paid to these agents and representatives for services to such performers who are under 21. Can they arbitrarily drop an agent without cause even after the agent has procured for the minor a term contract? May the minor arbitrarily discharge the agent? And, without further payment under the contract? Broadly spoken, the answer apparently is in the affirmative." But it was good business for an agent to work with underage actors. There were still plenty of them becoming stars and honoring their contracts.

Zeppo had taken a chance on another minor in December 1936. *Hollywood Reporter* publisher Billy Wilkerson asked him to see an attractive teenaged girl he had encountered in an ice cream parlor near Hollywood High School. (Why Wilkerson was ogling high school girls in an ice cream parlor is another matter.) Wilkerson had been a bootlegger, and the repeal of Prohibition moved him into the nightclub business. He owned several Hollywood clubs and restaurants including the Trocadero. One of his closest friends was Johnny Rosselli.

With permission from her mother, Wilkerson sent his malt shop girl to Zeppo's office. Armed with a letter from Wilkerson, fifteen-year-old Julia Jean Turner—whose friends called her Judy—went to see Zeppo. He agreed with Wilkerson that Judy Turner—later better known as Lana Turner—was beautiful and could become a star if she could learn to act. In her autobiography, she described their first meeting. After reading Wilkerson's letter, Zeppo

looked up and said, "Tell me Judy, how old are you?"

"Fifteen, Mr. Marx," I said. He slapped his hand down sharply on the desk, and he barked, "Oh no, you're not."

"Yes, I really am. Honest."

"Don't ever say that again. As far as this industry goes, you're eighteen."

We didn't know then why my age was so important, but later on I found out. Meanwhile Zeppo Marx agreed to represent me and assigned me to his agent Henry Willson. Henry took me around to meet the casting directors, but nobody offered me a job—not even as an extra. So, he turned me over to another young man named Solly Baiano.

Zeppo's insistence on her saying she was eighteen suggests an unpleasant motive. The age of majority in California was twenty-one, so for the purpose of protecting himself in contractual matters, Turner being eighteen still made her a minor and was of no help to Zeppo as an agent. The fifteen-year-old girl was not likely to pass for twenty-one, but there was a reason to pass her off as being eighteen: the age of sexual consent in California was eighteen.

Zeppo told Shirley Eder of the *Detroit Free Press* a version of the Lana Turner story that took Wilkerson out of the ice cream parlor and made him a friend of the girl's family. But the key points of the story were unchanged:

> [S]he was beautiful. A beautiful figure, and she had no experience at all. Mervyn LeRoy, who was just starting his own unit at Warner Bros. calls me and says . . . "anything new in talent, please give me first chance at it because I need some talent." I had a boy named Solly Baiano working for me, and I called Mervyn and said, "I got a girl here that I think has great possibilities as far as looks and a figure and everything. If you teach her how to act this girl could be a star." He says, "I've got a small part in a picture." I sent her over with Solly Baiano. She had a tight sweater on, and a tight skirt and he put her in the picture . . . and she immediately became known all over.

LeRoy had given the girl a small role in *They Won't Forget* and changed her name to Lana Turner. When the film was released in July 1937, Turner had only recently turned sixteen. In compliance with the law that protected studios but not agents, her contract with LeRoy was approved by a judge. It isn't clear what made them lie about her age and still have her be under the age of consent in the process. On March 12, 1937, the *Los Angeles Times* thought this noteworthy enough to report: "Approval was given by Judge Wilson to a contract between Mervyn LeRoy, producer, and Julia Jean Turner, 17 years of age, a recent discovery, who will be known in films as Lana Turner. The contract calls for from $50 to $600 per week over a seven-year period."

When LeRoy moved his production unit to MGM at the end of 1937, he convinced Warner Bros. to let him take Lana Turner with him. With a new contract from another studio about to be offered, Lana Turner's mother stepped in and decided that she no longer needed the services of Zeppo Marx. Having already been down this road with Olympe Bradna, Zeppo knew there was nothing he could do. He told Shirley Eder, "In those days you had no protection with a minor. You could sign a contract, but it didn't mean a thing. And her mother, who was really a pusher, made a deal with Metro." What Zeppo didn't see coming was his junior agent Solly Baiano leaving him to take a job in the Warner Bros. casting department—using the discovery of Lana Turner to his own advantage. The discovery of Lana Turner ended up on at least one other résumé. Henry Willson—a man prone to exaggeration—later claimed to have been responsible for getting her to LeRoy and even coming up with her name.

In her book Turner acknowledged the more nefarious explanation for Zeppo insisting she lie about her age. It was common practice for the studios to give attractive young girls six-month options with no intention of casting them in any movies. She wrote, "Word had gotten around that I was Mervyn LeRoy's protégé. Nobody ever made a pass at me. I was not just a six-month-option girl to be passed around the executive offices."

Zeppo was more focused on the money he could potentially make if Turner could be made into a star. He was not in the business of procuring girls for studio executives—as Frank Orsatti had been. But by the time she wrote her memoirs, Lana Turner had learned all about the young women who were used by Hollywood executives and didn't acknowledge Zeppo's concern about underage clients not honoring agency contracts. She wrote, "It had to be spelled out for me that those six-month-option girls would never go on to a movie career—they were for the benefit of the management. That was what Zeppo Marx had meant when he told me to say I was eighteen. If I had got one of those six-month-option deals, I'd better lie about my age for *their* protection." Zeppo was probably more worried about the possibility of a repeat of the Olympe Brada situation, but the other concern was certainly real.

Marwyck was becoming much more of a focus for Zeppo as the agency business kept getting uglier. Minor problems like clients refusing to pay commissions resulted in the occasional lawsuit. One such dispute was with one of his first clients, Norman Krasna. Zeppo also sued agent Jack Bachman over commissions for his former client, screenwriter Tess Slesinger. Even with the formation of a protective association there were still agents undercutting each other and raiding clients. By the spring of 1938 there were 273 licensed agencies in Hollywood. Ten years prior there were twenty-six. The top agencies that formed the Artists' Managers Guild became known around town as "the Big 13." A *Variety* story about the state of the agency business ran on March 2, 1938, under the headline "H'wood 'Big 13' to Purge Ranks."

Stormy days are ahead for Hollywood's over-manned army of talent agents. Finally awake to the fact that their own enterprises are being undermined by unhealthy conditions, more or less general throughout the percentage field, the 13 rich and powerful members of the Agents Guild are poised for a widespread putsch intended to rid the racket of . . .

some of the affluent 10%ers who are alleged to have gotten that way through unethical practices.

Zeppo's entrance into the agency business wasn't specifically scrutinized in the *Variety* article, but there was a comment that could certainly apply to his rise to the top of it. "Stories of amazing bankrolls being piled up resulted in a rush for agency licenses from all walks of life, current list of permit holders including a former chauffeur and two ex-waiters." *Variety* had the good taste to not add an unhappy straight man from a famous comedy team to the list. The rapid rise of the Zeppo Marx Agency was cryptically referenced in a *Hollywood Reporter* gossip item on April 9, 1937: "The fellow that offered Zeppo Marx $500,000 for his business, can't be found by Zeppo."

With several experienced agents in his employ and Gummo now working out of the Hollywood office, Zeppo scaled back his own activities as an agent—although he continued to personally handle a few prominent clients, most notably Barbara Stanwyck. Frustrated with his brothers, he'd handed them off to Gummo, but Zeppo handled negotiations for a radio deal for Groucho and Chico in December 1938. They would costar with Cary Grant and Carole Lombard on the NBC program *The Circle*.

Zeppo considered his brothers difficult, but he occasionally tolerated them—at least in part because of the high salaries they commanded. But his most important client continued to be Barbara Stanwyck. When she married Robert Taylor shortly after midnight on May 14, 1939, Zeppo and Marion drove with them to San Diego for the spontaneous, secret wedding. Marion was the matron of honor. The newlyweds rented a large house in Beverly Hills and began spending less time at Marwyck. Zeppo and Marion were going there less frequently as well.

Gummo's son Bob recalled a conversation between Zeppo and Stanwyck in which she wanted to sell her half of the ranch to him because his dogs were keeping her up at night. In July 1941 Zeppo bought her out and became the sole owner of Marwyck.[6] Harry Hart continued to run the stable and breeding operations at Marwyck until September 1943, when Zeppo sold the ranch to J. H. Ryan and his partners, who renamed it Northridge Farms.[7]

In the April 1942 issue of *Motion Picture*, Marion wrote of Stanwyck's desire to leave Marwyck:

[H]er drive to and from work every day began to lose its luster. Especially when the rains came. After every rain, there would be flash floods,

Julius, Minnie, Sam (top), Herbert, cousin Polly, and Milton (bottom), circa 1904. COURTESY JERRY SEINFELD

Herbert Marx and his Aunt Hannah, circa 1903.

A portrait of Herbert taken shortly after the family moved to Chicago.

Herbert in front of 179 East 93rd Street.

ORPHEUM Theatre
NOW PLAYING
4 MARX BROTHERS
18--People--18
MUSICAL COMEDY

TUESDAY NIGHT
SPECIAL ATTRACTION
HERBERT MARX
"The 5th Marx Bro."
Chicago's Boy Soprano

WEDNESDAY NIGHT—
—SPECIAL ATTRACTION
At the end of each performance
CHORUS GIRL CONTEST
Each Chorus Girl will do a specialty—The audience will pick the winner

COMING THURSDAY
Pepple & Shean present
THE PARISIAN REVUE
Just a rare and creamy cocktail of Mirth, Music and Song.

Herbert at age twelve in Chicago around the time of his stage debut.

Gary, Indiana, February 24, 1914: Herbert officially makes the Four Marx Brothers a quintet for one performance. *GARY EVENING POST* (2/23/14)

Joliet, Illinois, May 1, 1914: The Marx family behind the Orpheum Theatre on the occasion of thirteen-year-old Herbert's two-day appearance with his brothers. (Left to right, Arthur, Leonard, Sam, Herbert, Minnie, Milton, and Julius.)

In the summer of 1915, Herbert toured the W.S. Butter-field vaudeville circuit with his brothers. It was the only time they were ever billed as the Five Marx Brothers. The ad is for the quintet's opening engagement in Lansing, Michigan. *LANSING STATE JOURNAL* (8/13/15)

Herbert and Arthur around 1915, when the Marx Brothers company had a baseball team.

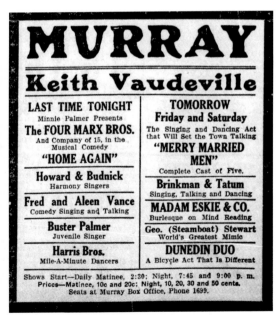

Fifteen-year-old Herbert at the beach on the shore of Lake Michigan.

Richmond, Indiana, September 4–6, 1916: Herbert appears as "Buster Palmer" on a bill with his brothers as Minnie prepares him for his own vaudeville career. *RICHMOND PALLADIUM ITEM* (9/6/16)

Fall 1916: The Juvenile Six: the Kashner Sisters—Marvel, Ida, and Fay—the Harris Brothers—George and Victor—and Herbert Marx. *SPOKANE CHRONICLE* (1/15/17).

Seattle, Washington, January 21–24, 1917: By the middle of their lone vaudeville season, the Juvenile Six was occasionally getting top billing. *SEATTLE STAR* (1/20/17)

St. Joseph, Missouri. March 29–31, 1917: An unusual billing for the Juvenile Six shows the members billed individually. *ST. JOSEPH NEWS PRESS GAZETTE* (3/30/17)

Leonard, Julius, and Herbert, around the time Herbert joined the Four Marx Brothers in 1918.

Spring 1921: Gummo, Groucho, and Ruth (front), *Humor Risk* producers Nathan "Nucky" Sachs and Oscar "Mike" Mirantz, and Zeppo, holding Chico's daughter Maxine.

Fall 1921: The Four Marx Brothers in what is possibly the earliest photograph of Groucho's greasepaint moustache.

Portrait of Zeppo just prior to the Four Marx Brothers' arrival on Broadway. COURTESY TIM MARX

May 1924: Zeppo, Chico, Groucho, and Harpo surround Minnie Marx as *I'll Say She Is* opens on Broadway.

Aspiring Broadway chorine Marion Bimberg (aka Marion Benda) around the time she met Zeppo. COURTESY TIM MARX

December 1925: Zeppo surrounded by chorus girls from the Broadway cast of *The Cocoanuts*.

August 14, 1926: Zeppo and Marion pose for the press as they announce their engagement. COURTESY TIM MARX

Marion and Zeppo again pose for the press to formally announce their marriage in April 1927. COURTESY TIM MARX

Groucho, Gummo, Harpo, and Chico strike a pose with Zeppo and Marion at their wedding on April 12, 1927, at the Chalfonte Hotel in New York. COURTESY TIM MARX

Zeppo on vacation at Camp Kenawa in Wood-
stock, New York, circa 1927. COURTESY TIM MARX

Zeppo in Boston, Massachusetts on
October 13, 1929, during the *Animal
Crackers* road tour that began a week
after the death of Minnie Marx.
COURTESY DAVID BRANDT/MARX
BROTHERS INC.

Zeppo, Marion, Harpo, Betty, Chico, Miriam, Ruth, Groucho, and
Arthur on board the *SS Paris*, en route to England in December 1930.

February 3, 1931, London: Zeppo and Marion walking Riff, Phyllis Robson's Afghan Hound, in Hyde Park.

Chico, Zeppo, and Groucho arrive in New York from Europe on February 14, 1931. Harpo had traveled separately and arrived a week earlier.

Harpo on the set of *Monkey Business* with Zeppo's Afghan Hounds, Omar and Asra.
COURTESY JOHN TEFTELLER/MARX BROTHERS INC.

Ruth Hall and Zeppo—the romantic leads in *Monkey Business*. COURTESY PAUL WESOLOWSKI/MARX BROTHERS INC.

March 1931. A *Monkey Business* publicity photo from the Marxes' first days in Hollywood.

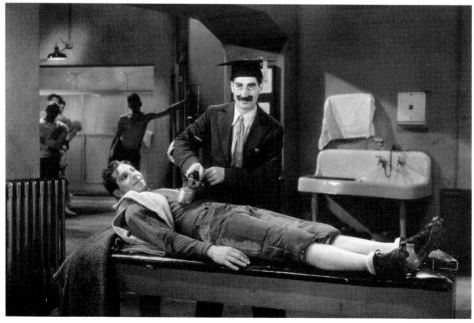

Zeppo and Groucho in a scene deleted from *Horse Feathers*. COURTESY JOHN TEFTELLER/MARX BROTHERS INC.

October 24, 1932: Zeppo addresses the crowd at the Los Angeles premiere of *A Bill of Divorcement* at the Hill Street Theatre. COURTESY DAVID BRANDT/MARX BROTHERS INC.

Zeppo at the February 4, 1933, birthday party for his friend and decorator Jetta Goudal at La Golondrina in Hollywood. COURTESY DAVID BRANDT/MARX BROTHERS INC.

Marion and Zeppo in Palm Springs.

May 15, 1933: Zeppo stops at Dearborn Station in Chicago with the train carrying his father's body to New York. COURTESY DAVID BRANDT/MARX BROTHERS INC.

Raquel Torres and Zeppo on the set of *Duck Soup*.

April 1932: Publicity photo for the unsold "Four Marx Brothers Radio Sketch."

Zeppo visits with Dorothy Mackaill on the set of Paramount's 1932 film *No Man of Her Own*—which featured his friends Carole Lombard and Clark Gable several years before their marriage.

September 3, 1932: Marion and Zeppo with friend and neighbor Alice Glazer at the "Gay Nineties" party celebrating Fredric March's birthday.

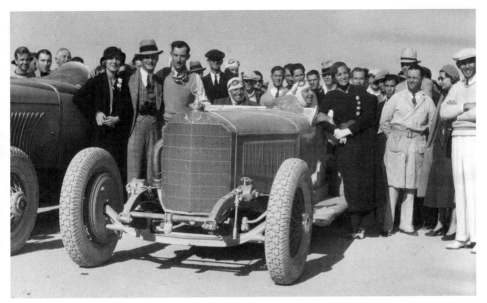

September 25, 1932: Leila Hyams and Phil Berg (left), Zeppo at the wheel of his Mercedes-Benz, and Marion, leaning on the car at the Muroc Dry Lake match race with Berg's Dusenberg. COURTESY DAVID BRANDT/MARX BROTHERS INC.

Zeppo in a scene deleted from *Duck Soup*. COURTESY JOHN TEFTELLER/MARX BROTHERS INC.

Glenda Farrell and Zeppo at Lake Arrowhead.

Lake Arrowhead, January 1933. COURTESY
PAUL WESOLOWSKI/MARX BROTHERS INC.

Zeppo at the November 13, 1933, premiere of *Only Yesterday* at the Pantages
Theatre in Hollywood.

The Hollywood bungalow that served as the first office for Zeppo's talent agency in 1934. COURTESY TIM MARX

September 6, 1934: Walter Lang, Zeppo, Bing Crosby, Gilbert Roland, and Stewart Peters (brother of Carole Lombard) are the pallbearers at Russ Columbo's funeral at Blessed Sacrament Church in Hollywood.

A mid-thirties portrait of Marion taken a few years after she'd abandoned any plans for her own movie career. COURTESY TIM MARX

Barbara Stanwyck and Zeppo Marx
invite you to attend the opening of
Marwyck Ranch
all day Sunday, February 28th, 1937

Devonshire and Reseda Blvds., No. Los Angeles, Calif.
2 Miles North of Reseda on Reseda Blvd.

Refreshments

Invitation to the February 28, 1937, opening of the ranch jointly owned by Barbara Stanwyck and Zeppo. COURTESY TIM MARX

Carole Lombard's gag gift to the proud owners of the Marwyck Ranch arrived shortly after the opening. COURTESY TIM MARX

Shortly after the opening of Marwyck Ranch, Groucho became one of the founders of the Beverly Hills Tennis Club. Harpo, Helen Vinson, Fred Perry, Barbara Stanwyck, Groucho, and Gloria Stuart at the club in July 1937.

Zeppo supports Barbara Stanwyck during her January 1938 court battle with her former husband, Frank Fay. Fay sought and won scheduled visits with the couple's five-year-old adopted son, Dion. COURTESY PAUL WESOLOWSKI/MARX BROTHERS INC.

Gummo at his desk at the Zeppo Marx
Agency with John Decker's portrait of the
Four Marx Brothers on the wall.
COURTESY DAVID BRANDT/MARX BROTHERS INC.

Zeppo's motorcycle riding group included
Norman Krasna and Robert Taylor.
COURTESY TIM MARX

Zeppo and Marion with Barbara Stanwyck and Robert Taylor, one of Hollywood's
most frequently seen foursomes in the early 1940s. COURTESY TIM MARX

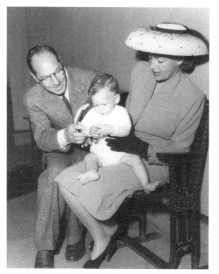

Zeppo and Marion adopted ten-month-old Thomas Marx on April 20, 1944. They would adopt ten-month-old Tim Marx on February 15, 1945. COURTESY TIM MARX

New father Zeppo inspecting aircraft parts at Marman Products, where he spent most of his time as Marion dealt with raising Tom and Tim. COURTESY DAVID BRANDT/MARX BROTHERS INC.

Marion with Tim and Tom shortly after Tim's adoption. COURTESY TIM MARX

The Marx Brothers—Tim and Tom, circa 1946. COURTESY TIM MARX

Zeppo at the Marman Products plant working on the Marman Twin motorized bicycle in 1948. COURTESY DAVID BRANDT/ MARX BROTHERS INC.

The photo of Zeppo seen with wire service reports about his January 1952 Hollywood street brawl with producer Alex Gottleib.

Marion, Zeppo, Tim, and Tom in Las Vegas, 1951. COURTESY TIM MARX

July 18, 1955: Tim and Marion return to Los Angeles for the rock throwing trial.
COURTESY TIM MARX

Zeppo in Indianapolis for his Federal Grand Jury testimony on August 22, 1958.

Zeppo and Barbara Blakeley at their September 18, 1959, wedding at the Riviera Hotel in Las Vegas.

Tim's 1965 visit with Zeppo in Palm Springs would be the last time he'd see his father.
COURTESY TIM MARX

Zeppo and Groucho on stage at the Gallery of Modern Art in New York for a Marx Brothers tribute on April 18, 1967.

Zeppo at home in Palm Springs around 1970.

Zeppo and Barbara at the bar in their Palm Springs home around 1970. COURTESY ROBERT MARX

Bobby Marx, Frank Sinatra, and Zeppo,
January 1971. COURTESY ROBERT MARX

Zeppo with Barbara's parents, Irene and
Charles Blakeley. COURTESY ROBERT MARX

Visible on the wall in Zeppo's Palm
Springs home office are photos of his
parents and the Four Marx Brothers.
COURTESY ROBERT MARX

Frank Sinatra and Zeppo, November 1971.
COURTESY ROBERT MARX

Zeppo in his home office in Palm Springs around 1973. COURTESY ROBERT MARX

Zeppo and Groucho at the American Film Institute's tribute to Orson Welles, February 9, 1975.

Zeppo at the Santa Monica courthouse to testify at the conservatorship hearing for Groucho, April 21, 1977.

Roxann Ploss and Zeppo in Tijuana in 1977. COURTESY ROXANN PLOSS

Roxann and Zeppo in Las Vegas in early 1979. COURTESY ROXANN PLOSS

Zeppo's signature from a 1956 legal document (top) and the signature on his will.

necessitating all kinds of unexpected detours between Northridge and Hollywood. Many a time I would hear Barbara drive out at 4 a.m., because it was raining. She was so conscientious, so thoughtful of others, she was panic-stricken at the thought that she might hold up production if she didn't set out before daylight, allowing for detours. Even in fair weather, she had to leave at 6 a.m. and wouldn't get home at night until after 8. That was pretty wearing. And after she and Bob married, and picture work kept them from having a honeymoon right away, they got thinking about how much more time they *could* spend together if they didn't live so far from work."

The end of the Marwyck partnership and the sale of the houses at the ranch resulted in Marion and Stanwyck beginning to see a lot less of each other. Inseparable friends for almost ten years, their relationship entered a slow fade-out period. Stanwyck had three big hits in 1941 with *The Lady Eve, Meet John Doe*, and *Ball of Fire*; and she became more focused on her suddenly exploding career. She also wanted to spend as much of her nonworking time as possible with her son.

Childless and approaching forty, Marion saw the joy Stanwyck got from being a mother. They still socialized on occasion but with Stanwyck a happily married mother, the nights on the town for the Taylors and the Marxes became infrequent. If Marion felt a sense of loss, she could at least be happy for her friend. Barbara Stanwyck had found what she was looking for in Robert Taylor, who was also an excellent father figure for Dion. Marion spoke privately to Susan Marx and wondered if Zeppo could take to fatherhood as Harpo had.

There was no silver lining when Marion lost another dear friend in one of the most profound tragedies in Hollywood history. Carole Lombard was returning home from a war bond rally in Indianapolis when she and her mother were killed in a plane crash near Las Vegas on January 16, 1942. Lombard was only thirty-three and had been happily married to Clark Gable for three years. Marion and Zeppo were longtime friends of both and had been amused and thrilled when they finally got together. They were among the small group of close friends who surrounded Gable with support in the days after the tragedy. Zeppo was one of Lombard's pallbearers at the private service on January 21. It was a difficult period for Marion who was now without two of the closest friends she had in Hollywood.

Zeppo had simultaneously operated Marwyck and his agency for almost five years. With Stanwyck out of the business, Marwyck was no longer a fun retreat that might make a profit. It was now strictly a business. With World War II shutting down California racetracks in 1942, the breeding side of it took a major hit. Marwyck had started to move away from breeding a year earlier to focus on boarding and training, so the ranch became much less interesting to Zeppo without any chance of seeing one of his horses become a champion. He'd only gotten into the venture because it was something Marion and Stanwyck wanted. But now there was another new venture to consider. An executive of the Douglas Aircraft Company had been boarding his horses at Marwyck and had something in mind that was right up Zeppo's alley.

CHAPTER SEVENTEEN

Whose Clamp Is It Anyway?

A HELP WANTED ADVERTISEMENT IN THE *LOS ANGELES TIMES* ON October 12, 1941, gave no indication that it had been placed by a celebrity.

DRILL PRESS & LATHE OPERATORS,
EXPERIENCED. CAPABLE.

ACTING AS LEAD MEN OR SET-UP MEN.
APPLY IN PERSON

TUES. 7 A.M. TO 6 P.M. MARMAN PRODUCTS CO,

940 W. REDONDO BLVD, INGLEWOOD.

As he had with each of his homes, Zeppo built a machine shop at his Marwyck house. He told Charlotte Chandler, "I was a mechanic. I love mechanical things, and every place I've had, I've always had a shop at the back of my house, because I love it." Zeppo met like-minded Albert Dale Herman. He'd been asking people to recommend good engineers for a new venture he was planning; and Herman, who was the General Manager of the Vickers Manufacturing Company, came highly recommended. The company founder, Harry F. Vickers, is known in mechanical circles as the father of industrial hydraulics. Among Vickers' inventions was the first automotive power steering system, which fascinated Zeppo.

A. Dale Herman, as he preferred to call himself, was invited to Zeppo's home and they began tinkering in Zeppo's shop in their spare time. They each had interesting ideas for inventions and worked well enough together that Zeppo invited him to be his partner in the new venture. But Herman wasn't prepared to give up his job with Vickers and could not make the financial commitment that Zeppo could. Herman, ten years younger than Zeppo and supporting a wife and two daughters, explained that he needed to remain at Vickers until he qualified for his pension. Nonetheless, Zeppo agreed to call the company Marman Products, using the same sort of amalgamation of names that gave Marwyck its name. In a sense, Herman was to Marman what Zeppo had been to the Four Marx Brothers—part of the name, but not an owner of the company. Herman would devote whatever time he could to Marman while continuing to work at Vickers.

Herman wasn't the only mechanically inclined friend Zeppo invited to tinker at his shop. "I had met a fella at RKO when I was going around to the different studios selling clients and getting jobs for my clients," he told Chandler.

> I always used to hang around the machine shop at RKO. Every studio had a machine shop. And I got very friendly and close with a fantastic machinist there. So, I said, "Charlie, I've got a little machine shop in the back of my house in the Valley. I'd love to play around with it with you. I have different ideas and inventions." And he said, "That's wonderful. I'd love to play around with it and work with you."

What set A. Dale Herman apart and made Zeppo want to form a company with him was Herman's ability to draft diagrams and patent applications.

Zeppo detailed for Chandler the sequence of events that turned a passion for all things mechanical into a company that would soon dwarf all his other business interests.

> I was out at Santa Anita one day, and we had a box right next to the vice president of Douglas Aircraft, who had some of his horses on our ranch. He said to me, "You know, we're very shy of machine shops and machinists." . . . "I hear that you have a machine shop. Well, we need some machine work very badly. . . ." I said, "All right. Send some stuff and the prints over, and we'll machine it for you."

Donald Douglas was one of the prescient manufacturers who knew the United States would be entering World War II sooner or later, and he ramped up operations at Douglas Aircraft well in advance of any urgent need for warplanes. He sent Zeppo several blueprints for parts from the DC-3 aircraft and Zeppo and his machinist buddies made them. Douglas was pleased and sent more plans and diagrams—and orders for quantities of these parts that could not be filled in a little home machine shop. Suddenly Zeppo found himself in his shop all night after handling agency business and Marwyck all day: "[W]e'd work until one or two o'clock in the morning machining these parts and getting them ready."

At first Marman hired unemployed actors, big band musicians between jobs, and guys from the RKO machine shop to meet the orders from Douglas Aircraft. But this became impractical. A large factory with a lot of manufacturing equipment was needed. Zeppo rented a building in Inglewood, got bank loans to buy the equipment, and hired around a hundred workers through his newspaper advertisement.

Once Marman was open for business Zeppo barely spent any time at the agency or Marwyck. Marion's brother, Alan Miller, had joined the agency in 1939 after having been its legal counsel for a few years. A graduate of Fordham University School of Law, Miller had first worked in Hollywood as an associate of Zeppo's Colonial House neighbor, attorney and agent Ralph Blum, the husband of actress Carmel Myers. With Blum and his partner Sherman Grancell, Miller represented agents Leland Hayward, Frank Joyce, and Myron Selznick as well as Zeppo. His clients also included actress Ruth Collier and producer Jed Harris, so Miller came to the Zeppo Marx Agency well qualified.

Gummo also took on a larger role. Zeppo told Charlotte Chandler, "I couldn't devote too much time to the agency business. I had this tremendous thing going." As Zeppo's business took off, Groucho told friends, "He's now running a very successful war plant for making some part of an airplane. I don't know just what part it is—but I think it's the hostess."

Like his agency and ranch before it, Zeppo's factory was operational quickly. And soon Marman Products would hire even more workers to keep up with the demand from Douglas Aircraft. Less than two months after Zeppo's initial help-wanted advertisement, the Japanese invasion of Pearl Harbor thrust the United States into World War II. Marman quickly became a government contractor.

"So now I'm in the machinist business. I've got five hundred people working, and we're working twenty-four hours a day, three shifts," Zeppo told Chandler.

> We're working like mad turning out these parts for all the aircraft companies. Finally, one day I started to take stock of myself. I said, "Look, I've got a machine shop here, and I'm machining things. If the war gets over very quickly, I've got a million dollars' worth of machinery here, and who's gonna use it? And what am I gonna do with it? We've got to

get a proprietary item—something we can split the government work with, something of our own."

He needn't have worried about the war ending quickly, but his concern about being stuck with all the additional equipment he purchased to meet the war time demand was legitimate.

This proprietary item that Zeppo sought to keep Marman viable after the war has become synonymous with Zeppo and his company. What came to be known as the Marman Clamp would make Marman Products very successful in a fairly short time. But who invented the Marman Clamp? Many assume that Zeppo did, but he had no hand in it apart from ultimately manufacturing it.[1] The story of the clamp as Zeppo told it to Charlotte Chandler has a few holes in it and may not be entirely truthful.

[O]ne day a fella came into the shop and to the office, and the girl came in and said, "There's a Mr. King out here who would like to talk to you." I said, "I don't know a Mr. King." She said, "Well, he's got an invention, and he wants to show it to you." I said, "Bring him in." Of course. I would see anybody. I brought him in, and he sat down. He had holes in the bottom of his shoes. Terrible looking man. He had a little clamp, a coupling device, and it appealed to me. He had his patents, and he said he'd been all over, but he couldn't get in to see anybody because on account of the war, they were so busy, and they didn't want to take on anything like that.

I said, "I'll make a deal with you. I'll take it on, and I'll give you the regular inventor's royalties." So, we made a contract, and I took this thing on. It was really a very good coupling or clamping device. As a matter of fact, right now, most everything that moves and some stuff that doesn't move has this item on it. We had it all over airplanes, we had it on boats, we had it in oil fields, we had it every place. This man finally became a millionaire. He rode around in a Cadillac with a chauffeur and had a yacht and everything due to his royalties from this thing, because it turned out to be so big.

The "Mr. King" in Zeppo's story was James Thomas King. He applied for the first two patents on his hose clamp in April and August 1941. These patents were granted in January and February 1942—around the time he brought them to Zeppo. King's design was a great improvement over previous clamps in that it could be applied and removed with the turning of a single nut. It could be applied quickly and provided even force around the perimeter of a hose or pipe. The ease of repeated removal and reattachment of the clamp made it very desirable in the aircraft industry.

Zeppo's description of King cannot be verified but based on what can be determined about him, King was quite accomplished. Born in England in 1890, he emigrated to Toronto, Canada in 1911 and worked as a carpenter before beginning a career in airplane manufacturing. He married in 1912 and had a son and daughter by 1918. He became an aeronautical engineer when Canada entered World War I in 1914 and was also involved in ground crew training.

When the United States entered the war in 1917, King taught aviation mechanics at Dunwoody Naval Institute in Minneapolis. In 1918 he was the coauthor of the book *Airplane Construction and Assembly*. After the war King supervised airplane manufacturing for Fokker and worked in the air mail business as an aviation inspector for Western Air Express. He eventually moved his family to Long Beach, California. When he applied for his clamp patents, he was living in Burbank, less than a mile from Lockheed Air Terminal—now known as Hollywood Burbank Airport. As an airport maintenance supervisor for Western Air Express, King earned an annual salary of around $2,400—which placed him squarely in the middle class.

On July 1, 1943, King signed an agreement granting Marman the exclusive right to manufacture, use, and sell the patented clamps throughout the world for the life of the patent. King was to be paid a percentage of the retail price of any clamps sold, but if his total revenue during any year failed to exceed $4,000, he had the power to terminate the agreement unless Marman paid the difference between his revenue and $4,000. Under the agreement Marman could not license King's patent to others or assign the agreement without King's permission. Marman did retain the right to institute patent infringement suits on King's behalf. Marman also had the right to purchase the patent for a lump sum.

King was involved with Marman prior to the signing of the agreement. On his April 1942 World War II draft registration, he listed himself as self-employed—but with the Marman plant in Inglewood as his place of business. King's deal with Zeppo looked much more promising than his future as a middle-class aircraft industry worker. After fifteen years with Western Air Express, James T. King was not getting rich.

On March 19, 1947, King filed an action against Marman in the Los Angeles Superior Court asking for an accounting for money due him as well as for damages for breach of contract. An out-of-court settlement was reached on

April 28, 1948, and the parties executed a new contract that was substantially the same as the 1943 agreement with the exception that Marman's right to purchase the patent for a lump sum was removed. James T. King would apply for and be granted a total of six patents associated with his clamp. None of his subsequent patents were assigned or licensed to Marman. There were, however, nineteen additional patents related to the clamp assigned to Marman by eight other inventors—including one by A. Dale Herman. But Marman certainly acknowledged the value of King's patents. Marman sued National Utilities Corporation for patent infringement in 1954 and cited four patents in the lawsuit—three of which were held by James T. King. The court would decide in favor of Marman in June 1957.

In 1947 James T. King became a founding director of Los Angeles Airways, Inc., a company that transported mail and cargo from airports to post offices by helicopter. He and his wife continued living modestly in their 1,700-square-foot house in Burbank. His son lived next door. Hardly the stuff of a chauffeur driven Cadillac and a yacht. If James T. King became a millionaire as a result of Marman's use of his patents, he certainly did not live like one. King clearly made some money, but the big winner on the Marman Clamp project was Marman.

With Zeppo usually at the Marman plant, Marion spent much of her time at Marwyck and the Beverly Hills Tennis Club. But she had also spent a lot of time with Barbara Stanwyck and her son, Dion. Stanwyck ultimately chose time with her son over the more frivolous aspects of her life—like shopping with Marion. And Susan and Harpo, after having adopted their son Bill in 1938, were planning to expand their family. Stanwyck doted on Dion, and Harpo and Susan were thrilled to be parents. Perhaps inevitably, Marion began thinking about having children—although her maternal instincts had probably not been stirred by playing tennis with Groucho's son Arthur.

Zeppo and Marion lived in a community filled with children—many of them adopted. There had been a lot of discussion of unwanted babies and adoption in Zeppo and Marion's circle of friends. In 1942 Zeppo turned forty-one and Marion thirty-nine. The clock was ticking away on parenthood, but the bigger obstacle for Marion and Zeppo was the fact that children—whether conceived by them or adopted—were of no interest to Zeppo, who barely had the energy to drag himself to the Clover Club to gamble while juggling three businesses.

At the Beverly Hills Tennis Club, manager Milton Holmes—surrounded by stars and producers—couldn't help but try to get back into the movie business. He started offering story ideas and initially found no takers. Zeppo could have easily taken him on as an agency client but did not. Holmes was in over his head gambling with the stars at the Clover Club as he peddled his story ideas there with the same results. He became closer with Clover Club manager Eddy Nealis and began inviting him to play tennis at the club. Several members were not amused—some because Nealis was part Mexican, and others because he was a notorious gangster and bookmaker. They didn't mind seeing Nealis at night in the Clover Club, but in daylight on the court at the Beverly Hills Tennis Club he seemed threatening. To make matters worse, Nealis was accused of skimming money from charity events he ran for some of the members at the Clover Club.

Eventually Milton Holmes's persistence paid off. He got Cary Grant interested in his short story "Bundles for Freedom," which had been published in *Cosmopolitan* in June 1941. Grant got RKO to pay Holmes $30,000 for the rights and it became the basis for the 1943 film, *Mr. Lucky*. Grant and his partner, played by Paul Stewart, operate a gambling ship and receive their draft notices. A dying associate is classified 4F—medically unfit to serve. The partners play a game of poker dice with the winner taking the dying man's identity—and 4F status. His partner cheats, but Grant's character wins anyway. Milton Holmes, engaged by RKO as a screenwriter, gave the cheating partner character the name "Zepp." Zeppo had a reputation in gambling circles for being uncompromising and many thought he didn't always play honestly. Some of the Clover Club crowd no doubt enjoyed a laugh when they saw *Mr. Lucky*.

Following the sale of their home at Marwyck, Zeppo and Marion rented a house on Devonshire Street in Northridge, not far from the ranch. But they were looking for something bigger and wanted to get back to Beverly Hills. After less than two years in Northridge they briefly rented a large house on Sunset Boulevard before buying 1001 North Rexford Drive, a large colonial style house built in 1921.

It was at that address that their lives would change dramatically. They were growing apart and there were the first signs of trouble in the marriage. Marion was generally understanding about Zeppo's gambling—his habit of mostly winning probably made that easier for her. But she was finding it harder to turn a blind eye to the womanizing, even though Zeppo was very discreet about it. The success of Marman Products and the Zeppo Marx Agency wasn't enough to keep Marion happy while her husband began to spend many evenings out of the house without her. She wanted something more and Zeppo reluctantly went along with her plan.

CHAPTER EIGHTEEN

Trouble in Paradise

The Cradle Society was founded in 1923 by Florence Dahl Walrath in Evanston, Illinois. The mission of the organization was to furnish needful care for homeless babies and aid in securing for them permanent homes and legal adoption. To help promote adoption as a positive way of building families, Mrs. Walrath reached out to Hollywood.

In the early 1930s Miriam Hopkins and Joe E. Brown were among the first movie stars to adopt children from the Cradle Society. George Burns and Gracie Allen followed. Later Bob and Dolores Hope would adopt four children from the Cradle Society. Over the next two decades adoptions from numerous agencies caused a minor population explosion in Hollywood. Walt Disney, Helen Hayes and Charles MacArthur, Hedy Lamarr, Bud Abbott, Irene Dunne, Jack Benny and Mary Livingstone, James Cagney, Joan Fontaine, Roy Rogers and Dale Evans, Milton Berle, Donna Reed, Fred MacMurray, and Henry Fonda all became adoptive parents.

In some cases, Hollywood adoptions did not go as planned—ranging from unhappy to disastrous. Al Jolson and Rudy Keeler's son was estranged from Jolson from boyhood until his father's death. Lana Turner's daughter stabbed her mother's mobster lover to death in what was deemed a case of justifiable homicide. Both children of Mary Pickford and Buddy Rogers were estranged from their parents, and their son made a widely reported suicide attempt in 1958.

On the far end of the disastrous adoption spectrum are the children who wrote books vilifying their parents—the daughters of Bette Davis and Joan Crawford being the leaders in that field. Closer to home, Zeppo and Marion saw the blissfully happy situation at Harpo and Susan's house as well as the traumatized boyhood of Dion Fay—most of the trauma coming courtesy of Frank Fay. Barbara Stanwyck was a devoted mother—at least in the beginning.[1]

While Susan and Harpo were making plans for their second adoption, Marion and Zeppo brought ten-day-old Thomas Marx home from an orphanage in Los Angeles on July 4, 1943. A month later Susan and Harpo brought home an infant they named Alexander from an orphanage in Salt Lake City. Tom's adoption became legal on April 20, 1944—thirteen days after the birth of a baby that Zeppo and Marion would adopt from the same Salt Lake City orphanage where Susan and Harpo found Alex.

In the summer of 1944 Harpo and Susan adopted two more children, Jimmy and Minnie. Zeppo and Marion named their second boy Tim, and his adoption became legal on February 15, 1945. Zeppo's sudden acceptance of fatherhood came largely as a result of Harpo's influence. Marion and Susan became even closer with five new babies between them. Zeppo was happy to be a father if Marion did most of the work. The only concession Zeppo made to fatherhood was giving up motorcycle riding. He'd been riding regularly for a few years with a group that included Robert Taylor, Van Heflin, Ray Milland, Andy Devine, and Clark Gable. In July 1944 Zeppo sold his motorcycle to Gable. Marion had been concerned about Zeppo's recklessness and thought he might get himself killed on the bike.

Things were busier than ever at Marman, and Alan Miller and Gummo were seeing much less of Zeppo. Henry Willson had been promoted to vice president in August 1942 and Miller, Willson and Gummo expanded their roles in the operation of the agency. Zeppo recognized Willson's value and when rumors of him taking a job at RKO made the rounds in 1940, Zeppo had given him a new contract and a raise. But the ambitious Willson quit in June 1943 and took Rhonda Fleming with him as he went to work for David O. Selznick.[2]

Gummo told Richard J. Anobile, "[W]e had quite an office, but Zeppo didn't pay much attention to it. It ended up that Miller and I ran the office and after a couple of years I finally told Zeppo, 'I'm not satisfied with being an employee. I either want a partnership or I want to get out.' So, we formed a partnership." Zeppo did for Gummo what Groucho, Harpo, and Chico had for years refused to do for him. They announced the news on May 15, 1945, with a full-page advertisement in *Daily Variety*:

Zeppo Marx Agency
Announces
A Change of the Firm Name
To
Marx, Miller & Marx, Inc.

The arrival of two children almost simultaneously had a significant impact on Zeppo and Marion's marriage. They met and got married at the height of the Roaring Twenties and lived for only themselves for nearly twenty years. For them the nonstop fun of the Roaring Twenties didn't end until Tom and Tim came along. Susan and Marion had playdates with five babies—and Harpo. Zeppo rarely participated. Tim Marx recalls,

> Zeppo was closer to Harpo than he was to anybody else. That was the house we all used to go to. We didn't go to Groucho's house much. We'd go to Chico's apartment occasionally, but we would always go to Harpo's house. Harpo was a clown, a funny guy that would make the funny faces that you see in the movies. He would have us sit next to him while he played the harp and he got us to try to play the harp, which we could not do, but he would laugh. He would think that was funny.

While his family played at Harpo's house, Zeppo was fully engaged at Marman Products. In addition to the Marman Clamp, which by this point was available in several sizes and varieties, Marman was manufacturing numerous aircraft parts and working on new inventions to keep the company relevant in the coming postwar manufacturing business. A large part of Marman's business during the war was supplying fighter planes and battleships with Marman Clamps to secure cargo—including bombs—during transport.

The parts and nuclear materials for the two atomic bombs dropped on Hiroshima and Nagasaki in August 1945—each weighing 10,000 pounds were first secured to the decks of transport ships by several very large Marman Clamps and brought to the remote island of Tinian near Guam, where they were assembled. The Boeing B-29 Superfortress aircraft—named the Enola Gay in honor of Enola Gay Tibbets, the mother of pilot Colonel Paul Tibbets—was fitted with what would ultimately be the most famous and important Marman Clamps ever manufactured. On August 6, 1945, the first atomic bomb, known as "Little Boy," was dropped on Hiroshima. On August 9 another B-29 Superfortress named Bockscar, similarly equipped with Marman Clamps dropped the second bomb, known as "Fat Man," on Nagasaki. Six days later Japan surrendered and the war in the Pacific was over.

Marman would remain a major defense contractor for the United States military, but the company also tried to make some useful products for everyday American life. Zeppo played around with a significant idea he eventually lost interest in and never patented. He should have. It was roll-on deodorant. Closer to his heart was the Marman Twin, a dual-engine motorized bicycle. The engine had been designed during the war by another defense contractor, Jack & Heintz. The thirty-pound engine produced 3.5 horsepower. There had been other motorized bicycles, but adapting the twin engine, which was originally designed for drone aircraft, was what set the Marman Twin apart from the earlier attempts.

Zeppo worked on the Marman Twin with Theodore A. Woolsey, one of the staff inventors at Marman. Woolsey, a trade school engineering teacher before being hired by Zeppo, had assigned his patent for modifying the Marman Clamp to the company. In April 1948, *Popular Science* wrote that the Marman Twin "provides an easy cruising speed of 35 m.p.h. without strain, leaving ample reserve power and speed for emergencies. . . . In tests it has given more than 100 miles on a gallon of gas."

The first Marman Twins were sold in 1948. They were expensive at $129.50 and more of an interesting novelty than an overwhelming success. Zeppo's enthusiasm for motorcycles and his motorized bicycle idea did not result in significant profits for Marman, but civilian life found plenty of uses for the Marman Clamp, which continued to lead the way for Marman's product line.

Tom Marx recalls, "I had heard about something called Marman Products, but I didn't know what he did. I never went there. I heard they made parts for airplanes." In the fall of 1948, Tom entered kindergarten at Hawthorne Elementary School and Tim followed a year later. By that time the atmosphere was starting to become tense at the Rexford Drive house. Zeppo bought a lot in Beverly Hills, very near Gummo's house, and planned to build a new house. Gummo's son Bob recalled building a fruit stand on an empty lot at the corner of North Beverly Drive and Carmelita Avenue in Beverly Hills:

In my yard we had grapefruit and lemons. Several neighbors had huge avocado and orange trees in their back yards. Well, I really wasn't stealing, because if I hadn't taken the fruit and avocados, they would have been allowed to rot on the trees. When the fruit was arranged professionally it looked quite good. Sometimes the people whose fruit it was, would buy it back from me and say, "I have avocado trees, but the fruit isn't nearly as good as what you sell." I did a really nice business for several months. One day a bulldozer came and leveled the lot and my little red fruit house with it. As it turned out, it was my own Uncle Zeppo that put me out of business, when he purchased the lot.

Looking back at that time, Tom Marx concludes Zeppo and Marion "liked the idea of having kids, but really, kids just got in their way. They didn't really want to have kids. I don't know why they did it. Probably because people would ask, 'How come you don't have any kids.' It was probably something to do with their status. But as far as actually wanting the kids, and playing with the kids, forget it." Tim Marx says,

Marion wanted kids. I'm not so sure that Zeppo did, but he went along with it. At that point, they were fine. On Rexford Drive they were, for the most part, a very compatible couple—lots of friends over, playing cards, they entertained quite a bit. They had the greatest relationship. She dressed him to the nines. He was always the paragon of style. Gambled a lot. She went everywhere with him, always on his arm. When I was in third or fourth grade, Marion and Zeppo started full tilt having problems. She alleged it was because he was running with everybody in town. He'd go to Las Vegas. Here's this woman, that woman. Word was getting back somehow.

By the time Tom and Tim came along the agency had become less interesting to Zeppo, and he considered it something of a burden. He told Charlotte Chandler,

[T]he agency business kept flourishing. Gummo kept bringing in clients, and my partner [Alan Miller] is bringing in clients, and I brought in clients, and I'm selling them. Now, we've got about 250 clients in this agency business doing fabulously. We were the third largest agency in the business. But in the meantime, I didn't like it because they drove me crazy, these actors and directors and everything. They came in and they said, "Why didn't I get that job? Gable got it!" Well, this little punk who was getting a hundred dollars a week with Goldwyn or something, he wanted Gable's part that was out at Metro. So, you had to contend with those things in the agency business. You had to be their manager, you had to be their analyst. You had to do everything for some of those people. And it got to me. So, I just sold out.

Zeppo's assessment that his agency was the third largest in the business is debatable. What's undisputed is that MCA, the Music Corporation of America, was the biggest. Founded in 1924 by ophthalmologist Jules Stein as a booking agency for orchestras, MCA opened an office in Hollywood in 1937. Stein and his young protégé Lew Wasserman began the process of dominating the talent agency business by buying their smaller competitors. Stein and Wasserman considered Marx, Miller & Marx a prime target for acquisition based on the value of such high-earning stars as Barbara Stanwyck, Joan Fontaine, and Ray Milland. The MCA model was to buy the agency, keep the top earners and sell off the less valuable clients to other agencies. MCA's plans didn't matter to Zeppo. He wanted out of the business and through Stein and Wasserman he turned what had become a burden into a sizable amount of cash.

Gummo had become resentful of the situation at the agency and was annoyed that Zeppo just stopped showing up. He told Richard J. Anobile, "I discovered that I was doing all the hard work and Miller the easy work. He'd represent the big stars like Barbara Stanwyck and Fred MacMurray, but I'd go out every night to little theaters looking for new people I thought could be developed. That's the hardest part of the business!"

Zeppo had started turning troublesome clients over to Gummo even before he stopped showing up at the agency. Writer Konrad Bercovici developed a reputation as a duplicitous troublemaker. He famously filed a lawsuit against Charlie Chaplin in 1941, claiming the story idea for *The Great Dictator* had been stolen from him. When Chaplin's lawyers sought information from Zeppo, they learned that Gummo had been representing Bercovici in his dealings with Chaplin for several years. He had previously tried to sell Chaplin an unrelated Bercovici story about musician Hector Berlioz in 1938.

Correspondence between the Chaplin representatives and the agency was handled by Alan Miller. Internal correspondence between Chaplin's lawyers Charles Millikin and Loyd Wright summarized their interview with Gummo on the Bercovici matter: "Mr. Marx said that he believes that if Bercovici is now claiming that he was the originator of the "Dictator" story for Mr. Chaplin, that such claims are made out of whole cloth. He said that he does not believe that Bercovici is 'too scrupulous.'" By June of 1940 Bercovici was no longer a client of the Zeppo Marx Agency. But during the brief period that he was with the agency, Bercovici caused enough trouble that after initially signing him, Zeppo had nothing to do with him.[3]

With MCA focused only on the top earners, Gummo's position had become expendable. Gummo recalled,

One day I walked into the office and found that between Zeppo and Alan Miller the agency had been sold out from under my feet. They had sold the agency without my knowledge! Miller made a deal with MCA to take over our clients and to go with them. He did turn back all his stock to Zeppo, which meant that Zeppo had two-thirds and I had a third. The agency was sold for $225,000 and that left me with $75,000. I was too old to work for MCA, so I decided to represent Groucho and a TV show called *The Life of Riley*, which I had helped create. Zeppo felt he should be in on *The Life of Riley*, but I said no. I ended up doing much better after the agency was dissolved.[4]

A report in *Variety* on October 22, 1947, did not indicate that Marx, Miller & Marx had been sold. The information presented publicly was that the agency had simply folded. Alan Miller joined MCA and brought several clients with him, including Barbara Stanwyck, Ray Milland, Dennis Morgan, and Evelyn Keyes. The *Variety* article said, "Lew Wasserman, head of MCA, stated that there had been no merger or purchase, but that Miller had moved into MCA." Zeppo did not just give away a lucrative business. In later interviews he'd admit that he'd sold the business to MCA.

Jules Stein and Lew Wasserman would not have had any trouble with the idea of hiding the value of the transaction. Aside from avoiding a significant tax bill on the sale, Zeppo got the added benefit of hiding the large sum of money from Marion as their marriage started to become contentious. The agency business was moving away from numerous smaller agencies and began consolidating itself with mergers and acquisitions. A couple of years after Zeppo sold out, Phil Berg and Bert Allenberg sold the Berg-Allenberg Agency to the William Morris Agency. The two sales ushered in the end of the era of the small independent agent in Hollywood. Zeppo's first agency partner Frank Orsatti had died on May 19, 1947, laying to rest another of the successful independent agencies.

It was Zeppo's friendship and brief partnership with Orsatti that led to his association with many key figures in the Los Angeles underworld. In her posthumously published memoir *Speaking of Harpo*, Harpo's wife Susan wrote of her husband's involvement in a secret fundraising effort to purchase military equipment for Palestine in its fight to become the independent state of Israel and break free from British colonial rule.

An event organized by Mickey Cohen, the most powerful organized crime figure in Los Angeles, was held at Slapsie Maxie's, a popular Hollywood nightclub. Susan wrote, "Zeppo and Marion joined us for the evening and arrived a little after we did. I was surprised to see Zeppo cruise around the room greeting many of the scariest looking of Mickey Cohen's pals as if they had been lifelong friends. I asked Harpo about it and all he said was, 'Yeah. That's Zep.'"

It was clear to anyone paying attention that Zeppo had quietly become richer than all his brothers—perhaps even more than all of them combined. At the April 16, 1949, Motion Picture Relief Fund benefit at the Shrine Auditorium, comic Lou Holtz, as noted in the *Hollywood Reporter*, introduced Zeppo in the audience: "This is the one they said had no talent. He's got 12 million and the other three haven't got to eat." Of this prosperous period Tom said, "We lived in a house on Rexford Drive. It was a colonial. They had famous paintings and all this antique furniture. Then they decided they wanted to go modern, so, they built the house on North Beverly Drive. They designed it. It was totally modern, totally the opposite of the Rexford Drive house. It took a few years to build."

Zeppo spared no expense on the construction. Among the features of the 10,000-square-foot house were eight bedrooms, twelve bathrooms, radiant floor heating, an oversized pool, an indoor botanical garden and a solarium—all on a half-acre lot in a prime Beverly Hills location. Neighbors on the street included Jimmy Durante, Joanne Dru, and John Ireland. It was the sort of house normally built by the head of a studio or a wealthy industrialist. But the new house did not ease the tension between Zeppo and Marion.

Tim remembers,

They used to have arguments like you wouldn't believe. When we moved into 524 North Beverly, Tom had a room, and I had a room. And these rooms each had lofts where the pillows and blankets would go above the closet. And they would get into incredible arguments. My brother and I would get up in the lofts and close the doors. We were scared to death. She's screaming at him, and Tom and I are saying, "What a mean bastard Dad is to Mom." There was an intercom in each room and suddenly, we hear through the intercom, "Boys, I'd like to see you in the living room." "Oh, shit. He heard us." The trouble really started after the Rexford Drive house got sold. I don't think Marion ever wanted to sell that house, and she was annoyed that he was getting rid of all these things that they'd worked so hard to accumulate.

In October 1949, Zeppo's modern art collection—including works by Thomas Hart Benton, Maurice Utrillo, and Paul Clemens—was sold at an auction in San Francisco. A second auction of his collection took place in Chicago in January 1950. When the Rexford Drive house was sold, the family moved into a furnished rented home owned by actor Richard Whorf on Canon Drive. In February 1951 the antique furniture from the Rexford house was sold at auction. Before the new house was completed, they moved into another rented house on Rodeo Drive. "Wherever we lived," Tim says,

> they never slept in the same room. When I was a kid, he was always up way earlier than she was. I can remember standing in the bathroom watching him shave. And he was ready to go. Out of the house very early. And sometimes I wouldn't see him in the evening. Zeppo never played quite the role that Harpo did in terms of family. Susan and Harpo had the family that Marion would have liked to have had. I found myself many times thinking I wish he was more like Harpo because Harpo was much more genuine, and he was visible, and he was there. Zeppo ran a lot, so he wasn't always around.

Tim and Tom grew up surrounded by celebrity and privilege, but barely experienced any of the benefits of that lifestyle. Tim recalls, "As a family, we existed, not as celebrity people, but just as a normal family, living in a town where everybody was a celebrity." Beverly Hills may have been full of celebrity children, but very few of them could say their uncles were the Marx Brothers. Tom remembers,

> We used to see Chico quite a lot. I remember him more than I do all the others. He and this woman he lived with, Mary Dee, would come over. As kids, we related to his sense of humor. Chico was one of the funniest people I knew. I just didn't get my father's sense of humor. It seemed mean and it just bounced off me. Probably the same reason I didn't really relate to Groucho. I only saw Groucho twice in my life—once in Beverly Hills and once in Palm Springs when we were older. We didn't see Gummo that much. He would come over maybe once a month. We used to call him Uncle Bubble-Gummo because he used to bring us bubble gum. We didn't have a lot of interaction with him, but he was a very nice man. He and Harpo seemed to me the nicest of all of them.

Tom's recollections of Zeppo and Marion are much darker than Tim's:

> They weren't around. We were raised by a bunch of maids and nannies. Every now and then we'd go out to dinner with our parents, maybe once every three or four months. And we had to be on our best behavior. We

were told what to wear. We couldn't order our own food. Total domination. Zeppo never went to a movie, or played baseball with us, he didn't come to any of my little league games. I would only see him every now and then at night. We ate in the kitchen. We were fed by maids.

Tim's experience in the same house with the same parents brings forth another *Rashomon*-like scenario in Zeppo's life. While Tom has no memory of sharing anything with Zeppo, Tim recalls

hanging out in the shop at the back of the house. It was a pool house, but that's where all his stuff was. It was fun to go back there and watch him work. Just sit and watch. He would put something together and I'd just say, "wow." I enjoy that. I think I got that from him. If I take something away from Zeppo, it's that I was always interested in seeing how things worked. He was fascinated by how things worked.

Tom remembers being forbidden from going near Zeppo's electric trains at the Rexford house. "Above the garage, Zeppo and some cop who was a friend of his, built a whole model train layout. It was huge. But of course, we couldn't play with it."

Tim recalls,

Zeppo had some friends that would meet in the evening to build trains, elaborate little towns, mountains, and things like that. At various locations on the platform, they could stick their heads up to see where the trains were and work on the thing. One of the guys who was scared to death of the dog would park in the alley next to the garage, come through the gate, sprint up the steps screaming "open the door"—barely escaping a nip or two as the growling dog chased him. Zeppo eventually pulled the guy aside and said, "Look, next time you come, bring a newspaper and the dog will back off and not bother you." The following week the guy shows up, parks, and comes through the gate with the same result. Zeppo says, "I told you to bring a newspaper to scare the dog." Barely able to speak and ashen, the guy says, "I did what you told me, Zep. I came in the gate, saw the dog and unfolded the paper, reading it as I got to the stairs. Your dog wasn't the least bit scared."

Tim recalls a few rare occasions when Zeppo would help them build model trains and let them run them on the track, but generally Zeppo's train set was off limits. Zeppo's enthusiasm for model trains was such that when a Beverly Hills train shop was expecting some new limited edition Lionel train cars to arrive, he and fellow model train lover Ben Hecht pestered the shopkeeper almost daily trying to get first crack at the new stuff. Hecht curried favor by giving the owner of the store signed copies of his books, and even getting his daughter a bit part in a movie he was writing.

The day the Lionel delivery arrived at the store Hecht was there before they opened. He was disappointed to walk in and see Zeppo behind the counter. Zeppo greeted him saying, "You're out of luck, Ben. I just bought the store." Another man with Zeppo's resources, two young sons, and a world class model train set would put that all together, somehow. But rather than bring him closer to Tom and Tim, the train set demonstrated, as well as anything else in his life, Zeppo's inherent selfishness and desire for control.

While Tom was more adversely affected by Zeppo's controlling nature, Tim came to understand it and was much better at dealing with it as they grew up. "He wanted things done a certain way," says Tim. "Zeppo at times was a 'my way or the highway' type of guy. He was orderly in that regard. You didn't much mess with that. He was the boss. He was in charge of our lives in every facet. There were a lot of people that knew Zeppo and Marion who said it was probably not a good idea for them to become parents." This perspective was an effective survival mechanism for Tim, who shared Zeppo's interest in mechanical things and enjoyed being with him in his workshop. Tom rejected the idea of doing anything his father enjoyed.

One aspect of childhood that Tom and Tim agree was similar for them was their Uncle Harpo. Tim envied life at Harpo and Susan's house. "Whenever I went to Harpo's house, and I'd see Minnie, Jimmy and Alex I almost felt like that was home." Tom concurs: "We were good friends with Jimmy, Alex and Minnie. We used to go over there quite a bit. They had a pool table, so we used to go over there and play pool. Sometimes my mother would be over there with us, but mostly we would just go. Or I would just go. My brother and I never really hung out together."

Beverly Hills was an insular community, and everyone knew each other. The boys had a certain amount of freedom as a result of having bicycles and Zeppo and Marion mostly not being around. They each had their own friends and although only ten months apart in age, there wasn't much if any overlap in their groups of friends. They rode their bicycles to and from Hawthorne Elementary

School and their days were generally without parental supervision. Zeppo was usually at the Marman plant in Inglewood and Marion was at the Beverly Hills Tennis Club almost every day.

As their marriage deteriorated, Zeppo and Marion showed even less interest in Tom and Tim. According to Tom, "Neither of them ever went to any of the things we did. Never went to parent-teacher nights at school, or any of that." Zeppo began spending a lot of time in Las Vegas, leaving Marion to deal with the boys. Tim remembers the heated arguments over Zeppo's frequent trips: "She would always scream at him when he got back from Vegas, 'You whore-monger, you bastard.' There was a big problem."

In April 1949, Zeppo had purchased an interest in the El Rancho Vegas hotel and casino on the Las Vegas strip. Opened in 1941, El Rancho Vegas was the first casino on Highway 91—before it was known as The Strip—to include a hotel. The original ownership group included Zeppo's old friend from the Clover Club, Milton "Farmer" Page. Zeppo bought Page's share—either with some of the surplus cash from the not-so-secret agency deal, or as payment for Page's gambling losses.

According to a June 9, 1949, *Los Angeles Daily News* story, Zeppo's time as a casino owner was brief. "Marx, in the past 60 days has been in and out of El Rancho Vegas Hotel. He reportedly bought in on behalf of himself and his more publicized brothers, and recently disposed of his interest to his partners in the operation, who include a group of the city's more prominent gamblers."

The quick turnaround certainly suggests there's something to the theory that Milton "Farmer" Page owed Zeppo a hefty amount of money and Zeppo sold Page's El Rancho Vegas shares to get his money. The same *Daily News* story told of a remarkable run of luck by Zeppo at the dice table of the Golden Nugget: "In an early morning session, at which Marx was at one time several thousand dollars in the hole, Zeppo capitalized on a fantastic 45-minute winning streak by a club shill and emerged with winnings admittedly in excess of $50,000."

On June 15, the *Daily News* published a letter from Zeppo: "On Thursday, June 9, you published a story stating that I had won in excess of $50,000 in some gambling hall in Las Vegas. Actually, the amount I won was $3,200. Since this published story is incorrect and has caused me some embarrassment, I would appreciate it very much if you would publish a correction of the story."

A year later when Zeppo had an amazingly similar run of luck, the story ran in papers across the country. Syndicated columnist Florabel Muir wrote in the *Los Angeles Mirror* on June 12, 1950, "Those 28 passes at the dice table you read about were made at the Desert Inn. Gus Greenbaum and Zeppo Marx were the two guys who lined their pockets betting with the lucky crapshooter. Gus got $35,000 and Zep $56,000 backing the guy's play."

Zeppo wrote no letters to the editor this time. Too many papers carried the story. He would have been asking hundreds of newspapers to run corrections. More concerning than the amount he won was the linking of Zeppo to notorious gangster Gus Greenbaum, a longtime associate of the even more famous gangster, Meyer Lansky. Greenbaum was one of the men who had taken over the Flamingo Hotel after the assassination of Bugsy Siegel. Zeppo's mob ties were at the highest level. Tim explains, "He wasn't a 'made' guy, but he was a connected guy. Connected all the way up to the top."

The company Zeppo kept was starting to worry his brothers, who according to Harpo's son Bill, threatened to disown him, a process by which the brothers could assure there would be no connection between Zeppo and their assets. Adding to his brothers' concerns, Zeppo was still getting attention in the press for his frequent involvement in public fistfights. When he attended the July 6, 1951 Manny Madrid–Chu Chu Jimenez fight at Hollywood Legion Stadium, Zeppo—not the boxers in the ring—made the headlines.

The *Los Angeles Times* reported on the action the next day: "The 3,500 fans were treated to a bonus bout of sorts during the seventh round of the feature. Zeppo Marx of the Marx Brothers got the bum's rush from the stadium cop after swinging a couple of times at *Mirror* photog Neil Clements. Marx complained that Clements's camera was obstructing his view. Clements didn't complain. He just kept shooting pictures."

When they weren't discussing the prospect of disowning Zeppo, his brothers liked the idea of being in business with him. In March 1950 all five Marx brothers became the largest individual investors in a limited partnership with around a dozen other investors called Stekoll Oil and Associates, Ltd. The plan was to develop land in Northern Texas for oil exploration. Texas oilman Marion Stekoll was the head of the operation and among the investors were friends George Burns and Norman Krasna. Drilling for oil was as much of a gamble as any game Zeppo played in Las Vegas, but many wealthy celebrities got into the oil business as a tax shelter, knowing they'd lose money for at least a little while. Chico, who always seemed to bet against the odds, might have been the only investor thinking he'd strike oil immediately. The other brothers—particularly Groucho and Zeppo—needed some business deductions that would ease their hefty tax burdens.

Zeppo's losses, as occasionally reported in the press, kept his balance sheet reconciled. In a December 1947 column from Miami, Ed Sullivan wrote,

In the top card games here, the big players insist on washable decks of cards—so none of the players yields to the temptation to mark them. Noted player who was reputed to have won $400,000 from Chico Marx, Zeppo Marx and coast bookies Mooney and Lou Levy at gin rummy a year ago, playing gin rummy for $40 a point, is the biggest bettor on the Florida scene, and his presence here is a cinch to attract other high rollers."

Zeppo's concern about his winnings getting into the press may not have been unfounded. On May 10, 1952, the British magazine *Picturegoer* ran this item:

It happened to Zeppo Marx. Somebody recognized him the night he was in on a lucky streak. The Marx "make" made print and Uncle Sam made more than 40,000 in additional taxes. Was Marx mad!

Zeppo had become an important and influential man in Las Vegas. For Labor Day weekend in 1952, he invited a group of friends to be his guests at the Flamingo Hotel. The group included Groucho and his new twenty-two-year-old girlfriend, and future third wife, Eden Hartford, Norman Krasna and his wife, and Arthur Sheekman and his wife, actress Gloria Stuart, who remembered the trip in her memoirs:

Zep was up in Vegas a great deal (we always wondered if he was in a gambling syndicate). It was a very crowded weekend, and our hotel, one of the most popular in town, was jammed with people. Reservations, of course, were very tight, but because we were with The Boys, we had a lovely room.

While I unpacked, Arthur went downstairs to the little credit kiosk, and they asked what his limit was. He didn't want to seem excessive—but he also didn't want to be extravagant. Instead of saying, "The sky!" which was his style, he said, "Two hundred dollars." Well, by the time he got back to the room, the hotel had made a terrible mistake! The manager had made a terrible mistake! The desk clerk had made a terrible mistake and our room had been rented! The message was we had to vacate by 3 PM! Of course, they wanted it for the high rollers. We had to get hold of Zeppo. It was early in the afternoon, Zeppo was nowhere in sight, and Groucho couldn't help us. It was only Zep that could. We had him paged, we left messages on his phone, we knocked on his door and slipped notes under it, and started repacking. Finally Zep surfaced and we were allowed to keep our room.

His friends needn't have worried. Zeppo was enough of a high roller to cover a few nice rooms at the Flamingo.

CHAPTER NINETEEN

Boys Will Be Boys

WHILE THE FAMILY LIVED AT 702 NORTH RODEO DRIVE, THE SEC-ond home Zeppo rented during the construction of the North Beverly Drive house, Tom became very close with one of his little league teammates, Robbie Sedway. Robbie's father was Moe Sedway, who had become Gus Greenbaum's partner in the Flamingo Hotel following the death of Bugsy Siegel a few years earlier. It may be coincidental that Zeppo rented a home just a short bike ride from the Sedways, but he was well acquainted with Moe Sedway from his frequent trips to Las Vegas.

Tom recalls,

The thing that I was happy about during my childhood was the friends that I had. I had this one friend, Robbie Sedway. He was the son of Moe Sedway, the manager of the Flamingo Hotel. In other words, he was mob. He was my best friend, and I was over there every day. We played baseball and football together.

Tom and Tim were too young to understand or have knowledge of the connection between the 1947 killing of Bugsy Siegel and the Sedway family, but Robbie Sedway shared details of the notoriously unsolved murder in the October 2014 issue of *Los Angeles Magazine*. It has generally been assumed that Siegel was killed by order of Meyer Lansky for spending the mob's money too freely—while probably taking some for himself—and going way over budget in building the Flamingo. Bee Sedway, wife of Moe and mother of Robbie, told a different story that she took to her grave. When Robbie was dying of cancer, he broke a long-standing promise never to tell.

Moe Sedway was the man watching the mob's money when Siegel brought his Las Vegas vision to life as elaborately as possible. Siegel tired of Sedway constantly bothering him about the spending and called a secret meeting with his associates. He told them he wanted to have Moe Sedway killed. Word got back to the Sedways. Bee and Moe realized they had to have Siegel killed first before he killed Moe. Bee suggested that they have Matthew "Moose" Pandza do the job. Moe knew that Pandza, a crane operator and small-time bookmaker with no connections to the mob, was having an affair with Bee. Moe wasn't much concerned with that since he himself was having as many affairs as time would allow during his frequent trips to Las Vegas. This was one of the main attractions to the town for Zeppo as well. Marion would have been relieved to learn that all Zeppo did in Las Vegas was gamble.

The theory that Lansky had Siegel killed over money is questionable. The Flamingo posted a $250,000 profit after a rough start just as Siegel was about to meet his fate, but some accounts suggest that the profitable period was temporary. Robbie Sedway provided his mother's proposal for a never-published book to *Los Angeles Magazine* in 2014. In it she quoted an attendee of the Siegel meeting in Las Vegas repeating Bugsy's plan to her: "I'll have Moe shot, chop his body up, and feed it to the Flamingo Hotel's garbage disposal." Bugsy Siegel was killed on June 20, 1947, when a lone gunman fired several shots through the living room window of his girlfriend's house in Beverly Hills as he sat on the sofa reading a newspaper. Bee Sedway died in 1996 with the secret that her boyfriend, Moose Pandza, was the gunman. It was only when Robbie Sedway was dying that he decided the secret should not die with him. Yet the Sedway story has not resulted in the Bugsy Siegel murder case being considered solved. But, of course, Bee Sedway's version of the events cannot be verified. It remains one of several theories.[1]

Moe Sedway suffered a heart attack in 1952 at the age of fifty-seven while flying to Miami with his mistress. He died the following day. Bee, who had married Moe when she was seventeen, became a thirty-three-year-old widow. At Sedway's funeral, Zeppo and his brothers were honorary pallbearers along with several other notable Hollywood figures including George Raft, Dean Martin, Jerry Lewis, Eddie Cantor, Danny Thomas, and Tony Martin. Moose Pandza was one of the actual pallbearers. When Zeppo and Marion finally moved into 524 North Beverly Drive, Bee Sedway and Moose Pandza were living at 614 North Beverly—the same house where Bee had lived with Moe. Eventually people in the neighborhood—including Tom and Tim—assumed that Moose was the father of Robbie and his older brother Richard. In Robbie's case people close to the family who knew Moe suspected that Moose was Robbie's biological father.

Robbie told *Los Angeles Magazine* that they were regularly visited by FBI agents after the Siegel murder. Neighborhood parents warned their children not to go to that house or to associate with those boys, but Zeppo and Marion made no such requests. They may not have even known about Tom's friendship with Robbie. Tim and Tom both recall Moose Pandza fondly as a neighbor who let them use his pool. If he was Bugsy Siegel's killer, he was also, by all other accounts, a very nice guy who occasionally played ball with the neighborhood kids. His only major brush with the law came in 1953 when he knocked Bee down in a Sunset Boulevard bar and assaulted the police officer who came in to assist her.

The FBI had other business in Beverly Hills in the wake of the Bugsy Siegel killing. The Clover Club remained one of the town's most popular gambling joints and offered a nearby convenience to its wealthy, famous customers—a very high-class brothel. Just above the Sunset Strip on Harold Way, less than half a mile from the Clover Club, Marie Mitchell—alias Brenda Allen—operated her business with the full knowledge and support of the Los Angeles Police Department. Several high-ranking members of the police force were on her payroll and many others were clients. She was also affiliated with Mickey Cohen, the most powerful mobster in town.

She was naturally shocked when her place was raided on May 4, 1948. She told the officers who arrested her that she would have their jobs. She was not entirely incorrect in that statement, as later there would be firings and resignations at very high levels of the department as a result of the case. But she had been too confident in her position and had offered an attractive young woman she spotted in the neighborhood an opportunity to make some easy money. The woman turned out to be a police officer who, without the knowledge that half of the vice squad was on Brenda Allen's payroll, thought she had discovered the biggest prostitution ring in the city.

The *Los Angeles Times* reported on May 6, 1948, "Hollywood was agog yesterday over a black card index file confiscated by vice squad policemen who late Tuesday night arrested three young women and a man on morals charges." The unfortunate man was not famous, but he was identified in the press as a movie producer. Benjamin Berk was actually a prop man and later a production manager at 20th Century Fox, hardly the type of Hollywood celebrity the newspapers implied would be named. *The San Francisco Examiner* reported that police "seized a 'little black book' which officers said would rock Hollywood to its foundations if its contents were revealed." The press ran daily stories about the Brenda Allen client file and there were demands it be released to the public. The *Times* report said, "On the cards containing names of many notables of the film colony, were written dates of the visits, the hostess who entertained the guest and the fees charged." There was no shortage of powerful people in city government, the police force and the organized crime community that did not want Brenda Allen's client file released. Mickey Cohen even had audio recordings of Allen discussing her business with high-level police department officials as insurance against this sort of problem. But the press would not let go of the story. The *Los Angeles Daily News* reported,

> [O]n occasion the entire organization was put at the disposal, for a staggering price, of some flush potentate of the moving picture mecca. …The hosts of such royal bacchanals as these supposedly were the men of wealth and prominence in Hollywood screen and radio circles whose names constitute the special gilt-edged client list detectives found among Brenda's carefully kept records.

While Brenda Allen's client list remained out of the public eye, men who knew they were on it had to notice an important line in the *Daily News* story: "[O]fficers may drop around at some of the movie city's most respectable homes in the course of the investigation."

Marion was aware by this point of Zeppo's chronic womanizing, but he had managed never to humiliate her publicly. To the relief of numerous important Hollywood figures, municipal judge Joseph Call sealed the file in August 1948, instructing the court clerk that the file "contains the names of dignitaries in the radio and motion picture field and of prominent executives. Public disclosure of its contents would be ruinous to the careers and private lives of these men. Seal it well, Mr. Clerk, and see that it stays sealed."

The names were never made public, but the FBI took an interest and made its own investigation. Among the names listed in the FBI files are stars Orson Welles, Mickey Rooney, and George Jessel; restaurateur Mike Romanoff; producer Hal Roach Jr., the owner of the Downbeat nightclub; the owner of the Orpheum theater chain; and several agents. Everett Crosby—brother and agent of Bing Crosby—Ernie Orsatti and Zeppo Marx were the most well-known agents in Brenda Allen's little black book. Zeppo's address was recorded as 8732 Sunset Boulevard, the office of Marx, Miller & Marx, so when the FBI came calling, the agency had been out of business for almost a year. But Zeppo was not difficult to find.

In June 1951, Marman Products was doing well enough to expand. The increased demand for aircraft parts coincided with the August 1950 congressional approval of $12 billion for United States military activity in Korea. The Defense Production Act of 1950 authorized the Reconstruction Finance Corporation to lend money to defense contractors that wanted to expand their operations. Zeppo applied for and received a $1.25 million loan to Marman, which he used to purchase the land and build a second plant at 11214 Exposition Boulevard in West Los Angeles. The new facility increased Marman's capacity by 300 percent.

Even though his company's success was primarily the result of being a defense contractor, Zeppo continued searching for that magical product that would secure a position for Marman as the manufacturer of something useful to the general population. On June 14, 1950, he submitted a patent application for his vapor delivery pad for distributing moist heat. The therapeutic use of heating pads presented challenges at this time and Zeppo's invention offered solutions for several of the problems. His application provides details for regulating constant temperatures and describes the use of flexible materials that would allow the pad to be wrapped around limbs. The patent was granted on March 18, 1952, but Zeppo did not go any further with the development of his heating pad. With a second plant in operation Zeppo employed a workforce of 450. It was the latest example of his inability to rest on his laurels. Tim says,

> Zeppo was the kind of guy who would ask an Olympic gold medalist, "What's your follow up? Where do you go from there?" Zeppo would build a house and collect all the paintings and all the fine furniture and then say, "Now what do I do for an encore?" So, the encore was, "I'll build a state-of-the-art house on North Beverly Drive that has an indoor tropical garden where it would rain at the flip of a switch." Every floor had a warming pipe underneath it where hot water would go through and warm the floors."

On January 14, 1952, Zeppo's picture was on the front page of the *Los Angeles Times*. It was not the sort of publicity that would make his brothers forget about disowning him. The *Times* reported, "An early morning sidewalk fracas involving one-time actor Zeppo Marx, youngest of the Marx Brothers, and film producer Alex Gottlieb was interrupted yesterday by Beverly Hills police. Officers said they found a strong argument in progress, complete with the swinging of wild roundhouse punches on the sidewalk at the corner of Rodeo Drive and Wilshire Boulevard."

After being hauled off to the Beverly Hills Police Station with their wives, neither combatant wanted to press charges. Marion told police that Gottlieb approached her and said, "If that punk husband of yours doesn't leave me alone, there'll be trouble." Gottlieb's wife Polly—the sister of producer Billy Rose—was knocked to the ground trying to break up the fight. Zeppo's explanation was that Gottlieb had threatened him over the phone about a gambling debt and the dispute had been festering for around a year. The day after the fracas Billy Rose was quoted in the *Hollywood Reporter* about his sister getting roughed up: "That Zeppo can lick any chorus girl in town."

Zeppo's temper had resulted in previous public brawls—and they always seemed to end up in the newspaper. But he also was known to become violent at home over the slightest infraction by Tom or Tim, who says, "You could fart and get hit. It was always with the big brush. He would say, 'Drop your pants. You're going to get hit.'" A fancy new house and the expansion of Marman Products did not make life at home any better for Zeppo, Marion, Tom, and Tim. Tom notes that Robbie Sedway enjoyed the benefits of being from a wealthy family:

> He always had the best of everything. With us they would say, "Do we have to buy him a new bike?" We had the same bikes for so long they became too small for us, and we couldn't even ride them. But we finally got new bikes. They hated to spend money on us.

Tim does not recall his bike ever being too small, but he had other problems at home. "Zeppo was the disciplinarian when we were young. Marion didn't like it at all. She thought he was over the top with it. And she would say, 'Zeppo, come on. Enough.'" Tom recalls, "Marion wasn't as strict as Zeppo. She'd say, 'Boys will be boys.' One time my friends and I got into a tulip fight in a park on Santa Monica Boulevard. The cops came and hauled us off and called the parents. That was $500. That was a big deal. I got punished a lot for that." Tim adds, "As we got older, Marion became the disciplinarian, and she had a terrible temper."

Tim has an indelible childhood memory of innocently setting off Zeppo's temper when his father asked him to fetch a beer. At around the age of six Tim wasn't even sure what a beer was. Zeppo explained, "It's Pabst Blue Ribbon. You'll see a big blue ribbon on the can." Tim found the beer in the refrigerator and put it on the floor. He kicked it toward the dining room where he picked it up and handed it to Zeppo, who had not noticed how Tim transported the can. Tim says,

He thanked me and opened it. The beer shot straight up to the ceiling and began dripping down on his head. He turned to me and said, "What did you do? Did you shake this up?" I said I hadn't and when pressed further I told him I had kicked it into the room. My mother was laughing hysterically, almost falling off her chair at the other end of the table. Tom was mortified, thinking I might get killed. My father was steaming and just couldn't say anything.

Zeppo was not the sort of parent who could find humor in a child not knowing the result of kicking a can of beer across the floor. Zeppo's hair-trigger temper could be set off by anything. Marion told Tim of an evening when she and Zeppo were watching *What's My Line?* on television. One of the panelists guessed the contestant's occupation a little too quickly for Zeppo. He began shouting that the game was rigged and hurled a shoe at the television set.

In consideration of the conditions at home described by Tom and Tim, it defies logic that Zeppo and Marion would find themselves defendants in a lawsuit that alleged they failed to exercise adequate parental control over one of their sons. But the fact that this happened essentially confirms the boys' recollections that they were on their own during the day once school let out.

On September 13, 1953, Tim was throwing rocks and hit eight-year-old Denise Singer, the girl who lived across the street at 517 North Beverly Drive, just above her left eye. Her father Mortimer Singer—described in the press as an oil company executive—filed a $300,000 lawsuit against Zeppo, Marion, and Tim. The suit claimed that Zeppo and Marion were negligent because they failed to control Tim's known penchant for throwing rocks at people. The extent of the girl's injury was not clear from newspaper accounts, but Denise Singer Vogel says,

I was struck above the eye, and it caused hemorrhaging behind the eye. I was in Children's Hospital for about ten days and ended up having four surgeries to save the eye. I had nothing but eye specialists for years after that. I was left with limited vision and a permanently dilated eye. As a child it was embarrassing because my eye looked different, and kids would tease me.

There's no doubt that Tim threw the rock that hit and injured Denise Singer. But there's a pretty good chance that the exorbitant financial recovery sought in the lawsuit may have had something to do with syndicated columnist E. V. Durling's September 5, 1953, item—published only days before the incident—that noted, "Zeppo Marx is by far the richest of the Marx Brothers." Denise recalls her father's reaction to the incident. "He was livid and was going to go as far as necessary to get revenge."

As for Tom and Tim, Denise recalls, "They were both little hellions in the neighborhood. Zeppo and Marion would go off on vacations and leave the housekeepers to watch them and they didn't watch them very closely." Mortimer Singer had every reason to be angry and was totally justified in filing a lawsuit. The timing of the incident and the newspaper article added up to an expensive problem for Zeppo.

To Zeppo it seemed as though everyone was after his considerable fortune. A year earlier there had been trouble with organized labor at the new Marman plant. The contract between Marman and the International Association of Machinists had expired on August 31, 1952. The union demanded a fifty-cent hourly wage increase for tool and die makers and a ten-cent hourly increase for all other workers. Marman offered a five-cent hourly increase for all workers and adjustments for some classifications of machinists. Tool and die makers were being paid $2.25 per hour at the time. Negotiations broke off and the workers went on strike at both Marman plants on September 14.

During the labor negotiations, A. Dale Herman retired from his position at Vickers and became the vice president and general manager of Marman. Zeppo began to see the growing company as too much trouble—a situation that replicated his experience with the Zeppo Marx Agency when he turned over the management of the company to Alan Miller. The strike at Marman came as news of the recently completed expansion of the West Los Angeles plant was reported in the *West Los Angeles Independent*:

> Increased demand for the company's line of engineered clamps, straps and couplings is given as the reason for the expanded facilities. . . . Today the largest manufacturer in its field in the United States, Marman has developed a line of standardized products which formerly required special designs. Among these is the famous V-Band coupling [the Marman Clamp] which has largely replaced the old bolt type of fastening device for ducting on aircraft. Production is now five times the pre-Korean level and employment has increased to 700.

Mass pickets and acts of violence at both Marman plants eventually resulted in a judge issuing a restraining order prohibiting the picketing. A. Dale Herman's daughter, Rita Mae Joyce recalls, "My father was worried. He told me and my sister to be careful going to the bus stop and around school." The Herman family lived in Encino, twenty miles from the picketing at Marman, but everyone was uneasy about the violence. Marman petitioned the National Labor Relations Board for an election to determine whether the union represented the Marman workers. The union withdrew its claim of representation and several of its members were cited for contempt of court for violating the restraining order. Could some of Zeppo's friends have used their influence with the union? He'd been involved in the organization of the Hollywood talent agencies and their affiliation with labor unions as a form of leverage with the studios, so he knew this game well. It was a mess, but Marman resumed normal operations.

Rita Mae Joyce would occasionally accompany her father to Marman:

I remember going on weekends. There would be nobody there. Dad had some business to work on and I would wander around. Zeppo had a very pretty office with sliding glass doors. Outside the glass doors was a Doberman Pinscher watchdog named Slim. Dad would say, "Don't get too close to the doors because Slim might throw himself into the glass and break it." It was a lavish, modern office. Very showy. Zeppo's desk was quite large, but he wasn't there that much. My father pretty much ran everything.

She also remembers Zeppo taking her and her father on a tour of the North Beverly Drive house during the construction. "We went over there a couple of times to see the progress on the house. Zeppo was very nice, walked us through the house and told us what each room would be."

Zeppo took a less active role in the company after the 1952 strike. In early 1954 he sold the Inglewood plant and consolidated Marman's business to the expanding West Los Angeles location. He commented on the company in the July 12, 1954, issue of *Newsweek*:

When a person can take his hobby and turn it into his primary business interest, as I have been fortunate enough to do, he has few worries over what he will do when he retires. Ever since I worked as a mechanic in an eastern automobile plant, I have been an avid home-workshop enthusiast.

With labor strife at Marman taken care of there was still the matter of Tim's rock-throwing case going to trial. Zeppo and Marion fought constantly during this period, and Zeppo frequently fled to Las Vegas as the marriage deteriorated. Tom recalls, "When we were on Rodeo Drive, I remember hearing them fighting a lot in that house. That was around a year before we moved into the new house. I don't think we lasted even six months on Beverly before they got divorced."

CHAPTER TWENTY

The Other Marx Brothers

O N MARCH 19, 1954, MARION TRAVELED TO LAS VEGAS AND FILED FOR divorce on the grounds of cruelty. The minimal six-week residency requirement in Nevada provided the fastest way out of the marriage. The barely lived in house at 524 North Beverly Drive was sold to producer Harry Tugend for $150,000—a relative bargain considering the opulence of the home and its features.

Zeppo rented an apartment in Beverly Hills and a house in Palm Springs. He made plans to build his new permanent residence at Tamarisk Country Club near Palm Springs. Regarding the divorce, Zeppo's statement to the press was short: "We're friends, but we're better living apart." He made no mention of what was better for Tom and Tim. Tom says,

> During this time we were being punished a lot. We were both getting into a lot of trouble. My mother didn't want to deal with two misbehaving kids and a divorce, so they just packed us off to military school. It was one of the things that totally ruined my life. I was never the same after that. A lot of freedom, and then suddenly—BAM! Military school where there's zero freedom. You're told what to do every minute of the day.

The boys were pulled out of Hawthorne Elementary School near the end of the spring semester, just before Marion left for Las Vegas. She and Zeppo sent them to Mount Lowe Military Academy in Altadena, around thirty miles from Beverly Hills. Ten-year-old Tom was in the fifth grade and nine-year-old Tim, the fourth. Set at the foot of the Sierra Madre mountains on thirty-six acres, the bucolic setting of Mount Lowe Military Academy offered no hint at what life there would be like for Tom and Tim.

Tim says, "When they were in the final stages of the divorce, we briefly visited Marion in Las Vegas and then we got sent away to this place that turned out to be a 24/7, twelve months a year tour for a couple of years. We never had any contact with Zeppo about it. We just got shipped out to Altadena." If the boys expected any of the comforts of home, the closest they came was the eavesdropping equipment installed in the dorm rooms. Like Zeppo, the headmaster of the school, Major John Hayden Dargin, listened in on the boys' conversations.

The atmosphere was more like a prison than a school, with barbed wire at the top of the fences. Other adopted children of Hollywood celebrities were also sent to Mount Lowe, including Roy Rogers Jr. and his brother Sandy. In July 1955, twelve-year-old Christopher Crawford, son of Joan Crawford, escaped from Mount Lowe with another cadet. They were apprehended five miles away by sheriff's deputies and brought back several hours later. It was young Crawford's fourth such escape. Other cadets were known to rub poison oak on their faces hoping it would get them sent home. For the peace of mind of having Tom and Tim basically incarcerated, Zeppo and Marion paid $95 per month for each boy. Tim says,

> When we got to military school, Tom took it very seriously. Within a year or so he was a second lieutenant. I got to be a sergeant or a corporal, or some crap like that. They had a battlefield, and there were bunkers, and we'd have war games. Tom blamed me for getting us sent to military school, probably because of the rock throwing incident. But it was Zeppo and Marion trying to figure out what they were going to do with their lives. They didn't want us around while they were figuring that out.

The divorce became final on May 17, 1954. It marked the end of an era during which Marion had carved out a place for herself in the Hollywood hierarchy without even an inkling of a career of her own. She was a dear friend and confidant to many and was trusted with the most sensitive information in Hollywood. Columnist Ed Sullivan, writing in the *Hollywood Citizen-News* in 1940, when leaving Hollywood to return to New York, praised Marion with words that would have seemed appropriate fourteen years later as she and Zeppo split up: "I'll miss pert Marion Marx, good-looking frau of the Zeppo, and her breezy ad libs on the passing parade of celebs."

There was a property settlement involving corporation stocks and other assets. Marion received a significant number of shares in Marman Products and half of the proceeds from the sale of 524 North Beverly Drive. It's unclear whether she was able to document any proceeds from the sale of the agency. Zeppo would pay $1,000 a month for Marion's support and $200 a month for child support—which basically covered the cost of Tom and Tim being at Mount Lowe. Marion rented an apartment on Doheny Drive and kept her membership at the Beverly Hills Tennis Club. Tom recalls, "The club was her whole life. All her friends were there, and she went every day. Zeppo never went there much. He had his own club, which was Hillcrest Country Club, where he played golf. I was there maybe once."

Marion would maintain relationships with Zeppo's brothers and their wives for many years. She'd been part of the family since the Broadway days and was especially close with Harpo and Susan. They all knew Zeppo hadn't treated Marion well for years and offered their support while remaining loyal to Zeppo. Loyalty ran deep in the Marx family, but a divorce didn't preclude them from staying in touch with an ex-wife or two.

Groucho had great respect for Marion and recognized all she had done for Zeppo. They had a warm, if intermittent, correspondence over the years. By the time Zeppo and Marion split up Groucho had a couple of ex-wives himself. Two months after their divorce was finalized Groucho married for the third time. Eden Hartford was born three years after Zeppo and Marion were married. She was forty years younger than Groucho. In an unpublished memoir she wrote in the early 1980s, Eden compared her husband and brother-in-law:

> Zeppo and Groucho were the most alike in temperament of the brothers but that is where the resemblance ended. Zeppo was an ardent card player for high stakes and a member of the Friars Club in Beverly Hills—a club especially for card players. Groucho could never understand how people could spend half the day and sometimes night playing cards. A congenial evening of five-card stud or draw poker at Harpo's mixed with an equal number of jokes was his limit. When Zeppo invited Groucho to the Friars Club for lunch one day he was appalled. Groucho came home after that lunch looking perplexed.
>
> "The Friars Club asked me to become a member. Do you know who I sat next to at lunch? My barber and my tailor. Afterwards they all played cards. I had to get a ride home. There wasn't a comedian in the crowd."

I had to laugh at the picture it brought to mind, but Groucho was serious. "Take a letter." I sat down at the typewriter. "Gentlemen, I don't care to be a member of a club where I have lunch with my barber and my tailor, and as for playing cards . . ." He stopped.

"If I write that letter, I'll never get a decent haircut or a suit that fits. Forget it. I'll sleep on it." He did and the next morning he had me write the oft-quoted line: "I do not care to belong to any club that will accept me as a member."

While Marion was in Las Vegas, Zeppo began dating Joyce Niven, a twenty-four-year-old model. Within a couple of weeks of the divorce decree coming through, they began being frequently seen together around Hollywood and Las Vegas. By the spring of 1955 the gossip columns began suggesting they would soon be married. If Miss Niven was interested in Zeppo's money, there would soon be a lot more of it. On March 31, 1955, Zeppo sold Marman Products to another defense contractor, the Aeroquip Corporation of Jackson, Michigan. The May 1955 issue of Aeroquip's company magazine *The Flying A*, described Marman's operation for its employees.

Marman Products Company manufactures clamps, couplings and straps and is recognized as a leader in that field. A line of check-valves and flanges was recently introduced for use with hot-air ducting and fuel lines on aircraft, chemical and food processing appliances.

Seventy-five percent of the Company's total volume goes to assemblers for inclusion on aircraft, and an additional ten percent is sold directly to air force bases and replacement depots. Industrial and commercial concerns in the United States, Canada, Europe and Australia account for the remaining fifteen percent of Marman's production. Practically all aircraft products are manufactured of stainless steel for airframe and engine application on jet aircraft. Gross sales for the last twelve months totaled approximately four and a half million dollars.

Marman had clearly become the most successful concern Zeppo was ever involved with. He liked and admired Aeroquip founder Peter F. Hurst, a German immigrant who started his company in much the same way that Zeppo started Marman. Most importantly for Zeppo, Hurst—like Lew Wasserman and Jules Stein in the MCA acquisition of Marx, Miller & Marx—agreed to keep the terms of the sale confidential. Veteran Aeroquip employees Mike Lefere and Al Wagner recall the deal being worth between $2.5 and $3 million in cash and stock.[1] Zeppo was proud that Aeroquip kept the Marman name active in its product line for decades and was pleased to maintain some interest through his Aeroquip stock.[2]

One small detail needed to be taken care of before the transaction could be completed. Marman's contract with James T. King stipulated that Marman could not transfer rights in King's clamp patent without his permission. On July 20, 1955, King and Marman agreed to retroactively terminate the 1948 contract effective May 31, 1955. This allowed King to make his own deal with Aeroquip. King would continue to receive royalties on the clamp, but Zeppo's assertion that King became phenomenally wealthy was greatly exaggerated. James T. King died in 1966 at the age of seventy-six with no indication that he became wealthy as a result of his association with Zeppo or Marman.

A. Dale Herman was not interested in working for Aeroquip and left to start his own company closer to his home in Encino. There were no hard feelings. Zeppo and Herman continued their friendship. Herman's daughter Rita remembers her father enjoying lunches at Hillcrest Country Club with Zeppo and friends like Edward G. Robinson, George Jessel, and of course, Zeppo's brothers. Herman's company was successful and did business with Lockheed and Boeing. And he would continue to tinker on various inventions with Zeppo in their off hours for many years. Herman and his family also visited Zeppo in Palm Springs.

Zeppo liked owning successful businesses, but the agency and Marman both had begun to cause problems that made him want to cash out. His next business venture was one that looked relatively easy. There would be no union trouble or spoiled, petulant actors. With Harpo, Gummo, and Marx Brothers business manager Alexander Tucker as his partners, Zeppo became a citrus rancher. They formed a partnership and called the property in Coachella—thirty-seven miles southeast of Palm Springs—the Martuc Ranch. Zeppo discussed the ranch in a March 1959 feature story in *Palm Springs Villager* magazine.

"We started from scratch four years ago and developed 250 acres of citrus groves from raw desert land," he proudly reports. The acreage is "double planted," supporting twice as many grapefruit, orange, lemon and tangerine trees, according to a new method of desert fruit ranching. First crops will be harvested this year.

They built two residences on the property and Zeppo added a large machine shop. Martuc would become the largest citrus grove in the Coachella Valley with 160 acres of Marsh Seedless Grapefruit, fifty acres of Temple Oranges, and thirty acres of Valencia Oranges. Zeppo also bought a fishing boat and kept it near the ranch at the North Shore Beach Yacht Club on the Salton Sea. Many Hollywood celebrities, fascinated by the opportunities for fishing, boating and water sports in the middle of the desert had flocked to the Salton Sea from their Palm Springs retreats. Zeppo's fellow yacht club members included Gregory Peck, Bing Crosby, Jerry Lewis, Clark Gable, and Edgar Bergen. As a resort community, the Salton Sea was short-lived, and it ultimately became an environmental disaster. Partially as a result of this, Zeppo would later become a supporter of Greenpeace and other environmental charities.

As a citrus rancher and part-time fisherman without the pressures of running Marman, Zeppo could focus his attention on women and gambling for a while. But first there was the matter of the trial in the rock throwing incident involving Tim. Tom and Tim were spending a brief summer vacation away from Mount Lowe at the Prescott Ranger Ranch in Arizona when the trial was to begin. Tim recalls being put on a plane by himself and being flown to Los Angeles during a bad storm.

The trial began on July 18, 1955. Zeppo did not attend. Marion appeared in court looking matronly in a black dress and wide hat. Tim wore his Mount Lowe uniform. The case presented by the Singer family attorneys was that "Tim was so negligently trained and supervised that he developed a belligerent and hostile nature." The suit was clearly drafted to place the blame for the incident on Zeppo and Marion—in other words, following the money.

While Tim was also named as a defendant, the case against him had an inherent problem. The law stated that "A minor . . . is civilly liable for a wrong done by him, but not liable in exemplary damages unless at the time of the act he was capable of knowing that it was wrongful." The defense posited that Tim could not know the act was wrongful because he was trying to hit a tree with the rock, and accidentally hit Denise Singer. Tim testified, "I was aiming at a tree and the stone slipped."

The Singer attorneys presented as a witness another neighborhood girl they claimed was Tim's intended target. Had Tim been trying to hit another person, rather than a tree, he would be liable to Denise Singer by the legal concept of "transferred intent." The Singers also offered the testimony of the previous occupant of their house, who testified that she had spoken to Marion about Tim's habit of throwing rocks a year before Tim threw the rock that hit Denise Singer.

She added that Tim and Tom had ruined her front door by throwing darts at it. Marion testified that she had no recollection of any such conversation with the neighbor and denied even knowing her. Marion did testify that she had been informed that Tim had thrown dirt clods at the car of the principal at Hawthorne Elementary School, and that he had been punished for it. Asked about Tim, Denise Singer testified, "He was always throwing rocks."

There was no disagreement on the basic fact that Tim threw a rock that hit Denise Singer near her eye. The legal questions as to Tim's intent, his parents' responsibility for the girl's injury and any negligence on their part were the ones that needed to be answered for the court to decide the case. On July 21 Superior Judge Caryl M. Sheldon dismissed the case, stating that there was no evidence that Tim was improperly supervised. Denise Singer Vogel recalls her family's attorney determining that Judge Sheldon was a fishing buddy of Zeppo's.

The Singers appealed and got a reversal of the decision in their favor against Marion and Tim, but not Zeppo. The appeals court decision, handed down by Judge Clyde C. Triplett—apparently not a fishing buddy of Zeppo's but still willing to give him something of a break—stated,

> It is fairly inferable that Mrs. Marx had notice of Tim's dangerous proclivities and did not administer effective discipline. . . . So far as the father, Zeppo Marx, is concerned, it does not appear that he had any personal knowledge of the rock throwing. The only evidence as to him is that he was consulted when punishment for any dereliction was due. That is not enough to make a prima facie case against him. The judgment of nonsuit is reversed as to defendants Tim Marx and Marion Marx and affirmed as to defendant Zeppo Marx.

Marion and Tim's petition for a hearing by the Supreme Court of California was denied on November 21, 1956. The $300,000 damage suit was ultimately settled for $22,500 on May 3, 1957, ending nearly four years of litigation in the matter.[3]

The extent of Denise Singer's injury notwithstanding, Zeppo felt that $300,000 was excessive—especially considering that Mortimer Singer was a compulsive gambler who was in Las Vegas almost as frequently as Zeppo was. The settlement amount was a relief to Zeppo and a huge disappointment to Mortimer Singer, who had a somewhat sketchy history and was always in need of money.

Singer was a used car salesman and a music publisher in the years before he filed the lawsuit against Zeppo. He acquired some oil leases in Osage, Oklahoma in 1953 and began putting equipment for oil exploration on the property. Presumably this is what made him an oil company executive. Within a couple of years Singer was on the receiving end of several lawsuits brought by the companies he purchased equipment from. He never paid for any of it. There was also a foreclosure on his oil leases.

Singer would get into further trouble. In March 1961 he was indicted by a federal grand jury on twenty-nine counts of mail fraud. He bilked would-be songwriters out of $159,713 in a scheme that promised he would set their poetry to music, get it recorded, and place the songs in movies to get them royalties. Singer ran advertisements in music trade publications using the alias Ralph Hastings and involved his son Stephen, who operated a recording company in Hollywood. The Federal Trade Commission also came after Singer's son for this scheme.

While awaiting trial, Mortimer Singer got back into the oil business, taking money from investors who all eventually sued him for non-payment. After a two-week trial, he was convicted on the mail fraud charges and sentenced to eighteen months in prison, followed by three years' probation and payment of a $4,500 fine. It isn't hard to believe that while his daughter's injury infuriated him, Mortimer Singer also saw Zeppo's wealth as an opportunity for a substantial payday in court.

By the time the Singer v. Marx case reached a final resolution, Marion, Tom, and Tim had left California, as had the Singer family. In December 1955 Marion abruptly took the boys out of Mount Lowe and moved to New York with them. According to Tim, "She wanted to be as far away from Zeppo as she could be." She rented an apartment at 933 Park Avenue, near East 84th Street. Tom and Tim were enrolled in New York City public schools. They were both thrilled to be out of Mount Lowe, even if it meant relocating to New York against their will. Construction on Zeppo's new house at Tamarisk was completed, and he moved in as Tom and Tim began the school year in September 1956.

The March 1959 *Palm Springs Villager* piece on Zeppo described the new house in unusually extreme detail.

Zeppo himself designed the new home, with the help of architect Wallace Neff. The theme is absolute symmetry.

The large hexametrical living room is perfectly balanced, both architecturally and in interior decor. Identical bedroom suites extend from opposite ends of its length. A long kitchen flanks the living room, servants' quarters adjacent. There is a wide-roofed patio overlooking the swimming pool.

By entering the living room well to the right of center, one is spared the impression of walking into a mirror and is only gradually conscious of the exact symmetry of the room's furnishings.

"Actually, it was the only sensible way to capitalize on both fireplace and view," Zeppo explained [of] the two-faced central unit, which he designed himself.

From a long-shelved centerpiece, red cushioned sofas arc widely on either side, edged with low tabletops and cupboard areas. The island's perimeter describes an interesting abstract shape, a pleasing combination of abstracts and curves. In front of each sofa-side stretches a long marble-topped coffee table.

Poolside, two giant white hassocks, each five feet in diameter, wing the view. Fireside, two organs—one a small black chord organ, the other a new electric console—are paired with a great curving fireplace in between.

Above the organs hang a pair of colorful Indian figures, copies of Far Eastern temple virgins. Lamps and a grinning brass lion repeat the Indian motif. Wall tones are white and shades of gray and are repeated together in the reed-and-cotton draperies which extend along the west wall of glass.

The western view seems to extend the house about three miles into the setting sun. The expansive patio, shady under a wide eave, is inviting and comfortable with cushioned wrought iron lounge chairs and ash trays bucket-size.

The pool is large (25' × 50') and rectangular—so that, according to Zeppo, "You can swim without bumping your head on all those abstract curves." Beyond the beautifully landscaped gardens stretch the fairways of Tamarisk golf course.

Zeppo had built one of the finest homes at Tamarisk and he was proud of it. The two organs prominently placed in his living room were an important feature of the house. Zeppo took a weekly lesson and frequently played for guests. Marion had settled comfortably in New York and wrote Zeppo a cordial and optimistic letter, letting him know, among other things, that the boys were pleased to be in public school and had received their polio vaccines. The letter

Zeppo sent back in October amused Marion so much that she saved it and passed it on to Tim:

Dear Marion,

Was happy to hear from you, and glad you're feeling well, also very pleased about the boys doing well in school. Strange that you should write me about the polio shots. I was about to ask you if they had received them.

About the house, believe me it has been a very tough job, I never realized how much work there is to it. I can now understand the running around you had to do in furnishing our other houses. Wow! Picking the colors for the carpets and furniture is about to drive me nuts. I don't think I will ever do it again. The decorators are all such thieves that I am doing the whole thing myself. Right now, I think the living room looks like a fruit salad and the two bedrooms look like the same fruit salad after I vomited. Anyway, I did it and am stuck with it, so if I ever wanted to sell it, I would have to get some schmuck who is completely blind, and that ain't easy. Bing Crosby, who is color blind, is the only one I know who has enough money to buy it, but my bar isn't big enough.

About the ranch I bought, it is raw land, and I am planting grapefruit. It will take about four years to bear fruit, and when it does, I hope to hell people will still want to eat them. If they don't, I'll be up to my ass in the stuff. Anyway, I will keep you posted. This will be all for now.
Love,
Zeppo

Nice letters notwithstanding, Marion was still angry at Zeppo and resentful about his not being around for Tom and Tim. In her mind, his absentee parenting even got him out of trouble in the court case, which certainly didn't make Marion any less upset. She felt he was rewarded by the court for not knowing about the behavioral problems of his children. Zeppo had reduced being a father to writing checks. Zeppo's attitude had always been that since Marion wanted children, she should deal with them. To him they were just a nuisance.

But in trying to start a new life in New York, Marion was not completely prepared to go it alone. She convinced her mother to move back to New York after having her move to Los Angeles twenty years earlier.[4] Marion was strongwilled and took charge of things once she accepted that Zeppo would not be any help with the boys. Tim says, "Once they separated, Marion became the boss.

Zeppo abdicated that and I didn't like it. I missed him. I didn't want to move to New York. I wanted to stay in California so I could see my father. At the time I couldn't figure out why Marion had to go to New York."

Had Tim stayed in California he wouldn't have seen much of his father. Zeppo was very interested in a new hotel and casino in Las Vegas. Among the original investors in what was to be called the Casa Blanca Hotel were Harpo and Gummo. It was originally set to open in 1953, but the Nevada Tax Commission would not grant a license when they learned that Meyer Lansky and Detroit mobster Willie Bischoff were involved. When it finally opened as the Riviera on April 20, 1955, it was plagued by financial problems and went bankrupt within three months. By July a new management team led by Zeppo's old friend Gus Greenbaum took over the operation of the Riviera with a group of partners that had been with him at the Flamingo.

Greenbaum had sold his interest in the Flamingo and retired, but he was pressured by high level organized crime figures to come out of retirement to save the Riviera. He refused at first but was convinced when his sister-in-law suddenly turned up dead in what was clearly a well-timed mob hit. Greenbaum had taken the unusual step of burying the Flamingo's ledgers in the Nevada desert along with the names of the Flamingo's Gold Club members, basically a list of the casino's high rollers. Zeppo's name was on that valuable list.

Before returning to Las Vegas from his home in Phoenix, Greenbaum stopped off in the desert to exhume the Flamingo paperwork, which would be useful in turning the Riviera around. The Nevada authorities expressed concern about the criminal past of Greenbaum and his associates but allowed them to take over the Riviera to save the new establishment. None of Greenbaum's partners were as notorious as Meyer Lansky (who remained a silent partner) and having some of the Marx Brothers involved made for better press.

Among the more colorful characters running the Riviera with Greenbaum would be Israel Alderman, alias "Icepick Willie," a name he picked up as a mob enforcer and hit man in Minneapolis. Gummo and Harpo were the Riviera's most—and probably only—respectable investors. Greenbaum's ownership stake was well known, but Nevada officials simply feigned ignorance on the matter. It was much nicer to say a couple of the Marx Brothers were part of the ownership group.

Gus Greenbaum invited Zeppo to be his guest for the opening of a new Spike Jones revue, *Musical Insanities of 1956*, which opened on August 3, 1955, in the Riviera's nightclub, the Clover Room.

Zeppo saw the show several times while it was at the Riviera. He also used his connection to the hotel management to watch the showgirls rehearse in the afternoon. One of the girls was Barbara Ann Blakeley, Zeppo's future second wife and Frank Sinatra's future fourth wife. In her 2011 autobiography, *Lady Blue Eyes: My Life with Frank*, she wrote about her first encounter with Zeppo:

> He was a well-tailored, middle-aged man who'd sit alone at the back of the theater to watch our rehearsals. He was a friend of the director Sammy Lewis, and I could tell he was important by the way the bosses reacted to him. Sammy came over to me one day and asked, "What have you done to Zeppo Marx? He's been asking questions all around the hotel about you."

The four-week engagement of the Spike Jones revue at the Clover Room was followed by nine weeks of Harpo and Chico Marx—booked by Riviera investor Gummo Marx. Zeppo caught the act so frequently his brothers may have thought he was reconsidering his disdain for show business. But he was more focused on one showgirl than anything else.

When Groucho came to Las Vegas to see Harpo and Chico's show, there was a rare public gathering of all five Marx Brothers. There would be another reunion of the five Marx Brothers on February 18, 1957, when the brothers all attended Chico's opening at the Hollywood Civic Playhouse in a touring production of *The Fifth Season*. On this occasion the reunion was filmed for broadcast on the NBC television show *Tonight: America after Dark*. Zeppo's ambivalence about making these appearances would probably have made it satisfying for him that the footage of this historic event is not known to survive. Zeppo's interest in show business at this point was limited to pretty chorus girls.

Barbara was a twenty-eight-year-old divorcée and former model with a nearly five-year-old son when she met Zeppo. She'd been pursued by numerous men during her time as a Las Vegas showgirl and had pursued a few wealthy older men in her search for a husband. But she had reached the point where she wanted to leave the city and find a better life for her young son. Zeppo complicated matters for her. She knew he was dating other women and would occasionally see him in Las Vegas with Joyce Niven. She'd no doubt seen the newspaper items suggesting Zeppo would soon marry Niven.

But Zeppo continued to pursue Barbara and told friends that the rumors about marrying Joyce Niven were nonsense. Zeppo's relationship with Niven would best be described as rocky. On May 29, 1957, Zeppo went to the Mocambo on Sunset Boulevard to see Connee Boswell perform at the legendary Hollywood nightclub. He was on his first date with Lillian Sherlock, a former model occasionally identified in gossip columns as a "Hollywood starlet" even though she never made it in the movies. One of the twice-divorced Sherlock's former husbands was a wealthy greeting card tycoon, so she may have seen more in Zeppo than his money. She was often described as an Ava Gardner lookalike, and Frank Sinatra had dated her during a break in his tumultuous marriage to Gardner.

When Zeppo and Lillian Sherlock arrived at the Mocambo that night, they were greeted by an incensed Joyce Niven, who accused Sherlock of stealing her boyfriend. Zeppo escorted Niven back to her table where her date for the evening grabbed Zeppo. A brief fistfight was broken up by some Mocambo waiters, and Zeppo yet again made headlines for getting into a public brawl. He was quoted in the *Los Angeles Times* as saying, "I got in a couple of good clouts. I'm glad no one was hurt." Niven's date was a former boxer, and Zeppo asked *Variety's* Army Archerd, "Why is it your pals always hold YOUR hands when they want to stop a fight? And the other guy's always way over six-foot?"

Lillian Sherlock was seen with Zeppo again when they caught comedian Mort Sahl's act at the Interlude, another Hollywood nightclub, but after that she was done with him. The following year she married comedy writer Harry Crane and remained with him for the rest of her life. But Joyce Niven persevered. She may have been justifiably upset when she saw Zeppo with another woman at the Mocambo. He had taken her there only weeks earlier to see Frank Sinatra. On the other hand, she was there with a burly ex-boxer.

A month after the Mocambo incident, Dorothy Kilgallen wrote in her "Voice of Broadway" column, "Zeppo Marx, recently headlined in a brawl involving two ladies, has forsaken both of them in favor of Betsy Duncan." Duncan was a twenty-five-year-old red-haired actress and singer. She had recently appeared in *Pal Joey* at the La Jolla Playhouse and appeared on television with Bob Hope and on the *Tonight Show*. She frequently performed at the El Mirador in Palm Springs. Zeppo caught her act at the newly opened Slate Brothers nightclub in Los Angeles and moved quickly, proposing marriage almost immediately. He told friends he was crazy about her.

Duncan had her sights set on marrying a wealthy man and didn't take Zeppo's proposal seriously. She was simultaneously dating clothier Sy Devore. Zeppo was so good at keeping his net worth a secret that Betsy Duncan had no idea how much money he had. She would ultimately marry Ever Hammes, the heir to the InSinkErator garbage disposal fortune. All was soon forgiven with Joyce Niven and Zeppo began dating her again in August 1957.

Three years after his divorce from Marion, Zeppo was searching for a wife. But he was mostly limiting his search to blonde models less than half his age. He had never let being married interfere with his longtime passion for chasing women, but the big difference for the post-divorce bachelor Zeppo was the public display of his social life. His frequent notices in the Hollywood and Las Vegas gossip columns, telling of various beautiful young women on his arm could be interpreted as a mid-life crisis, or an inexpensive way of advertising his availability to any young gold-diggers looking for a rich older man.

CHAPTER TWENTY-ONE

Barbara Moves In

ZEPPO HAD BEEN SUFFERING FROM HEARING LOSS FOR SEVERAL YEARS, and the situation became very noticeable during his bachelor years in Palm Springs. Gummo's son Bob, who was building homes in the area, saw Zeppo frequently during this time. He recalled, "I ran into Zep and whoever the blonde bimbo of the week was at the movies. She had a pair of coke-bottle eyeglasses and could barely see. He was hard of hearing. During the movie I heard him say loudly to her, 'What did they say?' Then she asked him, 'What are they doing?' I can't imagine why they bothered going to the movies."

Zeppo had learned about a new operation that could greatly improve his hearing. Developed in 1952 by Dr. Samuel Rosen, the procedure then known as the "Rosen stapes operation" offered a cure for otosclerosis, a condition that prevents sound waves from reaching the auditory nerve as a result of hardening of the soft tissue stapes bone. The operation, now known as a stapedectomy, replaces the stapes bone with a synthetic substitute. Zeppo had the operation in 1956 on one ear with good results. Asked by a reporter why he'd gotten the surgery Zeppo replied, "So I can hear the applause if I return to acting."

Zeppo never stopped pursuing Barbara Blakeley and saw her whenever he was in Las Vegas, but she read the gossip columns and seeing things like the Mocambo fistfight made it difficult for her to take Zeppo seriously as a romantic possibility. There were also reports that Zeppo was dating Nancy Valentine, a former model who'd recently signed a movie contract with Howard Hughes. Barbara had her young son to think about, and Zeppo didn't seem like a good influence. The compulsive high-stakes gambling was also problematic for a woman who was trying to get away from Las Vegas. But Barbara was looking for security and she also saw newspaper accounts of Zeppo's business and investment dealings.

In April 1956 there were reports of Zeppo purchasing a Safeway store in Redding, California, for $541,000. It was a more nuanced deal than the simple purchase of a retail store. Safeway was in business with Webb & Knapp, a large real estate development company owned by wealthy builder William Zeckendorf. Zeckendorf owned the Chrysler Building and the Astor Hotel in New York and was behind the land deals for such projects as Chicago's Magnificent Mile, Century City in Los Angeles and the United Nations building in New York. Webb & Knapp had $250 million in undeveloped properties in several cities around the United States and Zeckendorf had an interesting plan to turn these into revenue generating properties quickly.

His idea for Safeway stores offered an unusual opportunity for investors with cash or good credit. When Zeppo bought the Redding store it was already built and operational, but for future investors land would be purchased as a lot and a store would then be built to Safeway's specifications. Safeway would then sign a thirty-year lease with the owner that would include an option for the retail chain to buy the store at the end of the lease. Safeway's rent payments would cover the monthly mortgage and allow for some profit each month. For his Redding investment, Zeppo took a mortgage for $422,285.69 with the Safeway store and the land it was built on as security for the loan. It was easy enough for him to put up the initial investment of roughly $120,000 and start collecting rent from Safeway.

Zeppo liked the Safeway deal enough to buy additional stores in Blythe, California, and Kansas City, Missouri. He also purchased one in Portland, Oregon, as an investment for Marion, an indication that they had come through the divorce on reasonably good terms, and that he was looking after her financial future—notwithstanding the money he hid from her in the divorce.

Zeppo's Safeway stores provided net income each month and their mortgages were being paid off at the same time. He told friends the stores were a "hedge against inflation." Barbara admired Zeppo's largesse in setting up an investment for his ex-wife, but she also wondered why Zeppo had virtually no contact with his two sons. Things were better between Zeppo and Marion, but she was handling all decisions about Tom and Tim herself. In the spring of 1957 Marion pulled the boys out of Robert F. Wagner Junior High School on East 76th Street in Manhattan and sent them to the Peddie School in Hightstown, New Jersey.

Tim recalls,

We were sent off to boarding school. Marion wanted to have her own life and she didn't want my brother or me around. Tom was very serious in his studies. He was a very bright guy. I got thrown out of the Peddie School for using the common slur a thirteen-year-old kid would have used in 1957 to describe a professor whose sexual orientation seemed threatening. I wasn't out a week and was back at some other school in Connecticut.

Marion didn't want the boys at separate schools, so she sent them both to the Cheshire Academy, in Cheshire, Connecticut. Tom once again blamed Tim for the abrupt relocation. Other than agreeing to pay for the tuition, Zeppo remained uninvolved in the decision. Tom began blaming Tim, Marion, and especially Zeppo, for his troubles. Tim suggests, "Tom lost his sense of humor when Marion and Zeppo split. And he has always insisted that military school ruined his life."

By the fall of 1957 Zeppo was starting to tire of his on-again, off-again relationship with Joyce Niven. He renewed his efforts with Barbara and sent her a gift—a Ford Thunderbird convertible. The recently introduced car, which set Zeppo back roughly $3,500, had its engine ruined when Barbara's former boyfriend poured sugar in the gas tank. Barbara was more impressed in October when Zeppo sent her son Bobby a bicycle for his seventh birthday. The very wealthy man described by Tom and Tim as being tight with money when it came to his two sons would be almost unrecognizable to them. But Zeppo had an unlimited budget when it came to gambling and women.

Barbara found Zeppo charming and realized that he could offer a better life for her and Bobby. Her former husband, a bartender and would-be singer named Robert Harrison Oliver, never made any child support payments and had skipped town. Bobby Marx, then known as Bobby Oliver, recalls, "I had some pretty traumatic experiences in Las Vegas as a kid. I was bullied by some local kids who tied me up and almost burned me alive. My mom saved me, but said, 'That's it. We're out of Las Vegas,' and I was sent to military school." Barbara moved to Long Beach—close enough to Los Angeles to resume her modeling career. Initially she lived in her parents' house, but eventually found her own apartment. But she found it nearly impossible to find modeling work and was almost penniless.

In her book Barbara wrote, "One day Zeppo called to see how I was. When I told him the truth, he made me an offer. 'Come to Palm Springs,' he pleaded. 'I'll set you and Bobby up in your own place. You can commute back to L.A.

to model whenever you want.' With all other options running out, I had little choice but to accept." Bobby says, "I was still in military school at the time, and I think Zeppo was perfectly happy with that. I'm sure a seven-year-old kid was not in his vision of the future."

At first Zeppo rented a two-bedroom apartment for Barbara and Bobby near the Racquet Club in Palm Springs. Bobby was mostly out of sight in the beginning, but when he'd be home from military school Barbara had a room waiting for him. Eventually they moved into Zeppo's house at Tamarisk. Barbara wrote, "Bobby and I tried to settle into our new life, but it wasn't as easy a transition as I'd hoped." Zeppo gave Barbara a hard time whenever Bobby was home. She wanted to take him out of military school and have him live with them full time. Zeppo paid the tuition for military school and Bobby continued to be only an occasional irritant for him.

Zeppo may not have been aware of the devastating effect military school had on his sons—particularly Tom. Pressuring Barbara to keep Bobby in military school seems like he considered it the only option. He was willing to pay whatever the cost to keep Tom, Tim, and now Bobby, out of his way. Barbara wrote, "Zeppo had no paternal instincts whatsoever, despite having adopted two children in his previous marriage." He told friends he never wanted children and that his marriage to Marion was falling apart by the time she suggested that adopting a couple of kids could save it. His position was that if children helped their relationship, that would be okay. But if they didn't at least Marion would not be alone when they split up.

With Barbara in Palm Springs Zeppo was suddenly placed in the position of needing to mend his relationship with Tom and Tim. He wasn't going to convince Barbara that he'd be a good father figure for her son if he had no relationship with his own sons. Tim says,

> Marion did not want us to be on good terms with Zeppo. She thought he was responsible for screwing up their marriage. She blamed him for us having to be with her. That sort of screwed up her life. And he's fancy-free banging everything he can get his hands on, and she resented that. Zeppo called Marion and said, "Look, it's about time I see them. I haven't seen them. You've held them from me." To Marion at that time, we were pawns. I think he finally got fed up and said, "Send them." So, we went to Palm Springs at the end of the school year in 1958.

Tom and Tim were greeted by Zeppo's butler, a fifty-eight-year-old black World War II veteran named Ulysses Grant Sheffield, and his forty-eight-year-old wife Versa, Zeppo's maid. The Sheffields handled everything around the house, which the boys couldn't help but notice was even more opulent than the Rexford and North Beverly houses. Recalling the trip Tom says, "He wasn't married to Barbara yet. She was living in the house with him. She had her own bedroom, which we used when we stayed there. She slept with him, I guess. Her son wasn't there. He was in military school. That was what people did back then. If they didn't want you around, they just shipped you off to military school."

Tim's memories of the visit are dominated by a case of viral pneumonia that landed him in the hospital for several days. But otherwise, he recalls, "Zeppo was terrific. He couldn't do enough for us. Horseback riding, golf, whatever. His Weimaraner dog, Fleet, would jump into the pool with us." Tom remembers the trip quite differently. "He was placing bets on the phone all the time. After that visit, that was it for us. He hated us after that. He didn't want to have anything to do with us." It would be the last time Tom ever saw Zeppo. He was fifteen years old.

Zeppo wanting the boys to visit him may have seemed like a turning point to Marion, since he was usually trying to get them to be wherever he wasn't, but she was unaware that he was mostly concerned with showing Barbara that he had a good relationship with his sons. He was pleased that the boys were doing well at Cheshire Academy, but the reality of it was that he paid the bills for whatever school they'd most recently been shuttled off to and expressed little interest in their lives. The effect was devastating to Tom, but Tim was more pragmatic and accepted whatever Zeppo could offer without expecting more. Tim offers some insight about his brother. "Tom didn't think he got a fair shake out of life. Zeppo wasn't too interested. Tom would have had a whole different life if he could have looked at things a little bit differently. He was certainly a smart and talented guy, but he just couldn't get past some of the problems in our childhood."

The long-retired actor put on a great show demonstrating a good relationship with his sons for Barbara—who was understandably skeptical, since this show was going on while her son was away at military school. She had to wonder why it wasn't Bobby going horseback riding, playing golf, and splashing around in the pool with Zeppo's dog. When the boys went back to New York Zeppo showed off Barbara to his brothers at a big dinner party. He was preparing for Barbara to become a member of the family.

When Groucho married Eden, part of the ritual had been to introduce his new bride into the family at large gatherings filled with show business reminiscing and a lot of laughter. It was at these family dinners that Zeppo got the laughs he never got in the act. In his book Bill Marx recalls a gathering that took place at Harpo and Susan's house that he was lucky enough to witness when he was growing up.

> Zeppo was regaling us with stories of their vaudeville years. This one was about the time when the two guys who were to be the front and back end of a horse that was an integral part of some silly sketch, got sick at the last minute, so Zeppo and Groucho, who weren't in the sketch, agreed to fill in and be the horse for that performance. Unfortunately, neither one of them had ever been inside a horse to practice the coordination between the two that was required.
>
> As Zeppo was describing their ineptitude, Groucho started to laugh out loud, and when Zeppo got to the point where they couldn't see where they were going and wound up falling off the stage and onto the musicians in the pit, Groucho was himself falling off the couch with uncontrollable laughter. I turned to my mom and said, "I've seen Groucho crack a smile at a good joke. I've seen him even sort of laugh at a good story. But I've never seen him with tears in his eyes with laughter as I am seeing tonight."
>
> Mom told me that Zeppo was the only one she knew who could make Groucho laugh like that. Zeppo was a very funny, gifted raconteur and accomplished dialectician, who somehow was able to tweak Groucho's funny bone like no other person.

A dinner with all five Marx Brothers assured Zeppo that Barbara would see him at his funniest and most charming, but he didn't get the result he was hoping for after he introduced Barbara to the assembled Marxes. Barbara's generally whitewashed memoir is surprisingly candid on her introduction to the family.

> Zeppo took me to meet his family only because he was pressing me to be his wife. Whenever I saw him getting up steam to propose, though, I quickly changed the subject or began an argument—anything to distract him. I didn't want to be backed into a corner and have to turn him down, so I stalled him repeatedly. He was kind and generous, but I really didn't want to marry him. One of my chief reasons for avoiding his impending proposal, though, was that he wasn't great with Bobby. . . . Although he tried for my sake to connect with my son, he always

seemed relieved when Bobby went back to the military academy or to visit his grandparents.... Modeling in L.A. had never lost its allure and still seemed a realistic possibility, so after five months in this idyllic date palm oasis, I scooped up Bobby, kissed Zeppo goodbye, and headed a hundred miles west.

There might have been another reason for the timing of Barbara's departure. On July 31, 1958, newspapers across the country carried a story with headlines like, "Zeppo Marx Sought in Gambling Probe," "Zeppo Marx Sought for Questioning about Syndicate" and "G-Men Hunt Zeppo Marx to Testify." It shouldn't have been difficult to find him, but further headlines like "Zeppo Marx Proves Elusive" followed.

Treasury agents tracked down Gummo, who was quoted in the press saying, "He was around Los Angeles three or four days ago." He also added that they might find him at his ranch near Blythe. Gummo had to know that Blythe was a hundred miles from the Martuc Ranch, but Zeppo might have considered it noble for his brother to have thrown the feds off his trail. Gummo's son Bob recalled his father telling agents, "You're not looking too hard. He's either on a broad or a horse," but that quote did not make it into the newspapers. Some of Zeppo's friends told agents they last saw him leaving Hillcrest Country Club and that he might be heading for Palm Springs. Bill Marx recalls seeing Harpo hang up the telephone looking disconsolate. He asked his father what was wrong, and Harpo replied shaking his head, "It's your Uncle Zeppo. The feds are after him. He'll probably get away with it—whatever it is."

When he was finally located after agents had searched for him for thirty-six hours, Zeppo told a reporter, "I know none of the people named in newspaper stories concerning the syndicate." He added that he was dumbfounded as to why anyone would subpoena him. The following day Zeppo accepted the subpoena at the office of his attorneys, Laurence W. Bielenson and Allen E. Sussman, who issued this statement:

> Mr. Zeppo Marx has been subpoenaed as a witness to appear before a U.S. grand jury in Indianapolis. Mr. Marx is not a prospective defendant, but merely a witness. Since U.S. grand jury testimony is secret, it would be improper for him or us to comment on his testimony.

Zeppo's testimony was scheduled for August 22, 1958, which meant he would be unable to serve as the best man at Chico's wedding to his second wife,

Mary DiVitha, set to take place the same day.[1] He testified that he "operated a citrus farm and instead of being Chico's best man he was in Indianapolis to be the worst man," adding that he wished he was back on the farm.

Zeppo's hometown newspaper, the *Desert Sun* in Palm Springs, reported on his court appearance: "Marx spent only a few minutes behind closed doors of the jury room. When he emerged, District Attorney Don A. Tabbert indicated he had answered all of the jury's questions." Headlines described Zeppo as a cooperative witness, not necessarily a description his friends in Las Vegas would like.

The questions were about bets placed with an Indiana gambling organization that grossed a reported $3.5 million over a ten-week period in the fall of 1957 while operating above a downtown Terre Haute restaurant. The establishment was raided in November. Most bets were on football games and Zeppo, known to frequently bet on football, was revealed in the raid to be a regular telephone bettor. *The Indianapolis News* described Zeppo's appearance in court. "Attired in a black silk suit, black shoes and socks and a white knit tie, Zeppo could have been taken for a gangster at the grand jury hearings. A big scab on his nose is the result of running into a door, he said. 'Very corny,' he admitted, 'but true.'"

On August 27 the grand jury indicted eight men after hearing twelve days of testimony from 177 witnesses—including forty-two who refused to answer questions citing their Fifth Amendment right not to incriminate themselves. Almost a year later the trial was set to begin. On June 22, 1959, Zeppo was again subpoenaed as a witness. On July 10, 1959, the *Indianapolis Star* reported on the proceedings in Terre Haute:

> Zeppo Marx, film comedian turned rancher, played to a packed house in Federal Court here yesterday and candidly admitted he had bet "$10,000—maybe more" with a Terre Haute gambling syndicate during the 1957 football season.
>
> Marx, friendly and courteous, told the all-male jury he had heard in Las Vegas, Nevada that he could call Lincoln 6194 at Terre Haute to wager on football games. "Who told you?" asked Judge Cale J. Holder. "I don't know," Marx replied, "in Vegas any little girl in kindergarten can give you the name of a bookie."

Zeppo testified in open court—as opposed to his previous secret grand jury testimony—that he placed his bets with anyone who answered the phone in Terre Haute and that he usually bet between $100 and $2,000 on professional or college football and the World Series. He said he made some of the calls from the Riviera Hotel and some from his home in Palm Springs, and that he paid his various gambling debts once a year in Las Vegas: "I think it was at the Riviera Hotel where someone came up and said I owed so much. It was the right figure, so I paid him." Zeppo said he was unable to identify the bill collector but admitted to knowing two of the defendants. "I've met Mr. Gordon and Mr. Flippy—there, he's the good-looking guy standing up," Zeppo said while pointing to Irwin Gordon and Phillip "Flippy" Share from the witness stand. Share had twice been acquitted in murder trials. Zeppo also knew several of the witnesses, among them one of his former partners in the El Rancho Vegas, Beldon Katleman. Gus Greenbaum's partner in the Riviera, Sid Wyman, was also acquainted with Zeppo. Asked if he spent considerable time in Las Vegas, Zeppo testified, "To my sorrow, yes."

In between his trips to Indianapolis and Terre Haute, Zeppo got over Barbara moving out of his house by using his friendship with Gus Greenbaum to meet young, beautiful women at the Riviera. Diane Davies worked at the counter in the hotel flower shop. She was also a model—a minimum requirement for Zeppo—with aspirations for a singing and acting career. Depending on which gossip columnist had it right, she was either nineteen or twenty-two. They met in the spring of 1958—as Barbara was moving into Zeppo's house. In October, shortly after Barbara moved out, Zeppo and Diane announced their engagement. It was over by the New Year. Diane broke it off because they had "too many disagreements."

That was the least of Zeppo's troubles as a rough 1958 came to a close. On December 3 Gus Greenbaum and his wife were murdered in their Phoenix home. Greenbaum's throat was cut with a kitchen knife and when his wife arrived home during the assault, she met the same fate. A graphic photo of the crime scene appeared on the front page of the *Arizona Republic*.

Gus had a serious gambling problem and was suspected by his mob superiors of skimming a fair amount of money from the Riviera. The situation in Indianapolis made things even worse for Greenbaum. He was likely the man at the Riviera Zeppo paid off but wouldn't identify on the witness stand. Zeppo's secret testimony in 1958 was not all that secret within the organized crime community and was consistent with his public testimony a year later.

Greenbaum met his fate in between Zeppo's two Indiana court appearances.[2] If Greenbaum did nothing worse than pocket Zeppo's losses, he'd have picked up some significant cash, but he was stealing far more than that. The Terre Haute gambling operation had numerous ties to the Riviera and Greenbaum's role in it was probably what got Zeppo involved. The men Zeppo admitted to knowing—Phillip "Flippy" Share and Irwin Gordon—and their co-defendants were convicted on federal tax evasion charges and handed five-year prison terms and $25,000 fines on September 10, 1959. The excessive newspaper coverage of Zeppo's role in the case had Groucho, Harpo, and Gummo again imploring him to clean up his act. Chico, the family's other compulsive gambler, wasn't concerned, but he was probably impressed by Zeppo's ability to get credit at a Las Vegas casino.

Many people gambled—some for even higher stakes than Zeppo—without testifying before a grand jury about it or seeing their friend's corpse on the front page of a newspaper. Zeppo was certainly well connected to the underworld and socialized as easily with mobsters in Las Vegas as he did with movie stars in Hollywood. As charming as Zeppo could be, there was always the ruthless side of him that usually took over when he was at a crap table or in a card game. If people at a casino didn't recognize him and saw him with a casino boss, he could easily be mistaken for a well-dressed gangster. His friends Moe Sedway and Gus Greenbaum would have their names combined—in much the same way Zeppo named his companies, Marwyck, Marman, and Martuc—by author Mario Puzo in the book and film *The Godfather* as the name of a character, Moe Greene, based on them and Bugsy Siegel.

Tim was not surprised by the newspaper accounts of the events in Indiana, which he followed when he returned to New York from his Palm Springs visit with Zeppo.

> I didn't think anything was unusual. I knew what he was doing in Las Vegas, but I didn't really have a concept of money at that point. Okay. The guy's losing fifty or a hundred thousand, and then when you get a little older, you think "Geez, that's a lot of money." But when you're a kid you just take it for granted. It's stupid, but that's what he had and that's what he gambled. He always had loads of money. What I knew about guys like Moe Sedway and Gus Greenbaum was that they were friendly to me when I was a little kid.

Only eight days after the convictions in Terre Haute, Tim found a real surprise about his father in the newspaper. "I'm sitting in the study hall at Cheshire Academy in Connecticut, and somebody hands me the *New York Daily News*. There's a picture of him. He just got married. That's how I found out he'd married Barbara."

CHAPTER TWENTY-TWO

The Second Time Around

Z EPPO RETURNED TO PALM SPRINGS IN THE SUMMER OF 1959, AFTER HIS testimony in Terre Haute, and called Barbara who was living in a rented bungalow in Beverly Hills. They began dating again. Barbara wrote, "Whenever Zep was in town, he'd come around and take me out. He was witty and handsome, claimed to adore me, and nothing I could do or say seemed to distract him from his goal of making me his wife."

Frank Sinatra biographer James Kaplan wrote in *Sinatra: The Chairman*, "Barbara Blakeley, the daughter of a Bosworth, Missouri, butcher, was never brilliant, but she was beautiful and tough and reasonably clever about capitalizing on her dazzling good looks." Ed Walters, a pit boss at the Sands told Kaplan he remembered seeing Barbara there frequently, walking through the casino with another statuesque blonde, Dani Crayne, who later married the actor David Janssen. "'She was stunningly beautiful,' he recalled. . . . They cruised the Sands like barracudas, looking for wealthy older men who wanted to remember what it was like to be young,' he said. 'It wasn't about the money, and it wasn't about the sex; it was about improving their place in the world.'"

James Kaplan interviewed the renowned fashion designer and critic Richard Blackwell, for whom Barbara had briefly modeled. He said Zeppo "was the most famous and important man she had met up to that point and so she set her sights for him." Barbara and Zeppo were married on September 18, 1959, at the place where they first met four years earlier—the Riviera Hotel in Las Vegas. Barbara moved back into Zeppo's house in Palm Springs, which he modified for the occasion. In her book Barbara said, "[H]e immediately added a room outside for Bobby, which impressed me enormously until I realized that it was to keep my son out of the way." Blackwell added, "Zeppo brought her into a new world of money and social prominence that she had never known before. He wasn't the classiest man in the world, I'll grant you that, but he was the best that Barbara could do at the time."

Bobby Marx says,

They got married when I was almost nine. By the time I turned ten my mom said, "We should bring Bobby here." I don't think that was in Zeppo's plan, but she had a couple of years to work on him. When I enrolled in fifth grade at Cathedral City Elementary School, I was Bobby Marx. That came about because I didn't understand why my mom's name was Barbara Marx and I was Bobby Oliver. They said, "Well, you can be Bobby Marx." So that's when I became Bobby Marx. I remember going to visit my dad's parents and my grandfather gave me a hard time about it. He said, "What's this Bobby Marx stuff? What's wrong with Bobby Oliver?"

Barbara had convinced Zeppo to legally adopt Bobby, but, Bobby explains, "When we tried to make it official my father filed an affidavit with the court protesting the adoption by Zeppo, saying he's the rightful father. So, my name was not legally changed until I turned eighteen."

Zeppo's willingness to adopt Bobby wasn't the result of his being suddenly overcome with paternal instincts. Barbara once came home to find Zeppo screaming at Bobby with his hands around his neck. This is the Zeppo that Tim and Tom would immediately recognize and point out was "the real Zeppo" no matter how nice he was to Barbara and Bobby publicly. Bobby says, "I had some encounters with him that were a little difficult." He remembers the incident that resulted in Zeppo's hands around his neck.

He had these white rocks out in the driveway in the landscaping with the cactus plants. I had a can of black spray paint, and I was spraying the rocks black. He came out and was furious, and asked me, "Did you spray those rocks black?" And I could see that he was mad, so I said "No" with the can in my hand. He just exploded. My mom came and saved me.

The early part of Zeppo and Barbara's marriage was a mostly serene period, but Zeppo's notorious temper occasionally kept things off balance. Barbara wrote of an episode from a New Year's Eve party at the Racquet Club:

[W]e were just leaving when I spotted some friends I wanted to say good night to. Zeppo hated that and stood by the door impatiently. As I turned to go, I was goosed from behind by Victor Rothschild, playboy and baron. Before I could say anything, Zeppo ran at Victor like a bull. He knocked down two couples before he grabbed Victor by the throat.

Age had not mellowed Zeppo at all. While Harpo and Chico were starting to show signs of old age, their youngest brother was still getting into public brawls. Harpo had suffered a couple of heart attacks and was in semi-retirement. Chico had also suffered a heart attack and his health was more precarious. He had slowed down considerably and suffered another heart attack at his Hollywood apartment in July 1960. Zeppo and Barbara visited Chico while he was convalescing, and Zeppo was depressed at the sight of his brother looking so frail. Chico knew he was near the end. He told Barbara, "Every morning I wake up, Barbara, I feel like I'm on velvet because I'm still alive." Bill Marx recalls Harpo using the same phrase after surviving whatever his latest health scare was.

Bobby began having the sort of father–son relationship with Zeppo that had never really developed for Tom or Tim. He says, "I got along with him when he wasn't trying to strangle me. We went fishing in the Salton Sea and my mom and I would go waterskiing. He would just keep fishing. I would sometimes go with him and watch him play cards. He would tell me about the stars he represented at the agency and the girls he went out with. He was very proud of being a suave and debonair guy."

But Bobby could still occasionally light the fuse on Zeppo's quick temper. "I was told to never, under any circumstances, take the golf cart out. So naturally I got in the golf cart and went out for a ride, driving around as fast as I could. I was speeding back into the driveway, and I hit some gravel as I turned. The golf cart flipped over and came down on my arm. So, I had a big bruise on my arm. That was another occasion when I felt some of Zeppo's wrath."

Zeppo was now renting a penthouse at the elegant Charleville Apartments in Beverly Hills, and he and Barbara frequently drove in from Palm Springs—to visit an ailing brother, for socializing with friends, or when Barbara had modeling work in town. He also bought a new yacht, named it the *Barbara Ann* and introduced his new wife to the social scene at the Salton Sea.

In Palm Springs Barbara took golf and tennis lessons and played cards with Zeppo and his friends. She became close with some of the show business figures in the community, particularly Dinah Shore, with whom Barbara would remain friendly for many years. When Groucho was in Palm Springs, his wife Eden spent her afternoons at the Racquet Club with Barbara. In her unpublished memoir Eden wrote,

> [Barbara] was a charming, beautiful blonde and a born leader. Zeppo called the clique she was clearly the queen of, "Barbara's Racquet Club Mafia." We would play tennis, and then finish the day playing gin rummy and drinking bloody marys. Both Barbara and I had built-in alarms that went off at 6:30 PM, the time we had to rush home and report to our husbands or be paged on the phone by them.

Zeppo and Barbara also began socializing with their Palm Springs neighbor Frank Sinatra, with whom Zeppo had been acquainted since the days of the Zeppo Marx Agency. Sinatra and Zeppo shared much in common, including several mutual friends with criminal records and significant involvement in the casino business. Zeppo called these associates "the boys." Sinatra liked to call them "the Harvard boys."

In the spring of 1960, Sinatra and some friends—including Dean Martin—purchased a piece of the Cal-Neva Lodge, a summer resort and casino located in Lake Tahoe at the California-Nevada border. For the opening of the summer season in June, Sinatra arranged a private plane to take a large party there to see comedian Joe E. Lewis and to celebrate his new venture.

Zeppo and Barbara were among his guests and Chico and Mary were to join them. But Chico wasn't well enough to make the trip. Zeppo was disappointed. Chico was something of a Las Vegas pioneer, having bounced an $11,000 check at El Rancho Vegas in 1943, when the town had barely been built. Another plane full of celebrities traveled to Lake Tahoe the following June for the opening of another season. This time the show would be headlined by Zeppo's former client, Mickey Rooney. Once again Chico had to miss the trip. He had collapsed in his apartment in May 1961. He was rushed to Cedars of Lebanon Hospital and released after a few days.

Chico died at home on October 11, 1961. In her book Barbara wrote, "Zeppo was grief-stricken. Chico was his big brother, the eldest of them all, and Zeppo had worshipped him." This much is undoubtedly true, but Barbara's account quickly veers away from reality: "After the funeral we went back to Groucho's house for a wake. Crammed into the living room with scores of mourners, I noticed a strange woman staring at me. Zeppo noticed too and asked someone who she was. It was his first wife, Marion."

Tim Marx is certain that Marion was living in New York when Chico died and would not have traveled across the country for her ex-brother-in-law's funeral. Furthermore, Bill Marx is certain that the gathering after Chico's funeral was at Groucho's son Arthur's house. Perhaps Barbara was remembering the unexpected appearance of Groucho's former wife Ruth at the funeral. It is plausible that Zeppo may not have recognized Ruth, the woman he'd brought into the Marx Brothers' act as his dancing partner more than forty years earlier. The once lithesome beauty had not aged well, and Zeppo might not have recognized the matronly alcoholic she'd become. But it seems highly unlikely that Zeppo would not have recognized the woman he was married to for twenty-seven years.

Zeppo celebrated his sixtieth birthday almost eight months before Chico died and he lost several friends and associates in the space of around a year. Clark Gable had died in November 1960. In 1961 Gary Cooper died in May, George S. Kaufman in June, Frank Fay in September, and Joe Schenck in October. *Animal Crackers* stage and screen costar Louis Sorin and playwright Moss Hart, once a client of Zeppo's, both died in December. Hart had been living in Palm Springs and Zeppo, Harpo, and Frank Sinatra attended the funeral.

Zeppo was starting to feel old for the first time. His much younger wife liked to go to parties and stay out late, while Zeppo liked to get home early and go to bed. It didn't bode well for their future. In her book Barbara wrote, "[A]fter two years in Palm Springs, I began asking myself how much tennis, golf or gin I could play." Publicly Zeppo and Barbara seemed to be a very happy couple. The April 19, 1961, edition of *Palm Springs Life* carried this item: "Their home looks out on the second green at Tamarisk Country Club. Well, one day Barbara happened to see a golf ball fly through the air and land neatly in the cup. Excitedly, she ran out to congratulate the golfer who'd hit the hole-in-one. And who was it? None other than Zeppo himself."

Barbara wasn't going anywhere for the time being. She threw herself into charity work and volunteered to raise money for City of Hope, a cancer hospital in Duarte. The charity screening organized by Barbara that took place at the Plaza Theatre in Palm Springs on February 27, 1963, was made possible because of a very nice gesture by Frank Sinatra, who was asked by Zeppo to help with Barbara's benefit. Sinatra arranged for his just completed film *Come Blow Your Horn* to have its world premiere to benefit Barbara's City of Hope event. Sinatra brought everyone involved with the film to the event and it had all the glamour of an old-fashioned Hollywood premiere. It was a big success, and a lot of money was raised.

In her book Barbara picks up the story the following day:

Zeppo and I went to Tamarisk Country Club for lunch. I spotted Frank sitting at a table and said, "I'd like to go over to thank him personally." "Stay there!" Zeppo barked. "*I'll* go over and thank him." I stared at my husband for a moment. I remembered when Zeppo and I had watched Andy Williams perform in Vegas; it had somehow gotten into his head that Andy was singing directly to me. "Stop flirting with him!" Zeppo had snapped as I sat innocently in my seat. . . . I told Zeppo, "Then please thank Frank from me," and watched as he went over to the Sinatra table. I saw Frank look up and nod politely in my direction. I smiled, and he smiled back at me. Ridiculously, I felt myself blushing. Zeppo returned to our table with an invitation for dinner that night, which he couldn't possibly refuse after the favor Frank had done for me.

That dinner was the first time Barbara was inside Sinatra's house. She was aware of Sinatra's flirtations as well as Zeppo's fits of jealously. She wrote, "I knew that Frank's reputation as a hothead superseded Zeppo's, so I didn't relish the idea of a public showdown. . . . I hadn't been married that long and was determined my marriage to Zeppo would work. Bobby's future was at stake as much as mine." Although Zeppo was fully supporting Bobby financially, Barbara was frustrated that her former husband was delinquent in his child support payments. She did something about it that might have been payback for blocking the adoption. *The Long Beach Independent* reported on January 23, 1962, that

> Robert Harrison Oliver was convicted Monday of contempt of court for failing to make child support payments to his former wife who is now married to Zeppo Marx of Marx Brothers movie fame. Mr. and Mrs. Marx drove here to court from their home in Palm Springs. . . . Oliver . . . was jailed for one day . . . for willfully failing to make monthly $125 payments last September, October and November for support of his son Robert, now 11. Mrs. Marx has custody of the child. . . . Oliver testified that he took home $290 a month during the period in question from his job as a bartender in Belmont Shore."

Zeppo's jealousy and persistent infidelity were a dangerous combination for the marriage. Barbara once arrived at Newport Beach, where the *Barbara Ann* was docked, and found a party with several young women in progress. Zeppo was below deck with one of them. This indiscretion cost him a trip to Europe, which Barbara accepted as compensation. As he had with Marion, Zeppo controlled the money, so Barbara had to cooperate to get things she wanted. Zeppo was very good at hiding his money—from his wives and the government—and Barbara wasn't quite sure how rich he was. This was something he picked up from his mobster friends. He was also capable of losing large sums of money gambling and that had to take a toll no matter how rich he was. In her book Barbara claims he once told her he lost $6 million in one crap game. While that seems unlikely, he certainly had plenty of money after selling the agency and Marman. He not only gambled for high stakes, but Zeppo also bought expensive things and invested large sums of money into businesses and the stock market.

By the time Barbara had settled into life in Palm Springs, Zeppo had again lost contact with Tom and Tim following their 1958 visit. Tim made some effort to stay in touch, but Tom was through with Zeppo and wanted nothing to do with him. He says, "My brother kind of ingratiated himself to him, but I didn't have any interest. I couldn't even speak to Zeppo. If I said something to him that he didn't like, he could explode. I was glad to be out of the whole thing."

Zeppo didn't know that Tom had dropped out of Cheshire Academy in the spring of 1961. Tim says, "That's when Tom's musical career started to blossom. He got into the Berklee School of Music in Boston without a high school diploma, based on some tapes he had made playing percussion and piano. They thought he was incredible." Tom adds, "Zeppo knew nothing at all about my music, but Marion knew all about it. I got a little bit close to my mother, but not very close. She was very demanding. She knew everything. You knew nothing. One of the things she used to say was, 'Don't put me on the defensive.' You couldn't criticize her at all for anything."

Tim's relationship with Marion remained cordial. In 1960 she took him on a European vacation that included a trip to Rome for the Olympics. Tim recalls, "Tom did me a big favor at that time. He told Marion, 'Tim really needs to go back with you and go to school in New York.'" But his last semester at the Cheshire School didn't go well. In the fall of 1961, his deliberate effort to flunk out at Cheshire caused Tim to repeat the eleventh grade at the Rhodes School on West 54th Street in Manhattan. But living in New York with Marion greatly improved Tim's situation. She traveled extensively, leaving him alone in the apartment for weeks at a time.

In the spring of 1963, Tim was a member of the Rhodes baseball team and he pitched the opening game on April 1. Marion did not attend. Tim returned home after the game and when asked by his mother how he did, he told her he had pitched a no-hitter. She laughed it off as an April Fools' Day prank. But the next day Marion saw an item in the *New York Times*: "No-Hitter by Marx

Wins for Rhodes." The article said, "Tim Marx enjoyed the thrill of a lifetime by pitching an opening-season baseball no-hitter for Rhodes School yesterday. Marx twirled the prep school team from Manhattan to a 5–0 victory over Bronx Science High School. . . . He struck out nine batters." Marion a sentimental, if indifferent parent, carefully saved the newspaper clipping. If the news made it back to Zeppo in California Tim was not aware of it.

In October 1962 Marion's mother had died at the age of seventy-seven. She'd recently retired as an interior decorator, a profession she took up when she moved back to New York at Marion's behest. With her mother gone, Marion was grateful to have Tim in her life more regularly. By the time he graduated in 1963, the animosity between Marion and Zeppo had further diminished. Tim recalls, "I went away to college in Atlanta that fall, and Marion moved back to Los Angeles. She and Zeppo were friendly at that point. Things really started to get better between them when I was in high school." But Marion still held a certain level of resentment. Tim says, "She was very much annoyed that he married Barbara. Marion didn't like her at all. Barbara was a close pal of Dinah Shore, and they would turn up at the Beverly Hills Tennis Club. Marion used to snarl about it. It was an invasion of her space."

Zeppo and Barbara socialized with Shore frequently in Palm Springs while she was going through her divorce from actor George Montgomery. She married Maurice Smith, her mixed doubles partner from the Racquet Club, as soon as the divorce was finalized. A large group of friends, including Barbara and Zeppo, celebrated with her when she opened at Harrah's Lake Tahoe in August 1963. When Dinah was at the Riviera in October, another large group of Palm Springs friends made the trip, this time including actress Donna Reed and her producer husband, Tony Owen. Owen, a former agent, liked to gamble and was an acquaintance of Zeppo's. They had both been regulars at the Clover Club twenty years earlier.

Marion reconnected with Harpo's wife Susan after not being in touch for most of the eight years she spent in New York. She complained to Susan that Barbara was born the same year she and Zeppo had gotten married and called her ex-husband a dirty old man. Susan and Harpo were living near Zeppo and Barbara in Palm Springs and they liked Barbara. Harpo also didn't like hearing complaints about his brothers, no matter how justifiable they may have been. Marion's comments didn't impress Susan either. She was twenty years younger than Harpo and didn't see the twenty-six-year age difference between Zeppo and Barbara any differently. Susan and Marion remained friendly, but from a comfortable distance. With their children grown there wasn't much left in common for them.

Tim visited Marion in Los Angeles during his spring break from college in 1964. Marion was justifiably proud of Tim for having overcome a childhood that even she would have to admit was far from ideal. She tried to foster a relationship with Tom, but it was difficult. Tim says, "When we first moved to New York with Marion, Tom started getting high. That continued after high school, and it got worse. Marion recognized that military school messed up Tom."

During Tim's visit there was a brief awkward reunion with Zeppo. Marion and Tim went to see a movie in Westwood and Marion noticed someone in the lobby of the theater. "That old guy looks familiar," she jokingly said to Tim. Zeppo and Barbara stopped to say hello. Marion and Zeppo were very cordial, and everyone quickly moved on. Near the end of his visit, Marion surprised Tim with an expensive gift—the sort of thing that would never have come from Zeppo. She bought him a 1964 Chevrolet Corvair and asked when he needed to be back at school. "In four days," Tim answered. Marion suggested he hop in and start driving. Tim rushed back to Atlanta in his new car. He drove back to Los Angeles in the car that summer and visited Marion again. He didn't see Zeppo on that trip.

Zeppo liked to tell people that he was now a citrus rancher, so it was unexpected and caused a minor family crisis when Harpo and Gummo learned that he'd sold his share of the Martuc Ranch without telling his partners—just before a statement came showing the ranch needed additional investments by the partners. Zeppo's share, which had also briefly been partly owned by Groucho, was sold to Tony Owen. Harpo immediately wanted to sell his share of the ranch, since he only bought in because of Zeppo. But it proved difficult to sell for several years.[1] When they learned that Tony Owen was their new partner, Harpo and Gummo suspected that Zeppo had lost his piece of the ranch in a card game.

As Harpo's heart troubles worsened, he was told by his doctor in no uncertain terms to stop working. To Susan's dismay he became convinced that open-heart surgery would repair the damage to his heart and enable him to get back on stage. He was financially secure; he just missed the applause. He died on September 28, 1964, several hours after having had the operation. Per Harpo's wishes there was no funeral service or family gathering. The surviving brothers had been so depressed at Chico's funeral they were probably relieved to grieve privately.

There was no question that Harpo was the most beloved member of the family. While the brothers may have had serious issues with Chico's or Zeppo's behavior, none of them could ever view Harpo as anything other than a complete angel. For Zeppo it was another grim reminder that, although he was the youngest brother, he was—at the age of sixty-three—approaching the twilight of his life. In his 1968 memoir, *The Unimportance of Being Oscar*, longtime Marx family friend Oscar Levant wrote, "I saw Zeppo not long ago. 'Had any fistfights lately?' I asked him. 'Had one about a month ago.' he sighed. 'It was very tough.' Then, for the first time, I knew Zeppo was getting old."

CHAPTER TWENTY-THREE

With Friends Like These . . .

WHENEVER ZEPPO AND BARBARA WERE IN LOS ANGELES, ZEPPO spent his days at the Friars Club; while Barbara, to the consternation of Marion, was often at the Beverly Hills Tennis Club. Zeppo played high stakes gin rummy with fellow Friars including Phil Silvers and Tony Martin. There were also some wealthy noncelebrity Friars in his regular game. Harry Karl, who was married to Debbie Reynolds, made a fortune in his family's shoe business. Victor Lands was a Beverly Hills doctor with many famous patients. Maury Friedman was a Las Vegas real estate developer who had put together a $25 million deal for the Frontier Hotel. Ben Teitelbaum was the co-owner of Hollywood Film Service, a manufacturer of movie studio equipment. He owned an art collection estimated to be worth $3 million that included some items from Zeppo's collection purchased at auction. T. Warner Richardson had previously operated the Silver Slipper in Las Vegas and was currently with the Frontier Hotel. Ricky Jacobs, supposedly an investment counselor, was really a professional gambler and the owner of a card club in Santa Monica. Apart from hanging around at the Friars Club, they all had something else in common: they were reprobate gamblers. What would become clear later was that Lands, Friedman, Teitelbaum, Richardson, and Jacobs were cheating.

The game started in the summer of 1962 as a two-handed grudge match between Harry Karl and Maury Friedman. As the stakes got higher, they drew the attention of the others in the card room. It soon became a four-handed game with restaurateur Al Mathes and Ted Briskin, a millionaire playboy whose father made a fortune with the Revere Camera Company selling home movie equipment.[1] Other Friars started to sit in when one of the four players wasn't available, and the game evolved into the larger rotating group over several months. Zeppo and Kurt Frings, mostly known as Audrey Hepburn's agent, played frequently.

Sometimes Zeppo would win several thousand dollars. And he could just as easily lose twice as much the next time he played.

One Friar rarely played but observed the game frequently. His name was Johnny Rosselli. His membership in the Friars Club had been sponsored by Frank Sinatra, Dean Martin, and George Jessel. Most of the older Hollywood crowd at the club knew quite well that Rosselli had been indicted on federal labor racketeering charges in 1942 for attempting to extort the studios with threats of labor trouble and had spent nearly four years in prison for it. Zeppo certainly knew about it, having been part of the Artists' Managers Guild, which tried to quietly benefit from Rosselli's scheme.

It didn't take long for Rosselli to figure out what was going on in the Friars Club card room. He knew Friedman was a card cheat, and he asked him to explain how he was beating his rich fellow Friars out of so much money. The answer was in the ceiling. Friedman had hired an electronics expert named George Emerson Seach to set up a space in an air duct above the card table. Equipped with a telescope and a transmitter, Seach sent electronic signals from his position in the air duct to a receiver in Friedman's pocket. If Friedman wasn't to be that night's winner one of the other crooked players would have the receiver. Having Friedman occasionally come out the big loser made it look legitimate. Johnny Rosselli was impressed enough to make himself a partner in the scheme to the tune of 20 percent of the take. Friedman had no problem making Rosselli his partner because he preferred to remain alive.

Describing the game to Rosselli biographer Lee Server, Tony Martin said, "Most of those guys played for relaxation. . . . Small stakes. A few hundred dollars. But there were some guys, Zeppo, Harry Karl . . . some others, they took it very seriously, you know. Somebody like Harry Karl was a degenerate gambler. That's a guy who plays until he wins or loses everything. And if he wins, he goes on playing until he loses again."

Zeppo was known to occasionally separate Harry Karl from large sums of money without being in on the scheme—and both of them could also lose when playing at a table not located under the surveillance equipment. The game went on for five years before the FBI raided the Friars Club on July 20, 1967. They got a tip exposing the scheme from Beldon Katleman—Zeppo's one-time El Rancho Vegas partner and fellow Terre Haute grand jury witness. Katleman, himself a notorious card cheat, despised Maury Friedman. When George Seach told him about the Friars Club game Katleman called the FBI. George Seach cooperated, and his confession included the names of all the participants—including Edwin Gebhardt and Albert "Slick" Snyder, the men who worked in the air duct when Seach spent some time in prison for an unrelated burglary conviction or was otherwise unavailable.

Once again Zeppo received a subpoena in a gambling investigation. This time he didn't try to evade it. The Los Angeles County grand jury heard more than a hundred witnesses. Testimony revealed that Ted Briskin was the biggest victim with losses of $220,000. Harry Karl lost $80,000—including $9,200 in a single game. Ben Teitelbaum was said to have won $30,000 from bank executive Richard Corenson in one game. Total losses in the scheme were estimated at around $1 million.

It was Zeppo's turn to talk to the grand jury on November 30, 1967. During his fifteen-minute testimony, he acknowledged that he was a member of the Friars Club and that "I played a little gin rummy and lost," adding "my losses were nothing like those other fellows." He told reporters as he left the courtroom that he was "running a citrus grove in the southern part of the state." When pressed with more questions he replied, "You should've gotten Groucho. He'd have loved this."

Friedman, Jacobs, Lands, Teitelbaum, Richardson, and Rosselli were all indicted. Gebhardt, Mathes, and Snyder were named as co-conspirators along with a few other lesser players. Gebhardt and Snyder were indicted separately on perjury charges for repeatedly lying during the grand jury proceedings. Maury Friedman bribed a court employee and obtained the secret grand jury transcripts. He learned that George Seach had been granted immunity from prosecution in exchange for implicating everyone involved in the crooked game.

Friedman and Johnny Rosselli decided the only way to save themselves was to kill George Seach before the trial. If the jury never hears the star witness the case falls apart. Rosselli arranged for mob hit men Jimmy "the Weasel" Fratianno and Frank Bompensiero to eliminate Seach. The pair headed to Las Vegas to stalk their target, but Seach was whisked away from them and put into protective custody almost immediately. Rosselli and Fratianno naturally had no idea that Bompensiero was an FBI informant. George Seach would testify at the trial, which would begin on June 11, 1968.

Victor Lands made a deal and pleaded guilty to one count of filing a false income tax return and the case against him did not go to trial. He must have had a good lawyer because he was intimately involved with the establishment of the scheme. As the chairman of the house committee at the Friars Club, Lands had allowed the installation of the surveillance system in the card room ceiling under the guise of it being a burglar alarm. Zeppo testified in the trial of the other five defendants on July 3. The *Los Angeles Times* reported,

Zeppo Marx, who described himself as a retired manufacturer and part-time actor—"not a very good one"—told of playing as a partner of Karl or Briskin against Mathes and Friedman on a few occasions. He said he lost but could not recall how much or whether he paid by cash or check. Several years later, Marx said, he played in two games in which Jacobs was an opponent. He said he lost several hundred dollars each time. Marx described himself as an "average player" and said he never felt that the winners were taking advantage of him.

Phil Silvers was asked how much he lost, and he answered, "Let me put it this way. I'm hitchhiking home." All five defendants were convicted on December 2, 1968.

Shortly after he testified, Zeppo attended a Friars Club roast honoring Joey Bishop. Comedian Corbett Monica set the tone for the evening: "This dinner is so packed that a lot of Friars couldn't get in. They're watching the show through peepholes in the ceiling." Milton Berle presented Bishop with a bunch of gag gifts, including "a periscope from the boys in the card room." Zeppo's involvement in the scandal didn't amount to much more than publicly exposing his own recklessness as a gambler—again.

In the mid 1960s he'd managed to accomplish something that seemed impossible only a few years before. He'd gotten his name in the newspapers as much, or perhaps even more, than the semi-retired Groucho had. And it was almost always as a result of gambling or his association with mobsters. According to Tim these were the people he was comfortable with: "Gambling and mobsters were the normal course of business for Zeppo—his way of life. Those guys were his buddies." Citing one example of Zeppo's high stakes recklessness and impulsiveness, Tim recalls, "He was playing golf with somebody at Hillcrest, and the guy says to him, 'I'll bet you $10,000 you can't make that putt.' It's like thirty feet. Zeppo says, 'Just put your money down.' And he makes the putt. There wasn't a bet that Zeppo would turn down if he thought he could win. For Chico it was an addiction. For Zeppo it was a business."

Zeppo had grown into a comfortable relationship with Bobby who, as a teenager shared some common interests with him.

I remember going to Dodger Stadium with him a lot. He liked to see Sandy Koufax pitch. He was friendly with Lee Walls, who played for the Dodgers for a few seasons in the early sixties, so we'd get to hang with the players a little. When I was fifteen-and-a-half I got a small motorcycle when I got my learner's permit. Zeppo loved motorcycles. I was fascinated by his stories about riding. He had owned an Arial Square Four—a classic vintage British bike. He'd also owned a Vincent Black Shadow, which was another classic. He told me stories about going on rides with his friends in Hollywood.

After six years with Zeppo and Barbara, Bobby left Palm Springs to spend his final year of high school at a boarding school.

Tim spent the summer of 1965 with Marion and got a job in the mailroom at Universal Studios, courtesy of his uncle Alan Miller. After working as an agent at MCA following the sale of Marx, Miller & Marx, Miller moved on to become the vice president of production at Universal Television. Tim spent an evening with his father that summer. "He and Barbara took me to the Friars Club one night. I stayed with them at his apartment on Charleville. He gave me a sport coat to wear at the club and it was missing a button. My mother always kept him immaculately dressed and I remember thinking he would never have had a coat with a missing button when she was around." Tim made every effort to have a relationship with his father, but it seemed Zeppo was only marginally interested. Tim had managed to develop a good relationship with Marion—who occasionally questioned his interest in seeing Zeppo.

As far as a relationship with Zeppo was concerned, Tom could not have been less interested. And his contact with Marion was minimal at this point.

Once I got away from them and came to Boston, that was it for me. They had this idea that we were supposed to be businessmen. We were supposed to be successful—which my brother actually accomplished. But I had no interest at all in being a businessman. I had no sense of business at all. I still don't. I became interested in music when I was around fifteen or sixteen. I went to Berklee for two years and the people there basically hated me. So, I quit.

Tim suggests, "Tom started to think, 'They don't know as much as I do.' So, he blew himself out of Berklee and ended up playing drums in a strip club. Then he's heavy into drugs. Marion enabled Tom. Sent him money occasionally. Zeppo had no knowledge of his drug use at this point."

Tim was back in Los Angeles for Christmas in 1965 and visited Zeppo and Barbara in Palm Springs for a few days. He described them as "cordial, but somewhat distant." It would be his last visit with his father. He borrowed

Marion's car to go see him and recalls, "I'm not so sure my mother wanted me to go, but I wanted to see him. I was greeted at the door by their housekeeper who told me that my father and Barbara were taking a nap. I waited around a while and got to watch their butler pluck a chicken before I finally saw them. I didn't have much interaction with Barbara at all, but they arranged a date for me, so I took some young lady to a movie. I think Barbara set it up. My date was supposedly the runner-up in the Miss Palm Springs pageant."

Tim recalls Zeppo's incredulous reaction when he tried to return some of the money he had been given for the date. "I gave you the money. You can spend it now or spend it later. It's yours." Zeppo never issued refunds. He didn't expect his son to. Before Tim drove back to Los Angeles, he played a round of golf with Zeppo and Barbara. He ran into his Uncle Groucho at Tamarisk and recalls it as one of the handful of times he ever met Groucho.

Tim's visit essentially marked the end of Zeppo's relationship with his two sons. When Tim sent Zeppo and Barbara an invitation to his December 1967 wedding, he received a card back from Barbara with a short note saying they had other plans that day. When he sent an announcement of his son's birth in January 1969, he didn't even get a card back. Tim suspects Zeppo never saw the invitation or the announcement.

CHAPTER TWENTY-FOUR

The Night We Called It a Day

OR BARBARA LIFE IN PALM SPRINGS IN THE LATE 1960S WAS IDYLLIC AND at the same time boring. She was determined to remain married to Zeppo but wasn't exactly discouraging the flirtations of Frank Sinatra. In her book she wrote, "When we weren't seeing Frank socially, Zeppo and I muddled along with dinners and parties as well as keeping up with the constant rounds of gin, golf and tennis—the last often played on Frank's court, which was the closest." Zeppo's jealousy was somewhat hypocritical in light of his own constant infidelity, usually on his boat, but sometimes during trips without Barbara to Los Angeles or Las Vegas.

Zeppo and Barbara took a trip to New York with Groucho and Eden in April 1967. Groucho was promoting his latest book, *The Groucho Letters*, and one of the highlights of the trip was a tribute to the Marx Brothers at the short-lived Gallery of Modern Art. Zeppo was not especially interested in attending a tribute to the Marx Brothers, but he was fascinated by the founder of the Gallery of Modern Art, Huntington Hartford.

Hartford was one of the richest men in the world and was an heir to the A&P supermarket fortune. He built the museum on Columbus Circle to house his extensive personal collection of modern art. Zeppo had known him briefly when he came to Hollywood in the 1940s and tried to buy RKO and Republic Pictures. Hartford also briefly owned a talent agency. But as much as any of that, Zeppo was also interested in Hartford's father, who was a manufacturer involved with the invention of the shock absorber. Money, art, and cars were still among Zeppo's favorite things.

The two-week Marx retrospective began on April 18 and Groucho regaled the audience with stories in between film clips on opening night. Harry Ruby arrived on stage and accompanied Groucho on piano for a couple of songs as

Zeppo mostly watched from the audience. But he did contribute the story of Groucho and Harpo turning up at a bachelor party completely naked in the 1920s. It was a rare lapse in Zeppo's avoidance of anything close to show business.

A few years later he attended the 1970 Broadway opening of *Minnie's Boys* with Groucho. The musical about the early life of the Marx Brothers was cowritten by Groucho's son Arthur. Producer Arthur Whitelaw shared his recollection of the evening with Charlotte Chandler.

> Zeppo came to the opening of *Minnie's Boys* in New York. I'll never forget. I said to Zep, "At the curtain I'd love for you to get up on the stage and make an appearance." And he said, "No, no. I leave all that to Groucho." And Groucho got up at the end of the show, and he said to the audience, who was then standing and applauding him, "I only wish Harpo and Chico could have been here tonight to witness this."

When Groucho had acknowledged Zeppo at the Gallery of Modern Art event, Zeppo got up on stage, told a story and got some laughs. Groucho would not make that mistake twice. Thirty-six years after he left the act, there was still no room in the spotlight for the fourth Marx Brother—no matter how rich and successful he'd become.

With Groucho scheduled to do several newspaper and television interviews during the Gallery of Modern Art retrospective, Zeppo tried to keep a low profile. But when Vincent Canby came to the St. Regis Hotel to interview Groucho for the *New York Times*, Zeppo joined them for lunch at the hotel's King Cole Bar. Canby wrote, "Zeppo had lox and eggs and traded opinions and stories laced with reminiscence and vitriol." The article mentioned that Zeppo looked fit and after leaving the Marx Brothers had "become one of Hollywood's leading talent agents, then became an airplane parts manufacturer and is now the backer of a 'revolutionary new wristwatch.'"

Zeppo listed himself in the Palm Springs city directory as a fisherman but kept himself busy with occasional projects that interested him. With his old friend A. Dale Herman from Marman Products he was the co-owner of a pair of patents for an automatic pulse rate monitor wristwatch. Herman's daughter Rita remembers Zeppo suggesting the idea to her father because he was starting to have concerns about his own health, and he wanted to be able to monitor his heart on the golf course.

Zeppo reiterated one of his important business rules to Herman: "Never use your own money. Use other people's money." They sought an investor for their idea and on July 18, 1967, Zeppo and Herman signed an agreement with real estate developer and philanthropist Louis H. Boyar. Boyar invested $40,000 to develop a commercially satisfactory combination of their pulse rate monitor invention and a watch movement.

The joint venture, which they named the Lifeguard Watch, was set up with Zeppo owning 51 percent, Boyar 39 percent, and Herman 10 percent. They tried to bring the idea to market for several years, even issuing press releases pointing out that the invention was not yet in production. Herman's daughter says the project was abandoned when her father began to have serious health problems. Like Zeppo's idea for roll-on deodorant, the pulse monitor wristwatch was ahead of its time. Fifty years later—after the Marx-Herman patent was no longer viable—the idea came of age and would lead to successful products like the Fitbit and the Apple Watch.

Zeppo in retirement remained on the lookout for innovative ideas. His fellow Friars Club scandal victim Harry Karl was involved with a project that interested Zeppo. Karl owned a Santa Monica company called Sutton Research Corporation, which had started work on creating a nicotine-free cigarette in 1962. Karl offered Zeppo the opportunity to buy three hundred shares of Sutton Research stock for $600.

Six years later, with the idea having caught the attention of the R. J. Reynolds Tobacco Company, the value of the stock suddenly skyrocketed. Karl never took Zeppo's $600 and never turned over the stock. Zeppo claimed to have paid the $600 to Karl in April 1968, but Karl still had not turned over the stock when Zeppo sued him in December 1968 for $449,400 or the three hundred shares.

Zeppo's suit asked the Los Angeles Superior Court to order Karl to pay him either the value of the stock—minus the $600 payment—or to make Karl give him the stock. The lawsuit quietly disappeared the following spring when R. J. Reynolds completed its evaluation of Karl's product. On March 18, 1969, the *News and Observer* of Raleigh, North Carolina reported, "Reynolds dropped its experiments with the tobacco substitute made by Sutton Research Corporation . . . saying the substance produces health irritants of its own." An ironic ending for the chain-smoking Zeppo's quest for a healthy cigarette. Equally ironic was the end of Zeppo's long friendship with Harry Karl. On Zeppo's 1953 Friars Club membership application he had listed the Karl Shoe Company as a business reference.

His frustration with the notoriously difficult Harry Karl was exacerbated by Zeppo's serious approach to the stock market. Zeppo studied the market, always on the lookout for any competitive edge he could find. His brothers, knowing his tenacity in business, tended to follow Zeppo's investment advice. Groucho had lost a significant amount of money in the 1929 market crash and was careful once he started investing again, but his respect for Zeppo's business acumen had resulted in some profitable investments. Zeppo's latest discovery was Lewis A. Bracker, a brash young stockbroker and investment advisor. In September 1968 Zeppo's was one of the required member signatures on Bracker's application to join the Friars Club. Bracker was interviewed for a *Los Angeles Times* profile on January 24, 1969. The *Times* called Bracker a "superbroker" and quoted Zeppo as a satisfied client.

> "I'm one of the best deal men around," says Bracker matter-of-factly. "I can smell a deal a mile away. In the conventional sense, I'm not a good broker. I put people into deals I'm close to. I tell them what to buy and when to get out. If they're smart, they'll do as I say."
> One client who obeys is Zeppo Marx, of Marx Brothers fame. "He's excellent," Marx says. "A brilliant young fellow who does very well for us." Marx won't discuss details, but his brothers also deal with Bracker, and Bracker has done well for them.

Bracker did well enough for the Marxes to put Zeppo in front of yet another grand jury. In June 1971 Bracker was indicted on nine counts of grand theft and three of violating California corporate security laws. Zeppo was among thirty witnesses who were called to testify as victims of Bracker. Zeppo's initial attraction to Bracker may have come because he saw a younger version of himself in him. Bracker, a multimillionaire who drove a Rolls-Royce and lived in a Brentwood mansion, bragged to the *Los Angeles Times* that in college he majored in ping-pong and flunked math. If Bracker was slightly crooked in his dealings Zeppo may have even considered that a point in his favor. In November 1971 Bracker pled guilty to the securities violations and spent five months in prison. He paid $200,000 in restitution to clients and the grand theft charges were dropped. Shortly after his release from prison Bracker was charged with eleven new counts of grand theft, but by that time Zeppo had taken his business elsewhere.

Barbara's friendship with Dinah Shore put Zeppo in social situations he often would have preferred to avoid. He never objected to becoming acquainted with powerful people, but for the most part, the people he'd meet at these gatherings bored him. On March 1, 1970, Dinah was the guest of honor at a swanky Palm Springs party at the Thunderbird Heights home of Vondell and Fred Wilson. (Mrs. Wilson was the former child actress Vondell Darr.) The affair celebrated both Dinah's birthday and the conclusion of her annual tennis tournament. The now twice-divorced Shore was escorted by C. D. Ward, a handsome young aide to vice president Spiro Agnew. Dinah arrived at the affair with Ward, Agnew, and his wife, and Zeppo and Barbara.

The *Desert Sun* reported, "Before long the Vice President and Bob Hope and Zeppo Marx retired to the Wilsons' luxurious billiards room to shoot a game or two." Agnew visited Palm Springs frequently and this new friendship soon resulted in Zeppo being invited to dinner with President Richard Nixon in May 1971.

Zeppo still enjoyed Las Vegas and made frequent trips to the casinos. In the 1960s he'd become acquainted with Nate Jacobson, the president and part owner of Caesars Palace. When Jacobson opened the Kings Castle Hotel and Casino in Lake Tahoe, Zeppo was invited to the grand opening on July 1, 1970. Among the stars in attendance when comedian Buddy Hackett performed in the Camelot Room on opening night were Zeppo's former agency clients Lana Turner and Barbara Stanwyck, neither of whom he'd seen in years. While at Kings Castle, Zeppo gave a rare interview to *Detroit Free Press* columnist Shirley Eder in which it was revealed that he'd come to Lake Tahoe on Frank Sinatra's private jet.

By this point Zeppo had only occasional telephone contact with Tim, who was living in Philadelphia with his wife and son, and no contact at all with Tom, who had been living in Boston trying to make a living as a drummer since dropping out of Berklee. Tom remembers, "Marion wanted to get some tapes to my cousin Bill to see if he could help me because I wasn't working. I was playing with good musicians like John Abercrombie and Jan Hammer, but I wasn't working at all. We were all on welfare." Tom visited Marion in Los Angeles in 1971 and was adamant about not seeing Zeppo. Marion did not suggest the idea at all, but Tom still felt a need to reiterate his disinterest in his father. He made the trip to see his cousin Bill, who had an active career as a composer and pianist and fronted his own jazz trio.

The Bill Marx Trio was playing a long residency at the Etc. Club near the Sunset Strip. Marion and Tom dropped in one night to see Bill, who remembers getting some tapes from Marion: "He was playing very modern stuff—jazz-rock fusion, not at all the kind of music I was involved with. I just didn't know what to do with it. Tom was quite good, but it just wasn't my style, and I knew of no opportunities for a musician playing that stuff."

Tom's musical career was not going anywhere, and he recalls a soul-crushing experience in Boston that put an end to it for a while. "I sat in at one of the local clubs and the drummer came up and escorted me off the bandstand. At that point I just quit; didn't play for several years. I got back into it later." Marion remained committed to helping Tom and sent him money for several years, but he was still using drugs and dealing with ongoing mental and personal issues. He showed no signs of making a go of it in music. Tom says, "After a while she got really sick of me. She just said, 'I give up on you' and I just never heard from her for maybe the last ten years of her life. I had no contact with her at all."

Another musical career seemed to be ending in the spring of 1971. On June 13, Zeppo and Barbara attended Frank Sinatra's farewell concert. That Sinatra would perform hundreds of concerts after this did not change the fact that he had announced his retirement and was giving what he said would be his final show at the Ahmanson Theatre in Los Angeles. Around this time Barbara and the thrice-divorced Sinatra began having an affair. In her book she wrote,

I was as lost and lonely as he was. My marriage was all but dead. Bobby was grown and living abroad; I didn't have to protect him anymore. Whatever happened next between Frank and me—and I knew then that something would—I wouldn't try to stop it. I was happy again, for the first time in years, and it felt so good.

Bobby had moved to Switzerland to attend college, and Barbara planned to visit him and then see some friends in Monaco. Whether coincidental or deliberately planned, Sinatra would be in Monaco at the same time. In her book Barbara said, "Quite apart from what might happen in Monaco, I could only guess what Zeppo would get up to while I was away."

As the tensions mounted, Zeppo and Barbara continued to appear at events looking like a happily married couple. Bobby recalled Zeppo telling him years later that the frequent dinners at Sinatra's house caused him humiliation as it became obvious to others what he already knew. The dedication ceremony for the Eisenhower Medical Center in Rancho Mirage on November 27, 1971, brought out big names from the world of politics like governor Ronald Reagan and vice president Spiro Agnew, as well as former first lady Mamie Eisenhower. From the entertainment world, celebrity fundraisers for the hospital included Jack Warner, Greer Garson, Red Skelton, Bob Hope, Gene Autry, Hal Wallis, Ray Bolger, and—to the insanely jealous Zeppo's dismay—Frank Sinatra.

Sinatra biographer James Kaplan wrote of Frank's blossoming relationship with Barbara:

And then there was forty-three-year-old Barbara Marx, ever less married to Zeppo and increasingly present in [Frank's] life. Tina Sinatra, visiting the Riviera soon after Frank's farewell performance at the Ahmanson Theatre, saw her father and Marx together in Monte Carlo, looking a lot like a couple.

Sinatra's daughter wasn't the only person to observe Frank and Barbara in Monaco. Either by virtue of an amazing coincidence or some astute planning by Zeppo, Barbara was met by Greg Bautzer, Zeppo's attorney, as she slipped out of Sinatra's suite at the Hotel de Paris one morning. Zeppo appeared to treat the deterioration of his marriage like anything else—business. Although if it was his intention to accuse her of adultery, she would have had no trouble citing dozens of Zeppo's indiscretions.

Back in Palm Springs things were tense, and most of their friends knew what was going on. Barbara wrote,

Zeppo and I were still living in the same house, although not the same bedroom. We put up a good front and went out together as husband and wife, visiting our usual haunts. In spite of the fact that Frank and I weren't seeing each other (or perhaps because we weren't) there was still a constant frisson between us. Even sitting next to him made me jittery. When Zeppo began to pick up on that sexual tension, he became irrationally jealous even though *he* was far from faithful.

When they decided to separate, Barbara needed to move out of Zeppo's house but had no money and no place to go other than her parents' house in Long Beach. Groucho's now former wife Eden wanted to sell the house she got from Groucho in their 1969 divorce. It was a small house near the golf course at Tamarisk.[1] Sinatra bought it and put it in Barbara's name. Problem solved. She filed for divorce on December 27, 1972, five weeks after moving out of Zeppo's house.

Bobby says,

When Zeppo and my mom separated I kept up my relationship with him. And I was not exactly the kind of guy he wanted me to be. This was the age of hippies, rock and roll and long hair. But we had a good time. I remember going out to movies with him. My mom encouraged me to keep the relationship going. I remember her being worried about him being alone. As hurt as Zeppo was he would sometimes speak very highly of my mother to me, which I thought was odd. I always had a lot of sympathy for him because, at least with me there was no facade. He was clearly hurt and upset.

Barbara summed up her life with Zeppo in her book:

Although I'd loved Zeppo in the beginning and had truly wanted our marriage to work, I didn't feel sad about leaving him at that point, because I knew it was his behavior, not mine, that was to blame. If he hadn't been so unfaithful, if he'd been the stepfather Bobby deserved, if he'd been less tight with money and more generous with his attentions, then we might have remained married until the day he died.

After Barbara moved out, Zeppo could no longer bear being Frank Sinatra's neighbor. Barbara had privately joked to friends that she wanted to build a tunnel under the fairway at Tamarisk so she could avoid detection when making late-night visits to Sinatra while Zeppo slept. For his part, Zeppo—not really joking—said there wasn't a fence tall enough to keep his wife off the neighbor's property.

Barbara wrote of Zeppo initially being difficult in the divorce proceedings: "One day I was having lunch at the Bistro in Beverly Hills with Sidney Korshak, the husband of my friend Bee, when Zeppo's attorney Greg Bautzer leaned across from an adjacent table. 'Barbara,' he told me, 'The only thing you're going to get from Zeppo is the clap.'"

Barbara's characterization of a casual lunch with her friend's husband is—to be charitable—disingenuous. With Sinatra's help, Barbara retained Korshak as her attorney. Sidney Korshak was about as well connected in both Hollywood and organized crime circles as a person could be. He and Zeppo numbered among their mutual friends Lew Wasserman, who had purchased Zeppo's agency for MCA, and Moe Dalitz, a leading figure in the Las Vegas casino business. Zeppo respected Korshak and the divorce became yet another business deal for him. He agreed to pay Barbara $1,500 a month for ten years. And in a purely magnanimous gesture, allowed her to keep the 1969 Jaguar he had bought for her. There is no evidence to indicate one way or the other if he cared when Sinatra bought her a brand-new Jaguar when he heard about Zeppo's gesture.

With no commitment about marriage from Sinatra, Barbara still had concerns about her financial future. While she didn't see a big windfall from Zeppo in the divorce, she wasn't overly concerned. Her sights were clearly set on Sinatra. She could look back on thirteen years of marriage to Zeppo as an investment that didn't quite pan out. James Kaplan wrote that Frank's younger daughter Tina came to see Barbara "with a certain grudging admiration, as a 'relentless strategist, a professional survivor.'" She had a theory about Barbara regarding Frank's occasional mistreatment of her while they were dating: "as for why she would tolerate his abuse: she would hold on tight for as long as it took, no matter how tough the ride, until the prize was hers." While this could also be applied to her relationship with Zeppo, she ultimately saw a better prize in Zeppo's neighbor.

CHAPTER TWENTY-FIVE

The Lion in Winter

A BACHELOR ONCE AGAIN, ZEPPO ACCELERATED HIS RELENTLESS PURSUIT of attractive women decades younger. *Today* star Barbara Walters had written in a September 12, 1971, *Family Weekly* article,

> My husband and I recently vacationed in Palm Springs, California, where Groucho's brother, Zeppo, has a home. At lunch at the Racquet Club, we watched Zeppo Marx talk to various women he knew . . . wives of friends and friends of his own wife. In every case, he had a smile, a compliment, a sincere delight in seeing them again. I've never met Zeppo Marx, but I'd like to.

There had never been any doubt about Zeppo being charming. As his relationship with his wife deteriorated, he wasted no time looking for his next female companion.

Zeppo first met Roxann Ploss at a party he and Barbara attended at Frank Sinatra's house in 1971. Ploss was an attractive twenty-three-year-old high school teacher who had recently arrived in Palm Springs. Recalling the period, Ploss says,

> Palm Springs in those days was empty of single young females during the week. Busloads of them showed up for the weekends looking for rich potential husbands. Being college educated, young, and breathing made me a hot commodity. So, I was a regular at Sinatra's dinner parties and I started dating him. After Zeppo and Barbara split up he called me and asked if I'd be interested in going out with him. He told some-

one at a party that he and Frank had switched partners and that he'd gotten the better of the deal.

Roxann saw through Zeppo's jokes and felt he was quite broken up about losing Barbara. Roxann and Zeppo became very close despite their forty-seven-year difference in age. She got to know him as well as anyone could in his last years and recalls some of his quirks.

> He had an enormous closet filled with nice clothes but rarely wore anything but very casual attire, which wasn't really in style at that time. He had a Rolls-Royce but drove a little Honda around town. And he kept $5,000 cash in his safe out of force of habit dating back to when he and his brothers would have to bail Chico out of trouble late at night. I sometimes sorted his mail and found a charge from a Swiss bank. He told me he was storing some of his patents in a vault there.

She also remembers Barbara calling Zeppo to retrieve a very expensive Judith Leiber gold mesh handbag she had left behind at his house. "Zeppo fluffed her off, saying that it was in a safety deposit box in Los Angeles, and he'd let her know when he had a chance to get it. He turned to me and said, 'I paid for it. Maybe I should let you have it.'" Zeppo also told Roxann that he'd "never met anyone more self-disciplined than Barbara. She could have a raging fever and would still get out of bed to do her exercise routine every morning."

Zeppo turned down numerous interview requests as the Marx Brothers experienced a great revival in the early seventies. Groucho couldn't get enough of it, but the last thing Zeppo wanted to do was go on television to talk about his career as part of the act. He was invited to appear on *The Dick Cavett Show*. Business always being on his mind, Zeppo told Cavett he would appear on his show for $5,000. Talk shows paid union scale, which was around $200, so Cavett had to decline Zeppo's offer. In retrospect he says, "We should have paid it. He would have been a fascinating guest."

On the other hand, Zeppo agreed to a pair of print interviews at Groucho's behest without being paid. It was difficult for him to turn down requests from Groucho, who by this time was sending Zeppo a monthly check, believing him to be having money problems. With his health deteriorating, Groucho no longer visited Palm Springs, so he knew nothing about Zeppo's opulent lifestyle. He also didn't wonder how Zeppo was able to keep his penthouse in Beverly Hills while supposedly struggling to pay his bills.

Zeppo began making frequent visits to Beverly Hills to see Groucho. In 1971 Erin Fleming, an ambitious out-of-work actress, came into Groucho's life and took charge of what remained of it. She became his manager and started booking him on television. With no one else showing much interest, Groucho welcomed Erin into his life. She set up a physically demanding concert tour for Groucho in 1972 and wasn't shy about using his celebrity to enhance her own weak career prospects.[1]

Zeppo was among the many friends and relatives who objected to Groucho performing in his compromised state, but he stopped short of objecting to Erin because he would never risk alienating an attractive younger woman. Apart from that, he was still being paid by Groucho each month, and Erin had taken control of Groucho's checkbook. Groucho was also still facile enough to express displeasure at the mention of anything negative about Erin.

The two interviews Zeppo agreed to were for book projects Groucho was involved with. Talking to Richard J. Anobile for *The Marx Bros. Scrapbook*, Zeppo was short with his answers and at times rude. Anobile recalled, "Zeppo was a tough interview. He only did it because Groucho wanted him to. Gummo also told him he should talk to me. He didn't give me too much time. He kept looking over at the television and checking the stock market reports during the interview. It felt like he wanted to get through with it as quickly as possible."

Interviewed by Lyn Ehrhard (who used the pen name Charlotte Chandler) for her book *Hello, I Must Be Going: Groucho and His Friends*, Zeppo was friendly and accommodating. The Ehrhard interview is peppered with valuable information and insights about his life with the Marx Brothers and beyond. The reason for Zeppo's cooperation was simple. He wanted to date Lyn Ehrhard.[2] She wrote in the book, "Although Zeppo was then in his seventies, he looked much younger. He had fair hair and his voice sounded as it did in the Paramount comedies. He told me he was always 'a very shy person,' but I didn't know if I should completely believe him, because he had his hand on my knee at the time."

In the spring of 1973, Groucho spoke freely to Richard J. Anobile in his interviews for *The Marx Bros. Scrapbook* and was not aware that Anobile would include what he assumed were off-the-record, and occasionally profane or embarrassing, comments in the book. Zeppo got off relatively easy. Comparing him to Chico, Groucho said, "Chico was sort of a rascal and Zeppo isn't. He's just cold-blooded." At the last minute, Erin orchestrated a lawsuit in Groucho's name to prevent the book from being published, but the suit was unsuccessful. Zeppo also spoke freely to Anobile and was surprised to see his brutally frank comments about Groucho in the book. With Erin's by now familiar irrational behavior and quick temper, Zeppo's monthly stipend was clearly at risk.

In the book Zeppo said, "I think it is just terrible that he is still working. It's awful. Why the hell doesn't he just hang them up. He's 82 and going on 83, and he's got all the money he needs. He can't be that much of a ham that he wants to keep performing." Zeppo doubled down and called out a recent television appearance that alarmed many of Groucho's friends. "I don't know if it's the income he's worried about. He was on the *Bill Cosby Show* a few weeks ago. I had to turn it off. He didn't look like Groucho; he didn't act like Groucho, and he didn't talk like Groucho. He had this silly grin on his face, and he kept looking at Cosby, waiting for him to ask the next question." Anobile had provided Groucho with an advance proof of the book, which Groucho approved—but clearly without reading it.

The Marx Bros. Scrapbook also includes Zeppo's review of the final show of the *Evening with Groucho* concert tour at the Dorothy Chandler Pavilion in Los Angeles on December 11, 1972. It had been rescheduled after the original September date had to be postponed when Groucho suffered a stroke. Shows in Chicago and Detroit were canceled, but Erin insisted the Los Angeles show be played. She was not willing to give up her own opportunity in the spotlight in front of an audience filled with show business luminaries, since she had made herself part of Groucho's show. Zeppo's assessment of the performance was shared by many and borne out by the rarely shown film of the event, which was kept from release at the time due to Groucho's frail appearance.

Appalled by what he saw that evening, Zeppo told Anobile,

I went to see his one man show. He couldn't remember a goddamn thing. The piano player had to keep cueing him. After all, he had to do something for this man who couldn't remember what the hell he was going to do next. And he was reading the stuff and he couldn't do it well! Jesus, I think he's spoiling a great image. He's tearing down something it took years to build. Why does he have to do it?

If Groucho read Zeppo's comments he didn't hold a grudge. Zeppo met a teenaged Marx Brothers fan and collector named John Tefteller at the show and briefly corresponded with him. In a letter dated December 26, 1972, Zeppo wrote:

I was pleased to receive your letter at a time when I needed a little cheering up. My wife is divorcing me, and I was lonely this Christmas. It's nice to realize that our pictures are bringing a ray of happiness to the now generation. Shows there is not a generation gap, just a lack of communication between the generations. Your collection sounds fabulous. I never saved anything. I will have my secretary answer your questions at a later date. That was she sitting with me the night of *An Evening with Groucho* when you saw me in the audience. Cute, huh?

The cute secretary didn't write back to answer Tefteller's questions. Zeppo did. In a December 28 letter, he said his favorite Marx Brothers movie was *The Cocoanuts*, and that "Humor Risk" was a piece of junk, and he didn't know where it was. Zeppo closed the letter saying, "Well I'm practically single now and lovable, yes."

That evening at the Dorothy Chandler Pavilion brought another encounter with a young Marx Brothers fan. In his memoir, *Raised Eyebrows: My Years Inside Groucho's House*, Steve Stoliar wrote of spotting Zeppo in the parking garage after the performance.

I mustered all my courage, strode over to him and said, "Mr. Marx, I just wanted to tell you how much I've enjoyed your work over the years." "It wasn't *me* you enjoyed," he protested, "It was my brothers." However right he may have been, there was no denying how exciting it was to have been admonished by a genuine Marx Brother.

Zeppo and Barbara's divorce was finalized on May 1, 1973. Two days later he responded to a fan letter inquiring about the Marx Brothers, apologizing for his slow reply. "Sorry it took me so long to write to you. I recently went through a divorce. Harpo and Chico are deceased, and I have been lucky to carry on. I still enjoy life."

On July 13, the *Desert Sun* reported that Zeppo had moved into a new condominium in Palm Springs. "'It's ideal,' said Marx who is selling his lovely Tamarisk Country Club home to move into the Diplomat. 'It has everything I've been looking for, space, a beautiful view, every convenience, and privacy when I want it.'"

He had all of that at Tamarisk, but his view there included Sinatra's house, and he had seen enough of that. Zeppo would still have lunch at Tamarisk on occasion, but after he moved, he became a regular at the Canyon Country

Club—until he was banned from that establishment. Old habits die hard and Zeppo got into a fight with Rocco Zangari, a low-level organized crime figure thirty years younger. In Zeppo's view, Rocco violated the cardinal rule of gambling. He wagered more than he had and could not pay up after their gin rummy game. Zangari's brother Dominick was the owner of Dominick's Restaurant, a popular spot in Rancho Mirage and a well-known Sinatra hangout. For scuffling with Rocco, Zeppo briefly found himself unwelcome at Dominick's, but was eventually forgiven.

Steve Stoliar soon began working at Groucho's house sorting his archives and helping with fan mail. He had a few further encounters with Zeppo and wrote, "I found Zeppo to be charming, animated and very amusing. And he seemed about twenty years younger than he actually was." Zeppo also met Stoliar's girlfriend, and she instantly caught his eye. When she and Stoliar stopped dating and remained friends, Zeppo made his move. Stoliar wrote:

> Linda and I stopped seeing each other romantically. About that time, I'd found a couple of vintage photos of Zeppo that I wanted him to sign. . . . I sent the photos to Zeppo along with a note informing him that Linda and I had broken up and wanting to know if a man of his experience had any advice for the lovelorn.
>
> I should have seen it coming. Two days later, I received a long-distance call from the Tamarisk Country Club in Palm Springs:
> . . . "Steve? It's Zeppo Marx, how are you? I got those pictures you sent, and I'll be happy to sign them for you. *God*, I was good-looking back then. Listen, I'm sorry to hear about you and Linda, but I was wondering: Do you think she'd go out with me?"

Zeppo was seventy-four and Linda was nineteen. Zeppo described their one date to Stoliar. "I took her to dinner in San Diego and then to a jai alai game in Tijuana. But we didn't 'do' anything. I didn't even kiss her, Steve. I swear it. You know, she's very nice, but all she did was talk about herself all evening." When Zeppo saw Stoliar at a party or event he would introduce him to whoever was nearby by saying, "Have you met Steve? He and I went out with the same girl, but he got further with her than I did."

Zeppo had much more in common with Roxann Ploss, and they began vacationing together. She too was taken to a jai alai match in Tijuana. In Las Vegas, Zeppo took Roxann to shows with stars like Wayne Newton. She remembers a lengthy backstage visit with Jerry Van Dyke. And of course, they gambled.

She observed Zeppo playing chemin de fer and baccarat but suggests that he wasn't gambling all that much at this point.

He was most passionate about fishing and would occasionally make the thousand-mile drive from Palm Springs to Buena Vista on the Baja Peninsula in a motor home for a fishing vacation. He made a point of telling Charlotte Chandler that he was a commercial fisherman. When Zeppo took Roxann to the Salton Sea the fishing became less enjoyable for him when she caught more fish than he did. She says, "Fishing was never a business for Zeppo. The commercial fisherman thing was just his inside joke. He could just as easily have called himself a professional card shark."

Beginning in the early sixties, Zeppo had a regular group of fishing buddies that frequently joined him for trips to Mexico on his boat. Eddie Suisman, Leonard Krieger, and Charlie Lubin were wealthy businessmen. The group was rounded out by Chuck Flick, the skipper of Zeppo's boat. According to Roxann Ploss, none of them would ever discuss any details of what went on during these excursions. It was a very private club. There would have been no need to be mysterious about fishing and playing cards, so these mostly married fishermen probably had some female companionship on their top-secret fishing trips, which continued into the seventies.

Barbara was living in Eden's former home and had become Sinatra's constant companion. She wrote of an unusual encounter with Groucho shortly after she moved out of Zeppo's house.

There was only one person who dared to express his disapproval publicly—Groucho Marx. He came up to us at a charity event one day and said to Frank, "Why don't you let Barbara go? You don't want her. Let her go back to Zeppo." Everyone knew Frank had a trigger temper, but Groucho was a fearless octogenarian. Fortunately, Frank chose not to respond, and I didn't say a word either, so dear old Groucho repeated his statement before going off with that funny little walk of his. I was both astonished at his nerve and touched that he was still so protective of his little brother Zep.

Barbara would finally marry Sinatra on July 11, 1976.

Groucho's protective instinct was something Zeppo was not above exploiting. In the wake of the publicity about the Friars Club scandal and his second divorce, Zeppo convinced Groucho that he was in dire financial trouble. Groucho, like everyone else close to Zeppo, had no idea how much money he'd been paid for Marman Products, and the agency deal was mysterious enough that even Gummo's assessment of it was incomplete—he being unaware that Zeppo likely received an additional undocumented payment not shared with his partners. When a compromised Groucho in his early eighties agreed to pay some of Zeppo's gambling debts—separately and apart from the monthly stipend he was already paying him—he certainly didn't consider the steady and significant monthly income from his brother's Safeway stores. And Groucho probably didn't give much thought to why he was giving financial assistance to a guy who'd just purchased a new yacht.

Groucho wanted to see Gummo and Zeppo as often as possible and frequently hosted parties at his house. Erin made sure the affairs were filled with younger celebrities like Jack Nicholson, Sally Kellerman, George Segal, and Alice Cooper as well as old friends like George Burns, Harry Ruby, and George Jessel. Zeppo drove in from Palm Springs for as many of these parties as he could manage. It was an opportunity to flirt with young women. Gummo rarely made the scene at Groucho's house, preferring to avoid the circus-like atmosphere created by Erin. Once he began dating Roxann Ploss, Zeppo brought her to Groucho's house on occasion. She says, "Erin and I became quasi-friends, something Zeppo warned me against often. It ended as he predicted."

Apart from persistent problems with his hearing, Zeppo appeared to be a very robust physical specimen in his early seventies. But chain-smoking and less-than-healthy eating habits started to catch up with him. Bobby Marx recalls,

> He was always sensitive about his hearing problem. He didn't want to wear hearing aids. He would speak in a very loud voice and expected you to do the same because he couldn't hear. He was getting older, which was a tough thing for him. Still vital as a man but getting older. That was a struggle for him because that was a big part of his persona—that macho, virile, tough, attractive guy. A guy who could do whatever he wanted. It was only at the very end that he started to fail. You could see him losing weight and getting thinner, but his attitude was such that he was in control of the situation. He didn't go out as much. He didn't play as much golf.

Zeppo developed an aortic abdominal aneurysm—a weakening of the wall of the largest artery in the body. This was the same ailment for which Harpo had his fateful open-heart surgery nine years earlier. Harpo followed the medical advice offered by Gummo, who insisted the surgeons in Los Angeles were excellent and that there was no need to travel to Texas where the pioneers of open-heart surgery, Michael DeBakey and Denton Cooley, practiced. Susan had suggested going to Texas to see DeBakey, but Harpo took Gummo's advice. At his advanced age and with the newness of the procedure, there was a good chance Harpo would not have survived an operation in Texas either, but Zeppo was taking no chances.

Zeppo was three years younger than Harpo at the time of his operation, and Harpo had the added disadvantage of a history of heart trouble that included three heart attacks. Zeppo arranged for his operation to be performed by the man who had developed a new method for repairing aortic aneurysms. Dr. Denton A. Cooley was a professor of surgery at Baylor College of Medicine and founded the Texas Heart Institute. Zeppo flew to Houston with Bobby just before Christmas, and Cooley operated on him at St. Luke's Hospital on December 28, 1973.

Bobby says, "He really had no one else to go with him. My mom encouraged me to do it. He wouldn't tell anyone he was dating because he didn't want to show any vulnerability or weakness. He had a big room and I stayed with him." After initially being discharged, Zeppo and Bobby returned to Houston. Zeppo became ill as soon as they got back to Palm Springs. Bobby explains, "They left a sponge inside of him, or something stupid like that."

The operation was successful, and he was discharged for the second time in mid-January with instructions to do nothing strenuous—including golf and fishing—for the next several weeks. According to Tim, his father's well-known arrogance and self-confidence overruled Dr. Cooley's medical advice. Days after returning to Palm Springs, Zeppo took his boat out and went fishing. Casting a line, he immediately tore out his stitches. At the hospital in Palm Springs Zeppo angrily exclaimed, "It's not my fault they used cheap fucking thread."

In February 1974 the Academy of Motion Picture Arts and Sciences announced that Groucho would get an honorary Academy Award for his "brilliant creativity and the unequaled achievements of the Marx Brothers in the art of motion picture comedy." Groucho spoke to Associated Press writer Bob Thomas, who recorded his reaction to the announcement:

I only wish that Harpo and Chico could be here to share it. No—if only Minnie were here. None of us would have amounted to anything if it hadn't been for her. What a woman she was! She said that Sam, her husband, could cough all night and she wouldn't wake up. But if one of her sons coughed just once she would wake up immediately.

Asked if he would collect his Oscar in person at the Los Angeles Music Center, Groucho replied, "Certainly, unless they just want to shove it under the door." By the time a very shaky and frail-looking Groucho ambled onto the stage on April 2 to collect the award, the sentimental feelings expressed to the Associated Press had diminished—or he more likely followed Erin's instructions and thanked her while ignoring Zeppo and Gummo in his speech.

Zeppo, sitting in the audience, had no discernible reaction to the slight. In *My Life with Groucho*, Arthur Marx wrote of a dinner with Gummo and his wife a few days after the ceremony: "Gummo said that he was thoroughly disgusted with Groucho for mentioning Erin in his acceptance speech—'You'd think she had something to do with the success of the Marx Brothers,' he complained."

The ceremony was followed by a party a month later at Hillcrest Country Club thrown by Jack Nicholson, Bill Cosby, and Marvin Hamlisch. Zeppo, fully recovered from his surgery and appearing healthy, attended and mingled with the celebrities—showing a particular interest in any young women that might be willing to go out with him. On May 23, 1974, Groucho, Zeppo, and Gummo attended the premiere of the rerelease of *Animal Crackers* in Westwood. Zeppo was frequently seen at events with Groucho and attended the February 9, 1975, American Film Institute tribute to Orson Welles at the Century Plaza Hotel with him. Zeppo was accompanied by Marvin Hamlisch's sister, Terry Liebling. That was an awkward evening for Zeppo. Frank Sinatra was the master of ceremonies and Zeppo ran into Barbara at the event.

That fall Groucho celebrated his eighty-fifth birthday with a celebrity-filled party at his house. Gummo and Zeppo drove in from Palm Springs for the event. Chronicling the affair in *Hello, I Must Be Going: Groucho and His Friends*, Charlotte Chandler wrote:

Zeppo brought some tuna which he had personally caught and canned. Groucho accepted the token with his customary grace. "You needn't have bothered coming. You could've just sent the tuna." Zeppo understood and would, in fact, have been worried by any sign of greater sentiment from older brother Julius.

Whatever Zeppo does he does well—canning tuna, playing cards, inventing complex mechanical devices or creating businesses. Uninhibited, and relatively unexhibited, Zeppo had the talent and energy to have been a pioneer, an inventor, a businessman, an agent—even a Marx Brother.

Zeppo began spending even more time in Los Angeles with Groucho, who was deeply depressed over the 1974 deaths of Harry Ruby and Jack Benny. But he was still committed to living in the desert. He was also spending time in San Diego, where he'd moved his boat from the Salton Sea. He sold his Palm Springs condominium and moved to a complex in Rancho Mirage called Desert Island and joined the newly opened Desert Island Yacht Club.

On February 19, 1975, the *Desert Sun* reported, "The first annual yacht race was led by Zeppo Marx, who recently became a condominium owner at the posh Desert Island development. Marx served as honorary commodore of the Desert Island fleet." In *Son of Harpo Speaks!* Bill Marx recalled Zeppo's time at Desert Island:

> [H]e sold his house and moved to a place in Rancho Mirage called Desert Island, which was completely surrounded by a body of water that was always stocked with fish. Zeppo's no-nonsense approach toward people made him the perfect selection to be the Fish Commish of Desert Island. It was his job to see to it that the fishing limit was two fish per person per day. One day he saw a guy pulling out many more fish than the limit.
>
> Bristling with anger, Zeppo ran out to confront and admonish the man for breaking the rules.
>
> "You SOB! Don't you know there is a limit of only two fish per day?"
>
> "Yes, I do, but I'm only down here on weekends, so this is two for Monday, two for Tuesday, two for Wednesday . . ."
>
> Zeppo was about to haul off and deck him, when suddenly controlling his temper, he responded, "Hey, fella, you're good. Real good!" and walked away.

Roxann Ploss remembers the day of Barbara and Frank Sinatra's wedding. It was at the Annenberg Estate. "To Zeppo it was like adding insult to injury because the entrance was directly across from his balcony at Desert Island. He looked out as the guests arrived and said, 'I'm going fishing.' He would never admit it, but he was deeply hurt by the Sinatra-Barbara thing."

Zeppo had certainly mellowed by this time, but he was still capable of letting his temper get him into trouble. He was awaiting a court date related to an incident that occurred on April 30, 1973—the day before his divorce from Barbara was finalized. Zeppo had met Jean Bodul at the wedding of golf pro Ken Venturi on November 13, 1972, at Mission Hills Country Club in Rancho

Mirage. It was a star-studded event hosted by Frank Sinatra, who by this time was having an affair with Barbara. Zeppo and Barbara were among the five hundred guests who celebrated Venturi's marriage to Hazel "Beau" Wheat, the hostess at Ruby's Dunes restaurant, a favorite Palm Springs hangout of Sinatra's. Sinatra gave away the bride and introduced her friend Jean Bodul to Zeppo.

Bodul was a thirty-nine-year-old divorced mother of a teenaged daughter and lived in a trailer park near Zeppo's Tamarisk home. Jean had been in a long-term tempestuous relationship with notorious mobster Jimmy "the Weasel" Fratianno. In *The Last Mafioso*—Fratianno's authorized biography—author Ovid Demaris noted the reference to Jean in a January 10, 1969, Fratianno probation report:

> "In the summer of 1966," the report stated, without offering a shred of evidence, "it was learned that subject Fratianno had a girlfriend in San Pedro by the name of Jean Bodul, female, Caucasian. Investigation revealed that Bodul was a prostitute working out of the Hollywood area where she maintained an apartment for just that purpose. She was handling her customers through referral from a known pimp in the Hollywood area. Fratianno made frequent trips to the San Pedro area and was seen on many occasions in the company of Bodul."

In April 1969, Jean and Jimmy appeared before a Los Angeles grand jury investigating the death of a mobster who very likely died while chauffeuring Fratianno to the airport. Jean regularly pressured Jimmy for marriage. He'd been divorced a year earlier and had agreed to marry her but changed his mind at the last minute. Jean threw a heavy ashtray at his head and ran out onto the streets of Lake Tahoe, where she went on a violent drunken rampage that landed her in jail. In 1970 Fratianno made a plea bargain in an extortion case and became an FBI informant in exchange for his sentence being reduced to probation. The government reneged on the plea deal and sent Fratianno to Chino State Prison for three years. He stopped informing.

Jean didn't give up on Jimmy, but they still argued whenever they spoke. Demaris wrote, "Jean stopped coming to Chino on visiting days. During that period, Jimmy heard that her drinking problem had worsened. She was living in Palm Springs, only a short drive from Chino, and the rumor was that she was involved with Zeppo Marx. . . . In a pique of temper, Jimmy had removed her name from the list of approved visitors."

The trouble began for Zeppo when Jean called him in San Diego and demanded he marry her. She threatened to move to Australia if he didn't. Zeppo rushed back to Palm Springs and confronted her in the gift shop at the Tamarisk Country Club the next day, shouting, "You're not leaving." In the civil lawsuit Jean Bodul filed against Zeppo for assault and battery, she claimed he pulled her hair and threatened to break her nose as she attempted to get into her car. Zeppo claimed he was trying to get his house key and credit card back from her. The incident was kept quiet and didn't initially make the newspapers. But when the case finally made it to Indio Superior Court, Zeppo once again made headlines for his violent temper.

According to his authorized biography, when Fratianno got out of prison in August 1973, he spoke about Jean with Johnny Rosselli: "I don't know what to do about that broad. She's turning into a lush. Oh, Jesus. It's terrible. She gets violent and throws things, goes on rampages. I get out of there in a hurry. . . . She's got this obsession about getting hitched."

Jean Bodul's determination to marry a rich man paid off when she somehow convinced Fratianno to marry her in 1975. News coverage of the case against Zeppo described Bodul as being the estranged wife of notorious mobster Jimmy "the Weasel" Fratianno. They may have fought constantly, but she was anything but estranged from him when the trial finally began on November 11, 1978.

Fratianno cooperated with another author, Michael J. Zuckerman, on a second book. *Vengeance Is Mine* was published in 1987. Zuckerman wrote, "It amazed everyone in Rancho Mirage that anyone would have the audacity to beat up on Jimmy Fratianno's main squeeze. But the defendant was Zeppo Marx. . . . He apparently took Jean at face value. And he didn't seem overly impressed by the reports of her boyfriend."

Preparing for the trial, Bodul's attorney, Jacques Beugelmans, spent hours on the phone with Fratianno gathering information about Zeppo. Zuckerman wrote, Fratianno "was only too willing to help Beugelmans with this particular Marx Brother's not-so-comical reputation in Las Vegas and Palm Springs. Zeppo was known as a 'degenerate gambler,' he had been thrown out of Tamarisk after a cheating scandal, and had a reputation as a curmudgeon, womanizer, and a man with a violent temper, or so Jimmy said." Other than the false claim about being thrown out of Tamarisk, even Zeppo would have to admit that Fratianno's description of him was pretty accurate. Bodul describes meeting Zeppo in *Vengeance Is Mine*:

It was at the wedding reception. I was standing with my girlfriend Diane, and she was dragging me over with her to see Sinatra when Zeppo came over and Sinatra introduced us. . . . I thought Zeppo was really quite handsome and distinguished-looking . . . he found out where I lived—I was living with my father at the time. . . . Well, at first, I didn't want to go out with him because I thought he might be mean—just a vibration, a feeling, you know. Well, he wouldn't take "no" for an answer. He started sending me flowers and candy and things, and after a while I started going out with him.

She also detailed the incident that led to the lawsuit:

We were at Tamarisk. I was pretty drunk. I always drank stingers at Tamarisk. Anyway, he'd been after me to move in with him for several weeks and I just didn't want to. I guess I—no, I'm quite certain, I still loved Jimmy. Anyway, we started arguing at the clubhouse, and I staggered out, and we argued and pushed and shoved all the way up to his driveway, where I tried to get into my car, and he got absolutely crazy and began hitting me and grabbing my hair and pounding my head against the car door. He pulled clumps of hair out of my head. Oh, he's dreadful.

Apparently Bodul was attracted to violent men. Fratianno pled guilty to planning the 1977 car bombing murder of a Cleveland crime boss and, in exchange for a light sentence, became a government informant for the second time. Fratianno and his wife were placed in the Federal Witness Protection Program and moved to an undisclosed location—believed to be Oklahoma City—under assumed names.[3]

When she came to court to sue Zeppo, Jean Bodul was protected by federal agents, who had placed her in El Paso, Texas, while Fratianno was busy testifying for the government on the East Coast. Her attorney pushed the false narrative that she was no longer with Jimmy "the Weasel" Fratianno. The Bodul trial would be Zeppo's fourth tangential connection to Fratianno, who as an informant provided the true details of the 1937 Les Bruneman murder, and in 1968 was one of the hit men sent to eliminate the government's star witness in the Friars Club case. Fratianno was also personally close to Chico and told his biographer that he and Chico worked a horse racing betting wire scam together in the 1940s. Presumably Zeppo profited from their efforts.

While waiting for the Bodul trial, Zeppo saw headlines about other participants in the Friars Club case. Johnny Rosselli got out of prison in 1973 after serving three years of his five-year sentence. Albert "Slick" Snyder, who was not indicted for his significant role in the scandal, was found strangled in his apartment in November 1974. Snyder had been sent to prison on a perjury conviction, but as an unindicted coconspirator in the Friars Club case was believed to have avoided more severe punishment by providing evidence against his partners after some well-publicized reluctance to talk. Police investigating Snyder's murder announced they could find no motive for the crime. Johnny Rosselli had a pretty good motive. He'd just spent three years in prison—largely as a result of Snyder's testimony. Whether related to Snyder's murder or any number of other things, retribution soon came to Johnny Rosselli. In August 1976 his body was found in a large drum floating in a Florida bay.

Chapter Twenty-Six

It Was a Very Bad Year

ZEPPO DROVE TO LOS ANGELES WITH ROXANN PLOSS ON JANUARY 16, 1977, for what turned out to be Groucho's final public appearance. The Marx Brothers were inducted into the Motion Picture Hall of Fame in a ceremony at the Wilshire Hyatt House hotel. Roxann recalls, "Zeppo was on the dais near his brother, and I was a few feet away at a table of strangers. The whole evening made me quite uncomfortable. At one point Groucho tried to sing 'Hooray for Captain Spaulding' and was so frail he could barely be heard. Erin Fleming jumped up and finished the song with him. It is not a happy memory for me."

If Zeppo thought Groucho was in rough shape at the Dorothy Chandler Pavilion in 1972, more than four years later one can only imagine what he thought as Groucho struggled through the event. Roxann was embarrassed for Zeppo, who had agreed to make a rare public appearance for the occasion. She says, "He never once mentioned the evening again."

The spring of 1977 was a difficult time for the three surviving Marx Brothers. On March 6, Groucho underwent hip surgery and spent two weeks in Cedars Sinai Medical Center. Groucho's son Arthur had seen enough of Erin Fleming and her complete takeover of Groucho's life. On April 15 he asked Santa Monica Superior Court judge Edward Rafeedie to remove Erin Fleming as Groucho's conservator, saying that she was a threat to his life.

Arthur's attorney presented witnesses who had worked at Groucho's house. They described incidents in which Erin verbally and physically abused Groucho and administered unprescribed drugs to sedate him. The five-day hearing also included testimony praising Erin. Her star witness was Zeppo, who told reporters, "Groucho is in love with her. It would be detrimental to Groucho if she were taken away from him." Zeppo could not have been unaware of the abuse described by multiple witnesses during the hearing. His appreciation of attractive younger women may have clouded his opinion of Erin's effect on Groucho's welfare.

On April 21, Gummo died at Eisenhower Medical Center in Palm Springs after a month in the hospital. Groucho was never told of his brother's death. Gummo had made no secret of his feelings about Erin, and had he been well enough to get to Los Angeles, his testimony would have been diametrically opposed to Zeppo's. Zeppo made a short statement about Gummo's death to reporters at the Santa Monica courthouse saying, "I guess his heart just gave out."

The following day Judge Rafeedie removed Erin as Groucho's conservator, temporarily handing the responsibility for Groucho's welfare to his old friend, writer Nat Perrin. There would be a second hearing to select a permanent conservator for Groucho, and the court asked Arthur and Erin to each prepare a list of candidates. On June 5, Zeppo's old friend A. Dale Herman died after a long battle with cancer at the age of sixty-six. They'd been close since the early 1940s. There were few people in Zeppo's life that could say they were friendly with him for more than thirty-five years. Losing Gummo and A. Dale Herman in such a short span could not have made it any easier for Zeppo as he watched Groucho's health rapidly deteriorate.

Erin's list had only one name on it: Zeppo Marx. Arthur wrote in *My Life with Groucho* that "Zeppo wasn't acceptable to me for three reasons: (1) he lived too far away, and was too old to commute, (2) He was an incorrigible gambler, (3) He was beholden to Erin because she had prevailed on Groucho to give Zeppo $1,000 a month to live on now that he had no income of his own and had no savings." (Note to Arthur: Groucho had started paying Zeppo prior to Erin arriving on the scene, Zeppo still had monthly income from his Safeway stores, and certainly wasn't buying new condominiums, boats, and fancy cars with his monthly check from Groucho.) Arthur described Zeppo's day in court: "When Zeppo arrived in a Rolls-Royce and jazzy-looking sports jacket and slacks, he hammed it up for the benefit of the media on the courthouse steps. Questioned as to what he thought of Erin Fleming, he replied, 'I think she's a wonderful girl. She's been great for Groucho, and I'm all for her.'" Zeppo was immediately eliminated from consideration by the judge.

Groucho was soon back in the hospital. He had pneumonia and had reinjured his hip, requiring another operation on June 12. He was unaware of the ongoing hearing in Santa Monica in which Erin presented her case for being appointed Groucho's permanent conservator. Groucho came home from the hospital on June 21 and was taken back the following day when his labored breathing turned out to be lung inflammation.

On July 27 Arthur's twenty-seven-year-old son Andy was appointed by the court as Groucho's permanent conservator in a twenty-minute court session in Groucho's room at Cedars-Sinai Medical Center. Andy Marx recalls the atmosphere surrounding the controversy: "Obviously my father had no problem with me. Erin wasn't doing anything for me, so I wasn't beholden to her. We got along and I was at the house a lot. She was nutty, but she liked me. So, there were no objections to me as conservator."

Andy would not have to serve in the position for very long. He says, "He was in really bad shape at that point, so there really wasn't much to do. Zeppo would call to see how he was doing, and I got the impression that he wasn't fully grasping how seriously ill my grandfather was." Groucho died on August 19. Zeppo told reporters he spoke to Groucho for around fifteen minutes on the telephone the night before he died and added, "I turned on the TV the next day, and there it was. He was gone." Zeppo's favorable testimony for Erin resulted in Arthur excluding him from a small memorial service he held for Groucho in his Bel Air home. Zeppo defended his position saying, "I told the court she was a wonderful person, and she is. She kept Groucho alive for seven years." Asked why he thought so highly of the obviously irrational Erin Fleming, Zeppo said, "Because Groucho was so much in love with her."

Zeppo was the last surviving Marx Brother, and he was shunned by many members of the Marx family for his allegiance to Erin Fleming. Zeppo was particularly upset that Arthur seemed to be unaware that Groucho had wanted his ashes scattered in Israel. There would be a lengthy and protracted battle over Groucho's estate in the coming years, but Zeppo was left $50,000 in Groucho's will and that was not part of the dispute. Groucho had written his own epitaph: "I hope they bury me near a straight man." Zeppo knew his days were numbered and that it would not be too long before Groucho was reunited with his long-time stage and screen straight man.

Harpo's son Bill was one of the few members of the Marx family who remained in touch with Zeppo after the conservatorship hearings. He recalled an evening with his uncle and a girlfriend—possibly the same woman Gummo's son Bob saw Zeppo with at the movies when he described a similar incident. In *Son of Harpo Speaks!* Bill wrote,

> Zeppo's later years brought on serious ear problems. He had lost all hearing in one ear and was preparing for an operation to save his hearing in the other ear. He was dating a nice blonde girl named June who was blind as a bat without her "coke bottle" glasses, which she could

never find to begin with, and for obvious reasons. I was at Zeppo's house one night having cocktails, and this was the conversation I heard between the two of them:

"Oh, June darling, would you come here for a minute?"

"Where are you?"

"What?"

End of conversation.

More than a year after Groucho's death, Zeppo's day in court with Jean Bodul finally came. In her civil assault and battery lawsuit, Bodul claimed that being roughed up by Zeppo caused her to suffer from persistent back and shoulder pain. Zeppo's attorney, Robert Coppo, was given a difficult job. There was no denying what Zeppo had done to Jean Bodul. Coppo said the dispute was over the return of the house key and credit card and that Zeppo did what was "reasonably necessary" to get them back.

Bodul's attorney claimed in his opening statement that he would prove Zeppo threatened to break Bodul's neck, but no evidence of that was presented at the trial. It all came down to how much money this was going to cost Zeppo. One witness testified that he was worth more than $456,000. Bodul was suing him for $350,000—based more on Zeppo's perceived assets rather than the value of the case against him. If nothing else, the trial demonstrated that Zeppo was still very good at hiding his money. His three Safeway stores were each worth more than $400,000.

Bodul's attorney claimed her medical expenses were $690 and that she should receive $5,000 for pain and $15,000 for punitive damages. And that is exactly what the court awarded her. Zeppo paid Jean Bodul $20,690 and she quietly returned to her life in the Federal Witness Protection Program with her husband, Jimmy "the Weasel" Fratianno, with whom she remained until his death in 1993. Zeppo told reporters, "It's not the money so much. It's my reputation. The Marx Brothers never had a reputation for beating women. This is the first time I've been in court in my life." He added, "[I]f there's an opportunity to appeal, I will."

Zeppo's level of shameless audacity is as mystifying as his claim that the Bodul case was his first time in court. Zeppo was in more lawsuits than movies. He appeared before grand juries almost as frequently as he did movie cameras. During his agency days there were lawsuits involving Arthur Lyons, Al Boasberg, Norman Krasna, Olympe Bradna, and Jack Bachman. At Marman

Products Zeppo sued another manufacturer for patent infringement and James T. King sued Marman for breach of contract.

There were also the two very high-profile cases that made headlines—Zeppo's suit against Harry Karl over the cigarette investment, and the lawsuit against him and Marion over Tim's rock-throwing incident. Add Zeppo's appearances as a grand jury witness in the Terre Haute gambling trial, the Friars Club cheating scandal, and the Lewis Bracker case, and it becomes clear that Zeppo was a courtroom veteran by the time he claimed the Bodul case was the first time he'd ever been to court.

The Bodul trial ended in November 1978. Several months later Zeppo learned that he had lung cancer. Roxann Ploss recalls, "He'd never been sick a day in his life so he delayed going to the doctor when he couldn't shake a persistent cough. When he finally got checked out, they found an inoperable cancer." Roxann was unaware that Zeppo had been through a previous bout with cancer in 1975. Zeppo had kept it secret from almost everyone.

Barbara's parents, Irene and Charles Blakeley, had recently relocated to Palm Springs and helped Zeppo through his treatment in 1975. They took him to his medical appointments and offered general assistance and friendship. Zeppo had always been generous to them, and they maintained a cordial relationship with him after their daughter divorced him. This is the point at which Bobby Marx believes his mother's sister, Patricia Jo Welch, became close to Zeppo and began helping him. In her book Barbara wrote, "He called me . . . one day and asked me to drive him to his doctor in Los Angeles, who informed me for the first time that my ex-husband was in remission from cancer."

Zeppo kept a low profile and by 1978 he didn't travel or go out much. But the *Hollywood Reporter* still bothered to keep track of him and mentioned in their "Rambling Reporter" column on February 3, 1978, that he and Roxann were a couple. That was hardly a new development by that point. He still enjoyed fishing, but the lengthy trips on his boat became infrequent. He rarely consented to interviews, but in late 1978 he filmed the BBC interview with Barry Norman that would be seen in the episode of the series *Hollywood Greats* devoted to Groucho. Broadcast the following summer, the interview shows Zeppo looking robust and healthy near the water at Desert Island. He'd only agreed to the interviews requested by Groucho in recent years, but he had obviously softened his position on being questioned after Groucho's death—at least for this one instance with the BBC.

In March 1979 he spoke on the telephone to a pair of Minnesota college students researching the Orpheum Theatre in St. Paul. David Fantle and Tom

Johnson immediately recognized that the narrow nature of their topic wouldn't draw much out of Zeppo. To most vaudevillians, every small town and theater seemed the same. Zeppo did recall it being cold in St. Paul, and when asked what he and his brothers did with their free time in the city, the not unexpected response was, "Usually we'd go to the poolroom, shoot some pool, or we might stand out in front of the theatre and try to pick up girls." The less than ten-minute conversation would be Zeppo's last interview.

Zeppo's second cancer diagnosis came so late there was no time to reach out to many people. Tim learned that his father had died when he heard the news on the radio in Philadelphia. Marion, who had remained in touch with Zeppo, had no idea he was sick and learned of his death from a news report. Tom was informed by Tim and, not surprisingly, had no reaction to the news.

Zeppo had entered the Eisenhower Medical Center in Rancho Mirage on November 25, 1979, as the cancer in his lungs spread and incapacitated him. It all happened very quickly. Zeppo died shortly after midnight on November 30. The following day Barbara told the *Desert Sun*, "He had been told it was terminal and inoperable two months ago." Roxann recalls, "We had Thanksgiving dinner on November 22, and I talked to him the next day. Then nothing. I wasn't sure what I'd done to make him angry and was trying to get hold of him when Erin Fleming called me to ask why Zeppo was in the hospital."

Bobby was one of the few visitors allowed to see Zeppo that week. "I went to the hospital maybe a day or two before he died. I remember him trying to talk, and he could barely get a word out." On November 26, Zeppo signed a new will with the assistance of Patrick Winans, the practical nurse who cared for him during his final days. Zeppo's attorney, Robert Schlesinger, and Winans signed the will as witnesses. Zeppo's signature on the will, which superseded one signed only a month earlier, is just short of indecipherable. The most notable changes in the new will were the elimination of any bequest to Marion and the inclusion of one for Barbara's sister, Patricia Jo Welch.

In her book Barbara wrote, "A few days before he died, I went to visit Zeppo in the hospital. He had an awful rattle in his throat, which told me the end was near. I'd loved him once, so it was horrible to see the dashing gambler who'd wooed me in Vegas looking old and frail." It is very possible that Barbara's visit to Zeppo on his death bed was on the day the new will was signed. Roxann says,

I wanted to go to the hospital, but I was told I couldn't see him because I wasn't a relative. I talked to him finally on the phone, and we were making plans for how to handle each day once he came home. I was working at the Indian Wells Hotel, and I told him I would quit my job to spend some real time with him and that pleased him. I was getting ready for work one morning when the phone rang, and a reporter asked for my reaction to the death of Zeppo Marx.

On December 2 around a hundred people attended a memorial service for Zeppo at Wiefels and Son Mortuary Chapel in Palm Springs. Along with Barbara and Frank Sinatra, mourners included Susan Marx, Bill Marx, Eden Marx, Erin Fleming, and Roxann Ploss. Baseball great Leo Durocher, comedian Ukie Sherin, composer Frederick Loewe, and actor William Demarest were also in attendance.

In his eulogy Bobby Marx said Zeppo was "not only a father figure, but a friend. . . . I am grateful for his care, concern and advice. My gratitude, love and prayers go with him." Rabbi Joseph Hurwitz of Temple Isaiah conducted the service and said it marked "the passing of the final member of one of the greatest institutions—the Marx Brothers, as well as the passing of Zeppo himself."

Rabbi Hurwitz seemed to have little personal knowledge of Zeppo. He paid tribute to him saying, "He believed in decency and honor. He was a feisty guy. He fought anti-Semitism in the country clubs and in the media. . . . There we see the character of the man. In Hollywood he was a fashion plate, on covers year after year. When he moved to Palm Springs the opposite took place. He wore baggy pants . . . after all, how can you fish in a double-breasted suit? He hated to dress up, hated formal affairs. He loved the peace and solitude fishing gave him." Marion, Tom, and Tim could have provided the perspective the rabbi lacked, but they were not invited to the service.

Longtime fishing buddy Eddie Suisman, who had met Zeppo in 1956, told the *Desert Sun*, "I went on fishing trips with him to Mexico and the Salton Sea. . . . He was a good person, pleasant company to be with and a considerate person. He's a good friend I'm going to miss. We played a lot of golf together, a lot of cards together." Susan Marx told the *Desert Sun*, "He had a wonderful life and I think he enjoyed it. . . . although he did feel the pressure of the family name."

On December 8, *Desert Sun* columnist Bruce Fessier eulogized Zeppo. He interviewed several of Zeppo's friends including Roxann Ploss, who was described in newspaper obituaries as his girlfriend. She called Zeppo a "walking library of jokes," adding "[h]e was not a practical joker. He loved telling stories. He was a kidder. . . . He loved to flirt and make people joke and be outrageous. He'd do something that was just not apropos to the moment."

Fessier wrote, "Several of Zeppo's friends in the Palm Springs area said Zeppo was the master storyteller. But one of his gin rummy buddies from the Tamarisk Country Club" told Fessier a story about Zeppo pulling a silly gag during a gin rummy game. Zeppo drew gin, but rather than call it, he left the table to make a phone call. He called the club, had his opponent paged, and called gin over the phone.

More than forty years after Zeppo's death, Roxann Ploss said, "Zeppo had a wicked sense of humor. For many years he was my best friend. He and I traveled together on occasion, went out to dinner or to parties at least once a week and talked almost every day. I adored him and missed him terribly for the longest time after he was gone."

Zepilogue

A s soon as the details of Zeppo's will became known, Marion contested it. In a petition filed in Indio Superior Court on January 4, 1980, Marion claimed the will was fraudulent and that Zeppo was "unduly influenced by a young and pretty girl." Patricia Jo Welch—Barbara's sister—it was asserted, "suggested the contents of the document." Zeppo left Welch his Safeway store in Kansas City and his Rolls-Royce, writing in the will that the bequest was "in consideration of the many kindnesses she has shown me during my lifetime." The Safeway store in Redding was left to Jacqueline Elam, a manager at Security-Pacific National Bank in Cathedral City. She managed Zeppo's accounts for several years and later married Gene Autry. Zeppo had occasionally joked with friends about Elam backing him into the vault, eager for him to propose marriage.

The Safeway store in Blythe, the Honda automobile, and $10,000 went to Roxann Ploss, who was also named by Marion in the court filing. Roxann says, "Anyone who knew Zeppo knew he simply could not be manipulated that way. I was told he had changed the will close to the end—during his time in the hospital when I was not allowed to see him. I didn't even know I was in his will. I truly didn't know what his assets were. I thought he probably had money in the bank, the condo at Desert Island, the motorhome, the Rolls-Royce—things like that. The Safeway stores were a complete surprise to me." Marion's accusation against Roxann was based solely on her being a young woman who was involved with Zeppo.

Roxann offers a more plausible and less nefarious reason for Zeppo removing Marion from his will. For several years Zeppo attempted to get out of paying Marion alimony based on her living with Harry Kitson, the son of a British navy commander, whose alcoholism prevented him from having his own naval career. In England he had worked in the film and television industry and was known to socialize with legendary drinkers like Peter O'Toole and Richard Burton. By the time he became Marion's companion, his drinking destroyed any career he might have had in the United States. Tim says Kitson "underwent electric shock therapy to cure his alcohol addiction but it didn't work. Nonetheless, he was a good companion for Marion. He was charming and debonair and all of Marion's pals liked him very much. He was her constant companion and was there for her at the end." Zeppo learned that Marion and Kitson had traveled to Mexico, checked into hotels together and were essentially living as man and wife. Zeppo resented supporting Kitson's lifestyle but his efforts to have the courts relieve him of Marion's alimony payments went nowhere.

Zeppo's collection of first editions was left to Gummo's son Bob. It included many signed books, among them several by Willa Cather—an author recommended to Zeppo by his one-time client Upton Sinclair. Books signed by Sinclair, George S. Kaufman and Moss Hart, Robert Benchley, Dorothy Parker, and former Zeppo collaborator S. J. Perelman were included in the collection along with fine copies of works by Mark Twain and Robert Louis Stevenson. Bob was also left $5,000 and allowed to choose any paintings, sculptures, and objects of art from Zeppo's collection.

Marion and Tom were not provided for in any way, but Tim was left $5,000—the same amount Zeppo left for both Larry Martindale and Elizabeth Cole, two employees of Alexander Tucker, his financial advisor. Fishing buddy Chuck Flick also received $5,000 in addition to getting Zeppo's boat and fishing gear. Erin Fleming received $10,000. Tom says, "He hated me. In his will he put, 'I have a son Thomas.' That's it. That's the only time I'm ever mentioned. I guess that's so I couldn't sue for not being mentioned." Bobby was given Zeppo's diamond ring and gold belt buckles as well as $25,000. According to the will, the primary purpose of the monetary gift was to make possible Bobby's legal education, but he was allowed to "use the funds for whatever purpose he deems best." Bobby says, "I had no legal relationship with Zeppo. He hadn't adopted me, and I wasn't expecting anything. I was told I'd been left some of his personal effects, but I found out that when they opened his safe everything was already gone."

Members of Barbara's family were collectively the largest benefactors of Zeppo's will. Her parents, Charles and Irene Blakeley, received forty shares of International Leisure Corporation. In 1969, Zeppo invested in a Las Vegas construction project spearheaded by his friend, billionaire businessman Kirk Kerkorian. The project would result in the building of the International Hotel, which was the largest hotel in the world when it opened. The original value of Zeppo's investment was $44,000. Kerkorian sold his shares, and the hotel became the Las Vegas Hilton in 1971. Zeppo retained his shares and their value increased under the Hilton management. The investment paid regular dividends and would continue to provide income to Barbara's parents. Along with the Safeway stores it was one of the most generous bequests in Zeppo's will.

The will provided charitable donations to environmental and animal rescue organizations Save-a-Paw, Greenpeace, and Save the Whales. Proceeds from the sale of the Desert Island condominium and its furnishings also went to Zeppo's designated charities. Marion claimed that Zeppo was "not of sound and disposing mind" when the will was written. The problem with Marion's claim was that the bequests were not unusual or unreasonable. The estate was valued at approximately $1.1 million. (The value was understated due in part to the equity in the Safeway properties not being properly accounted for.) Patricia Jo Welch and Roxann Ploss—whether they influenced Zeppo or not—weren't left anything close to the bulk of the estate. Months before the trial date, one of Marion's attorneys, Samuel Norton, said his client was only contesting the bequest of the Safeway stores in St. Louis and Blythe, which he said were valued at about $100,000. But that was not consistent with the actual complaint that was filed. Marion's representation bordered on incompetent. For starters, the Missouri Safeway Store was in Kansas City, not St. Louis. Furthermore, the mortgage documents on the Safeway properties indicated a much higher value.

Marion's day in court came on September 23, 1980. Zeppo's attending physician at the time of his death, Dr. Phillip Driesbach, testified that neither his illness nor prescribed drugs—including narcotics—would individually incapacitate Zeppo mentally. Zeppo's attorney Robert Schlesinger testified that Zeppo was attentive and absorbed when signing his will, and that Zeppo informed him that he would be revising it approximately five days before he signed it. Larry Martindale, who had handled Zeppo's business affairs through the Alexander Tucker office, testified that Zeppo told him he was planning to leave the Kansas City Safeway store to Marion as late as early November—only a few weeks before he died. But no evidence was offered that the change in the will was the result of any action by Patricia Jo Welch or Roxann Ploss.

Attorneys Samuel Norton and Roy Murray presented a case for Marion that suggested Welch had a sexual relationship with Zeppo and accused her of living with him. But they offered no evidence to support their allegations. Welch testified that in her twenty-two-year friendship with Zeppo, at no time did the relationship go beyond "a kiss on the cheek or the mouth."

Welch's attorney John Blumberg argued that Marion's accusations against Welch were "totally without a shred of evidence" and that there was "a wealth of evidence to the contrary." After two days of testimony the judge dismissed the case immediately after Norton and Murray's presentation. The defense didn't even need to present opposing testimony. Zeppo's will was valid. Blumberg called Marion's allegations "totally frivolous and malicious." Roy Murray vowed to appeal the decision and Blumberg countered, saying that an appeal would be "even more frivolous."

It appeared this would be the last time Zeppo made headlines, but four years later Patricia Jo Welch sued both of Marion's attorneys for malicious prosecution. Welch told the *Desert Sun*, "I'm suing because of all the lies and allegations released to the newspapers." Welch had initially included Marion in the lawsuit, but they settled out of court. Welch said, "I feel Marion Marx was as much a victim as I was." Robert Schlesinger, the executor of Zeppo's will, and Roxann Ploss each filed separate civil suits against Marion that were settled quietly. Roxann wanted to be done with the entire mess and was happy to just have Marion pay her legal fees, saying, "The whole thing was a coda to Zeppo's story which he did not deserve."

Bobby Marx theorizes that "Zeppo took pride in being a strong, competent man. As he weakened and started to get frail it doesn't take a lot of imagination to think of what sort of kindnesses Zeppo might have received from Patricia Jo Welch. My mom and her had a falling out at that time. I can't say it was over Zeppo's will, but it might have been. I think that's probably why Roxann got a bad rap. There's an industry that's built up around people as they grow frail and as they get older. People hang around and are very kind and very nice and see what rewards come from it. That's where that whole suspicion probably came into play."

In any case, Marion's accusations were legally baseless and on September 7, 1984, a Superior Court jury in Indio awarded Patricia Jo Welch $312,500 for suffering caused when she was wrongly accused of improper meddling in Zeppo's will. Samuel Norton was responsible for two-thirds of the damage award and Roy Murray one-third. Norton and Murray's attorney Steve Levy argued that discrepancies in the will—including the shakiness of Zeppo's signature and the fact that a nurse had to help him sign his name—justified contesting the will.

Levy acknowledged that his clients may have been guilty of negligence or incompetence, but they believed Marion's complaint was legitimate. One look at Zeppo's signature on the will and the fact that Welch essentially replaced Marion as a beneficiary would suggest that contesting the will was justified. Marion simply hired a pair of terrible lawyers. Zeppo had cheated on her one last time from the grave.

Marion died on February 26, 1986, at the age of eighty-two. Zeppo had made his last headline. Marion's death went without notice in the press. She

left a holographic will—a handwritten document with no witnesses or law-
yers involved—bearing only her own signature. She assured Tim it was legal.
Marion had no faith in the traditional document after the debacle surrounding
Zeppo's will.

Being thrown into the Four Marx Brothers may not have been what
seventeen-year-old Zeppo Marx had planned, but he did later admit that being
taken away from the street life in Chicago probably saved his life. He wasn't
initially bitter about taking the job or even being relegated to straight man
status. He lived a lucrative and extravagant life as a celebrity and that was not
something he would have automatically achieved on his own.

What put a permanent chip on his shoulder was being an employee of his
brothers for the entire time he was in the act. From 1918 until 1934, there never
came a point when anyone even suggested cutting him in as a partner. Remaining loyal to his brothers while carrying this slight for the rest of his life created
a paradox that motivated and drove Zeppo. His son Tim concludes, "He was
always trying to prove himself. 'Screw show business. I'm getting a pittance here.
I'll show you how much money I can make for other people and for myself.'"

Narcissism, self-indulgence, and selfishness permeated all aspects of Zeppo's
life after he left the Four Marx Brothers. This had no more harmful effect than
what it did to the people who tried to love him. Although he spent more than
forty years in his two marriages, he was far from a good husband in either of
them. He was successful in almost everything he touched, yet he was a woeful
failure as a father. Tom Marx certainly was the person most damaged by Zeppo's
insensitivity and callousness. While his brothers may have threatened to disown
Zeppo, Tom was the guy who did it: "If you were in Beverly Hills and you had
famous parents, that's who you were. That's always who I was. Zeppo Marx's son.
That's why later in life and to this day I still don't tell anybody about it. I didn't
really want to be that for the rest of my life." The best lesson Tom learned from
Zeppo was to be nothing like him.

Tim survived a childhood that devastated Tom. He developed an understanding of his father at a young age. It didn't make things any better; he just
came to expect less. Tim recognized the forces that made his father a surly man
with a violently quick temper—and he noticed that it all had a lot to do with
his famous uncles:

Zeppo thought he was better than they were in many ways. He was
funnier. He would do things that they had yet to think of. Pranks
and things like that. His mind worked in a way where he could do

these types of things and they couldn't. "I'm an inventor, I'm this, I'm that. They're not." This drove him to be the best at whatever he was doing—golf, gambling, machinery, even a grapefruit ranch. Whatever. He always had this bug up his ass to be the best and to be noticed for being the best.

It seems never to have occurred to Zeppo that he could also have tried to be the best husband and the best father. But that would benefit others and that never seemed especially important to Zeppo. Even when he had proven himself a success in several areas, he still couldn't bring himself to let Tom and Tim enjoy his electric train set. It was part selfishness and part control. After leaving the Four Marx Brothers, Zeppo never had another employer. He was always self-employed and answered to no one. The only venture Zeppo ever pursued that he didn't control was gambling—and he was arrogant enough to believe that he did.

Maxine Marx, who'd been around Zeppo for roughly the first forty years of her life, wrote in *Growing Up with Chico*, "I didn't know Zeppo at all. He was a big playboy around town, but I found him a cold potato." In an April 23, 2000, *Los Angeles Times* story about the Marx family Maxine was more succinct: "Nobody liked Zeppo." In *Speaking of Harpo*, Harpo's wife Susan summed up Zeppo as well as anybody could:

A strange man who even his brothers never completely understood, Zeppo could entertain a party of friends with uproariously funny anecdotes. He had style, taste, and good looks, but there simply hadn't been room for a fourth comic Marx Brother, and Zep had to settle for the humiliation of straight roles. The funniest Marx Brother off screen couldn't get a laugh on screen. He left the team to become a highly successful agent, representing some of the biggest names in Hollywood, but his lack of success as a member of the Marx team was a psychological problem he struggled with to the end.

Zeppo made no demonstrable personal sacrifices after being drafted into the act at the age of seventeen. Zeppo lived for Zeppo. The rest of his life played out like payback for that moment in 1918.

Appendix I: Zeppo Marx on Stage

Acomprehensive and more detailed stage chronology of the Marx Brothers can be found in *Four of the Three Musketeers: The Marx Brothers on Stage*.

Guest Appearances with the Four Marx Brothers (1914–1915)

Jan. 11, 1914   Chicago, Ill.   Willard Theatre
Six weeks shy of his thirteenth birthday, Herbert makes his stage debut when he joins his brothers on the final day of their week at the Willard in the double bill "Fun in Hi School" and "Mr. Green's Reception."

Feb. 24, 1914   Gary, Ind.   Orpheum Theatre
On February 23, Herbert is advertised in the Gary *Evening Post as the fifth Marx Brother, "Chicago's Boy Soprano." He appears for only one day during the four-day engagement of the Four Marx Brothers.*

May 1–2, 1914   Joliet, Ill.   Orpheum Theatre
Herbert appears on the final two days of the Four Marx Brothers' three-day engagement. He is advertised locally as "Chicago's sixteen-year-old tenor."

June 1–5, 1915   Grand Rapids, Mich.   Empress Theatre
The Four Marx Brothers, starring in their new show Home Again, *open their week in Grand Rapids on May 31 as a quartet, but Herbert travels from Chicago as the school year ends and makes them a quintet for the rest of the week.*

Appearances as a Member of the Five Marx Brothers (1915)

The 1915 fall vaudeville season opens early with Herbert joining his brothers in *Home Again* for a late summer tour of the W. S. Butterfield circuit in Michigan. The act is billed as the Five Marx Brothers for the only time. In advance of the tour Herbert makes an unscheduled July 25, 1915, appearance at the Cabaret at Lake Goguac while visiting his cousin, Lou Shean, who is vacationing in Battle Creek.

Aug. 15–18, 1915	Lansing, Mich.	Bijou Theatre
Aug. 19–21, 1915	Saginaw, Mich.	Franklin Theatre
Aug. 22–25, 1915	Kalamazoo, Mich.	Majestic Theatre
Aug. 26–28, 1915	Jackson, Mich.	Bijou Theatre
Aug. 29–Sept. 1, 1915	Bay City, Mich.	Bijou Theatre
Sept. 2–4, 1915	Flint, Mich.	Majestic Theatre
Sept. 5–8, 1915	Battle Creek, Mich.	Bijou Theatre
Sept. 9–11, 1915	Ann Arbor, Mich.	Majestic Theatre

Appearances as Buster Palmer (1916)

As the fall vaudeville season begins in the late summer of 1916, Herbert—billed as Buster Palmer—is given a solo spot on four bills featuring the Four Marx Brothers as headliners in *Home Again*. Minnie showcases Herbert as she works on creating a new act that will include him.

Aug. 21–26, 1916	Chicago, Ill.	LeGrand Theatre
Aug. 31–Sept. 2, 1916	Elkhart, Ind.	Orpheum Theatre
Sept. 3, 1916	Hammond, Ind.	Orpheum Theatre
Sept. 4–6, 1916	Richmond, Ind.	Murray Theatre

Appearances as a Member of the Juvenile Six / the Juvenile Sextet (1916–1917)

Minnie sends Herbert out on the road as a member of the Juvenile Six. They are occasionally billed as the Juvenile Sextet. Along with Herbert, the act features the Harris Brothers—George and Victor—who had previously been with the Four Marx Brothers, and the Kashner sisters—Fay, Marvel, and Ida—who billed themselves as the Karlmer sisters. From December 1916 through May 1917, the Juvenile Six toured the Ackerman and Harris circuit, one of the most arduous in vaudeville. Cities not listed here but almost certainly played include Jamestown, North Dakota; Livingston, Montana; Wallace, Idaho; Chico, California; Provo, Utah; and Aberdeen, South Dakota.

Sept. 21–23, 1916	Chicago, Ill.	Lincoln Hippodrome
Oct. 2–4, 1916	Lincoln, Nebr.	Lyric Theatre
Oct. 5–7, 1916	St. Paul, Minn.	Princess Theatre
Oct. 16–18, 1916	Richmond, Ind.	Murray Theatre
Oct. 19–21, 1916	Kokomo, Ind.	Sipe Theatre
Oct. 23–25, 1916	Lexington, Ky.	Ada Meade Theatre
Oct. 30–Nov. 1, 1916	Charleston, W.Va.	Plaza Theatre
Nov. 6–8, 1916	East Liverpool, Ohio	American Theatre
Nov. 13–18, 1916	Buffalo, N.Y.	Olympic Theatre
Nov. 20–22, 1916	Hornell, N.Y.	Majestic Theatre
Nov. 23–25, 1916	Hamilton, Ont.	Grand Theatre
Nov. 27–Dec. 2, 1916	Penn Yan, N.Y.	Cornwell Theatre
Dec. 11–13, 1916	Chicago, Ill.	Grand Theatre
Dec. 14–16, 1916	Kenosha, Wis.	Virginian Theatre
Dec. 18–20, 1916	Grand Forks, N.D.	Grand Theatre
Dec. 25, 1916	Billings, Mont.	Babcock Theatre
Dec. 26, 1916	Lewistown, Mont.	Judith Theatre

Heavy snow caused their train to be delayed and the Juvenile Six did not appear.

Dec. 28, 1916	Great Falls, Mont.	Grand Theatre
Dec. 29, 1916	Helena, Mont.	Liberty Theatre
Dec. 31, 1916–Jan. 2, 1917	Butte, Mont.	Empress Theatre
Jan. 3, 1917	Missoula, Mont.	Bijou Theatre
Jan. 7–9, 1917	Spokane, Wash.	The Hippodrome
Jan. 12–13, 1917	Walla Walla, Wash.	Liberty Theatre
Jan. 14–15, 1917	Yakima, Wash.	Empire Theatre
Jan. 18–20, 1917	Tacoma, Wash.	Regent Theatre
Jan. 21–24, 1917	Seattle, Wash.	Palace Hippodrome
Jan. 25–28, 1917	Portland, Ore.	The Hippodrome
Jan. 31–Feb. 3, 1917	Sacramento, Calif.	Empress Theatre
Feb. 4–10, 1917	San Francisco, Calif.	Empress Theatre
Feb. 11–17, 1917	San Francisco, Calif.	The Hippodrome
Feb. 22–25, 1917	San Diego, Calif.	Spreckels Hippodrome
Feb. 26–Mar. 3, 1917	Los Angeles, Calif.	The Hippodrome
Mar. 17–24, 1917	Denver, Colo.	Empress Theatre
Mar. 25–27, 1917	Pueblo, Colo.	Princess Theatre
Mar. 29–31, 1917	St. Joseph, Mo.	Electric Theatre
Apr. 2–4, 1917	Kansas City, Kan.	Electric Theatre
Apr. 5–7, 1917	Joplin, Mo.	Electric Theatre

Apr. 9–11, 1917	Springfield, Mo.	Electric Theatre
Apr. 12–14, 1917	Little Rock, Ark.	Majestic Theatre
Apr. 22–25, 1917	Des Moines, Iowa	Empress Theatre
Apr. 26–28, 1917	Marshalltown, Iowa	Casino Theatre
Apr. 30–May 2, 1917	St. Paul, Minn.	The Hippodrome
May 3–5, 1917	Fargo, N.D.	Grand Theatre
May 10–13, 1917	Janesville, Wis.	Apollo Theatre
June 4–10, 1917	Detroit, Mich.	Miles Theatre
June 11–13, 1917	Pontiac, Mich.	Oakland Theatre

APPEARANCES AS A MEMBER OF THE FOUR MARX BROTHERS (1918–1932)

Herbert quits his job at the Ford Motor Company at Minnie's insistence and joins his brothers in Rockford, Illinois to learn Milton's part and replace him in the act as Milton prepares to join the army.

Home Again

June 6–8, 1918	Rockford, Ill.	Palace Theatre
June 10–12, 1918	Madison, Wis.	Orpheum Theatre

Milton gives his final performances as a member of the Four Marx Brothers as Herbert makes the act a quintet for the last time as the vaudeville season draws to a close.

The Cinderella Girl (The Street Cinderella)

Sept. 26, 1918	Benton Harbor, Mich.	Bell Opera House
Sept. 28, 1918	Benton Harbor, Mich.	Bell Opera House

Additional scheduled Michigan performances of the ill-fated show are canceled in Grand Rapids, Battle Creek, and Lansing. Illinois bookings in Ottawa, Streator and Chicago are canceled as are Milwaukee, Wisconsin and Fort Worth, Texas performances.

Home Again / 'N' Everything

Nov. 1, 1918	North Chicago, Ill.	Great Lakes Auditorium
Nov. 4–9, 1918	Gary, Ind.	Gary Theatre
Nov. 18–20, 1918	Springfield, Ohio	New Sun Theatre
Nov. 21–24, 1918	Chillicothe, Ohio	Majestic Theatre
Nov. 28–Dec. 1, 1918	Muncie, Ind.	Star Theatre
Dec. 7–8, 1918	East Chicago, Ind.	Hartley Theatre
Jan. 9–11, 1919	Bloomington, Ill.	Majestic Theatre

Jan. 13–18, 1919	Chicago, Ill.	Wilson Ave. Theatre
Jan. 20–21, 1919	Valparaiso, Ind.	Memorial Opera House
Jan. 24, 1919	Goshen, Ind.	Jefferson Theatre
Jan. 27–Feb. 1, 1919	Grand Rapids, Mich.	Empress Theatre

The Winter Garden Revue

Feb. 3–8, 1919	Chicago, Ill.	Palace Theatre
Feb. 10, 1919	Logansport, Ind.	Nelson Theatre
Feb. 11, 1919	Portland, Ind.	Auditorium Theatre
Feb. 12, 1919	Elwood, Ind.	Grand Theatre
Feb. 13, 1919	New Castle, Ind.	Grand Theatre
Feb. 14–15, 1919	Muncie, Ind.	Star Theatre

'N' Everything

| Feb. 17–22, 1919 | Cincinnati, Ohio | Keith's Theatre |
| Feb. 23–Mar. 1, 1919 | Louisville, Ky. | Mary Anderson Theatre |

Herbert takes Arthur's role for one performance when Arthur is too ill to go on.

Mar. 3–8, 1919	Youngstown, Ohio	The Hippodrome
Mar. 10–15, 1919	Cleveland, Ohio	The Hippodrome
Mar. 24–29, 1919	Toledo, Ohio	Keith's Theatre
Mar. 31–Apr. 5, 1919	Akron, Ohio	Colonial Theatre
Apr. 7–12, 1919	Erie, Pa.	Colonial Theatre
Apr. 14–19, 1919	Indianapolis, Ind.	Keith's Theatre
Apr. 21–26, 1919	Dayton, Ohio	Keith's Theatre
Apr. 28–May 3, 1919	Milwaukee, Wis.	Majestic Theatre
May 5–10, 1919	Chicago, Ill.	State-Lake Theatre
May 18, 1919	Union Hill, N.J.	Hudson Theatre
May 19–24, 1919	New York, N.Y.	Palace Theatre
May 26–31, 1919	Bronx, N.Y.	Keith's Royal Theatre
June 2–8, 1919	Washington, D.C.	Keith's Theatre
June 9–14, 1919	New York, N.Y.	Alhambra Theatre
June 16–21, 1919	Brooklyn, N.Y.	Henderson's Music Hall
June 23–28, 1919	Boston, Mass.	Keith's Theatre
June 30–July 5, 1919	New York, N.Y.	Riverside Theatre
July 7–12, 1919	Brooklyn, N.Y.	Orpheum Theatre
July 14–19, 1919	Brooklyn, N.Y.	Bushwick Theatre
July 21–26, 1919	Rockaway Beach, N.Y.	Morrison's Theatre

July 28–Aug. 2, 1919	Philadelphia, Pa.	Keith's Theatre
Aug. 4–6, 1919	Newark, N.J.	Palace Theatre
Aug. 7–10, 1919	Mount Vernon, N.Y.	Proctor's Theatre
Aug. 11–16, 1919	New York, N.Y.	Palace Theatre
Aug. 18–23, 1919	Newark, N.J.	Palace Theatre
Aug. 25–30, 1919	Philadelphia, Pa.	Nixon's Grand Opera House
Sept. 1–6, 1919	Montreal, Que.	Princess Theatre
Sept. 8–13, 1919	Hamilton, Ont.	Lyric Theatre
Sept. 15–20, 1919	Detroit, Mich.	Temple Theatre
Sept. 22–27, 1919	Rochester, N.Y.	Temple Theatre
Sept. 29–Oct. 4, 1919	Buffalo, N.Y.	Shea's Theatre
Oct. 6–11, 1919	Toronto, Ont.	Shea's Theatre
Oct. 13–18, 1919	New York, N.Y.	Keith's 81st St. Theatre
Oct. 20–26, 1919	Yonkers, N.Y.	Proctor's Theatre
Oct. 27–Nov. 1, 1919	New York, N.Y.	Proctor's 5th Ave. Theatre
Nov. 2, 1919	New York, N.Y.	Proctor's 5th Ave. Theatre
Nov. 3–8, 1919	New York, N.Y.	Colonial Theatre
Nov. 10–15, 1919	New York, N.Y.	Hamilton Theatre
Nov. 24–29, 1919	Bronx, N.Y.	Keith's Royal Theatre
Dec. 1–3, 1919	Troy, N.Y.	Proctor's Theatre
Dec. 4–6, 1919	Albany, N.Y.	Proctor's Theatre
Dec. 8–13, 1919	Syracuse, N.Y.	Temple Theatre
Dec. 15–20, 1919	Lowell, Mass.	Keith's Theatre
Dec. 22–27, 1919	Portland, Maine	Keith's Theatre
Jan. 5–10, 1920	New York, N.Y.	Alhambra Theatre
Jan. 12–17, 1920	New York, N.Y.	Colonial Theatre
Jan. 19–24, 1920	New York, N.Y.	Palace Theatre
Jan. 25, 1920	New York, N.Y.	The Hippodrome
Jan. 26–28, 1920	Brooklyn, N.Y.	Prospect Theatre
Jan. 29–Feb. 1, 1920	Newark, N.J.	Proctor's Theatre
Feb. 8–14, 1920	Minneapolis, Minn.	Orpheum Theatre
Feb. 15–21, 1920	Duluth, Minn.	Orpheum Theatre
Feb. 23–28, 1920	Winnipeg, Man.	Orpheum Theatre
Mar. 1–3, 1920	Calgary, Alb.	Orpheum Theatre
Mar. 4–6, 1920	Victoria, B.C.	Orpheum Theatre
Mar. 8–13, 1920	Vancouver, B.C.	Orpheum Theatre
Mar. 15–20, 1920	Seattle, Wash.	Moore Theatre
Mar. 21–24, 1920	Portland, Ore.	Orpheum Theatre

Mar. 28–Apr. 10, 1920	San Francisco, Calif.	Orpheum Theatre
Apr. 11–17, 1920	Oakland, Calif.	Orpheum Theatre
Apr. 18–21, 1920	Sacramento, Calif.	Clunie-Orpheum Theatre
Apr. 22–24, 1920	Fresno, Calif.	White Theatre
Apr. 26–May 8, 1920	Los Angeles, Calif.	Orpheum Theatre
May 9, 1920	Long Beach, Calif.	Hoyt Theatre
May 12–16, 1920	Salt Lake City, Utah	Orpheum Theatre
May 17–22, 1920	Denver, Colo.	Orpheum Theatre
May 24–29, 1920	Lincoln, Nebr.	Orpheum Theatre
May 30–June 5, 1920	Kansas City, Mo.	Orpheum Theatre
June 7–12, 1920	Milwaukee, Wis.	Palace Theatre
June 14–20, 1920	Chicago, Ill.	Majestic Theatre
June 28–July 3, 1920	Chicago, Ill.	Palace Theatre
July 4, 1920	Chicago, Ill.	Woods Theatre
July 5–10, 1920	Chicago, Ill.	State-Lake Theatre
July 12–17, 1920	St. Louis, Mo.	Rialto Theatre
July 18–24, 1920	Canton, Ohio	Meyers Lake Park Theatre
Aug. 14, 1920	Union Hill, N.J.	Pastime Theatre
Aug. 16–21, 1920	New York, N.Y.	Palace Theatre
Aug. 23–28, 1920	New York, N.Y.	Keith's 81st St. Theatre
Aug. 30–Sept. 4, 1920	Brooklyn, N.Y.	Brighton Coney Island Theatre
Sept. 5, 1920	Brooklyn, N.Y.	Orpheum Theatre
Sept. 6–11, 1920	New York, N.Y.	Keith's Jefferson Theatre
Sept. 13–18, 1920	New York, N.Y.	Keith's AlhambraTheatre
Sept. 13–18, 1920	New York, N.Y.	Hamilton Theatre
Sept. 20–25, 1920	Newark, N.J.	Proctor's Theatre
Sept. 27–Oct. 2, 1920	New York, N.Y.	Keith's Colonial Theatre
Oct. 4–6, 1920	Brooklyn, N.Y.	Keith's Prospect Theatre
Oct. 7–10, 1920	Mount Vernon, N.Y.	Proctor's Theatre
Oct. 11–17, 1920	New York, N.Y.	Proctor's 5th Ave. Theatre
Oct. 18–23, 1920	New York, N.Y.	Palace Theatre
Oct. 25–27, 1920	New York, N.Y.	Proctor's Coliseum
Oct. 28–30, 1920	Elizabeth, N.J.	Proctor's Theatre
Nov. 1–6, 1920	Bronx, N.Y.	Keith's Royal Theatre
Nov. 8–10, 1920	New York, N.Y.	Moss' Regent Theatre
Nov. 11–14, 1920	New York, N.Y.	Proctor's 5th Ave. Theatre
Nov. 15–20, 1920	Brooklyn, N.Y.	Keith's Bushwick Theatre
Nov. 22–27, 1920	Brooklyn, N.Y.	Moss' Flatbush Theatre

Nov. 29–Dec. 4, 1920	New York, N.Y.	Moss' Broadway Theatre
Dec. 6–11, 1920	New York, N.Y.	Keith's Riverside Theatre
Dec. 12, 1920	New York, N.Y.	The Hippodrome
Dec. 12, 1920	New York, N.Y.	Apollo Theatre
Dec. 13–18, 1920	New York, N.Y.	Keith's Colonial Theatre
Dec. 19, 1920	New York, N.Y.	New Amsterdam Theatre
Dec. 19, 1920	New York, N.Y.	The Hippodrome
Dec. 20–25, 1920	New York, N.Y.	Keith's Alhambra Theatre
Dec. 27, 1920–Jan. 1, 1921	New York, N.Y.	Keith's Jefferson Theatre
Jan. 3–8, 1921	New York, N.Y.	Keith's Hamilton Theatre
Jan. 16, 1921	New York, N.Y.	Manhattan Opera House
Jan. 17–22, 1921	New York, N.Y.	Keith's 81st St. Theatre

On The Mezzanine Floor / On The Balcony

Feb. 14–16, 1921	Hartford, Conn.	Poli's Capitol Theatre
Feb. 17–19, 1921	Worcester, Mass.	Poli's Theatre
Feb. 21–23, 1921	Springfield, Mass.	Poli's Palace Theatre
Feb. 24–26, 1921	Bridgeport, Conn.	Poli's Theatre
Feb. 28–Mar. 2, 1921	New York, N.Y.	Moss' Coliseum
Mar. 3–5, 1921	Mount Vernon, N.Y.	Proctor's Theatre
Mar. 10–12, 1921	New York, N.Y.	Proctor's 5th Ave. Theatre
Mar. 13, 1921	New York, N.Y.	Proctor's 5th Ave. Theatre
Mar. 14–26, 1921	New York, N.Y.	Palace Theatre
Mar. 20, 1921	New York, N.Y.	Hotel Pennsylvania
Apr. 7, 1921	New York, N.Y.	Tom Healy's Jungle Room
Apr. 11–17, 1921	Washington, D.C.	Keith's Theatre
Apr. 18–23, 1921	New York, N.Y.	Keith's Hamilton Theatre
Apr. 25–30, 1921	New York, N.Y.	Keith's Jefferson Theatre
May 2–7, 1921	Brooklyn, N.Y.	Moss' Flatbush Theatre
May 9–14, 1921	Brooklyn, N.Y.	Keith's Bushwick Theatre
May 16–21, 1921	Newark, N.J.	Proctor's Theatre
May 22, 1921	New York, N.Y.	The Hippodrome
May 22, 1921	New York, N.Y.	Manhattan Opera House
May 30–June 4, 1921	New York, N.Y.	Palace Theatre
June 6–11, 1921	Brooklyn, N.Y.	Keith's Orpheum Theatre
June 20–25, 1921	Baltimore, Md.	Maryland Theatre

Harpo is unable to perform due to illness. Zeppo takes his role for this week and the weeks that follow in Philadelphia and Boston.

June 27–July 2, 1921	Philadelphia, Pa.	Keith's Theatre
July 4–10, 1921	Boston, Mass.	Keith's Theatre
July 11–16, 1921	Brooklyn, N.Y.	Brighton Coney Island Theatre
July 18, 1921	New York, N.Y.	Palace Theatre
July 18–23, 1921	New York, N.Y.	Keith's Riverside Theatre
July 25–30, 1921	Bronx, N.Y.	Keith's Royal Theatre
Aug. 1–6, 1921	Atlantic City, N.J.	Garden Pier
August 26, 1921	Rockaway Beach, N.Y.	Lorraine Hotel
Sept. 5–10, 1921	New York, N.Y.	Palace Theatre
Sept. 12–17, 1921	New York, N.Y.	Moss' Franklin Theatre
Sept. 19–24, 1921	New York, N.Y.	Moss' Broadway Theatre
Sept. 26–28, 1921	Bronx, N.Y.	Keith's Fordham Theatre
Sept. 29–Oct. 1, 1921	Brooklyn, N.Y.	Keith's Boro Park Theatre
Oct. 3–5, 1921	New York, N.Y.	Moss' Coliseum
Oct. 10–12, 1921	Dayton, Ohio	B. F. Keith's Strand
Oct. 16–22, 1921	Minneapolis, Minn.	Hennepin Theatre
Oct. 24–30, 1921	Chicago, Ill.	Majestic Theatre
Oct. 31–Nov. 6, 1921	Chicago, Ill.	State-Lake Theatre
Nov. 7–12, 1921	Milwaukee, Wis.	Majestic Theatre
Nov. 14–19, 1921	Chicago, Ill.	Palace Theatre
Nov. 21–27, 1921	St. Louis, Mo.	Orpheum Theatre
Nov. 28–Dec. 3, 1921	St. Louis, Mo.	Rialto Theatre
Dec. 11–17, 1921	Kansas City, Mo.	Main Street Theatre
Dec. 18–24, 1921	Des Moines, Iowa	Orpheum Theatre
Dec. 26–31, 1921	St. Paul, Minn.	Orpheum Theatre
Jan. 2–7, 1922	Winnipeg, Man.	Orpheum Theatre
Jan. 9–11, 1922	Edmonton, Alb.	Orpheum Theatre
Jan. 12–14, 1922	Calgary, Alb.	Orpheum Theatre
Jan. 16–21, 1922	Vancouver, B.C.	Orpheum Theatre
Jan. 22–28, 1922	Seattle, Wash.	Moore Theatre
Jan. 29–Feb. 1, 1922	Portland, Ore.	Orpheum Theatre
Feb. 5–18, 1922	San Francisco, Calif.	Orpheum Theatre
Feb. 19–25, 1922	Oakland, Calif.	Orpheum Theatre
Feb. 26–Mar. 1, 1922	Sacramento, Calif.	Clunie-Orpheum Theatre
Mar. 2–4, 1922	Fresno, Calif.	White Theatre
Mar. 6–19, 1922	Los Angeles, Calif.	Orpheum Theatre
Mar. 20–22, 1922	Long Beach, Calif.	Hoyt's Theatre
Mar. 29–Apr. 4, 1922	Denver, Colo.	Orpheum Theatre

Apr. 9–15, 1922	Kansas City, Mo.	Orpheum Theatre
Apr. 16–22, 1922	Omaha, Nebr.	Orpheum Theatre
Apr. 23–29, 1922	Minneapolis, Minn.	Hennepin Theatre
May 1–7, 1922	Chicago, Ill.	Majestic Theatre
May 8–14, 1922	Milwaukee, Wis.	Palace Theatre
May 15–21, 1922	Chicago, Ill.	State-Lake Theatre
May 21, 1922	Chicago, Ill.	Colonial Theatre
May 29–June 3, 1922	New York, N.Y.	Palace Theatre
June 19–24, 1922	London, UK	London Coliseum
June 26–July 1, 1922	London, UK	London Coliseum
July 3–8, 1922	London, UK	Alhambra Theatre
July 10–15, 1922	Bristol, UK	The Hippodrome
July 17–22, 1922	Manchester, UK	The Hippodrome
Sept. 1922	Hoboken, N.J.	Lyric Theatre
Sept. 11–16, 1922	Jersey City, N.J.	State Theatre
Sept. 18–20, 1922	New York, N.Y.	Keith's Jefferson Theatre
Sept. 21–28, 1922	Far Rockaway, N.Y.	Columbia Theatre

The Twentieth Century Revue

Oct. 8–14, 1922	Chicago, Ill.	Englewood Theatre
Oct. 15–21, 1922	Detroit, Mich.	Detroit Opera House
Oct. 23–28, 1922	Toronto, Ont.	Princess Theatre
Oct. 30–Nov. 4, 1922	Buffalo, N.Y.	Criterion Theatre
Nov. 13–15, 1922	Worcester, Mass.	Worcester Theatre
Nov. 16–18, 1922	Fall River, Mass.	Bijou Theatre
Nov. 20–25, 1922	Boston, Mass.	Majestic Theatre
Nov. 30–Dec. 2, 1922	Hartford, Conn.	Shubert Grand Theatre
Dec. 4–10, 1922	New York, N.Y.	Central Theatre
Dec. 11–17, 1922	New York, N.Y.	Harlem Opera House
Dec. 18–24, 1922	Brooklyn, N.Y.	Shubert Crescent Theatre
Dec. 25–27, 1922	Astoria, N.Y.	Astoria Theatre
Dec. 28–31, 1922	Brooklyn, N.Y.	Boro Park Theatre
Jan. 1–7, 1923	Newark, N.J.	Shubert Theatre
Jan. 8–13, 1923	Philadelphia, Pa.	Chestnut St. Opera House
Jan. 14–20, 1923	Washington, D.C.	Belasco Theatre
Jan. 22–27, 1923	Pittsburgh, Pa.	Aldine Theatre
Jan. 28–Feb. 3, 1923	Cleveland, Ohio	State Theatre

Feb. 4–10, 1923	Chicago, Ill.	Garrick Theatre
Feb. 11–17, 1923	Cincinnati, Ohio	Shubert Theatre
Feb. 18–24, 1923	St. Louis, Mo.	Empress Theatre
Mar. 1–3, 1923	Indianapolis, Ind.	Shubert Murat Theatre

Following the unexpected confiscation of the scenery in Indianapolis, a one-night booking at the Grand Theatre in Anderson, Indiana, scheduled for March 4, is canceled.

Apr. 15–18, 1923	Brooklyn, N.Y.	Premier Theatre

I'll Say She Is

May 31–June 2, 1923	Allentown, Pa.	Lyric Theatre
June 4–Sept. 1, 1923	Philadelphia, Pa.	Walnut St. Theatre
Sept. 3–29, 1923	Boston, Mass.	Shubert Theatre
Oct. 1–6, 1923	Pittsburgh, Pa.	Alvin Theatre
Oct. 7–13, 1923	Detroit, Mich.	Garrick Theatre
Oct. 14–Dec. 22, 1923	Chicago, Ill.	Studebaker Theatre
Dec. 23, 1923-Jan. 12, 1924	Kansas City, Mo.	Shubert Missouri Theatre
Jan. 13–19, 1924	St. Louis, Mo.	Shubert Jefferson Theatre
Jan. 20–26, 1924	Cincinnati, Ohio	Shubert Theatre
Jan. 27, 1924	Hamilton, Ohio	Jefferson Theatre
Jan. 28, 1924	Springfield, Ohio	Fairbanks Theatre
Jan. 29, 1924	Zanesville, Ohio	Weller Theatre
Jan. 30–31, 1924	Wheeling, W.Va.	Court Theatre
Feb. 1, 1924	East Liverpool, Ohio	Ceramic Theatre
Feb. 2, 1924	Sharon, Pa.	Columbia Theatre
Feb. 4–9, 1924	Buffalo, N.Y.	Shubert Teck Theatre
Feb. 11–16, 1924	Toronto, Ont.	Royal Alexandra Theatre
Feb. 18–20, 1924	Rochester, N.Y.	Lyceum Theatre
Feb. 21–23, 1924	Syracuse, N.Y.	Wieting Opera House
Feb. 24–Mar. 1, 1924	Cleveland, Ohio	Hanna Theatre
Mar. 3, 1924	Akron, Ohio	Goodyear Theatre
Mar. 4–5, 1924	Canton, Ohio	Grand Opera House
Mar. 6–8, 1924	Youngstown, Ohio	Park Theatre
Mar. 10, 1924	Johnstown, Pa.	Cambria Theatre
Mar. 11, 1924	Altoona, Pa.	Mischler Theatre
Mar. 12, 1924	Cumberland, Md.	Maryland Theatre
Mar. 13–15, 1924	Wilmington, Del.	Wilmington Playhouse
Mar. 17, 1924	Harrisburg, Pa.	Orpheum Theatre

Mar. 18, 1924	York, Pa.	Orpheum Theatre
Mar. 19, 1924	Reading, Pa.	Orpheum Theatre
Mar. 20, 1924	Easton, Pa.	Orpheum Theatre
Mar. 21–22, 1924	Allentown, Pa.	Lyric Theatre
Mar. 24–29, 1924	Atlantic City, N.J.	Nixon's Apollo Theatre
Mar. 30–Apr. 5, 1924	Washington, D.C.	Poli's Theatre
Apr. 7–19, 1924	Baltimore, Md.	Auditorium Theatre
Apr. 21–26, 1924	Brooklyn, N.Y.	Shubert Crescent Theatre
Apr. 28–May 17, 1924	Philadelphia, Pa.	Walnut St. Theatre
May 19, 1924–Feb. 7, 1925	New York, N.Y.	Casino Theatre

After a year on the road, I'll Say She Is *has a 313-performance run on Broadway.*

Feb. 9–Mar. 28, 1925	Boston, Mass.	Majestic Theatre
Mar. 30–Apr. 4, 1925	New Haven, Conn.	Shubert Theatre
Apr. 6–8, 1925	Springfield, Mass.	Court Square Theatre
Apr. 9–10, 1925	Hartford, Conn.	Parsons' Theatre
Apr. 12–May 30, 1925	Chicago, Ill.	Apollo Theatre
May 31–June 13, 1925	Detroit, Mich.	Shubert Detroit

The Cocoanuts

Oct. 27–Nov. 21, 1925	Boston, Mass.	Tremont Theatre
Nov. 23–Dec. 5, 1925	Philadelphia, Pa.	Forrest Theatre
Dec. 8, 1925–Aug. 7, 1926	New York, N.Y.	Lyric Theatre

The Cocoanuts *has a 276-performance run on Broadway.*

| Sept. 20–25, 1926 | Washington, D.C. | National Theatre |

The first road tour of The Cocoanuts *begins with Zeppo's fiancé Marion Benda in the chorus.*

Sept. 27–Oct. 2, 1926	Baltimore, Md.	Ford's Opera House
Oct. 4–9, 1926	Cincinnati, Ohio	Grand Opera House
Oct. 11–Dec. 18, 1926	Chicago, Ill.	Erlanger Theatre
Dec. 19–25, 1926	Milwaukee, Wis.	Davidson Theatre
Dec. 26, 1926–Jan. 8, 1927	St. Louis, Mo.	American Theatre
Jan. 9–15, 1927	Kansas City, Mo.	Shubert Theatre
Jan. 17–22, 1927	Louisville, Ky.	Brown Theatre
Jan. 24–29, 1927	Indianapolis, Ind.	English's Opera House
Jan. 30–Feb. 5, 1927	Dayton, Ohio	Victory Theatre
Feb. 6–19, 1927	Detroit, Mich.	New Detroit Theatre
Feb. 21–26, 1927	Columbus, Ohio	Hartman Theatre

Feb. 27–Mar. 12, 1927	Cleveland, Ohio	Ohio Theatre
Mar. 14–26, 1927	Pittsburgh, Pa.	Nixon Theatre
Mar. 28–Apr. 9, 1927	Boston, Mass.	Colonial Theatre
Apr. 11–16, 1927	Newark, N.J.	Shubert Theatre

On the afternoon of April 12, Marion and Zeppo are married at the Chalfonte Hotel in New York.

Apr. 18–23, 1927	Brooklyn, N.Y.	Werba's Theatre
Apr. 25–30, 1927	Atlantic City, N.J.	Nixon's Apollo Theatre
May 2–14, 1927	Philadelphia, Pa.	Garrick Theatre
May 16–June 4, 1927	New York, N.Y.	Century Theatre

Sept. 26–Oct. 1, 1927	Buffalo, N.Y.	Erlanger Theatre

The second road tour of The Cocoanuts *begins, and Marion has graduated from the chorus to a featured role.*

Oct. 3–8, 1927	Rochester, N.Y.	Lyceum Theatre
Oct. 10–15, 1927	Toronto, Ont.	Princess Theatre
Oct. 17–22, 1927	Pittsburgh, Pa.	Nixon Theatre
Oct. 24–29, 1927	Cleveland, Ohio	Ohio Theatre
Oct. 31–Nov. 2, 1927	Akron, Ohio	Goodyear Theatre
Nov. 3–5, 1927	Youngstown, Ohio	Park Theatre
Nov. 7–9, 1927	Columbus, Ohio	Hartman Theatre
Nov. 10–12, 1927	Indianapolis, Ind.	English's Opera House
Nov. 13–19, 1927	St. Louis, Mo.	American Theatre
Nov. 20–26, 1927	Kansas City, Mo.	Shubert Theatre
Nov. 27–Dec. 3, 1927	Denver, Colo.	Broadway Theatre
Dec. 5–6, 1927	Ogden, Utah	Orpheum Theatre
Dec. 7–10, 1927	Salt Lake City, Utah	Salt Lake Theatre
Dec. 12, 1927–Jan. 14, 1928	Los Angeles, Calif.	Erlanger's Biltmore Theatre
Jan. 16–Feb. 4, 1928	San Francisco, Calif.	Columbia Theatre

Spanish Knights

Feb. 9–15, 1928	Los Angeles, Calif.	Metropolitan Theatre
Feb. 20–25, 1928	San Francisco, Calif.	Granada Theatre
Mar. 29–31, 1928	Rockford, Ill.	Coronado Theatre
Apr. 2–7, 1928	Chicago, Ill.	Chicago Theatre
Apr. 9–14, 1928	Chicago, Ill.	Uptown Theatre
Apr. 16–21, 1928	Chicago, Ill.	Tivoli Theatre

Animal Crackers

Sept. 25–Oct. 13, 1928	Philadelphia, Pa.	Shubert Theatre
Oct. 15–20, 1928	Philadelphia, Pa.	Erlanger Theatre
Oct. 23, 1928–Apr. 6, 1929	New York, N.Y.	44th St. Theatre

Animal Crackers *has a 191-performance run on Broadway.*

Scenes from Animal Crackers

Apr. 13, 1929	Brooklyn, N.Y.	Madison Theatre
Apr. 14–27, 1929	New York, N.Y.	Palace Theatre
Apr. 28–May 4, 1929	New York, N.Y.	Riverside Theatre

Animal Crackers

Sept. 20–21, 1929	New Haven, Conn.	Shubert Theatre
Sept. 23–Oct. 19, 1929	Boston, Mass.	Shubert Theatre
Oct. 21–26, 1929	Newark, N.J.	Shubert Theatre
Oct. 28–Nov. 2, 1929	Baltimore, Md.	Maryland Theatre
Nov. 3–9, 1929	Washington, D.C.	Poli's Theatre
Nov. 11–23, 1929	Pittsburgh, Pa.	Alvin Theatre
Nov. 24–Dec. 14, 1929	Detroit, Mich.	Cass Theatre
Dec. 22, 1929–Mar. 1, 1930	Chicago, Ill.	Grand Theatre
Mar. 2–8, 1930	St. Louis, Mo.	Shubert-Rialto Theatre
Mar. 9–15, 1930	Kansas City, Mo.	Shubert Theatre
Mar. 17–21, 1930	Indianapolis, Ind.	English's Opera House
Mar. 23–Apr. 5, 1930	Cleveland, Ohio	Hanna Theatre

July 11, 1930	Asbury Park, N.J.	Paramount Theatre

The Four Marx Brothers make a personal appearance at the grand opening of the newest Paramount Theatre.

The Schweinerei

Oct. 1–3, 1930	Flushing, N.Y.	RKO Keith's Theatre
Oct. 4–9, 1930	Brooklyn, N.Y.	RKO Albee Theatre
Oct. 11–24, 1930	New York, N.Y.	RKO Keith's Palace Theatre
Oct. 31–Nov. 6, 1930	Philadelphia, Pa.	Stanley-Warner Mastbaum Theatre
Nov. 8–13, 1930	Chicago, Ill.	RKO Palace Theatre

Groucho undergoes an emergency appendectomy the night before the opening. Zeppo capably fills in for him for the entire week. The following week's engagement in Cincinnati is canceled.

Nov. 22–28, 1930   Cleveland, Ohio   Palace Theatre

The RKO circuit is assured of Groucho's full recovery, but the Marxes get caught using Zeppo as Groucho for half of the performances and a second week in Cleveland is canceled.

Dec. 5–10, 1930   Boston, Mass.   Metropolitan Theatre

Dec. 12–18, 1930   Detroit, Mich.   Michigan Theatre

Jan. 5–Feb. 1, 1931   London, UK   Palace Theatre

The Schweinerei *is presented as part of Charles B. Cochran's 1931 Varieties.*

April 22, 1931   Los Angeles, Calif.   Shrine Auditorium

The Four Marx Brothers appear at the Ninth Annual National Variety Artists Benefit.

Napoleon's Return

October 16, 1931   Union City, N.J.   Capitol Theatre

Oct. 17–20, 1931   Flushing, N.Y.   RKO Keith's Theatre

Oct. 23–29, 1931   St. Louis, Mo.   RKO St. Louis Theatre

Oct. 31–Nov. 5, 1931   Columbus, Ohio   Keith's Theatre

Nov. 7–12, 1931   Cincinnati, Ohio   Albee Theatre

Nov. 14–19, 1931   Chicago, Ill.   Palace Theatre

Nov. 21–26, 1931   Cleveland, Ohio   Palace Theatre

Dec. 4–10, 1931   Buffalo, N.Y.   Shea's Buffalo Theatre

Jan. 2–7, 1932   New York, N.Y.   RKO Keith's Palace Theatre

Jan. 9–14, 1932   Brooklyn, N.Y.   RKO Albee Theatre

May 2, 1932   Los Angeles, Calif.   Shrine Auditorium

The Four Marx Brothers appear at a benefit for the Guaranty Depositor's Restoration Association.

Sept. 24, 1932   Los Angeles, Calif.   Olympic Stadium

The Four Marx Brothers appear at the Motion Picture Parade and Sports Pageant to benefit the Marion Davies Relief Fund.

Appendix II: Zeppo Marx on Film, Radio, and Television

FILM

Humor Risk

Caravel Comedies Company—April 1921 (unreleased)
Directed by Dick Smith
Written by Jo Swerling
Photographed by A.H. Vallet

In early April 1921 the Four Marx Brothers made a silent two-reel comedy at the Victor Studio in Fort Lee, New Jersey. With some friends as investors, they formed the Caravel Comedies Company and announced that they would star in a series of short films, going so far as to name the next two: "Hick, Hick, Hooray" and "Hot Dog." All parties involved agreed that "Humor Risk" was terrible and future filmmaking plans were scrapped. No print of the never-released "Humor Risk" is known to survive.

A Kiss in the Dark

Paramount—April 6, 1925
Directed by Frank Tuttle
Screenplay by Townsend Martin
Based on *Aren't We All* by Frederick Lonsdale
Photographed by Alvin Wyckoff

During the Broadway run of I'll Say She Is *Zeppo visited the Paramount Studio in Astoria and filmed a brief sequence with some other Broadway stars at a garden party in this Adolphe Menjou romantic comedy. Only two reels of the film are known to survive. The garden party sequence is not on either of those reels.*

The Cocoanuts

Paramount—May 23, 1929
Directed by Robert Florey and Joseph Santley
Based on the play by George S. Kaufman

Screen Adaptation by Morrie Ryskind
Music by Irving Berlin
Photographed by George Folsey
The Four Marx Brothers' first film is the adaptation of their second Broadway stage hit. Zeppo's role in the play is greatly reduced in the screen adaptation.

Animal Crackers

Paramount—August 28, 1930
Directed by Victor Heerman
Based on the play by George S. Kaufman and Morrie Ryskind
Screenplay by Morrie Ryskind
Music and Lyrics by Bert Kalmar and Harry Ruby
Photographed by George Folsey
The transition of another Broadway musical to the screen again eliminates a fair amount of Zeppo's already minimal role from the play. But Zeppo shines as Captain Spaulding's secretary Horatio W. Jamison when the captain dictates a letter to the honorable Charles H. Hungerdunger in one of the memorable highlights of the film.

The House That Shadows Built

Paramount—April 15, 1931
This promotional film celebrating the twentieth anniversary of Paramount features clips from films made during the studio's first twenty years, including some that were still in production at the time of the film being screened. The Four Marx Brothers had just arrived in Hollywood to film Monkey Business. *Since production on the new film had not yet begun, they shot the "Theatrical Manager's Office" sketch that they had done on the stage for many years. The footage is a rare example of the quartet as they interacted on the stage—with Zeppo an equally contributing member.*

Monkey Business

Paramount—September 19, 1931
Directed by Norman McLeod
Screenplay by S. J. Perelman and Will B. Johnstone
Additional Dialogue by Arthur Sheekman
Photographed by Arthur L. Todd
The first Marx Brothers film not adapted from a Broadway show gives Zeppo his most significant role to date. The film is loosely based on the vaudeville show Home Again *in which Zeppo had replaced Gummo. In* Monkey Business *Zeppo has far*

more to do than he or Gummo ever did in Home Again. *Here Zeppo is the romantic lead and plays the hero in the climactic scene. He even gets a few laughs.*

Horse Feathers
Paramount—August 10, 1932
Directed by Norman McLeod
Screenplay by Bert Kalmar, Harry Ruby, S. J. Perelman, and Will B. Johnstone
Music and Lyrics by Bert Kalmar and Harry Ruby
Photographed by Ray June
Zeppo again has a significant role as Groucho's son and the romantic lead. He even gets to sing a solo—as he had frequently on stage.

Duck Soup
Paramount—November 17, 1933
Directed by Leo McCarey
Screenplay by Bert Kalmar and Harry Ruby
Additional Dialogue by Arthur Sheekman and Nat Perrin
Music and Lyrics by Bert Kalmar and Harry Ruby
Photographed by Henry Sharp
As originally conceived, Duck Soup *would have continued featuring Zeppo in the same manner as he had been in* Monkey Business *and* Horse Feathers. *He was to play Groucho's son, be the romantic lead, and have a featured song. But the Marx Brothers walked out in a contract dispute as production was starting. By the time they ironed out their differences with Paramount, Zeppo was well on his way to leaving the Four Marx Brothers. The film was rewritten upon their return and Zeppo was again relegated to his earlier marginal status.*

Hollywood on Parade (B-5)
Paramount—December 1933
Directed by Louis Lewyn
Zeppo is seen at a Hollywood costume party thrown by Marion Davies. He's wearing the toupees of several stars on his jacket in what the narrator calls "toupee or not toupee." Chico and Groucho are also seen, as is Zeppo's friend and decorator Harold Grieve who accompanies his wife Jetta Goudal.

Screen Snapshots (Series 16, Number 11)
Columbia—June 25, 1937
Directed by Ralph Staub

The Screen Snapshots *series celebrates its seventeenth anniversary with footage of a party at the home of columnist Harriet Parsons. Guests include Buddy Rogers, Wallace Reid, George Raft, and Marie Provost. The Four Marx Brothers are seen in unrelated newsreel footage.*

Grand Opening of Del Mar Racetrack

Just about every studio and newsreel company covered the opening of Bing Crosby's Del Mar racetrack near San Diego on July 3, 1937. Celebrities seen watching Reigh Count win the Del Mar Inaugural Handicap along with Crosby and sportscaster Clem McCarthy include Lee Tracy, Bob Burns, Pat O'Brien, Una Merkel, Oliver Hardy, Robert Taylor, and Barbara Stanwyck. If they were even recognized by the producers, Zeppo and Marion—seen in several of the newsreels seated in a box with Stanwyck and Taylor—were not mentioned by any of the newsreel narrators.

Screen Snapshots (Series 17, Number 1)

Columbia—September 17, 1937

Directed by Ralph Staub

A compilation of newsreel footage featuring Clara Bow, Gary Cooper, Marion Davies, Janet Gaynor, Myrna Loy, Jackie Cooper, Lew Cody, Joan Bennett, and Theda Bara, also includes footage of the Four Marx Brothers' handprints and footprints being preserved in cement at Grauman's Chinese Theatre in 1933.

Screen Snapshots: Hollywood's Famous Feet

Columbia—July 20, 1950

Directed by Ralph Staub

In a compilation of newsreel footage showing various stars placing their hands and feet into cement at Grauman's Chinese Theatre in Hollywood, Sid Grauman is seen with the Four Marx Brothers, Al Jolson, Edgar Bergen, the Ritz Brothers, John Wayne, and Tom Mix. Jolson is the narrator.

RADIO

January 27, 1923   Pittsburgh, Pa.   WCAE

On their final day at the Aldine Theatre in The Twentieth Century Revue, *the Four Marx Brothers make what is believed to be their radio debut from the studio of WCAE.*

June 9, 1924   Newark, N.J.   WOR

A few weeks into the Broadway run of I'll Say She Is, *the Four Marx Brothers and the cast of the show make a radio broadcast from the WOR studio at Bamberger's department store.*

July 8, 1924   New York, N.Y.   WHN

A special late-night broadcast—starting at 11:30 p.m. after the evening perfor-mance of I'll Say She Is *concludes—features the Four Marx Brothers and other cast members performing selections from the show.*

December 30, 1924   New York, N.Y.   WNYC

The Four Marx Brothers appear at the Newspaper Club Clubhouse before their performance in I'll Say She Is *that evening. The event is broadcast as* Old Timers' Night at the Newspaper Club.

February 25, 1925   Boston, Mass.   WBZ

A few weeks after I'll Say She Is *closes on Broadway, the show is back on tour and the Four Marx Brothers appear on a radio broadcast celebrating the first anniver-sary of the WBZ radio studio at the Hotel Brunswick Roof.*

April 7, 1925   Springfield, Mass.   WBZ

The cast of I'll Say She Is *appears on a broadcast from the Kimball Studio at the Westinghouse Hotel.*

Mar. 10, 1929   New York, N.Y.   WMCA

The Four Marx Brothers are among the many stars performing as the Jewish Theatrical Guild honors its vice president, Eddie Cantor.

Mar. 15, 1929   New York, N.Y.   WMSG

The Four Marx Brothers appear at the premiere of Texas Guinan's Vitaphone film, Queen of the Nightclubs *at the Strand Theatre. The event and the broadcast benefit the Theatrical Press Representatives of America.*

October 4, 1930   Brooklyn, N.Y.   WBBC/WCGU

On the afternoon of their opening in The Schweinerei, *the Four Marx Brothers appear on a broadcast over two stations from the RKO Albee Theatre.*

April 17, 1932   Hollywood, Calif.   CBS network

Zeppo sings with the Raymond Paige Orchestra on California Melodies, *a new nationally broadcast series.*

September 1933   Hollywood, Calif.   Paramount Studio
Paramount creates a series of radio promotion discs for the upcoming release of Duck Soup. *The shows, called* The Paramount Movie Parade *are distributed to radio stations around the country. Excerpts from the film included on the discs differ from the versions heard in the finished film. In the second disc, songs from the film are heard, but in versions that don't feature the Four Marx Brothers. These unusual outtakes are probably from the period after the Marx Brothers walked out on the film in a contract dispute. Paramount had originally planned to continue the production with actors replacing the Four Marx Brothers. Other outtakes in the shows are from the early production when Zeppo was to play Groucho's son. The voice over announcer says Zeppo is "the only one of the Four Marx Brothers cursed with common sense."*

Fall 1933   Hollywood, Calif.   Syndicated
Zeppo makes two appearances on the five-minute transcribed interview show, Kay Parker in Hollywood. *In one he promotes Perry's Brass Rail. The other is from the set of* Duck Soup.

October 6, 1963   Palm Springs, Calif.   NBC
Zeppo provides a brief recorded message for the Monitor 63 *birthday salute to Groucho.*

TELEVISION

Feb. 18, 1957 *Tonight: America after Dark* NBC
The Five Marx Brothers participate in a filmed interview when they gather at the Hollywood Civic Playhouse for Chico's opening in a touring production of The Fifth Season. *The film is broadcast later that evening and then promptly lost.*

February 17, 1975 *The American Film Institute Salute* CBS
          to Orson Welles
Groucho and Zeppo are briefly seen in the audience at the event taped on February 9 at the Century Plaza Hotel in Los Angeles.

August 9, 1979 *Hollywood Greats: Groucho Marx* BBC
Zeppo's interview with Barry Norman, filmed outside his Desert Island condominium in Rancho Mirage, is featured in an hour-long documentary about Groucho.

NOTES

CHAPTER 1

1. Minnie's sister was at Blackwell's Island at around the same time *New York World* reporter Nellie Bly famously got herself committed to the institution as part of an undercover assignment to expose the horrific and squalid conditions there. Her newspaper reports describing patients tied together with ropes, ice cold baths in filthy water, beatings, rancid food, and rat infestation were compiled in 1887 as the book *Ten Days in a Mad-House.*

2. The illnesses associated with the deaths in Minnie's family were particularly horrific in an era without the benefit of antibiotics and future advances in medicine. Julius LeFevre suffered from articular rheumatism, which led to double hypostatic pneumonia. He died within three weeks of the diagnosis. Pauline LeFevre died from an epileptic seizure after five months in the asylum with dementia.

3. Minnie's sister Celine—known in America under her Americanized married name, Selena Walker—died of nephritis on August 31, 1893. She is erroneously listed in immigration and census records as the daughter of Minnie's sister Pauline and her husband Julius LeFevre.

4. Although Groucho would claim to have been named for Hannah's third husband, Julius Schickler, he was in fact named for Julius LeFevre, Minnie's sister Pauline's husband who had died in 1886. Hannah married Julius Schickler well after Groucho's birth.

5. Al Shean entered vaudeville at age sixteen in 1884 when he formed the Gotham City Quartet. In 1890 he formed the Manhattan Quartet, later renamed the Manhattan Comedy Four when they started to add comedy bits in between songs. In 1900 Shean left the Manhattan Comedy Four and started working with Charles Warren as the team of Shean and Warren. They become a great success in vaudeville with two classic sketches, "Quo Vadis Upside Down" and "Kidding the Captain." They split up a few times before permanently ending their partnership in 1910 and paving the way for Al Shean's greatest success as half of the team Gallagher and Shean with Ed Gallagher.

6. Harry would have another child, Harry Shean, Jr., in 1916 with his second wife.

7. The twins were born prematurely on July 28, 1900. Marie Julia Schoenberg died the same day. Selma Ruby Schoenberg died on August 22, 1901.

8. After Harry and Marie divorced, Marie and the widowed Sara Heyman lived together in their later years.

Chapter 2

1. Adolph changed his name to avoid confusion with Adolph Marks, a Chicago attorney notorious for bringing legal action against vaudevillians on behalf of circuit and theater managers.
2. Previous hired hand Lou Levy had been replaced in the Four Nightingales by Manuel Frank prior to the Marx family moving to Chicago. Frank not relocating with them resulted in the hiring of Fred Klute.
3. Grand Boulevard has been renamed South King Drive, but the Marx house still stands at 4512 South King Drive.
4. Minnie's choice of the name Palmer was occasionally explained as being taken from the Palmer House Hotel, but Minnie promoted the confusion of herself with actress and musical comedy star Minnie Palmer (1857–1936).

Chapter 3

1. In the 1950 Federal Census, Zeppo noted that he had completed the eighth grade.
2. One of the Five Rose Maids, Mary Orth, had previously appeared in T. Dwight Pepple's *Follies of the Cabaret*. She would continue working for Minnie for several years. She joined the Four Marx Brothers company in the fall of 1914—and remained with them until January 1921. She appeared in *Home Again*, *The Cinderella Girl*, *'N' Everything*, and *The Winter Garden Revue*.

Chapter 4

1. There were 350,000 casualties at Argonne. The forty-seven-day battle ended with the signing of the Armistice on November 11, 1918. Sergeant Alvin York's heroic exploits at Argonne were depicted in the 1941 film *Sergeant York*, for which Gary Cooper won an Academy Award as Best Actor in 1942.
2. Chico and Betty claimed March 22 as their wedding date in the interest of promoting the idea that Betty became pregnant after the wedding. They picked March 22 because Chico was not likely to forget his fake wedding anniversary if it was also his birthday.
3. Groucho may not have known that William Henry Johnson had died at the age of sixty-nine only a few weeks before that *Brooklyn Daily Eagle* interview.

Chapter 5

1. No formal rule was implemented to prevent the married Chico from moving in on the girlfriends of his unmarried brothers—not that such a rule would have prevented this activity.
2. Note that Groucho created a comic version of the wedding for his December 30, 1930, *Collier's* piece, "My Poor Wife," that is not interrupted by any facts.
3. There's nothing about Zeppo fixing up Jack Benny with a fourteen-year-old schoolgirl as a gag that doesn't ring true, but this simple story came to include several fabricated details in memoirs by Benny's longtime writer Milt Josefsberg, his manager Irving Fein, and even one cowritten by Mary Livingstone and her brother Hilliard Marks. In

these books the various inaccuracies include varying ages for Mary, the placement of the event in 1922, and assertions that the Marx Brothers were distantly related to the Marcowitz family. The notion that the dinner was a Passover seder was introduced in the Josefsberg and Livingstone-Marks books, but the first night of Passover in 1920 was April 2. The Marx Brothers and Jack Benny celebrated the holiday during their two-week engagement in San Francisco.

4. A version of the "Theatrical Manager's Office" sketch was filmed in 1931 for the Paramount promotional film *The House That Shadows Built*. It demonstrates unequivocally that Zeppo was better utilized on stage than he was on film.

CHAPTER 6

1. *A Kiss in the Dark* has long been considered a lost film, although in recent years two of its six reels have been discovered. The garden party sequence with Zeppo's appearance is not contained in the two known surviving reels.

CHAPTER 7

1. Thomas Meighan starred in four films for Famous Players-Lasky that were shot at Paramount in 1925 and three of them are lost. Marion was not billed in any of these films.

2. In an interesting twist, Marion appeared with the show at the Lyric Theatre in Allentown, where nearly six months earlier, the Four Marx Brothers gave the debut performance of *I'll Say She Is*.

3. Oddly, the other Marion Benda appeared in the Broadway production of *Rio Rita*, which featured Harpo's future wife Susan Fleming in the cast.

4. Marion took the important role of Penelope Martin, one of the villains in the show. In the Broadway production Penelope had two featured musical numbers, "Minstrel Days" and "Tango Melody." By the time Marion had assumed the role on tour, "Tango Melody" had been given to another character. Kay Francis played Penelope in the film version of *The Cocoanuts*. Penelope's musical numbers were not included in the film.

CHAPTER 8

1. Minnie and Frenchy had lived just down the street at 217 East 78th Street around the time that Chico and Harpo were born.

CHAPTER 9

1. Harris sold his theater to the Shubert Organization in 1926 but it would bear his name until it closed in 1994.

CHAPTER 10

1. Upon his return to Boston, George S. Thomas sold Omar and Asra to the highly respected breeder, Q. A. Shaw McKean. Thomas kept Omar and Asra's first litter and McKean began breeding Afghan Hounds. Asra lived to be fourteen and produced seventy puppies. Zeppo is frequently credited with bringing Afghan Hounds to North

America, but it was Q. A. Shaw McKean who was principally responsible for popularizing the breed.

2. There's no doubt that the "Mrs. Marx" in Sheilah Graham's book is Marion, although Graham incorrectly states that Harpo was living at the Garden of Allah with his wife Susan, who never lived there and hadn't yet married Harpo at the time he lived there.

CHAPTER 11

1. The dispute over the Marx Brothers' financial participation in *Monkey Business* and *Horse Feathers* was finally settled on April 6, 1962, for $38,500—roughly $357,000 in the modern economy.

CHAPTER 12

1. Hard liquor remained prohibited until December, so speakeasies continued to operate after the passage of the Beer Act.

2. The planned duet—"Keep Doin' What You're Doin'"—was instead used in the Wheeler and Woolsey film *Hips, Hips, Hooray!*

CHAPTER 13

1. Orsatti also had other debts he couldn't pay. He would be greatly embarrassed when *Variety* published the details of his bankruptcy filing on November 3, 1931, under the headline "Orsatti's Debts."

2. Louis Bimberg continued to be plagued by the scandal that caused several members of his family to use his wife's maiden name (or in Marion's case, the stage name Benda). He had been separated from his wife for several years when he died at the age of fifty-six on February 2, 1937. He had been living at the Hotel Ruxton on West 72nd Street in New York and had worked as a real estate broker during the final years of his life. Marion had little or no contact with him during that time.

3. After dodging the case for several years by fleeing to Chicago and Miami, Voiler finally went to trial in 1938. The case was dropped when Friedman, by this time serving his sentence for the crime, would not testify against Voiler after recanting the confession in which he implicated him. Smart way to stay alive since Friedman knew Voiler well.

CHAPTER 14

1. Zeppo Marx, Inc. issued one thousand shares of capital stock in August 1934. In addition to Zeppo and his attorney, Loyd Wright, the directors of the company were S. Earl Wright and Herschel B. Green, two other attorneys at the firm Wright, Wright, Green & Wright. The company names "Zeppo Marx, Inc." and "the Zeppo Marx Agency" became interchangeable.

2. Bing Crosby's combined earnings from movies, radio, and records would eclipse MacMurray's income, but MacMurray had the top income among male stars from motion picture work.

CHAPTER 15

1. The success of *A Night at the Opera* in 1935 resulted in Paramount rereleasing *Horse Feathers* in 1936—almost immediately following the untimely deaths of two of the film's stars. David Landau died on September 20, 1935, at the age of fifty-six, and Thelma Todd died on December 16, 1935, at the age of twenty-nine.

2. Joey Bass would spend his later years in Canada. He may have been in hiding, since he was living under the name Joseph Cowan. He died under that name in Toronto on December 8, 1976.

3. Warner took the punishment a bit too far by claiming that the time de Havilland spent on suspension should not count toward the fulfillment of her contract. RKO didn't go quite this far with Barbara Stanwyck.

CHAPTER 16

1. An advertisement in the *1938 Film Daily Yearbook* listed the members of the Artists' Managers Guild as H. E. Edington–F. W. Vincent Inc.; Hawks-Volck Corporation; Leland Hayward, Inc.; Lyons, McCormick & Lyons; M. C. Levee; Myron Selznick & Company, Inc.; Phil Berg-Bert Allenberg, Inc.; Sam Jaffee, Inc.; The Small Company; The Feldman-Blum Corporation; The Orsatti Agency; William Morris Agency, Inc.; Zeppo Marx, Inc.; and a fourteenth member, Artists and Authors Corporation of America.

2. Testimony at the 1943 extortion trial of the participants in the protection scheme revealed that Paramount, MGM, 20th Century Fox and Warner Bros. had each paid $50,000 a year between 1936 and 1940 to assure they'd have no union trouble. Smaller studios paid lesser amounts.

3. On January 15, 1935, the *Hollywood Reporter* noted that Jack LaRue had signed a management contract with the Zeppo Marx Agency.

4. The check for $2,000 was found in Bruneman's pocket. The additional $200 was a collection fee. The notion of the check being found in a safe deposit box by Bruneman's widow is contradictory to the original police report. The matter was ultimately settled for $257.

5. The man convicted for the Bruneman murders, Peter Pianezzi, was another low-level mobster. He spent thirteen years of a double life sentence in Folsom Prison before being paroled in 1953. The key witness against Pianezzi later said that he knew Pianezzi was not the gunman, but that he testified against him anyway because "he has done enough things in life to deserve the gas chamber." Pianezzi maintained his innocence for the rest of his life and was pardoned based on his rehabilitation in 1966 by governor Edmund G. Brown, Sr. Pianezzi was pardoned again in 1981 by Brown's son, governor Edmund G. Brown, Jr. based on the evidence of Pianezzi's innocence. Pianezzi died in 1992 at the age of ninety.

6. At the same time, they both sold their houses to Jack Oakie who moved into the Stanwyck house with his wife Venita Vardon. They operated Oakvardon Kennels at the property and bred Afghan Hounds descended from Omar and Asra. Shortly after acquiring the property, Oakie sold Zeppo's house to retired oil man Thomas Quine.

A year later Janet Gaynor and her husband, MGM costume designer Gilbert Adrian, bought the house from Quine.

7. J. H. Ryan would buy Zeppo's former house from Janet Gaynor and Gilbert Adrian in 1952. Harry Hart stayed on at Northridge for a short time before going to work at Louis B. Mayer's Riverside County ranch in Perris, California.

CHAPTER 17

1. There are patents for similar clamps dating as far back as 1881.

CHAPTER 18

1. Barbara Stanwyck and her son became estranged as a result of her authoritarian treatment of him. A succession of military schools fostered a feeling of abandonment in him, and by the time he turned nineteen, Dion Fay had virtually no relationship with his mother.

2. Henry Willson would go on to great success as the agent who discovered several of the major stars of Hollywood's so-called beefcake industry of the 1950s. The homosexual Willson's most prominent discovery was Rock Hudson, and his clients also included Tab Hunter, Rory Calhoun, Troy Donohue, John Derek, Guy Madison, and Robert Wagner.

3. Gummo's interview with Chaplin's lawyers also revealed that Bercovici was believed to have stolen a story he sold to Samuel Goldwyn. Bercovici's $6,450,000 plagiarism suit against Chaplin was settled in 1947 for $95,000.

4. The sale price of Marx, Miller & Marx that Gummo related, adjusted for the current economy, equates to $2.8 million.

CHAPTER 19

1. There are many theories of who killed Bugsy Siegel and why, but none are any more plausible then the Sedway story. Most mob experts agree that an authorized hit would not have been made from outside the house through a window. And a sanctioned mob hit would have needed the approval of Charlie "Lucky" Luciano—who would not have given permission due to Siegel's close relationship with the powerful Meyer Lansky. Siegel was essentially untouchable as far as the mob was concerned. An outsider—like Moose Pandza—certainly could be the killer.

CHAPTER 20

1. A current valuation of the Marman sale would place the value at between $25 and $30 million dollars.

2. The Eaton Corporation, the current owner of Aeroquip, still maintains a Marman product line of couplings.

3. The Singer family netted $12,581.79 after legal fees of $6,998.33, court costs of $1,505.47, and medical bills totaling $1,414.41 were paid.

4. Marion's mother had changed her name from Rebecca Bimberg to Eleanor Miller, using her middle name and maiden name, to further disassociate herself from Louis Bimberg—even though they never divorced.

CHAPTER 21

1. Chico had been living with Mary (generally known by her stage name Mary Dee) since moving out of his house and leaving Betty in 1941, but he didn't marry Mary until 1958 because Betty would not agree to divorce him until she wanted to remarry.
2. Greenbaum had been offered a chance to divest himself of his interest in the Riviera by his mob superiors. His life would have been spared, but he refused to sell. Johnny Rosselli brought the offer to Greenbaum. Rosselli would later say that the hit on Gus Greenbaum was ordered by Meyer Lansky.

CHAPTER 22

1. Susan was finally able to divest of Harpo's portion of the Martuc ranch when the entire property was sold in 1970.

CHAPTER 23

1. Ted Briskin's claim to fame was marrying three Hollywood actresses—Betty Hutton, Joan Dixon, and Colleen Miller—between 1945 and 1955.

CHAPTER 24

1. Groucho had become one of the first homeowners in Tamarisk Ranchos in 1958. The community of sixteen homes near the Tamarisk Country Club, but not actually part of it, was built by Groucho's friend, developer Lou Halper. The house had three bedrooms and three bathrooms and was roughly 2,000 square feet.

CHAPTER 25

1. Using Groucho's influence, Erin was able to get a small part in Woody Allen's *Everything You Always Wanted to Know about Sex* (*But Were Afraid to Ask.)* She also appeared with Groucho on episodes of *The Dick Cavett Show*, *The Merv Griffin Show*, and *The New Bill Cosby Show*. These would be her most high-profile appearances. She also had small television roles on *Marcus Welby, M.D.* and *Adam-12*, and she appeared as an extra in a few films, including *Sheila Levine Is Dead and Living in New York* and *Conquest of the Planet of the Apes.*
2. Zeppo's interest in Lyn Ehrhard represents a rare instance of him pursuing a woman somewhat closer to his age than his usual girlfriends—although she was twenty-six years younger than him. Ehrhart, who shrouded herself in mystery and provided no details of herself anywhere, was born on September 21, 1927—only a few weeks before Barbara.
3. Fratianno was relocated to Sudden Valley, Washington, and eventually removed from the Federal Witness Protection Program in June 1989 when he—under the name James Thomas—was arrested for pointing a loaded gun at Jean Bodul and threatening to blow her head off.

Bibliography

1. Periodicals

Agee, James. "*The Marx Brothers* by Kyle Crichton." *Films in Review*, July-August 1950.

Anonymous. "Making Ready *The Cocoanuts*: Chat with the Four Marx Brothers amid Hectic Excitement in Their Dressing Room." *Boston Globe*, November 1, 1925.

Anonymous. "Aeroquip Acquires Marman Products, Prominent West Coast Manufacturer of Aircraft Clamps and Allied Components." *The Flying A*, April 1955.

Anonymous. "Introducing . . . Marman Products Company: Meet the Most Recent Addition to Aeroquip; a New Subsidiary in Los Angeles, California." *The Flying A*, May 1955.

Anonymous. "Zeppo Marx: Comic at Home in Palm Springs." *Palm Springs Villager: The Magazine of Fine Desert Living*, March 1959.

Benny, Mary Livingstone. "Where My Heart Is." *Radio Mirror: The Magazine of Radio Romances*, March 1945.

Beranger, Clara. "The Woman Who Taught Her Children to Be Fools." *Liberty*, June 3, 1933.

Borgeson, Griffith. "Madness at Muroc: The Great Duesenberg—Mercedes Match Race." *Automobile Quarterly* 18, no. 3 (1980).

Cervin, Paul. "Marwyck." *Turf and Sports Digest*, December 1937.

Eder, Shirley. "Talking with Zeppo: The Handsome Marx." *Detroit Free Press*, July 20, 1970.

Ellis, Allen W. "Yes Sir: The Legacy of Zeppo Marx." *The Journal of Popular Culture*, August 2003.

Golden, Sylvia B. "Confessions of the Marx Brothers." *Theater*, January 1929.

Hall, Gladys. "Barbara's Advice to Girls in Love." *Radio Stars*, March 1937.

Hamilton, Sara. "The Nuttiest Quartet in the World." *Photoplay*, July 1932.

Hempstead, Susan. "It's 'Duck Soup' for the Marx Brothers." *Shadoplay*, November 1933.

Hopper, Hedda. "Marx Brothers Story—Saga of Their Clan." *Los Angeles Times*, September 4, 1938.

Kaufman, George S. "How Minnie's Five Boys Made Their Marx." *New York Times*, June 18, 1950.

Kutner, Nanette. "Her Neighbors—The Taylors." *Modern Screen*, December 1939.

Marx, Groucho. "Our Father and Us." *Redbook*, March 1933.

Marx, Gummo. "The Fifth Marx Brother." *Daily Variety*, November 2, 1953.

Marx, Marion (as told to James Reid). "My Pal Barbara." *Motion Picture*, April 1942.

McDermott, William S. "Telling a Tale of Those Droll Marx Boys and How They Got That Way." *Cleveland Plain-Dealer*, March 30, 1930.

Moffitt, John C. "The Marx Brothers, Four Lunatics at Large in Hollywood, Keep Movie Capital Gasping with Their Audacious Exploits." *The Hartford Courant*, August 27, 1933.

Moffitt, John C. "Further Adventures of the Marx Brothers in Hollywood, Wedding Bells for Groucho—The Love Affairs of Harpo." *The Hartford Courant*, September 3, 1933.

Mook, Samuel Richard. "Barbara Lets Go." *Picture Play*, September 1937.

Newnham, John K. "Four Crazy People." *Film Weekly*, June 2, 1933.

Norman, Barry. "Zeppo's Last Interview." *The Freedonia Gazette*, Winter 1981.

Olsen, Richard L. "The Mob and the Movies." *Los Angeles Times*, July 5, 1987.

Perelman, S. J. "The Winsome Foursome." *Show*, November 1961.

Prelutsky, Burt. "The Last Marx Brothers Movie." *The Chicago Sun-Times*, December 10, 1972.

Rittenberg, Louis. "Four of a Kind." *The American Hebrew*, January 22, 1926.

Ross, Betty. "The Four Marx Brothers: How They Rose from Vaudeville to Electric Lights on Broadway." *The Jewish Tribune*, September 5, 1924.

Sammis, Edward R. "Those Mad Marx Hares as Revealed by the Fifth Marx Brother to Edward R. Sammis." *Photoplay*, February 1936.

Saunders, Hortense. "Dodging 'Tank Town' Tomatoes Trained the Four Marx Brothers for Broadway." *The Yonkers Statesman*, July 24, 1926.

Shanklin, Gertrude. "Missy Is No Sissy." *Movieland*, September 1946.

Sherwood, Robert E. "The Moving Picture Album: *Monkey Business*." *New York Evening Post*, August 9, 1931.

Stein, Edwin C. "Marx-ing Time: Chico Reveals Life Story and Harpo Goes in for Backgammon in the Grand Manner." *The Brooklyn Standard-Union*, September 4, 1931.

Sullivan, Ed. "A Quarter of a Century of the Marx Brothers." *The Chicago Daily Tribune*, October 30, 1938.

Swanson, Pauline. "The Life of Jack Benny." *Radio and Television Mirror*, April 1948.

Wallace, Amy. "Who Killed Bugsy Siegel?" *Los Angeles Magazine*, October 2014.

Welkos, Robert W. "Is the Monkey Business Over at Last?" *Los Angeles Times*, April 23, 2000.

Wilson, B. F. "From Duck Soup to 'ОРѢШКИ'." *Screen Book*, February 1934.

Woollcott, Alexander. "A Mother of the Two-A-Day." *The Saturday Evening Post*, June 20, 1925.

2. BOOKS

Allen, Fred. *Much Ado About Me*. Boston: Little Brown and Company, 1956.

Arce, Hector. *Groucho*. New York: G.P. Putnam's Sons, 1979.

Bader, Robert S. *Four of the Three Musketeers: The Marx Brothers on Stage*. Evanston, Ill.: Northwestern University Press, 2016.

Balaban, Carrie. *Continuous Performance: Biography of A. J. Balaban.* New York: A. J. Balaban Foundation, 1964.

Bartlett, Tom. *Motorized Bicycles: From Motorbikes to Mopeds to eBikes.* Piedmont, N. C.: lulu.com, 2010.

Benny, Jack, and His Daughter Joan Benny. *Sunday Nights at Seven: The Jack Benny Story.* New York: Warner Books, 1990.

Benny, Mary Livingstone, and Hilliard Marks with Marcia Borie. *Jack Benny: A Biography.* Garden City, New York: Doubleday, 1978.

Berlin, Irving. *The Complete Lyrics of Irving Berlin.* Edited by Robert Kimball and Linda Emmet. New York: Knopf, 2001.

Brecher, Irving, as told to Hank Rosenfeld. *The Wicked Wit of the West.* Teaneck, N. J.: Ben Yahuda Press, 2009.

Carey, Gary. *All the Stars in Heaven: Louis B. Mayer's MGM.* New York: E.P. Dutton, 1981.

Chandler, Charlotte. *Hello, I Must Be Going: Groucho and His Friends.* Garden City, N.Y.: Doubleday & Company, Inc., 1978.

Crichton, Kyle. *The Marx Brothers.* Garden City, N. Y.: Doubleday, 1950.

Demaris, Ovid. *The Last Mafioso: The Treacherous World of Jimmy Fratianno.* New York: Times Books, 1981.

Eliot, Marc. *Cary Grant: A Biography.* New York: Harmony Books, 2004.

Eyles, Allen. *The Marx Brothers: Their World of Comedy.* New York: A.S. Barnes, 1969.

Eyman, Scott. *Lion of Hollywood: The Life and Legend of Louis B. Mayer.* New York: Simon & Schuster, 2005.

Fein, Irving A. *Jack Benny: An Intimate Biography.* New York: G.P. Putnam's Sons, 1976.

Goldstein, Malcolm. *George S. Kaufman: His Life, His Theater.* New York: Oxford University Press, 1987.

Gordon, Max with Lewis Funke. *Max Gordon Presents.* New York: Bernard Geis Associates, 1963.

Graham, Sheilah. *The Garden of Allah.* New York: Crown Publishers, Inc., 1970.

Green, Abel. *The Spice of Variety.* New York: Henry Holt and Company, 1952.

Hofler, Robert. *The Man Who Invented Rock Hudson: The Pretty Boys and Dirty Deals of Henry Willson.* New York: Carroll & Graf Publishers, 2005.

Hurst, Peter F. *I Came to Stay: The Journey That Led to the Founding of Aeroquip.* Jackson, Mich.: The Hurst Foundation, 2016.

Josefsberg, Milt. *The Jack Benny Show: The Life and Times of America's Best-Loved Entertainer.* New Rochelle, N. Y.: Arlington House, 1977.

Kanin, Garson. *Hollywood.* New York: Viking Press, 1974.

Kaplan, James. *Sinatra: The Chairman.* New York: Doubleday, 2015.

Levant, Oscar. *The Unimportance of Being Oscar.* New York: G.P. Putnam's Sons, 1968.

Lewis, Brad. *Hollywood's Celebrity Gangster: The Incredible Life and Times of Mickey Cohen.* Charleston, S. C.: BookSurge, LLC, 2009.

Lloyd, Herbert. *Vaudeville Trails Thru the West.* Philadelphia: Herbert Lloyd, 1919.

Marx, Arthur. *Life with Groucho: A Son's Eye View.* New York: Simon and Schuster, 1954.

Marx, Arthur. *Son of Groucho.* New York: David McKay, 1972.

Marx, Arthur. *My Life with Groucho.* London: Robson Books, 1988.

Marx, Bill. *Son of Harpo Speaks!* Montclair, N. J.: Applause Theatre & Cinema Books, 2011.

Marx, Eden Hartford. *Groucho.* Unpublished manuscript, 1980.

Marx, Groucho. *Groucho and Me.* New York: Bernard Geis Associates, 1959.

Marx, Groucho. *The Groucho Phile: An Illustrated Life.* Indianapolis: Bobbs-Merrill Company, Inc., 1976.

Marx, Groucho. *Love, Groucho: Letters from Groucho Marx to His Daughter Miriam.* Edited by Miriam Marx Allen. Boston: Faber and Faber, 1992.

Marx, Groucho, and Richard J. Anobile. *The Marx Bros. Scrapbook.* New York: Darien House, 1973.

Marx, Harpo, with Rowland Barber. *Harpo Speaks!* New York: Bernard Geis Associates, 1961.

Marx, Maxine. *Growing Up with Chico.* Englewood Cliffs, N.J.: Prentice-Hall, Inc., 1980.

Marx, Robert. *Son of a Gummo: Growing Up the Son of a Marx Brother.* Privately published, 2002.

Marx, Susan Fleming, with Robert S. Bader. *Speaking of Harpo.* Lanham, Md.: Applause Theatre & Cinema Books, 2022.

Mast, Gerald. *The Comic Mind: Comedy and the Movies.* Indianapolis / New York: The Bobbs-Merrill Company, Inc., 1973.

McDougal, Dennis. *The Last Mogul: Lew Wasserman, MCA and the Hidden History of Hollywood.* New York: Crown, 1998.

Meredith, Scott. *George S. Kaufman and His Friends.* Garden City, N.Y.: Doubleday & Company, Inc., 1974.

Miller, Constance O., and Edward M. Gilbert, Jr. *The New Complete Afghan Hound, 4th Edition.* New York: Howell Book House, 1988.

Riche, Melissa. *Mod Mirage: The Midcentury Architecture of Rancho Mirage.* Layton, Utah: Gibbs Smith, 2018.

Rose, Frank. *The Agency: William Morris and the Hidden History of Show Business.* New York: Harper Collins Publishers, 1995.

Rosenberg, Bernard, and Harry Silverstein. *The Real Tinsel.* New York: The MacMillan Company, 1970.

Russo, Gus. *Supermob: How Sidney Korshak and His Criminal Associates Became America's Hidden Power Brokers.* New York: Bloomsbury, 2006.

Ryskind, Morrie, with John H. M. Roberts. *I Shot an Elephant in My Pajamas.* Lafayette, La.: Hunting House Publishers, 1994.

Server, Lee. *Handsome Johnny—The Life and Death of Johnny Rosselli: Gentleman Gangster, Hollywood Producer, CIA Assassin.* New York: St. Martin's Press, 2018.

Sinatra, Barbara, with Wendy Holden. *Lady Blue Eyes: My Life with Frank.* New York: Crown Archetype, 2011.

Stoker, Sgt. Charles. *Thicker 'N Thieves: The 1950 Factual Expose of Police Pay-Offs, Graft, Political Corruption and Prostitution in Los Angeles and Hollywood.* Los Angeles, Calif.: Thoughtprint Press, 2011.

Stoliar, Steve. *Raised Eyebrows: My Years Inside Groucho's House.* Los Angeles, Calif.: General Publishing Group, 1996.

Stuart, Gloria, with Sylvia Thompson. *I Just Kept Hoping.* Boston: Little Brown and Company, 1999.

Teichmann, Howard. *George S. Kaufman: An Intimate Portrait.* New York: Atheneum, 1972.

Teichmann, Howard. *Smart Aleck: The Wit, World and Life of Alexander Woollcott.* New York: William Morrow and Company, 1976.

Turner, Lana. *Lana: The Lady, The Legend, The Truth.* New York: E.P. Dutton Inc., 1982.

Woollcott, Alexander. *While Rome Burns.* New York: Grosset & Dunlap, 1934.

Zuckerman, Michael J. *Vengeance Is Mine: Jimmy "The Weasel" Fratianno Tells How He Brought the Kiss of Death to the Mafia.* New York: MacMillan Publishing Company, 1987.

3. SCRIPTS AND TREATMENTS

Johnstone, Will B. *I'll Say She Is.* Library of Congress, copyright registration number D-68674, August 2, 1924.

Johnstone, Will B. *I'll Say She Is.* November 10, 1924.

Kaufman, George S. *The Cocoanuts.* 1925.

Kaufman, George S., and Morrie Ryskind. *Animal Crackers.* 1928.

Marx, Zeppo and Gouverneur Morris. *Tom, Dick and Harry.* 1932.

Marx, Zeppo and Gouverneur Morris. *A Pair of Shoes.* 1932.

Marx, Zeppo and S. J. Perelman. *Roller-Coaster.* 1932.

Marx, Zeppo. *Muscle-Bound.* 1932.

Ryskind, Morrie, and Will B. Johnstone. "Four Marx Brothers Radio Sketch." 1932.

Timberg, Herman. *On the Balcony.* 1921.

4. ADDITIONAL SOURCES

Billy Rose Theater Collection
New York Public Library of the Performing Arts, Dorothy and Lewis B. Cullman Center, New York.

Charlie Chaplin Archive
www.charliechaplinarchive.org/en.

Groucho Marx Collection (1911–1978)
Smithsonian Institution, Archives Center, National Museum of American History, Washington, D.C.

Groucho Marx Papers (1928–1971)
Wisconsin Center for Film and Theater Research, Madison, Wis.

Hollywood Greats: Groucho Marx. BBC-TV, August 8, 1979.

The Keith—Albee Vaudeville Theater Collection (1890–1952)

The University of Iowa Libraries Special Collections and University Archives, Iowa City, Iowa.

Sol M. Wurtzel Papers, Correspondence (1917–1961)

Margaret Herrick Library, Academy of Motion Picture Arts and Sciences, Los Angeles, Calif.

Loyd Wright Papers (1924–1971)

Hoover Institution Library and Archives, Stanford University, Stanford, Calif.

Palm Springs Historical Society

Welwood Murray Memorial Library, Palm Springs, Calif.

The Marx Brothers in a Nutshell. PBS-TV, March 10, 1982.

Betty Marx interview. Conducted by Robert Weide. Recorded but not used for *The Marx Brothers in a Nutshell.* 1981.

Zeppo Marx interview. Conducted by Shirley Eder. Recorded July 1970, Lake Tahoe, Calif.

Zeppo Marx interview. Conducted by David Fantle and Tom Johnson. Recorded March 21, 1979, Palm Springs, Calif.

Acknowledgments

THIS BOOK EXISTS IN LARGE PART BECAUSE OF TIM MARX. TIM ENCOURaged me to write Zeppo's story after a couple of other well-meaning authors had expressed interest. Tim's contribution to the book goes beyond giving enlightening interviews. He shared his mother Marion's archive of documents, letters, and photos, and provided insights about her that no one else could. It was the next best thing to interviewing Marion.

I would be remiss if I failed to acknowledge the kindness and patience of Tim's wife Laura, who has learned a lot about the Marx Brothers in recent years. Tim was also able to help me secure an interview with his brother Tom. Tom Marx would rather not talk about his father, but he was gracious and generous with his time and spoke freely about the difficult relationship he had with Zeppo and Marion. It would not have been possible to tell Zeppo's story without the cooperation of his sons.

Other members of the Marx family shared information and stories about Zeppo that could not have come from any other source. Harpo's son Bill, with whom I've maintained a more than thirty-five-year friendship, shared tales of Zeppo that revealed several aspects of his personality. (e.g., "Zeppo could make you laugh like you'd never laughed before, and he could also beat the crap out of you a minute later.")

Gummo's son Bob knew his Uncle Zeppo as well as anyone. He grew up around Zeppo and spent a lot of time with him in his later years in Palm Springs. Bob Marx was an enthusiastic supporter of my work, and a great resource in my research on the Marx family. Sadly, Bob passed away as this book was nearing completion. He loved to talk about his father and his uncles, and I'm fortunate to have gotten to know him and to have been his friend.

Bobby Marx, the son of Zeppo's second wife Barbara, while never legally adopted by Zeppo, was as much a son to him as Tim and Tom. In fact, they would say Bobby got more of a father-son relationship out of Zeppo than either of them ever did. I'm particularly grateful to Bobby for providing a realistic and balanced view of his mother, who all too often is portrayed as a caricature and a stereotype. Bobby also filled in some critical gaps in Zeppo's story.

One of the more challenging aspects of writing a Zeppo Marx biography was the lack of information about his final years in Palm Springs. Roxann Ploss was among the closest friends Zeppo had during that period. Her initial reluctance to talk about her relationship with Zeppo somehow morphed into an easy ongoing conversation and a new friendship. Roxann revealed the sweet side of a man everyone else described as a tough guy with a ruthless streak. Without her unique perspective, the book would have been incomplete. I'm very grateful to Roxann for allowing me to use her precious memories of Zeppo in this book.

Researching the life of Zeppo Marx took me into areas I would not have imagined (the United States Patent Office, the Chicago Juvenile Court Archive, and the Kefauver Committee Hearings, to name a few). I was fortunate to find two men who worked for the Aeroquip Corporation during the 1950s when the company purchased Zeppo's company, Marman Products. Mike Lefere and Al Wagner provided information about the transaction and, amazingly, copies of the Aeroquip company newsletters with details of the Marman acquisition. A. Dale Herman's daughter, Rita Mae Joyce, provided additional information about Marman and shared insight on her father's decades-long friendship with Zeppo.

Sharon McKibben, the daughter of Zeppo's childhood friend Joey Bass—initially skeptical about my inquiry—graciously decided to share personal memories that filled in gaps in the story that would have remained gaps without her help. Denise Singer Vogel, who was injured by a rock thrown by Tim Marx when she was eight years old, hung up on me when I first called her. But that was because she assumed I was a telemarketer. Once we established that I wasn't trying to sell her anything, Denise was incredibly gracious and forthcoming in discussing an incident that caused her pain and suffering for many years.

My longtime Marx Brothers fan friends were especially helpful with research on this book. Paul Wesolowski and I go back more years than either of us want to count. As he has with my previous books, Paul freely shared his research and his sizable archive. John Tefteller not only provided some rare photographs, but he also shared his correspondence with Zeppo.

Robert Moulton scares me a little. When I think I've researched something to the point where nothing else can be found, Robert will ask if I'd spoken to so and so's grandson. His ability to find things and people I either missed or didn't know I cared about is humbling. I hesitate to ever say my research on something is complete until Robert has signed off on it.

I've known Paul, John, and Robert for a long time, but there's a Marx fan I've known longer than all of them. Charlie Kochman was among the earliest and most enthusiastic supporters of the idea of me writing a biography of Zeppo. While others may have thought it was a nice concept, Charlie said that I *must* write the Zeppo book. As far as this book is concerned, these guys are Four of the Three Musketeers.

My mother, Sandy Bader, has finally given in and become a devoted Marx Brothers fan. A lifetime of support from her has gone a long way. Among the many friends and associates who've offered either a piece of research or just some much appreciated support, are Jeff Abraham, David Brandt, Mark Brodka, Steve Buschel, Dick Cavett, Will Coates, Michael Crain, Mary Crosby, Noah Diamond, Scott Eyman, Allan Falk, David Fantle, Frank Ferrante, Arne Fogel, Jeff Friedman, Paul Friedman, Howard Green, Gregg Hawks, Tom Johnson, Steven Lasker, David Leopold, Stan Levin, Laura Liebowitz, Matt Luxenberg, Alice and Leonard Maltin, Andy Marx, Barry Mitchell, John Myhre, Andrea Orlando, Jim Pierson, Jonathan Pont, Katie Pratt, Marc Ribler, Lynn Surry, Amy Thorsen, Jay Wartski, Robert Weide, Morris Weiss, Timothy Weng, Dan Wingate, and Dave Zobel.

Richard J. Anobile—who sadly passed away as this book was nearing completion—deserves special mention for always being kind to me whenever I contacted him. He was many years removed from his work on Marx Brothers projects and would politely let me know that he had moved on to other things. Then he would patiently answer my questions. Richard was a very nice man whose work in the 1970s was incredibly important to a generation of young Marx Brothers fans.

Research for my previous books certainly led me to writing *Zeppo: The Reluctant Marx Brother*. My deepest bow of gratitude is to the people who were interviewed or provided other assistance for those books but passed away before this book was even a thought. Matt Hickey, Bob Birchard, Toby Ruby Garson, Florence Mirantz, Maxine Marx, Minnie Marx Eagle, Miriam Marx Allen, and Susan Fleming Marx have all managed to posthumously contribute to this book.

INDEX

54–55; Marx, H., as straight man for, 64; Marx, H., filling in for, 75–76; Marx, H., financial trouble and, 248–49; Marx, H., getting laughs frowned on by, 234; Marx, H., interviews with, 243–44; Marx, H., making, laugh, 212; Marx, H., New York trip with, 233; Marx, H., on, still working, 245–46; Marx, H., on Johnson, R., relationship with, 42; Marx, H., role explained by, 44; Marx, Marion, respected by, 195; Marx, Milton, close relationship with, 11; Marx, Milton, representing, 174; on Marx, H., departure from act, 104–5; on Marx, H., nickname, 33; on Marx, Minnie, 250; *The Marx Bros. Scrapbook* co-written by, 63–64, 244–45; names origin of, 293n4; oft-quoted line of, 196; Paramount contract payable to, 77; professional debut of, 20; Sinatra, F., confronted by, 248; stock market losses of, 72; Stoliar working for, 247; stroke suffered by, 245; in Tamarisk Ranchos, 299n1; vaudeville singing by, 9; Weber described by, 108

Marx, Leonard ("Chico"), 5–6, 119; act control taken by, 15; death of, 220–21; DiVitha marrying, 213–14, 299n1; as gambler needing money, 74–75; heart attacks suffered by, 219; Jones complaints to, 129; Karp dated

by, 32; Marx, Adolph, show with, 204; Marx, H., awestruck by, 11; Marx, H. spending time with, 16; new wife of, 34; as robbery victim, 115; Shean, Al, teamed with, 14; wedding date of, 294n2; as womanizer, 60

Marx, Marion Ruth (Bimberg), 295n4; Afghan Hounds and, 78–79; background of, 57–58; Berg and Hyams socializing with, 93; in Broadway shows, 58–59; children adopted by, 169; children decisions made by, 208–9; close friends lost by, 159; court testimony by, 199; death of, 268–69; divorce filed for by, 193–94; divorce thoughts of, 97; equestrian interests of, 58–59; Gable good friend with, 106–7; home design and, 86; honeymoon of, 60–61; Lombard friendly with, 97; Marman Products shares received by, 195; marriage trouble for, 167; Marwyck Ranch home sold by, 167; Marx, Arthur, tennis game against, 152–53; Marx, H., apartment with, 69; Marx, H., engagement with, 56; Marx, H., letter to, 201–2; Marx, H., marrying, 59–60; Marx, H., meeting mystery, 59, 61–62; Marx, H., resentment from, 202; Marx, H., will contested by, 265–68; Marx, J., respecting, 195; Marx, Susan, relationship with, 224–25; Marx, Thomas,

Muroc Dry Lake, 91
"Muscle-Bound" (song), 88
Music Corporation of America
(MCA), 172–73
My Life with Groucho (Marx, Arthur),
251, 258
"My Poor Wife" (article), 294n2

"Napoleon's First Waterloo" sketch,
83
National Utilities Corporation, 166
NBC, 88
Nealis, Eddy, 136, 152
Ned Wayburn's Training School, 10
'N' Everything, 38, 46
Nicholls, George, 143
nicknames, 13–14, 19, 32–34
nicotine-free cigarette, 235
A Night at Maxim's (tabloid musical),
26
A Night at the Opera (film), viii,
127–28, 133
Nitti, Frank, 148
Niven, Joyce, 196, 204–5, 209
No Man of Her Own (film), 107
nonskid tire, 92
Norman, Barry, 8, 30, 40, 44, 261
North Beverly Drive, 175, 184, 191,
193
North Rodeo Drive, 183
no wives in act rule, 60

Oakie, Jack, 297n6
Oakley, Annie, 138
Oakvardon Kennels, 297n6
O'Banion, Dion, 116
O'Brien, Margaret, 134
O'Donnell, Mabel, 10

Of Thee I Sing (musical), 144
Oliver, Robert Harrison, 222
On the Mezzanine Floor (Timberg),
46; dialogue from, 47–50; Marx,
H., expanded role in, 47, 50;
Marx Brothers buying, 51; two-
tiered set of, 50
On the Stroke of Twelve (film), 7
Orange Blossoms, 15
organized crime figure, 149–50
Orpheum Theatre, 18, 43, 50–51
Orsatti, Ernie, 109
Orsatti, Frank, 94; background of,
109; debts of, 296n1; Mayer
firing, 122; Mayer setting up as
agent, 110–11; as Mayer's liquor
supplier, 110–11
Orsatti, Jesse, 116–17, 121
Orsatti, Morris, 109–10
Orsatti, Vic, 109, 134
Orsatti Agency, 134
Orth, Mary, 294n2
O'Sullivan, Maureen, 80
otosclerosis, 207
Owen, Tony, 225

package deal, invention of, 91
Page, Milton ("Farmer"), 152, 179
"A Pair of Shoes" script, 86–87
Palace Theatre, 39, 68
Palinkas, Steve, 117
Palmer, Minnie, 294n4; in hub of
vaudeville, 25; inexperienced
relatives used by, 39–40;
self-promotion by, 29; tabloid
musicals success of, 25–26;
as vaudeville manager and
producer, 15–16
